THE ECOLOGY OF CHILDHOOD

FAMILIES, LAW, AND SOCIETY SERIES
General Editor: Nancy E. Dowd

Justice for Kids: Keeping Kids Out of the Juvenile Justice System
Edited by Nancy E. Dowd

Masculinities and the Law: A Multidimensional Approach
Edited by Frank Rudy Cooper and Ann C. McGinley

The New Kinship: Constructing Donor-Conceived Families
Naomi Cahn

What Is Parenthood? Contemporary Debates about the Family
Edited by Linda C. McClain and Daniel Cere

In Our Hands: The Struggle for U.S. Child Care Policy
Elizabeth Palley and Corey S. Shdaimah

The Marriage Buyout: The Troubled Trajectory of U.S. Alimony Law
Cynthia Lee Starnes

Children, Sexuality, and the Law
Edited by Sacha Coupet and Ellen Marrus

A New Juvenile Justice System: Total Reform for a Broken System
Edited by Nancy E. Dowd

Divorced from Reality: Rethinking Family Dispute Resolution
Jane C. Murphy and Jana B. Singer

The Poverty Industry: The Exploitation of America's Most Vulnerable Citizens
Daniel L. Hatcher

Ending Zero Tolerance: The Crisis of Absolute School Discipline
Derek W. Black

Blaming Mothers: American Law and the Risks to Children's Health
Linda C. Fentiman

The Politicization of Safety
Edited by Jane K. Stoever

The Ecology of Childhood: How Our Changing World Threatens Children's Rights
Barbara Bennett Woodhouse

The Ecology of Childhood

How Our Changing World Threatens Children's Rights

Barbara Bennett Woodhouse

NEW YORK UNIVERSITY PRESS
New York

NEW YORK UNIVERSITY PRESS
New York
www.nyupress.org
© 2020 by New York University
All rights reserved

References to Internet websites (URLs) were accurate at the time of writing. Neither the author nor New York University Press is responsible for URLs that may have expired or changed since the manuscript was prepared.

Library of Congress Cataloging-in-Publication Data
Names: Woodhouse, Barbara Bennett, 1945–   author.
Title: The ecology of childhood : how our changing world threatens children's rights / Barbara Bennett Woodhouse.
Description: New York : New York University Press, [2019] | Also available as an ebook. | Includes bibliographical references and index.
Identifiers: LCCN 2019006913 | ISBN 9780814794845 (cl. ; acid-free paper) | ISBN 081479484X (cl. ; acid-free paper)
Subjects: LCSH: Children's rights. | Child welfare. | Children—Government policy. | Child development. | Sustainable development. | Globalization. | Children—Florida—Cedar Key. | Children—Italy—Scanno.
Classification: LCC HQ789 .W66 2019 | DDC 323.3/52—dc23
LC record available at https://lccn.loc.gov/2019006913

New York University Press books are printed on acid-free paper, and their binding materials are chosen for strength and durability. We strive to use environmentally responsible suppliers and materials to the greatest extent possible in publishing our books.

Manufactured in the United States of America

10 9 8 7 6 5 4 3 2 1

Also available as an ebook

To Sacha and Zoe and all the world's grandchildren

CONTENTS

List of Figures	ix
Preface	xi

PART 1. COMPARATIVE ECOLOGIES

1. How a Comparative Study of Childhood Became a Story of Global Crisis	3
2. Tools for Studying Childhood	14

PART 2. MICROSYSTEMS AND MESOSYSTEMS

3. A Tale of Two Villages	41
4. The Magic of Mesosystems, Seedbeds of Solidarity	74

PART 3. EXOSYSTEMS AND MACROSYSTEMS

5. Falling Birth Rates and Rural Depopulation	97
6. The Role of Family-Supportive Policies in the Decision to Have Children	112
7. Children of the Great American Recession	131
8. The Great Recession Crosses the Atlantic	151
9. Globalization: The Elephant in the Playroom	171

PART 4. TRANSFORMING THE ECOLOGY OF CHILDHOOD

10. The Role of Children's Rights	207
11. How the CRC Affects Actual Children's Lives	225
12. Building Small Worlds in Urban Spaces	260
13. Charting the Way to a World Fit for Children	283

Acknowledgments	303
Bibliography	309
Index	341
About the Author	357

LIST OF FIGURES

Figure 1.1. Ecology of childhood diagram, microsystems and mesosystems. B. B. Woodhouse, adapted from Bronfenbrenner (1979). 4

Figure 1.2. Ecology of childhood diagram, exosystems and macrosystem. B. B. Woodhouse, adapted from Bronfenbrenner (1979). 5

Figure 2.1. Multiple generations sharing a public space as mass lets out in the Italian mountain village of Scanno. Cesidio Silla. 16

Figure 2.2. Panorama of Scanno nestled in the mountains of the Abruzzo National Park. B. B. Woodhouse. 31

Figure 2.3. View from No. 2 Bridge, crossing from mainland Florida into Cedar Key. B. B. Woodhouse. 35

Figure 3.1. Scanno children delivering firewood during Festival of Saint Anthony. B. B. Woodhouse. 46

Figure 3.2. Birds-eye view of Cedar Key, Florida, Levy Co. 1884. Library of Congress, G3934, C 315A3 1884. 57.1884. 77–69024. 49

Figure 3.3. City of Cedar Key park and beach. B. B. Woodhouse. 52

Figure 3.4. View north on G. Street with water tower and Cedar Key School in background. B. B. Woodhouse. 55

Figure 3.5. View west on Second Street from Island Hotel, Cedar Key. B. B. Woodhouse. 57

Figure 3.6. Preschool-age children playing in Piazza Santa Maria della Valle with the Asilo Buon Pastore in the background. B. B. Woodhouse. 59

Figure 3.7. Preschool-age boy at a Cedar Key church Easter egg hunt. B. B. Woodhouse. 60

Figure 3.8. Children playing dancing game in Piazza dell'Olmo with older neighbors looking on. B. B. Woodhouse. 61

Figure 3.9. A kid's-eye view of modern Cedar Key. B. B. Woodhouse. 62

Figure 3.10. Girl in Scanno traditional costume hosting visiting students from another village. B. B. Woodhouse. 66

Figure 4.1. Cedar Key School students entertaining guests at Madrigal Dinner. B. B. Woodhouse. 82

Figure 4.2. Massimo and Gaia and their parents in their First Communion procession. B. B. Woodhouse. 84

Figure 4.3. Cedar Key elementary school students dressed as favorite superheroes for Homecoming Spirit Week. Cedar Key School Facebook. 86

Figure 4.4. Girl from La Plaja in a mask of charcoal dust from her *contrada's* San Martino bonfire. 90

Figure 4.5. Cedar Key School Safety Patrol students selling soft drinks at the grand opening of the Nature Coast Biological Research Station. B. B. Woodhouse. 91

Figure 9.1 Scanno schoolchildren clowning around after perfectly executed earthquake drill. B. B. Woodhouse. 184

Figure 11.1. Map of Scanno in Abrruzzo, Italy, seventeenth Century. DEA/A DE GREGORIO/ De Agostini Editore/age fotostock. 228

Figure 11.2. Girls playing *bancarella*. B. B. Woodhouse. 231

Figure 11.3. Boys playing *bancarella*. B. B. Woodhouse. 232

Figure 11.4. Genny, youth mayor of Scanno. B. B. Woodhouse. 235

Figure 11.5. Frattura earthquake logo. Photograph by B. B. Woodhouse. Design by Scanno fifth graders. 247

Figure 11.6. Gaia cradling baby lamb. C. Nannarone. 253

Figure 11.7. Massimo herding Sheep. C. Nannarone. 254

Figure 11.8. Gaia and friend at a regional dialect poetry competition. B. B. Woodhouse. 255

PREFACE

This book project occupied more than a decade, from 2007 to 2019. It unfolded on two continents and utilized a wide range of methods, from legal research and comparative law to site visits and ethnographic fieldwork, and it introduces narratives and case studies from the author's work as examples. The purpose of this preface is to assist readers in navigating the book by providing a brief overview and roadmap. This is especially useful for navigating a complex, multidisciplinary, and multiyear project such as this one.

This book began as a relatively simple comparative study of childhood in two developed countries, using the ecological model of childhood as its framework. An unanticipated event—the Great Recession—reshaped the project almost as soon as it was started. The devastating effects on children and families of global economic crisis left no doubt that global forces, instead of being distant and abstract from the ecology of childhood, could threaten the welfare of children even in economically advanced countries. In response, I expanded the project to consider these potentially toxic forces, gathered under the umbrella of globalization. These global phenomena include unrestrained capitalism, technological change, rising inequality, mass migration, racial conflict, and, most global of all, the human-made juggernaut of climate change. These forces are already at work, destabilizing and degrading the social and physical environments necessary to the survival and well-being of the young. Not only this generation of children but succeeding generations are at risk.

In these pages, I argue for a radical change in value systems. If human society is to survive, we must place the well-being of future generations at the top and not the bottom of our social agenda. A society's welfare is not captured by measures such as a rising GDP or a higher competitiveness index. As I have argued in my prior writings, which introduced the theory of "ecogenerism," the true measure of a just and sustainable society is whether it meets the basic needs of its children and whether its policies foster environments in which children, young people, and families can flourish. Without these preconditions for sustainable communities, a society's human capital dwindles and, eventually, disappears. A far better benchmark than GDP is found in evidence-based research into child well-being and a far better value system than short-term efficiency is found in the UN Convention on the Rights of the Child, which identifies children's most important needs and assigns responsibility for their nurture and protection not only to parents but to the larger community. The book ends by proposing ways in which each reader, wherever and however situated, can contribute to the goal of building a better world for children on the theory that a world fit for children will be a world fit for everyone.

The analysis in this book is grounded in the ecological model utilized by many disciplines in studying childhood. Pioneered by social scientists studying children's development, this model is designed to place children's lives in social context. It imagines children at the center of a constellation of social institutions and social structures that include and surround them, as represented schematically in the ecology of childhood diagram (see figure 2.1). The systems in which children are embedded are the "microsystems" where they spend their days, such as the family, peer group, faith community, neighborhood, and school. Where these microsystems intersect and overlap, they create social spaces that are called "mesosystems." Conditions in the microsystems are influenced by spaces where children may rarely or never go. These are the encircling "exosystems" of institutions and structures such as the parents' workplace, economic markets, and health care, as well as social welfare and judicial systems. Permeating every part of this universe is the "macrosystem," the ever-present climate of ideas, values, prejudices, and powers that create hierarchies that are often damaging to children. In addition to providing insights into fostering the development of children, both as individuals and in groups, the ecological model can provide insights into larger environments for rearing children as well. The ecological model recognizes that childhood is dynamic, not static, and thus events unfolding in any of the systems affecting childhood will have spillover effects into the others. It also recognizes that macrosystemic values, like H_2O in a natural ecological system, are not static but flow up from the microsystems as well as down from on high. Unlike laws of gravity or physics, macrosystemic laws, both written and unwritten, are generated by human societies. In sum, the cultural macrosystem is created by us and can be reformed and reshaped by us.

Roadmap

The ideas presented above recur throughout the book, but what follows is a basic roadmap to aid readers in understanding the book's structure and to assist teachers who might want to assign selected chapters. Using the ecological model as a framework, I have divided the book into four parts, with a total of thirteen chapters. The sequence of parts and chapters is structured to take the reader from the center of the ecology diagram to its outer reaches and back.

Part 1, "Comparative Ecologies," is intended to introduce the project and to orient the reader to the tools and methodologies utilized in the project.

Chapter 1, "How a Comparative Study of Childhood Became a Story of Global Crisis," explains the genesis of the project as a comparison of childhoods and child-welfare policies in Italy and the United States that was transformed by unforeseen events, leading to the project's expansion. In addition to the economic turmoil of the 2008 financial crisis and its fallout, these events included advances in the science of brain development and new research into DNA that shed new light on the roles of nature, nurture, and environmental stressors in the cognitive and emotional growth of infants and children.

Chapter 2, "Tools for Studying Childhood," introduces the reader to the methodological tools and analytical theories I have employed. In addition to exploring ecological and other models of inquiry into children's development, I discuss the central theory animating my approach: the child-centered and environmentally informed perspective of "ecogenerism" introduced in my prior writings. I also explain how and why I selected Scanno, in the Abruzzo Region of Italy, and Cedar Key, in the US state of Florida, as petri dishes for a longitudinal ethnographic comparative study.

Part 2, "Microsystems and Mesosystems," focuses on the most intimate levels of children's worlds—the places where children actually go. It examines the various microsystems where childhood unfolds and the social dynamics children experience in the mesosystems, those zones where microsystems intersect and overlap. It, too, utilizes the two villages as a petri dish for examining these intimate systems.

Chapter 3, "A Tale of Two Villages," provides detailed portraits of the two villages under study and explores their similarities and differences from a child-centered perspective. It utilizes demographic data and historical materials as well as ethnographic field observations, and it employs the comparative method developed by comparative law scholars to compare similarities, differences, and overarching values within the microsystems of family, school, faith community, neighborhood, and peer group.

Chapter 4, "The Magic of Mesosystems: Seedbeds of Solidarity," examines how the social institutions that constitute children's microsystems overlap and intersect. It uses examples from both villages to illustrate how these zones of interaction generate personal and group identity and values of solidarity that can transform "other people's children" into "our" children.

Part 3, "Exosystems and Macrosystems," moves outward from the intimate zones of family and community to examine the larger institutions, such as employment markets, health care, and child-welfare policies, that encircle these microsystems and indirectly, or sometimes quite directly, impact children's lives. It highlights how these exosystems, when they fail to meet children's and families' needs, can threaten the ecology of childhood. It also shows how macrosystemic forces—those ideas, values, prejudices, and powers that permeate the ecosystem—distort our policies and our politics to the detriment of children and of humankind.

Chapter 5, "Falling Birth Rates and Rural Depopulation," looks at two current crises that are largely attributable to exosystemic factors: the sharp decline in birth rates in developed countries, and the migration of young people from rural to urban areas, rupturing their social and family bonds. Young men and women in rich countries want babies, but they are not having them. They want to put down roots but they cannot afford to. The chapter examines the reasons behind this decline, and the consequences of this "baby bust" for young people and for society.

Chapter 6, "The Role of Family-Supportive Policies in the Decision to Have Children," explores how government policies such as day care, affordable health care, parenting leave, and income supports can influence the decision whether to have children. Such policies can make the climate for child-rearing warmer and more child-friendly, or colder, more hostile, and more stressful. Comparisons indicate that the United States lags behind peer nations in providing support to working parents. This phenomenon is part of an American culture of rugged individualism that treats child-rearing as a private matter and sees supports as a slippery slope to socialism.

Chapter 7, "Children of the Great American Recession," considers the role of market systems in shaping the ecology of childhood and determining whether a nation's children are lucky or unlucky. The chapter begins with an overview of benchmarks commonly used to measure a nation's success. It then traces the impact of the Wall Street meltdown on child poverty, food security, housing stability, child health, and child maltreatment. In each of these areas, children of the US recession were harmed as a result of parental loss of employment, cuts in family-supportive government programs, and fiscal policies that hurt the most vulnerable and further damaged an already frayed safety net.

Chapter 8, "The Great Recession Crosses the Atlantic," shows how a crisis made in America metastasized to Europe, with dramatic consequences for families and children in Italy. As a member of the Eurozone, Italy lacked the power to use monetary policy to fight the recession, and children's lives were even more deeply affected in Italy than in the United States. Utilizing sources such as UNICEF Report cards and OECD studies, this chapter documents the disproportionate effects of austerity policies on children in Southern European countries such as Italy. It closes with an account of the backlash that the fiscal crisis generated in both the United States and Italy, resulting in sharp increases in racism and hostility toward immigrants and refugees, as well as in the alarming rise of radical populist parties and autocratic strongmen.

Chapter 9, "Globalization: The Elephant in the Playroom," presents a critique of the dominant macrosystem. It argues that a set of macrosystemic forces, which I group under the umbrella of globalization, have been the elephants in the room of contemporary social policy. These forces include unrestrained capitalism guided only by short-term profit, the destabilizing forces of technological change, rising inequality even in developed nations, mass migration, the rise of racial and ethnic discrimination, and paralysis in the face of climate change. When examined through the lens of the ecology of childhood, these seemingly separate issues are revealed as collectively apocalyptic. I argue that these ills are produced or exacerbated by a set of misguided beliefs, prejudices, myths, and individualistic values that have come to dominate global policies and have eroded social solidarity. The climate they create is unsustainable and threatens both the small worlds of children and the larger ecology of human societies.

Part 4, "Transforming the Ecology of Childhood," moves from explorations of the ecological model to proposals for macrosystemic transformation and reform. It proposes a child-centered value system as the measure of how well a given society or community is functioning. Grounded in the theory of "ecogenerism" introduced in chapter 2, its guiding philosophy regards a commitment to the welfare of future generations as the mark of a mature, just, and sustainable society. This final part considers how to flesh out and implement these ideals.

Chapter 10, "The Role of Children's Rights," asks the metrics question, "How do we decide what is good for children?" I offer the UN Convention on the Rights of the Child as an example of a scientifically sound and highly developed scheme of children's essential needs and inalienable human rights. Known internationally as the CRC (Children's Rights Convention), it is the most rapidly and universally accepted charter of human rights in history. This chapter explains the basic concepts of the CRC, in both child-friendly and legalistic terms, and describes its spreading influence in the world beyond the United States.

Chapter 11, "How the CRC Affects Actual Children's Lives," rebuts a criticism often aimed at this charter and at human rights charters in general. The charge is that lofty human-rights principles are simply powerless to affect real world change. This chapter provides concrete examples from the Italian and

EU contexts of how implementation of the CRC has improved the lives of real children, giving them voice and furthering recognition of their rights to family, play, education, participation, protection from discrimination, and inclusion. It introduces children's own voices to tell their stories.

Chapter 12, "Building Small Worlds in Urban Spaces," is inspired by E. F. Schumacher's classic 1973 book *Small Is Beautiful: Economics as if People Mattered*. Schumacher was prescient in proposing a humanist alternative to the school of economics that has dominated recent policy. In this chapter, I draw upon insights gleaned from studying the ecology of childhood at the village level to advocate focusing on the small and local levels and learning to bring the strengths of smallness to bear on larger problems. The chapter concludes with evidence of how the virtues of smallness are not limited to rural communities but can be introduced into challenging urban settings. It describes and compares two projects, La Sanità in Naples and the Harlem Children's Zone in New York, aimed at improving the lives of at-risk children and youth by building supportive small-scale communities.

Chapter 13, the book's closing chapter, "Charting the Way To a World Fit for Children," begins by highlighting some of the "big ideas" that inform the "small is beautiful" approach. Clearly, action is needed at a global level. But in this book, instead of offering a grand solution for altering the dominant macrosystem from the top down, I close by challenging readers to take action at the grassroots level, reminding them that macrosystems are built from the bottom up. I propose a very accessible menu of strategies for action at the local, municipal, and regional levels, aimed at advancing child-friendly institutions and communities, combatting the myths and prejudices that undermine solidarity in microsystems like schools and faith communities before they take root, and embedding the values of the CRC at every level of the ecology of childhood. Through active engagement, I argue, each one of us can contribute to building a world fit for children.

PART 1

Comparative Ecologies

1

How a Comparative Study of Childhood Became a Story of Global Crisis

This is the story of an environmental crisis on an unprecedented scale. It examines how the very environments necessary to the regeneration and survival of the human species are being placed at risk by destructive human forces. It is not the story I set out to write. When I began this project over a decade ago, I was on sabbatical from the University of Florida, where I was director of the Center on Children and Families at the Levin College of Law. The year was 2007 and, having won a Fernand Braudel Senior Research Fellowship at the European University Institute in Florence, I was embarking on a multiyear research project.

My project was relatively straightforward. In studying comparative and international family law, I had observed how human-made laws and policies at the macro level affect the intimate environments in which children grow. Children in developing nations are especially at risk of harm from the effects of poverty, war, famine, and environmental degradation. However, developed nations have no cause for complacency.

Too many children in rich countries are also suffering from political, economic, and environmental neglect. A series of "Report Cards" from UNICEF's Innocenti Research Centre measuring child well-being in developed nations highlighted the wide variations among developed nations in rates of child poverty, access to education, health, infant mortality, and many other measures of child well-being (UNICEF 2000; 2001a; 2001b; 2002; 2003a; 2005; 2007; 2008; 2010; 2012; 2013; 2014b; 2016; 2017; 2018a). Using the ecological model of child development, a widely accepted method of studying children in social context, I had designed a research project that would compare the ecologies of childhood in two contrasting "first-world" environments. The ecological model, introduced by sociologist Urie Bronfenbrenner, asks us to examine child development in the context of the "systems" in which children are embedded (Bronfenbrenner 1979). The first diagram represents the *microsystems* where children spend their time, from family and faith community to neighborhood, school, and peer group. Often these microsystems overlap and intersect. Consider a school where faith community, neighborhood, family, and peer group overlap; these

Microsystems and Mesosystems

Microsystems: where children's daily lives unfold.

[Diagram with overlapping circles labeled: Family, School, Neighborhood, Peer Group, Faith Community, Child]

Mesosystems: where microsystems overlap and intersect.

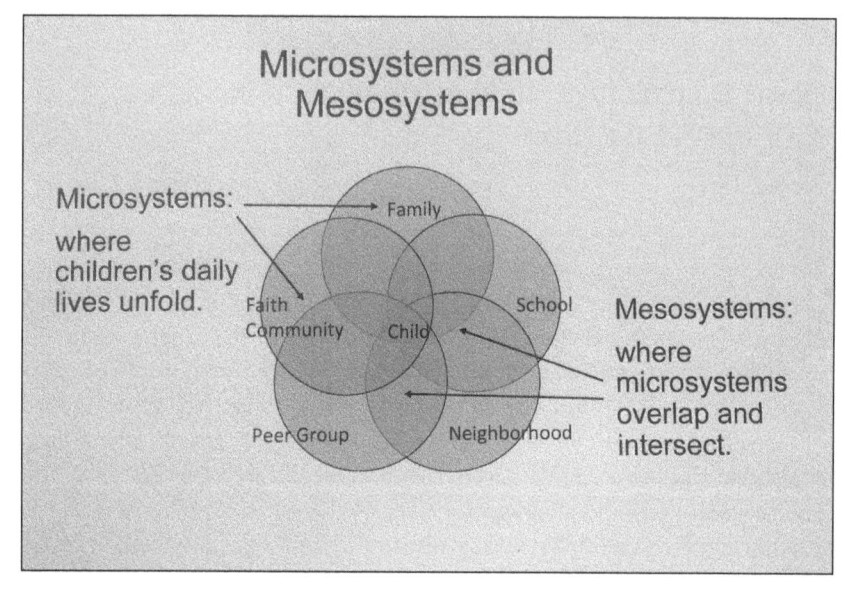

Figure 1.1. Ecology of childhood diagram, microsystems and mesosystems. B. B. Woodhouse, adapted from Bronfenbrenner (1979).

zones of intersection are called *mesosystems* and are especially important to children's social development.

In figure 1.2 we see that the ecological model acknowledges the indirect impact on children of *exosystems* that encircle the children's intimate worlds but are where children may rarely go. Examples include parents' workplace, health-care systems, housing and financial markets, and justice systems. Finally, the ecological model identifies the overarching influences of the social *macrosystem*, identified by a permeable line of dashes at the outer circle of the diagram. The macrosystem is defined as the complex of ideas, values, prejudices, and powers that permeates a particular ecosystem.

My research question would be, "How do social policies (those exosystemic factors) affect the ecology of childhood?" Of course, I realize that there are many childhoods. "Childhood" is a socially constructed concept and differs from place to place, time to time, and child to child (Woodhouse 2008a). But the term "childhood" remains a useful category for thinking about policies affecting children. My thesis, supported by the Innocenti Report Cards, was that policies such as universal health care, robust labor laws, access to child care, and early childhood education, as well as family supports such as paid parenting and medical leave, when supported by progressive tax policies and a commitment to children's human rights, were associated with higher rates of child well-being and lower rates of children's exposure to deprivation and trauma. I proposed to use Italy as an example of a European style social welfare approach, and the United States to exemplify a more individualistic free-market approach.

Why Italy? Why not Sweden or Finland? Because Italy is not perfect. Italy, like the United States, belongs to the Organization for Economic Cooperation and Development (OECD). In short, both countries are members of the international club of affluent nations. Italy, as a founding member of the European Union (EU), differs from the United States in that its laws and policies are shaped by EU law and international human-rights principles that do not bind the United States. But Italy is far from being a socialist "children's paradise" like Finland or Sweden, and thus it is less easily dismissed as an unrealistic comparison. Many middle-class families in Italy, as in the United States, have trouble making ends meet and struggle to overcome social, ethnic, and regional inequalities. Both Italy and the United States have relatively high rates of child poverty, but in Italy these rates have generally been somewhat mitigated through social-welfare spending. Of course, my choice of Italy was also influenced by the match between my skills and the projected research. I am fluent in the Italian language and familiar with Italian culture, having spent three years studying in Italy before attending law school and I have

Exosystems: external to the child's microsystems but powerfully influencing child and family well-being.

parent's work place
housing markets
healthcare systems
financial markets,
etc.

Children's Microsystems

The Macrosystem: climate of ideas, values, prejudices and powers that surrounds and permeates all levels of the ecology of childhood.

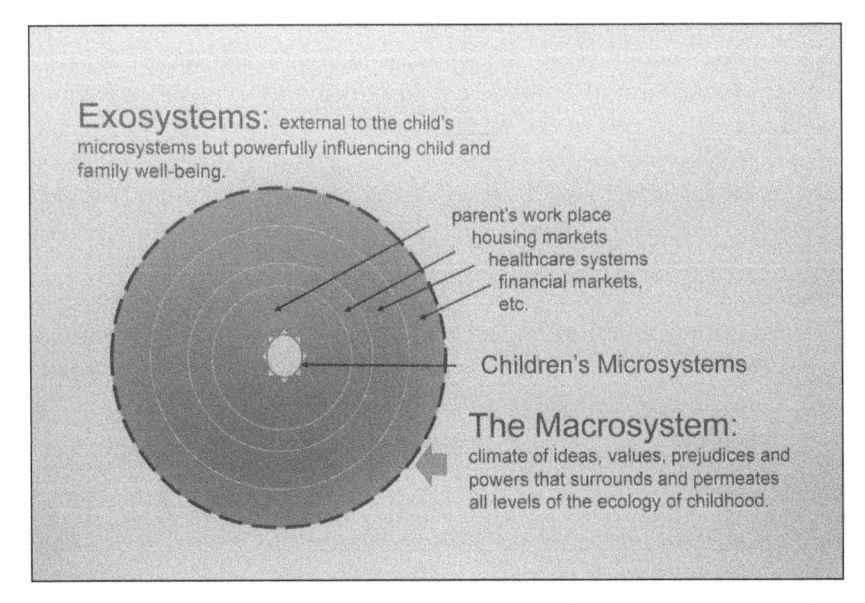

Figure 1.2. Ecology of childhood diagram, exosystems and macrosystem. B. B. Woodhouse, adapted from Bronfenbrenner (1979).

maintained my ties with Italy over the past four decades, putting down roots in the Italian academic community.

As I studied child law and policy in both countries, I was struck by many examples of concrete situations in which differences between the individualistic policies in the United States and the more communitarian policies in Italy resulted in starkly different outcomes. Here is but one example: a case study I used to illustrate my grant proposal was that of a low-income family with two children, where the mother was the sole breadwinner and the father primary caretaker because of unemployment. Add to this scenario that one of the two children was terminally ill with cancer and the father was struggling with substance abuse and had been caught stealing to support his habit. When I presented the fact pattern to seasoned child advocates in the United States, they invariably predicted that the unavoidable tragedy of the child's death would be compounded by an avalanche of other troubles. A year from now, they predicted, the father would be incarcerated and the mother would have lost her job for missing too many days of work to care for her dying child. She would lose her home to foreclosure or be evicted, if she were renting, and, lacking housing and income, would be at great risk of having her surviving child removed to foster care by Child Protective Services, an event that would start the statutory clock ticking toward termination of her parental rights. The laws in most states require child-protection agencies to move for permanent termination of the rights of a parent who has not corrected the situation within fifteen months of the child's placement in care (Woodhouse 2002).

Then I asked my US colleagues to imagine the outcome in an environment where the family has access to free medical care, paid family and medical leave, job protection for caregivers dealing with family crisis, access to low-income housing, free, timely, and effective residential drug-treatment programs, as an alternative to incarceration of the addicted parent, and in-home social services including nurses and teachers for children unable to attend school. When I posed these changes to our hypothetical, my colleagues laughed and asked, "Where are we? In paradise?" "No, we are in Italy," I would reply. This example illustrated more clearly than any string of data points the differences that can be made by robust and responsive social-welfare policies.

I anticipated challenges to my assessments of the relative benefits of social welfare versus free-market approaches. Anyone who surfs the web or listens to the news understands the philosophical and political divide between those who advocate social-welfare spending and those who condemn it as a waste of money and a drain on a nation's economy. However, at the start of my project, the storyline seemed straightforward. It would be a tale of two systems—one committed to social-welfare rights and the betterment of society through public support of the vulnerable, and the other committed to individual rights and betterment of society through personal freedom and market competition.

What I did not anticipate when I started my project was the bursting in 2008 of the US housing bubble and the near-collapse of American financial markets. Economic crisis and soaring inequality revealed the fragility and vulnerability of social environments and social policies, much as global warming and species extinctions have exposed the fragility of our natural environments. Humankind has clearly overestimated the resilience of forests and oceans when exposed to stressors created by industrialization and technological change, and the same may be true of the resilience of humans when exposed to economic and social stressors. Common sense tells us that even the strongest organism is susceptible to the toxic effects of a degraded ecosystem. The more vulnerable the organism, the greater the harm. This is what I see happening to the ecology of childhood.

When Wall Street crashed, I did not foresee the effects this would have on children in Italy. I should have known better. As the Italians like to say, "When the United States sneezes, Italy catches pneumonia." There were certain obvious differences between the economies and cultures of the two countries. Granted, Italy had a rather high national debt in comparison to its GDP, and Italy's greedy political class had been spending way beyond its means. But the Italian people, unlike the people in the United States, had avoided a housing bubble and had a high rate of personal savings and very little consumer debt. The bedrock of the Italian economy was not big banks and multinationals, but small family businesses and traditional farms. It was not long, however, before the spillover effects of our Great Recession triggered an even deeper economic crisis in Europe. By 2009, Italy was in deep trouble (Coletto 2010).

Differences between the two countries have become more pronounced in the wake of the crisis. In the United States, the Republican Party's focus on reducing the national debt and opposition to government spending on social programs and infrastructure prevented the robust response many experts contended was needed to overcome the effects of the crisis. The size of the Obama administration's initial fiscal stimulus was limited, and subsequent developments, including the "Sequester," resulted in deep cuts to social programs that were not strong to begin with.

As my research project progressed, the political environment in both Italy and the United States evolved rapidly and in unexpected directions. In the United States, the Obama administration (2009–17) had managed to enact and defend the Affordable Care Act against strong pushback from Republicans. Advocates for stronger social-welfare programs and greater investment in infrastructure and trade expected that the election of 2016 would strengthen their hand. Instead, front-runner Hillary Clinton won the popular vote but lost the Electoral College, for reasons too complicated and clouded in mystery to address in these pages. Donald Trump's anti-elitist, anti-immigrant, and anti-trade messages hit a nerve among voters who had suffered during the recession and demanded radical change. With promises to "drain the swamp" in Washington, DC, create jobs, and enact tax cuts for the middle class, real-estate magnate Donald Trump carried several postindustrial "rust belt" states that had traditionally gone to Democrats. In its first six months, the Trump administration, despite the distraction of the "Russiagate" investigation, acted aggressively to clamp down on immigration and to suspend, repeal, or obstruct many of the social-welfare programs of the Obama administration. The Trump administration's first budget proposed drastic cuts to social welfare programs, including health care, nutrition assistance, public housing, and public education. Critics claimed that these cuts, rather than increasing efficiency, would increase the national debt while giving massive tax cuts to the very rich.

In Italy, meanwhile, during the first years of the recession, there was no stimulus to counter rising economic distress. Italy could not use deficit spending or monetary policy to cushion the shocks of recession because Italy had no control over the euro, which is controlled by the EU. Instead, austerity measures, forced upon the Italian leadership by Germany and other fiscal conservatives in the EU, were the only tools available. By 2014, it had become increasingly clear that these austerity measures were tearing at the very fabric of the Italian society that I had been studying. Existing social welfare programs had been slashed, and even commitments that were explicitly embedded in the Italian constitution, including protections for workers and families and rights to education and health care, were on the chopping block. While the United States was slowly climbing out of recession, the EU was still deep in crisis. Italy was seen as one of the EU's sickest members, with a youth unemployment rate twenty points higher than the average among euro currency countries. As of 2016, the youth unemployment rate in the United States had fallen to 10.9 percent while in Italy it was at 38.3 percent (World Bank: Unemployment, youth total 2016).

In a rapid succession of new governments, a string of different Italian leaders tried to unite the country behind a policy that would relieve the fiscal crisis and turn the economy around. By April 2017, Italy declared that the recession was at last over, but the country, hampered by lingering political and economic stressors, was still struggling to catch up to other EU nations. The Movimento Cinque Stelle (Five Star Movement), an upstart left-of-center populist party founded by Italian comedian Beppe Grillo, had dominated many of the headlines and captured the popular imagination of many dissatisfied citizens. The crisis also strengthened a right-wing, fiercely anti-immigrant separatist movement, called the Lega del Nord (the Northern League), which originated in the northern provinces. In Italy's March 2018 elections, these two antiestablishment parties won half of the vote in what observers characterize as a "wake-up call" for the European establishment (Mazzini 2018).

In addition to the economic crisis, another development has complicated my storyline. In the past decade, the study of the relative roles of nature and nurture has been revolutionized. Scientists have learned that exposure to social and physical trauma can inflict permanent brain damage and even result in changes to the victims' genes—changes that are transmitted to succeeding generations (National Scientific Council on the Developing Child 2010; Delude 2014). We once drew lines between nature and nurture, or the effects of genetics and effects of environment. During the past decade, scientists have made quantum leaps in the study of how physical and social environments affect child development. We already knew that a healthy childhood begins long before birth and even before conception and that we had to address the health of future parents if we wanted healthy children.

Recently, however, scientists have discovered unimagined ways in which environment and nature interact to shape human development. Epidemiologists, neuroscientists, and other developmental scientists have established a correlation between adverse experiences in childhood (ACEs) and the risk of poor health and social outcomes in childhood and adulthood (Centers for Disease Control and Prevention 2010; Landrigan 2016). ACEs include domestic and neighborhood violence, sexual abuse, separation from caregivers, parental divorce or separation, and various other traumas. While adverse experiences are not uncommon for children, multiple such experiences can reach a toxic level. If such compounded trauma is not attended to, children may not just heal and get on with their lives. ACEs do not dictate consequences etched in stone; fostering resilience can counteract the effects. But without purposeful and strong support, the effects of trauma—especially during the period of explosive brain development in early childhood—can lead to lasting and quantifiable damage to individuals and to society. Thanks to the work of biologists and neurologists, we now also understand that the DNA of an individual is not set at birth; it is actually vulnerable to mutations due to adverse conditions, just as it can be positively affected by a supportive environment. Neurologists can now map changes in the human brain as it develops and can show the actual effects of trauma and adversity on the architecture of the developing brain (National Scientific Council on the Developing Child 2010; Delude 2014).

These discoveries, in both the economic and scientific spheres, call into question some widespread conceptions of the individual as an autonomous, discrete organism operating freely in an environment where the major variable is individual merit and strength of character. The reality is inescapable: social and political developments and these scientific discoveries affirm the importance of an environmental perspective on the study of childhood. Any such inquiry must begin by recognizing the role played by intimate physical and social environments, but must extend to macro forces such as globalization, inequality, climate change, market economics, and the dislocations caused by migration.

These events and ideas have reshaped my initial project, just as the economic crisis overtook my initial premise. Instead of a story about how we in the United States might learn from Italian child and family policy, it has become a tale of a spreading global crisis. An environmental crisis is threatening humankind not only on the grand scale of global warming, but in the many small worlds of childhood. Fundamental differences still remain between the United States and the European powers; for example, the decision of President Trump to withdraw the United States from the Paris Accord on climate change has only sharpened the determination of Europeans to move aggressively to address this threat. But it is clear that we face common challenges on a grand scale as well as on an intimate level.

During the decade of my research project, certain other global factors emerged as existential threats that compounded the economic and political crises in both the United States and Italy. A short list would include the effects of unrestrained capitalism, racism, technological revolution, rising inequality, and mass migration. Many of these factors predated the Great Recession, but when the economic crisis struck, the impact of these factors on children became even more stark. Loss of employment and migration of workers to better labor markets may make sense from an economist's standpoint, but they take a terrible toll on children. Stockholders may improve their bottom lines through an emphasis on efficiency, but working families suffer profound collateral damage when labor and trade policies privilege efficiency and resource mobility at the expense of job security and social stability. Technology makes people redundant even as it saves human lives. Soaring inequality erodes the sense of solidarity that creates communities and nations. Together, they seemed to add up to a perfect storm whose effects are felt throughout the ecology of childhood.

As my research evolved, I came to see that these challenges were all, in some way, related to a much larger phenomenon. If any single word is sufficient to encompass all of the practical and cultural dimensions of these challenges, it would be "globalization." Globalization has been the dominant characteristic of the global macrosystem that shapes children's small worlds. Inevitably, I found my inquiry into the ecology of childhood entangled in examination of this relatively new, complex phenomenon.

I call this a story of small worlds not to imply that children's worlds are unimportant. Rather, I use the term "small" in the sense of being intimate, and "worlds" to indicate places that are located in a particular time and space. When ecologists explore reproduction and nurture of the young in the natural context, they focus first on the immediate environment: a frog in a pond, a bird in a woodland glade. What are the factors that make the pond or glade a good or a poor environment for survival and thriving of this species? Like any organism, a child has certain irreducible needs for survival. I will use the ecological model to explore these needs and see how well or poorly the environment meets them. As with any small world, external forces and events may affect the conditions in a pond or a glade and the creatures born or hatched there may leave for other streams and even migrate to other continents. It is the same with humans. Still, we start small in order to build a base of understanding, while always recognizing that a specific ecological system is subject to many external influences.

It may seem counterfactual to suggest that children are an endangered species. Demographers tell us that the human animal, far from disappearing from the Earth, is reproducing at an alarming rate (World Population Trends UNFPA; Dimick 2014). But the threat to humankind of degraded environments for the rearing of our young is very real. We are not immune to the laws of nature, and as a species we will survive or become extinct, accordingly. A sustainable environment for reproduction and rearing of the young is essential to the survival of any species. In common with other observers, I fear the consequences of our collective indifference to children's needs, evident on a global as well as a local scale. An environment that is toxic to its young is a world without a future (Landrigan 2016; Louv 2008; Edelman 2016; Miller, Marty and Landrigan 2016; UNICEF Office of Research 2014).

As my study evolved, I realized I must focus on the intimate and local as well as the global. As explained earlier, the ecology of childhood is the study of systems and environments surrounding and affecting children. As with any ecosystem, it is best studied in a real time and in a real place. Therefore, my research project, which compared the effects on children and families of laws and policies in Europe and the United States, involved substantial fieldwork. I have focused my field research at the micro level, studying two small villages that offer insights into the ecology of childhood in two different cultures.

In describing these small worlds, I will use narratives and case studies and draw upon data, social science, and legal sources to examine and evaluate specific ecologies. I will also provide examples from other countries or regions in order to place these childhoods in a comparative and international frame. In evaluating systems, I will use as a touchstone of values those principles articulated in international human-rights treaties—and, more specifically, children's rights as established by the UN Convention on the Rights of the Child—as my overarching framework. While others might view the issues through a different lens, I am persuaded that children's human rights provide the best template for measuring how well we are doing at meeting the needs of children.

Much of what I will report has been learned through observing children and talking with them and their families. For example, the case I used above of the family with a terminally ill child is a real case from the region of Umbria, in Italy. I will also introduce you to the world of children in the Italian mountain village of Scanno, in the Abruzzi region, and compare it with that of children in Cedar Key, a Gulf Coast community in north central Florida. I will take you to one of the oldest and poorest quarters of Naples to meet courageous young people building alternatives to the lure of the Mafia. We will also visit the Harlem Children's Zone in the United States and examine the similarities and differences between these two urban initiatives. I will let the young people of Wales show you how they used the United Nations Convention on the Rights of the Child to elect their own parliament and push through many reforms. I will introduce you to Angelo, a teenager in trouble with the law who was saved from jail by a child-centered juvenile justice team. We will visit what may be the largest drug treatment community in the world and see how families can survive addiction and start new lives. I hope to make these children, their families, and their communities come alive in the pages of this book. Throughout, I will strive to draw connections between these individual stories and specific environments, and the larger forces of globalization, inequality, violence, environmental stress, and economic crisis that affect them.

Make no mistake; the most serious threats we face are not from natural but from human causes. Admittedly, humankind has achieved remarkable victories over some of its natural enemies: think of discoveries such as high-yield crops, antibiotics, and childhood vaccinations for diphtheria and polio. Our worst threats are self-inflicted: think of starvation, armed conflict, inequality, pollution, and global warming. What a legacy to leave to our children!

I wish I could promise solutions. I do propose several strategies. I fear that humankind may be reaching or may already have passed a tipping point in the ecology of childhood, much as it has in the setting of climate change. Nevertheless, perhaps some hope can be found in ecological theories of sustainability. Maybe we can build, if even on a very small scale, multiple sustainable environments that fully meet the needs of children born into them. This project is not only about children. They may be the canaries in the mine, signaling a toxic environment, but they also hold the secret to achieving a healthy planet. To borrow a phrase coined by youth delegates to the United Nations: "We want a world fit for children, because a world fit for children is a world fit for everyone" (UNICEF 2003b, 3).

Ultimately I call for a fundamental reformation of today's dominant macrosystemic values, at home and at the global level, to reduce the emphasis on individualism and materialism and to foster values of solidarity, sustainability, and mutual support, on which the survival of the human species depends. In closing, I propose specific ways in which each of us, wherever situated and however skilled, can play a role in creating a better environment for children.

2

Tools for Studying Childhood

Model: A schematic description of a system, theory or phenomenon . . . that may be used for further study of its characteristics.

Method: A means or manner of procedure, especially a regular and systematic way of accomplishing something.

Value: A principle or standard, as of behavior, that is considered important or desirable.

—*American Heritage Dictionary*

In this chapter I will provide some background on the methods, models, and value metrics that I have used in my studies of childhood. These are not the only models and methods developed by experts in childhood studies, nor is my value metric the only contender for evaluating child policy. However, they are the tools that proved to be most useful for my project. Initially, I began with the ecological model and the comparative method as my basic tools for studying childhood. The role of a model is not to duplicate reality but rather to facilitate and structure the study of reality. Likewise, the role of a method is not to substitute for analysis but to provide a framework for analysis that employs consistent measures and practices. Comparative method, as used by those who study law and policy, is a tool for exploring different legal, cultural, and political systems, with the goal of learning from their differences and similarities. Drawing lessons from these models and methods entails identifying a value system that provides a metric for judging what is important and desirable and what is not. The value metric I propose in these pages is neither that of efficiency beloved by economists nor that of preserving the status quo of tradition beloved by conservatives. Rather, it is a new philosophy of "ecogenerism" that reflects the most rapidly and universally accepted charter of human rights: the United Nations Convention on the Rights of the Child (CRC).

The Ecological Model

My embrace of the ecological model for this project—and for my scholarship in general—came only after first adopting, and then becoming dissatisfied with, the doctrinal model of constitutional law. I began my teaching career thirty years ago, after having clerked at the US Supreme Court for the first female justice, Sandra Day O'Connor, so I naturally gravitated toward the models for teaching US constitutional law. I always started the first family law class by drawing on the board a model representing the constitutional doctrine of family privacy: an isosceles triangle, with an S for State (meaning government) at the apex and the letters P and C for Parent and Child at each end of the base. Next, I would draw a line a few inches above and parallel to the base and then shade in this area, explaining that it represented the zone of family privacy. I would next draw an arrow shooting downward from the top of the triangle, to represent action by the State; when it hit the boundaries of the zone of privacy, it would be deflected. I would then draw a second arrow, this time thicker and more forceful. This arrow would pierce the zone of privacy. Using this model, I could provide a graphic illustration of a core principle of American constitutional law. Under US constitutional doctrine, the individual enjoys rights of family privacy and liberty and the State may only intrude on these rights if it is necessary to accomplish a compelling goal and if the means adopted are narrowly tailored to accomplish this goal. I still use this model for illustrating constitutional principles of family autonomy, but I became dissatisfied with it as a model for the broader study of children's law and policy. It had two major flaws: first, it showed only what the State must not do to families and did not show what it ought to do for families; and, second, it focused on the law and the individual child and parent to the exclusion of surrounding relationships and systems that affect children's well-being. My Child/Parent/State triangle failed to account for the complex reality of children's development and children's welfare.

I soon realized that my colleagues in the social sciences had developed other, more complex, and richer models. The ecological model that I adopted was pioneered by social scientists such as Urie Bronfenbrenner (1979) and James Garbarino (1985, 1995) (Woodhouse 2008a). Ecology involves the study of a living environment in which a specific organism or family of organisms is growing. As these experts understood, the ecological research methods and models developed for studying natural environments are useful to the study of childhood because they do not stop at abstractions, but examine how an organism interacts and is affected by its surroundings. The ecological model captures a basic truth about human development: there is no one "childhood," just as there is no one "adulthood." Instead, every childhood is shaped by and experienced within a living context. A particular social, cultural, and physical geography sets the stage on which childhood is played out.

Figure 2.1. Multiple generations sharing a public space as mass lets out in the Italian mountain village of Scanno. Cesidio Silla.

Childhood, understood as a stage of human development, exists in every society, but its boundaries and specifics vary widely. History and anthropology teach us that childhood is, to a large extent, a "social construct" (Aries 1962). It is defined by natural, cultural, demographic, and economic factors that shape a community's understanding of the role of the young in a given social order. Chronological age still plays an important part. There is no culture in which human infants are expected to fend for themselves at birth. All human beings go through stages of cognitive and physical development as they mature and develop autonomy. All human beings are born with basic needs for food, protection, socialization, instruction, shelter, and, most important, nurturing relationships. If these basic needs are not met, an infant cannot survive, much less thrive and grow into "adulthood."

How children's basic needs are met and the pace of their transition from dependency to increasing levels of autonomy differs from time to time and place to place (Woodhouse 2008a). Aboriginal or other traditional cultures follow oral customs or religious beliefs that determine at what age it is appropriate for a child to, for example, be married or sent into the bush to hunt or tend livestock. In modern societies, these boundaries often consist of laws establishing benchmarks based on chronological age. The law may state a specific age before which a child cannot be charged with a crime, drive a car, consent to sex, work, vote, or sign a binding contract. The law may specify a general "age of majority," marking with a bright line the end of legal childhood. In Italy and in most US states, that age is now eighteen, but for many centuries it was twenty-one. Even in modern rule-based societies, there are exceptions to every written rule. The exceptions are context-dependent and culturally dependent, differing from place to place. To use one stark example, in many US states children of any age who commit a criminal act can be deemed "adults" and tried in the adult courts under the theory that "a child who commits an adult crime deserves adult time." In Italy, no child younger than fourteen may be charged with a crime because they are presumed to be too immature to truly intend and understand the consequences of their acts (Bapat and Woodhouse 2016).

Ecology and childhood are interactive. The environment in which the child grows plays a role in setting benchmarks on the road to adulthood. In a simple agrarian society family economics dictate that children must work in the fields as soon as they are able to, if the family or tribe is to survive. In a technological society where young people need advanced education and training to enter the workforce, adulthood (defined by reaching self-sufficiency) may be delayed until well past twenty-one (Woodhouse 2001). External factors may influence the timing of the transition from childhood to adolescence to adulthood. Poverty, war, and natural calamities can force an early end to childhood, while, historically, enslavement and gender hierarchies have imposed a perpetual childhood on whole groups of people. Until very recently, such systems of oppression were reinforced by laws subjugating women and enforcing servitude on peasants in Italy and racial minorities in the United States. Their influence continues to this day (Levi 1983). Clearly, it is impossible to state an age at which childhood ends for all peoples and for all places and times. Contemporary human rights laws such as the CRC set age-based benchmarks but leave some margin for variation. The CRC avoids the thicket of defining when life begins and instead it treats all "persons" under eighteen years of age as "children" covered by its rights and protections. A particular nation may set a lower age of majority without violating the CRC (Article 1). The CRC also sets certain bright lines of age. For example, no person may be condemned to death or life in prison without parole for a crime committed before age eighteen (Article 37).

Psychologists and sociologists define childhood by stages of development. They may assign age ranges to various stages but are clear that each child develops at his or her own pace. Europeans and Americans have different cultural attitudes to childhood but tend to study the same scientific texts and theories and be guided by a shared body of scientific knowledge based on experiment and empirical research. Probably the most influential of all modern theories on child development was that of Swiss researcher Jean Piaget (1958), who defined the stages of human development according to his observations of children's behavior and cognitive capacity. Erik Erikson (1963), another famous researcher, defined stages slightly differently, according to children's psychological maturation. Modern parents are familiar with terms defining stages of maturation, such as infancy, early childhood, preadolescence, adolescence, and young adulthood, although they might find that the experts disagree on when these stages begin and end.

The ecological method, developed by Urie Bronfenbrenner (1979) and used by many contemporary experts in childhood such as James Garbarino (1985, 1995), accepts as a given that all children go through various cognitive and developmental stages on their way to adulthood and focuses attention on the surrounding environment. Like other organisms, young humans may find certain environments especially compatible with their flourishing at different stages of development, and they may find certain environments toxic and even deadly. No child, not even the child growing up in an affluent gated community, is immune to the effects of the surrounding physical and social environment (Woodhouse 2006a).

As illustrated in figure 1.1, the ecological model for the study of childhood uses a diagram as an aid to conceptualize children's environments. The diagram places the subject of study, the child, at the center (Siegler et al. 2017). In our diagram, the social systems in which the child actually participates are represented by intersecting circles called *microsystems*. Examples of microsystems might include family, neighborhood, school, peer group, and faith community. For a very sick infant, the ICU may be the space where all these microsystems converge. For a child growing up in a very simple culture, microsystems may be similarly coextensive. For example, in a culture where the family is defined as the entire tribe or village, the child's family life, education, peer-group interactions, religious life, and work training may all occur in the same spaces. Microsystems embedded in more complex societies and in urban locations may be harder to identify and study, but they still are present and critical to development. For a child growing up in a city, the circles representing the microsystems of childhood may be scattered across large areas with very few overlaps. The microsystems of children's lives may be far easier to trace and study in smaller, geographically isolated communities such as those I will use as examples.

In our ecological diagram, the spaces where two or more microsystems intersect are labeled *mesosystems*. What happens in these mesosystems is extremely important. Imagine the microsystems of religion and family intersecting and overlapping with, for example, a school in a religiously diverse community. If the microsystems are in harmony, the experience is relatively conflict free. If the child's school teaches religious tolerance and diversity while the family and faith community practice shunning and condemnation of nonbelievers, the mesosystem where these microsystems intersect can feel very conflicted and confusing to the child. The conflict may be constructive rather than harmful, but it exists and it affects the child. The crucial role played by mesosystems in building community solidarity will be further explored in chapter 5.

The diagram of childhood includes many places where children rarely go, but that nevertheless exert a powerful effect on the child's life. These are called *exosystems* (Siegler et al. 2017). In modern times, when many parents work outside their home community, the parent's workplace is usually a good example of an exosystem. A workplace that pays the parent a living wage and offers paid parental leave and good health-care benefits can have a very positive effect on the child's quality of life. A workplace that requires mandatory overtime and provides no health care can have a negative effect (Woodhouse 2008a). In modern Italian cities, as in the United States, many workers commute to their jobs. In small communities, children are more likely to spend a significant amount of time at their parents' workplace. Sometimes home and workplace share the same space; this is true of farming and fishing families, crafts workers, and small business enterprises where the family lives above the shop and children help their parents at work. Other exosystems are more or less separated from children's daily lives—the health-care system; the market economy; the transportation system; the welfare, pension, and retirement systems; and the systems governing natural resources as well as energy production and consumption. In a comparative ecological study, the indirect effects of these exosystems, often missing from a simpler analysis, become readily apparent (Siegler 2017). What differences do universal health care, universal preschool and subsidized maternity leave make in children's lives? What about clean air and water and safe, nutritious food?

The final element in the ecological diagram is called the *macrosystem*. The macrosystem is the patterning by history, power, and ideas of the broader society in which the child lives. It includes prejudices, politics, ideologies, religions, moral values, and even the concept of childhood itself (Woodhouse 2005; Woodhouse 2008a). The best analogy for the role of macrosystem values within our ecological model of childhood is the way in which water permeates our natural ecosystems. Like water, the values of the macrosystem flow throughout all levels of the environment and, having the capacity to either nourish or pollute it, shape its contours and dictate which organisms will survive in the environment and which will wither. But where does law fit into this picture? A group of social workers to whom I presented my work provided me with an excellent metaphor. They suggested that laws (and I would include public policies and deeply entrenched customs) are the conduits that channel macrosystemic values throughout the environment, influencing the exo-, meso-, and microsystems and thus shaping the realities of children's lives. As Glen H. Elder Jr. of the University of North Carolina argues, neither the macrosystem nor the ecology of childhood is static; childhood has a temporal dimension. Elder's work highlights the effects on children as a society moves through phases of stability and change (Elder 1996)—an insight that plays a large role in my study. We shall see how the interplay of internal stages of growth, external events, and societal forces in the period of rapid change between 2008 and 2018 has affected the childhoods under study.

While the concept of macrosystems may seem vague in the abstract, a comparative study reveals the powerful role they play. The environments of childhood may be very different in a society that places a high value on rugged individualism and competition compared with one that places a high value on mutual assistance and solidarity. Even the language for discussing values may be different. In Italy, "social solidarity" is the term used to describe government programs of social support that Americans call "welfare." In the United States the term "welfare" is often used as a pejorative, as in "ending welfare as we know it" or "welfare queen." In the United States, the term "solidarity," rather than having a positive meaning, is associated with communism and the redistribution of wealth. In Italy, the term "solidarity" is strongly positive, evoking unity of purpose and sticking together and helping others, especially those who are less fortunate.

Methods

While the ecological model provides the framework for my study, I utilize a number of methods developed in a variety of disciplines—including comparative law, sociology, history, economics, ethnography, and environmental science—as tools for exploring the ecology of childhood. I also relied on research, theories, and data from all of these disciplines.

Comparison as a Method

My work is grounded especially in comparative legal method. Comparative studies must be more than merely descriptive (Reitz 1998). They should drive home similarities as well as differences. They should force us to look beneath surface differences for functional equivalents—ways in which different systems accomplish the same or similar goals. They should investigate reasons why a particular law or social structure exists. Comparative studies of other systems can serve to heighten self-awareness and force us to challenge our own accepted wisdoms. For example, most Americans (and, indeed, most Italians) think of the United States as a land of opportunity, a wealthy country that is especially lavish in support of its children. Comparative studies show otherwise. A series of reports from UNICEF (UNICEF 2000; 2001a; 2001b; 2002; 2003a; 2005; 2007; 2008; 2010; 2012; 2013; 2014; 2016; 2017; 2018a) and the OECD (2009) measuring child well-being put Italy near the middle of the pack of developed nations and the United States either near or at the bottom. Studies of economic mobility measuring the likelihood that a child born in one economic class will rise to a higher one rank Italy above the United States (Acciari 2017). In a study of child mortality in twenty OECD nations, the United States ranked lowest of all, with rates of mortality 50 percent above the median, while Italy's child mortality rates were substantially below the median (Thakrar et al. 2018).

Comparison is one of the most basic tools of research. Scientists establish norms and primary-care doctors compare test results with these norms—a cholesterol test result is either low, normal, or high according to these comparisons. In studying children, we compare groups with each other when we measure scholastic achievement and health status. A child is in a lower or higher percentile of height compared to the national norm. In this book, I use several tools for comparison. Comparative ethnography opens the door to comparison of systems of social relations, while comparative law takes us outside the norm of a single country's laws to examine other possible normative systems. I use comparative methods to explore and explain the differences and similarities between children in different countries growing up under different legal and social systems.

In my work, I follow the method suggested by John Reitz (1998) in his article "How to Do Comparative Law." He identifies nine principles to be followed in any international legal comparison. The six most important for our purposes are: (1) draw explicit comparisons and do not just describe; (2) pay attention not only to similarities and differences but also be alert for functional equivalents; (3) develop conclusions based not only on distinctive characteristics of the specific legal systems but in commonalities they share in dealing with a particular subject matter; (4) use functional equivalents to push the analysis to broader levels of abstraction; (5) draw upon fields such as history and culture to shed light on reasons behind differences and similarities; and (6) always be guided by a spirit of respect for the other (Reitz 1998).

Most of these principles are easily understood. One should not merely describe two laws or two legal systems without delving explicitly into their differences and similarities. Nor can systems be understood in a vacuum, without reference to history, culture, and tradition. And, of course, respect for the unfamiliar "other" is a basic requirement of any comparative project. Indeed, the last item on Reitz's list is the most essential. Without respect for the "other" we are dealing in mere curiosities and making superficial judgments; we are likely to learn nothing worth knowing. I tell my comparative-law students to suspend their disbelief until they get used to a new idea. By taking time to study, appreciate, and respect other ways of doing things, we gain valuable insights into our own ways and are coaxed out of an exceptionalist stance that assumes our way is the best or only way (Walt 2011).

The concept of a "functional equivalent" perhaps requires more explanation. This concept tells us to look past form and focus on function. A good example is found in the realm of adoption. Adoption as we know it in the United States is not recognized in Islamic law (Todres 2006). However, standing back and looking at the underlying purposes of adoption, we quickly see that *kafala* is a functional equivalent in Islamic legal systems. *Kafala* does not erase the child's former name, lineage, or identity, but establishes a legal relationship between the child in need of a home and the adult who is committed to seeing that the child's needs are met. The search for functional equivalents leads us to a higher level of analysis: rather than studying "adoption" we might wish to study "systems for meeting the needs of children who have lost or are separated from their parents."

Functional equivalents will be highlighted throughout this book. To take but one example, it will become clear that Italian grandparents of every social class do the lion's share of caring for grandchildren from ages zero to three while their parents are at work. There may be no binding legal duty, but this is the reality of who provides infant and toddler daycare. As Italians often remark, we don't have a universal crèche system of baby nurseries like the French—we have *Nonna e Nonno* (Grandma and Grandpa). Looking for functional equivalents between the United States and Italy, we see that Italy's pension system can be thought of as the functional equivalent of US day-care subsidies and tax deductions. Policy-makers should hesitate before deciding that Italians who retire at sixty are lazy. By and large, they stay close to family and pool their resources with the next generation. This is a common practice in many extended families in the United States who live below the poverty line, whereas more affluent retirees often move to retirement communities that do not allow children. This realization pushes us to explore and compare the larger abstraction of "systems of intergenerational support" as they intersect with fiscal and family policies.

As suggested by principle 5, many other "methods" are useful in comparative and international study, especially for the study of childhood. As noted above, the methods I have used in this book come from many fields. Sociology and ethnography, in particular, have informed my study of childhood in the two villages, Scanno and Cedar Key, which serve as my petri dishes for studying childhood in specific social contexts.

Sociology and Ethnography as Methods

According to Lisa J. McIntyre, in *The Practical Skeptic: Core Concepts of Sociology*, "Sociology is the scientific study of interactions and relations among human beings" (McIntyre 2014, 2). Sociologists focus on the social rather than on the individual. Recognizing the power of social institutions, sociology examines social structures and interpersonal and group relationships. Sociology can be quantitative (e.g., numbers and data) or qualitative (e.g., narrative and case histories) or a combination of both. While sociology is a fact-based science, it examines a special kind of facts. As the French sociologist Emile Durkheim (1858–1917) explains, sociologists study social facts, a "category of facts which present very special characteristics: [social facts] consist of manners of acting, thinking and feeling external to the individual, which are invested with a coercive power by virtue of which they exercise control over him" (Durkheim 1895, quoted in McIntyre 2014, 14). Sociology plays a large role in the study of law because law is such a potent form of coercive power. When a legislature enacts a law it embodies social fact in its most coercive and explicit form. But even when a social fact is not embodied in formal law, it exerts coercive power. Consider the social facts (now prevalent in both the United States and Italy) that marriage proposals are expected to involve the offering of a ring and that guests at a wedding are expected to provide a gift, whether in cash or in household goods. Neither is enshrined in law in Italy or the United States. The details of social fact may change from era to era and place to place, but their coercive power persists.

A core concept of sociological research is "triangulation"—the strategy of utilizing a variety of methods to study a particular social phenomenon (McIntyre 2014, 95). Since various methods each have strengths and weaknesses, employing several different methods can produce a more balanced picture. Among the tools of sociology that I use in this project are the survey and the interview. It stands to reason that if you want to know what people think, ask them. Surveys and interviews cannot tell us what people actually do or think, but they can provide a local, subjective, first-person perspective. My survey of Scanno was designed in collaboration with an Italian colleague, Maura Cosenza. It was composed of ten open-ended questions and administered by the interviewer to a "convenience sample" (McIntyre 2014, 97). This method of sampling is random only in the sense that people are chosen at random by the interviewer. Interviewees could decide whether to use a pseudonym or their own first names. We made an effort to collect responses from a variety of people of different ages, marital status, and genders. The questions all aimed at discovering participants' views about what makes a good environment for raising children. I attempted to use the same survey method in Cedar Key, translating the questions and answers from Italian to English and adapting them slightly to the different physical and social context. I discovered that people in Cedar Key do not like surveys and formal interviews. Where interviewees in Scanno were voluble and spoke eagerly and with apparent candor, many ordinary Cedar Keyans whom I approached with a survey or a request for an interview "clammed up." It was not just me—as one older man said bluntly to my husband when he asked for information that might be controversial, "This is Cedar Key. We don't say nothing to nobody." This experience taught me to respect the high value placed on personal and family privacy and also to appreciate the habits of conflict avoidance that are characteristic of even a laid-back and outwardly informal community in the American South. The experience also spurred me to utilize public sources such as institutional Facebook pages (especially the Cedar Key School and the Cedar Key Beacon) and to use less formal methods myself. Often having a low-key chat about life in Cedar Key or asking a specific question rather than presenting people with a daunting survey were more effective ways of gaining insights.

The central method I used in my studies of the two villages was ethnography. Ethnography is a branch of sociology particularly adapted to studying social facts in a specific context. It is a research "process" that uses fieldwork and observation to learn about a particular community or culture. An "ethnography" is also the name given to the final product—the written description and analysis of the researcher's observations. Cultural and social ethnographers such as Margaret Mead (1901–1978) and Bronislaw Malinowski (1858–1942) believed that a researcher, rather than standing aloof, should immerse himself or herself in the culture under study for long periods of time. Ethnography began as a method of understanding exotic or primitive cultures, but it has spread to other fields and places closer to home. Carol B. Stack used the tools of ethnography to study a contemporary American community in her pioneering work *All Our Kin: Strategies for Survival in the Black Community* (1974). Unlike methods that require complete objectivity (the double-blind study, for example), ethnography encourages researchers to be participants as well as observers, in order to more fully understand local context and meaning (McIntyre 2014, 89). The goal of ethnography is to make sense of the social world by studying the meaning it has for the people who inhabit it. Ethnographers utilize a variety of approaches, ranging from historical research and data mining to unobtrusive observation and interviewing, but the key to success is remaining open minded and avoiding presumptions. As one expert explains, "The goal [of ethnography] is not proving a theory or testing a hypothesis; the goal is surprise" (McIntyre 2014, 93). My own experience confirms the value of an ethnographic approach, not only when studying a foreign culture but when studying one closer to home. Before embarking on fieldwork in Cedar Key, my understanding of its culture of childhood was shallow at best, despite my familiarity with the village as a longtime resident, because I had never intentionally immersed myself in its culture as researcher and as a participant observer.

Developing a Value System

In addition to methods, models, and perspectives, it is important for any study to be explicit about its overarching values. No field of study is entirely free of values and all have some ethical endpoint, even if it is not explicitly articulated. As the legal realists and critical legal scholars taught us, we need to dig beneath the surface of dominant norms and expose their underlying values and assumptions to critical examination. Seventeenth-century abolitionists challenged the dominant value systems that condoned slavery. Feminists in the nineteenth century challenged laws that discriminated against women. The twentieth century saw environmentalists challenging the rights of owners of natural resources to exploit them without regard to environmental impact. Each of these movements not only exposed but changed dominant value systems. The metric I have adopted in my work is the extent to which a particular environment meets children's essential needs (Woodhouse 2008a). While the notion of "what children need," like that of childhood itself, is a social and cultural construct, a large measure of consensus has developed around certain needs all human children have in common (Waldfogel 2006; Brazelton and Greenspan 2000). These needs go beyond basic survival and include the essential elements that allow a child to flourish. In Europe, where the CRC is universally accepted, these types of goods would be described as "rights" of the child, and these rights are recognized in European national as well as international law. The US legal tradition looks to the United States's own Constitution in defining rights. Since the Bill of Rights in the US Constitution is about what government *may not do to* its citizens, not about what it *must do for* its citizens, we tend to treat these as benefits government may choose or not choose to provide (Woodhouse 1999). While the United States does not classify a child's needs as positive "rights" that governments are obligated to protect, the impact on children of failure to meet their needs is equally harmful, regardless of the name we give it. In either case, our inquiry is the same: How well does the ecosystem fulfill children's essential needs? Is the ecosystem healthy? Is the ecosystem sustainable?

An Environmentalist Perspective on Values

Just as the ecological model, the comparative method, and ethnography offer important tools and lessons, the environmentalist perspective offers important insights into the value systems for determining what is important and desirable in an ecosystem. As I have argued in prior writings, the principles developed by environmentalists for protecting natural environments and endangered species are highly relevant to the development of law and policy protecting the young of our own species (Woodhouse 2004). Whether faced with degradation of the small worlds in which they live or faced with threats on a global scale, children can benefit from the environmentalist's holistic and protection-oriented perspective. Environmentalists have developed a number of principles and methods of study that deserve replication. These include methods such as examining problems in ecological context, and principles such as "sustainability" and "the precautionary principle."

The precautionary principle describes a commitment to erring on the side of caution in situations posing serious risks. As the EU consumer safety laws explain,

> The precautionary principle enables rapid response in the face of a possible danger to human, animal or plant health, or to protect the environment. In particular, where scientific data do not permit a complete evaluation of the risk, recourse to this principle may, for example, be used to stop distribution or order withdrawal from the market of products likely to be hazardous. (European Commission, for summaries of EU legislation)

While many areas of law and policy require clear evidence of actual harm before any protective action can be taken, an environmentalist perspective would err on the side of caution in protecting children from environmental harms.

Sustainability is another important tool for assessing goals and directions in environmental policy. It has been described as a commitment to "creat[ing] and maintain[ing] the conditions under which humans and nature can exist in productive harmony, that permit fulfilling the social, economic and other requirements of present and future generations" (National Environmental Policy Act, 42 USC 4321, 1970). Sustainability is the opposite of instant gratification. It requires us to focus beyond the short term and promotes justice for future generations.

Environmentalism also includes a commitment to evidence-based decision-making. All the tools of science must be brought to bear in order to understand the functioning of systems and to evaluate potential solutions to problems. In the area of childhood studies, these tools include the physical sciences such as neurology and epidemiology and the social sciences such as demographics and sociology. The very concept of childhood is a social construction as well as a physical reality, and its study must be multidisciplinary if it is to be meaningful.

Introducing Ecogenerism as a Value System

Inspired by both feminism and environmentalism, in my prior writings I have articulated a value system I call *ecogenerism* (Woodhouse 2004, 2005, 2009a, 2010). The "eco" in "ecogenerism" invokes the methods and principles of an ecological or environmental approach described above, while the term "generism" invokes a value called "generativity." In this value system, the needs and rights of the next generation are central rather than marginal (Woodhouse 1993). The term "generativity" was coined by developmental theorist Erik H. Erikson. Erikson, in his highly influential writings, identified a series of life stages, from infancy to old age, during which human beings face particular challenges. The primary task of "adulthood," Erikson theorized, is to develop a sense of commitment to caring for others as opposed to lapsing into self-absorption and stagnation. It is this quality of dedication to the flourishing of coming generations that exemplifies human maturity (Erikson 1963, 1976; Evans 1995). As reflected in the environmentalist perspective, this principle must be a core value of human societies. Obviously, ecogenerism was not invented when I coined the term. The same values of protection of the vulnerable are found in every religion and most systems of ethics.

Vulnerability Theory

As I was starting my project in Italy, my colleague Professor Martha Albertson Fineman, the leading feminist theorist in the United States, launched an exciting new project called the Vulnerability and the Human Condition Initiative

(2008). She argued that vulnerability, not autonomy, is the single universally shared human experience and that the role of society is to mitigate vulnerability and nurture resilience (Fineman 2008, 2010, 2013; Fineman and Shepherd 2016). As Fineman explains, "Even before the moment of birth, human beings are embedded in webs of economic, cultural, political and social relationships and institutions. . . . They are the legitimate means through which we can gain the assets or resources necessary to mediate, negotiate, or cope with our human vulnerability" (Fineman 2017, 61). During the decade of my study, Fineman's vulnerability theory has grown into an international movement with global reach. As the above quotation illustrates, Fineman's approach is richly contextual and rooted in an ecological vision of the human condition. Her pathbreaking work has influenced many scholars around the world, including myself.

Childhood in a Petri Dish

The combination of ecological, comparative, environmental, sociological, and ecogenerist models and methods brought me to the final step of choosing the village level as my medium for an ethnographic study of the culture of childhood. It is important to stress that selecting a site for ethnographic fieldwork is a very different enterprise from identifying a community that is "representative." The tools involved in attempting to define a "representative national childhood," if such a thing exists, are large-scale studies that mine various sources of data. UNICEF, with its Innocenti Report Cards, is an example of how researchers generalize a picture of national childhood. Part 3 of this book will focus on these forms of generalizing conclusions from large-scale data. The goal of an ethnographic study such as mine was to create a petri dish in which to study one small, specific, and isolated sample of a living social organism.

The petri dish was invented by German bacteriologist Julius Petri in 1890. Still used in laboratories all over the world, it is a shallow, cylindrical, lidded glass dish that serves as an enclosed space for growing and examining living organisms. To be useful, it must offer a good medium for study and generalization. In order to make a comparison between Italy and the United States, I needed to find two petri dishes—two communities that were sufficiently similar to allow children's environments to be compared and sufficiently different to expose differences in the two contexts. Why did I choose to focus my fieldwork on the relatively small and isolated microecology of the village? I began my project with a bias toward studying small towns. I have always been intrigued, as an academic researcher and as a parent and citizen, with the critical roles played by neighborhood and community in creating sustainable environments for children and families. I grew up in a small town and returned there to raise my own children. So, in pursuing my research in the comparative ecology of childhood, I naturally gravitated toward smaller communities. The oft-quoted African proverb says that "it takes a village to raise a child." The point of the ecological model (and of the proverb) is to break away from a myopic focus on the structure and dynamics of the family of origin. Endless studies have dissected the influence on children of variations on family structure—single-parent families, divorced families, LGBTQ families, blended families, and extended families. While family systems are important factors in the ecology of childhood, this narrow focus can obscure the influence of the other systems highlighted by the ecological model.

But the villages of the proverb come in all shapes and sizes, including the indigenous tribe, the inner-city neighborhood, and the suburban bedroom community. Why not examine urban villages as opposed to rural ones? I seriously considered this option. I began my project in Florence, Italy, a medium-sized city with many distinctive neighborhoods. I teach in Atlanta, Georgia, a modern city with a highly diverse population. In Italy, as in the United States, urban communities have been a rich source of research of the hidden strengths as well as the persistent problems of raising children in urban settings (Stack 1974; Tough 2009; Loffredo 2013). One might assume that urban neighborhoods deserve special attention because they present a risk-intensive environment for children, with higher crime rates, more socially marginalized residents, and greater concentrations of poverty. Contrary to common assumptions in US culture, child poverty in the United States is higher in rural areas than in urban areas, at 26 percent versus 21.5 percent. In addition, more children live in rural than in urban areas—only one-third live in urban areas with the other two-thirds evenly divided between large and small rural areas (US DHHS 2015). The same is true in Italy and the EU, with the incidence of poverty higher among families with minor children and higher in rural than urban areas (Bertolini 2008, ISTAT 2017).

Moreover, I was especially anxious to gain as clear a comparative picture as possible of an Italian and a US microsystem and mesosystem in action. I learned the hard way how difficult it is to study a small community in a rapidly urbanizing setting. I began my field research in 2008 in Lacugnano, a small community on the outskirts of Perugia, the capital of the province of Umbria. I had longstanding connections to the community and an entrée into local institutions. But within the first two years I realized the community was being so rapidly erased by urban sprawl and its boundaries were becoming so porous and blurred that it was losing its identity. It became too hard to screen out the static. This experience set me looking for a more isolated community—a true petri dish.

Another reason to study small communities is that the researcher, not to mention the reader, can really get to know the place and the cast of characters. A model, like a short story or a one-act play, is a bridge between abstraction and real life experience. The purpose behind my detailed pictures of life in these villages is to create a place in the mind of readers where they can see the ecology of childhood actually functioning. "The child" at the center of the diagram becomes a specific child or group of children embedded in a specific community; the abstract "microsystems" take on a real life of their own, becoming more accessible and relatable. The reader, not to mention the researcher, recognizes and draws connections between lived experience and theory. Let me be clear: descriptions and narratives such as I provide in this section of the book are not a substitute for macro-level research in social sciences. They do not pretend to provide data to support predictions or establish correlations or causation. As noted, many of the chapters that follow the ethnographic study will mine the social science data to extract large-scale insights. The purpose of my ethnographic studies is to provide context for understanding the ecology of childhood. In addition, they provide contextual frames for assessing observed similarities and differences, many of which are also supported by macro-level data. The process of transforming a two-dimensional ecological model and a mass of dry macro-level data into a three-dimensional understanding of childhood involves placing the data and the model in concrete context, through the use of images, narratives, and case histories.

Finding Scanno

By 2011, three years into my project, at the top of my agenda was the task of locating an Italian community to serve as my Italian petri dish. It had to be small enough to study in fine-grained detail and yet sufficiently prototypical to serve as a bridge between the theoretical model and the real lives of children and families. I happened upon the Italian mountain village of Scanno by accident, while on my way to southern Italy in May 2011. I had spent the past three years visiting children's centers and schools, interviewing parents, lawyers, judges, and social workers and observing juvenile courts and social-services outreach in Florence, Verona, Perugia, Turin, Lecce, and Rome. My companions on this adventure had been my husband, Charley, at the wheel of our various rental cars, and our pug dog, Jane. Jane was not just along for the ride; she served as a magnet for children and a great conversation starter with adults. Along with my fluency in Italian, Jane has been my secret weapon.

Figure 2.2. Panorama of Scanno nestled in the mountains of the Abruzzo National Park. B. B. Woodhouse.

The evening when we first saw Scanno, we had been travelling on the Italian A-24, a modern highway that bisects the Italian peninsula from Rome on the Mediterranean coast to Pescara on the Adriatic coast. Called the Highway of the Parks (Autostrada dei Parchi), this marvel of engineering tunnels through the Abruzzi mountains, part of the Apennine chain that runs from the crown of the Alps to the toe of the Italian boot-shaped peninsula. We were on our way to Lecce, in the province of Puglia, located at the heel. As evening approached, we needed a convenient spot to spend the night. Looking at our map, Scanno seemed ideal–just twenty kilometers off our route. What our map did not reveal was the hair-raising adventure ahead. Between the superhighway exit and Scanno lay thirteen miles of narrow road—often wide enough for only one car—snaking up the spectacular Sagittarius Gorge, climbing steeply around hairpin curves, clinging to the edges of steep precipices, and tunneling through galleries hewn by hand in rocky cliffs. It took forty-five minutes of heart-in-mouth driving for us to reach our destination.

Finally, the village of Scanno came into sight, tucked in a narrow valley and encircled by seven-thousand-foot mountains.

We skirted the alpine lake (Lago di Scanno), headed for the town center, checked into a dog-friendly hotel, and took Jane out for her evening walk. As we expected in this part of Italy, the town center was a warren of cobblestone streets, connected by pedestrian steps, winding among ancient stone buildings and punctuated by church towers. What we did not expect to see was dozens and dozens of children. As will be discussed in chapter 5, the birth rate in Italy had recently hit an all-time low, well below the replacement level. While large families remain common in southern Italy, family size in central and northern Italy has fallen sharply. There is enormous irony in the fact that babies are becoming a scarce commodity in a culture that worships babies. I had grown used to the lament that children were disappearing from the Italian *piazza* (public square). But the central piazza of Scanno was alive with children: in parents' arms and on grandparents' knees, in strollers and on tricycles. We saw toddlers practicing their first steps, as well as kids riding bikes and scooters, kicking balls, and playing with dolls, while adults chatted nearby and old folks rested on benches. As if to drive home the centrality of children in this community, one whole side of the piazza was devoted to the Good Shepherd Children's Nursery (Asilo dell Infanzia Buon Pastore), the community's day nursery and kindergarten. As we explored the narrow streets, we saw many doors with rosettes of ribbons announcing, in blue or pink, the arrival of a new infant.

Why was Scanno so full of children? I began my field research that evening by asking this question of people we met in the piazza. Their responses showed a common theme: Scanno was a good place to raise children. This was a friendly environment (*ambiente*) for children and families. We could see this for ourselves. With streets and piazzas largely free from traffic, children could play together in the same spaces where grandparents and teenagers also congregated. Economic and age segregation seemed to be at a minimum. Young families were not isolated from each other behind walls and fences; they were an integral part of the community, and they experienced the support of neighbors and extended family. This sense of community was driven home to us next day when we found all the restaurants in town were closed for lunch because the town was celebrating the first communion of this year's crop of the town's children.

Scientists who study child well-being have documented the risks associated with the isolation and marginalization of young families. Yet it is rare to see a situation of inclusion and solidarity so clearly illustrated. In our increasingly fragmented economically developed societies, much of family life takes place in private and in age-specific and class-segregated spaces. Families are increasingly mobile and geographically isolated from extended family, putting more stress on nuclear family relationships. Moreover, the sheer detail and complexity of modern childhood, in Italy as well as the United States, can be overwhelming. In affluent urban or suburban environments, children's agendas are so packed with lessons, sports, and play dates that children and parents really do need their personal iPhones to keep track of everybody's whereabouts and to schedule transportation.

The next morning, to learn more about Scanno, I stopped by the Palazzo Comunale (town hall) and was encouraged by what I learned. The mayor was out of town, but the ladies who worked there suggested I contact Don Carmelo, the parish priest. "He knows everything there is to know about family life in Scanno," they told me. They assured me that I would find him in church and sent me back to the main piazza to knock at the sacristy door of Santa Maria della Valle (St. Mary of the Valley). Monsignor Carmelo Rotolo, who was just finishing mass, was a short, stocky, white-haired man in his eighties with a welcoming smile. Although he had been promoted to Monsignor, he still preferred the simple parish priest's title of *Don* (Father). He was born in Scanno and had been its parish priest for over thirty years. When I told him about my idea of studying childhood in Scanno, he encouraged me to come back the following spring and promised ("God willing") that he would be there to help me get started.

I went back in the spring of 2012. Don Carmelo was as good as his word. He entrusted me to a lady named Anna who took me across the square to the Good Shepherd Nursery (the Asilo) that I had noticed on my earlier visit. I had assumed it was a religious institution. In the United States, where we have a tradition of separation of church and state, the lines between secular and sectarian are fairly clear. A hybrid institution like the Good Shepherd Nursery would be an anomaly in the United States. Good Shepherd is a community nursery and children's center, supported by private donors as well as by the Catholic Church and state funding. It has a citizen board but is staffed by an order of teaching nuns. Its big, airy, three-story home was built with labor and money donated to the children of Scanno by a group of citizens in the 1930s. The Good Shepherd Nursery has touched the life of virtually every Scanno child for eighty years. As I later learned, my visit to the Asilo reverberated in kitchens all over town as children reported to their parents and grandparents that a *Professoressa Americana* (American lady professor) had come to their school. They had sung her a song in English and she had talked to them in Italian.

As word of my research project spread, I was able to expand my contacts to a wide variety of citizens, teachers, children, and parents. I visited schools, attended festivals and sports events, and spent many hours observing children at play. I also studied the history, culture, and economy of Scanno. As readers will learn, my first impressions of Scanno, albeit naïve and oversimplified, were basically correct. It is a good place to raise young children. In social science terms, which will be explored in detail in coming chapters, the ecological systems affecting Scanno's children seem to function in synchrony, with a minimum of stressful risk factors and a maximum of supportive protective factors. It became my Italian petri dish.

In fact, Scanno resembles many small communities the world over. As one of my colleagues back in the United States remarked, after I gave a presentation on my Italian field research, "Take away the Italian local color, great food and spectacular scenery and you could be back in my hometown in Iowa in 1955." He spoke movingly of a lost world where everyone knew your name. But it would be very wrong to think of Scanno as some sort of Italian Brigadoon. While a visitor experiences a feeling of stepping back in time, Scanno is definitely part of the modern world. It has televisions and parking fines, cellphones, high-speed internet and webcams, and a tourist industry that attracts visitors from all over the world in both winter and summer. When we first came to Scanno, there were some forty elderly women who still donned the traditional costume of headscarf and long full skirt every morning, recreating the image immortalized by photographer Henri Cartier-Bresson. But their granddaughters drive cars and wear the latest fashion in track shoes and form-fitting leggings. Except for festival days, when many girls and young women put on the traditional wedding dress and reenact the old traditions for visitors, the young women of Scanno look thoroughly modern. In Scanno I had found the mixture of history and modernity that I hoped would capture the essence of Italian family life.

Rediscovering Cedar Key

Having decided on Scanno for my Italian site, I set about looking for a comparable petri dish for studying childhood in the US context. After considering several possibilities further afield, I realized I had one in my own backyard: the island community of Cedar Key, Florida, which has been my home since 2002. Actually, my first Cedar Key visit dates back to 1995, when my husband and I "discovered" it while driving from Tallahassee, the capital of Florida, to Tampa, a big modern city further south along Florida's Gulf of Mexico coastline. We were travelling south on US Highway 98, which runs from Tallahassee to Tampa. This highway is forced to stay twenty-five miles inland to avoid the swamps, hammocks, and inlets that honeycomb the mostly

Figure 2.3. View from No. 2 Bridge, crossing from mainland Florida into Cedar Key. B. B. Woodhouse.

uninhabited stretch of land known as Florida's "Nature Coast." Hoping to find a lunch stop with a view of the Gulf, we turned off Highway 98 onto a narrow road that runs straight out to the island village of Cedar Key, twenty-five miles due west, without a single turn, a single stoplight, or a single crossroads. After miles of wilderness, the dense swampland and pine forests suddenly opened out to reveal a string of small islands connected by a series of bridges. Crossing several bridges, we arrived in the Island City of Cedar Key.

It is a cliché to say that we felt as if we had stepped back in time. But sometimes life delivers clichés. We saw battered fishing boats tied up at wooden docks, modest tin-roofed wood houses painted in sun-washed colors, and a few old motels and tourist cottages with names like Mermaid's Landing and Pirates' Cove. We saw a white clapboard church shaded by live oak trees dripping with Spanish moss crowning the one small hill in the center of the tiny island. We spent an hour exploring the village, admired the classic old Island Hotel, which was built out of oyster shell, limestone, and sand in 1859 by the first European settlers. We ate seafood at a restaurant on Dock Street and promised ourselves we would return.

We could not have predicted that in 2001 I would receive an invitation to found the David H. Levin Center on Children and Families at University of Florida's Levin College of Law, just fifty miles inland from Cedar Key. The following year we bought a rustic house in Cedar Key and eventually became official Cedar Key residents.

I titled this subsection "Rediscovering Cedar Key" because I have been struck by how differently I approached this by-now-familiar village once I began to consider it as a site for field research. First I had to determine if it was a good match for a comparative study. Like Scanno, Cedar Key is geographically isolated from any large commercial hub, so it presents a relatively self-contained and self-sufficient site for studying the ecology of childhood. Like Scanno, Cedar Key is surrounded by extensive tracts of unspoiled natural beauty among the islands of the Cedar Key National Wildlife Refuge. Like Scanno, Cedar Key has retained its own distinct identity and has not become absorbed by urban or cultural sprawl. In the next chapter I will provide other examples of commonalities between Scanno and Cedar Key and explore the many differences.

I also had to navigate the passage from semiretired seasonal resident to researcher. This passage was both more interesting and more difficult than I had imagined. It was more interesting because the research process revealed how little I knew as a mere resident and prompted me to ask questions and delve into facts and relationships I had either never noticed or had taken for granted. The passage was more difficult than I expected because my relationship with Cedar Key was subtly altered. While Cedar Key had been my legal residence for a decade, my professional life and much of my personal life was based in the Northeast, where I was born and have family ties. My working home was Atlanta, where I have been a faculty member at Emory Law School since 2009. I always knew I would never be an insider in Cedar Key in the same way as those who are born and raised there. Here was another commonality with Scanno, where I am distinctly a respectful presence but an outsider who comes from somewhere else. But, as I noted earlier, strategies that had been successful in Scanno, such as structured surveys and interviews, fell flat in Cedar Key. I was no longer a "snow bird," as Floridians call northerners who come south to get away from the snow. Suddenly, I was a researcher, with all the invasiveness that the label implies. In the end, this difference between the research environments in Scanno and Cedar Key provided important insights. In chapter 3 I will provide more detailed, systematic comparisons of the two villages. My "Tale of Two Villages" will serve to provide a real-life context in which to anchor and illustrate my observations about the ecology of childhood

The previous discussion illustrates the range of models, methods, and values metrics that go into studying social phenomena. During the past few decades, however, these humanistic methods and models have taken a back seat to a faith in free-market economics. Efficiency became the preferred measure for policy-makers. Good things were expected to trickle down to workers when capital and labor markets operated efficiently. Instead, inequality has risen and working-class people have suffered. There have always been dissenting voices raised against unregulated capitalism, in books by former academics like Senator Elizabeth Warren (2017), political scientists like Robert Reich (2015), Nobel Prize–winning economists like Joseph Stiglitz (2015, 2016) and Paul Krugman (2012), and French researcher Thomas Piketty (2014). Perhaps the most widely known critic of unrestrained capitalism is an Argentinian who emigrated to Italy, the land of his ancestors, in 2013: former Cardinal Jorge Bergoglio, who was elected to head the Catholic Church. He took the name of Francis because of his concern for the poor and vulnerable and for the environment. *Time* magazine named him its Person of the Year in 2013 and one of the one hundred most influential people in its 2014 edition.

Pope Francis is also a master of social media. According to one 2014 study, "Pope Francis has by far the most clout of any world leader on Twitter because he is so widely retweeted" (Fowler 2014). It must be admitted that the institution he leads is deeply flawed in many ways. For every Francis of Assisi or Cardinal Romero, critics can point to a venal Renaissance pope or a brutal Spanish inquisitor. Presently, the Catholic Church is struggling to adequately confront and atone for a tragic legacy of child abuse by priests, an evil that was enabled and compounded by cover-ups and denial in the Church hierarchy (Grand Jury Report 2018; Goodstein and Otterman 2018). Yet Pope Francis, with his humility, ecumenical outreach, and common touch, has brought a breath of fresh air and modernity to the Vatican. The same qualities that have offended and infuriated conservative Catholics have inspired others, who welcome his message of concern for the poor and vulnerable, openness to change, and greater inclusiveness (Horowitz 2018).

Collecting "Francis quotes" has become an international pastime, and not just among Catholics. Certain themes appear repeatedly in his speeches and writings. In May 2014 he gave an address on the role of science in preserving precious human and natural resources. Gazing out over a massive crowd gathered in front of the Basilica of Saint Peter in Rome, he said, "The gift of knowledge helps us to avoid falling prey to excessive or incorrect attitudes. The first lies in considering ourselves masters of Creation. Creation is not a property, which we can rule over at will, or, even less, the property of only a few. . . . If we destroy Creation, in the end it will destroy us!" (Vatican Radio 2014). On July 5, 2014, he addressed thousands of young people gathered at a youth pilgrimage to a shrine in the mountains of Abruzzo and Molise:

> We cannot resign ourselves to losing a generation of young people who do not have the dignity of work! . . . A generation without work is a future defeat

for the country and for humanity . . . we must fight against this, and help each other find a solution, through help and solidarity. . . . Solidarity is a Christian word which means forging ahead alongside one's brother to help and overcome problems. (NCR 2014)

He exhorted them to "be courageous, with hope and solidarity" (NCR 2014). Under Pope Francis's guidance, in May 2014 the Joint Workshop of the Pontifical Academy of Science and the Pontifical Academy of Social Sciences linked "Sustainable Humanity" with "Sustainable Nature," defining both of these values as a collective responsibility of all (Dasgupta, Ramanathan, and Minnerath 2014). He has called us to resist the "economy of exclusion" and the "globalization of indifference" to human suffering (Magliano 2013) and denounced the "throw away culture of globalization and called for new ways of thinking about poverty, welfare, employment and society" (MacKenzie 2015). Pope Francis's words have struck a chord in many listeners, within and outside the Christian community, who share his concern for the future of the planet and for the future of humanity. As President Barack Obama wrote in *Time* magazine, referring to Pope Francis, "Rare is the leader who makes us want to be better people" (Obama 2014). In the past few years I have formed the habit of collecting "Francis quotes" and including them in my writings.

Perhaps the most apt quotation, as I move forward in describing my ecological project of renewal, is the following, taken from Pope Francis's encyclical on the environment, "Laudato Si': On Care for Our Common Home":

> The urgent challenge to protect our common home includes a concern to bring the whole human family together to seek sustainable and integral development, for we know that things can change (Pope Francis 2015c).

PART 2

Microsystems and Mesosystems

3

A Tale of Two Villages

I bambini di Scanno stanno bene dove stanno.
(The children of Scanno are doing very well right where they are.)
—Bruno Lauzi, "I bambini di Italia—I testi delle tradizionale filastrocche"

It's a shame one day the modern ways will overrun our shore
The progress of the concrete's bound to change our island world,
And people when they pass won't take the time to say "Hello,"
But not as long as tin roof shanties dot the coastline of our home.
—Bob Cooper, "Notes on the Song 'Tin Roof Shanties,' Cedar Key's Very Own Ballad"

Each of the two villages in this study is unique, yet both are rich with examples of the ecology of childhood. The two epigraphs with which I begin the chapter are emblematic of each village's particular ethos. The first is from a patter song describing childhood in various Italian towns and boasting that children born in Scanno have no desire to leave their native village. Scannesi are fond of quoting the song, and associate it with the value of growing up in a place where children play freely on their own from an early age, with nature at their doorstep (D'Alessandro 2017).

The second epigraph is from a country-music ballad about Cedar Key. The shanty, a one-room, metal-roofed shack made of wood, is just the kind of structure that is anathema to developers who want to pave over the state of Florida. The song represents Cedar Keyans' pride in the authenticity, down-home informality, and lack of pretension of their little island city. While the song first appeared in the 1980s, those tin roof shanties still line the Cedar Key shores thirty years later (Cooper 2017).

In part 2 of this book we explore the microsystems and mesosystems of childhood in these two concrete contexts. The first part of this chapter is devoted to detailed portraits of the two villages. These portraits will set the stage for the second part, which applies a comparative method of study. In chapter 4, we will focus on the mesosystems, where children's worlds overlap and intersect with community institutions, and consider their crucial role in building community identity and solidarity.

Portrait of Scanno

Scanno is located in south central Italy, in the province of Aquila, region of Abruzzo. Scanno's elevation is 1,050 meters (3,440 feet) above sea level. The modern town, which began as a fortified hilltop settlement, has expanded beyond its ancient walls onto surrounding slopes but retains its distinct identity. The mountain valley where Scanno is situated is surrounded by a ring of mountains rising another 3,000 feet above the town, part of the National Park of Abruzzo, Lazio, and Molise. The surrounding forests are home to the *Orso Bruno Marsicano* (marsican brown bear), *Lupo Appenninico* (appennine wolf), and herds of animals similar to small mountain goats and known as *camosci* (chamois). Scanno is governed by a popularly elected mayor (*Sindaco*) and citizen council composed of both majority and minority party representatives ("Scanno, Abruzzo" n.d.).

In Scanno, children's schooling begins at age three in the Good Shepherd Nursery, described in the prior chapter. At age six, children move on to the public schools. Control of Italian public schools is vested in regional and national authorities, with significant local input. Scanno's school buildings, which also serve children from the nearby town of Villalago, have been a focal point of both pride and anxiety. In the six years of my study, the location of the primary- and middle-school classes was changed three times because of concerns about the earthquake resistance of existing structures. For high school (*Liceo*), Scanno's young people still travel via the regional public bus service to the city of Sulmona. Sulmona, with a population of 24,454, is located forty minutes down the mountain, through the Sagittarius Gorge and across a wide valley ("Sulmona, Aquila" n.d.). Graduating from the Scanno schools and going to Sulmona is a major rite of passage, both for children and their parents.

The residents of Scanno, called *Scannesi,* are overwhelmingly white and Catholic, with a few Muslims and Jehovah's Witnesses. The village's population has been shrinking: Scanno was home to 1,883 residents in 2013, but by 2018, with deaths outpacing births, the population was only 1,780 (Tuttitalia 2018). At Scanno's historic zenith, in the year 1706, there were 2,736 residents (Caranfa 2010).

As I described my first visit to Scanno in chapter 2, you may have wondered how this remote spot produced such a rich stock of handsome stone dwellings and baroque churches. The answer is, in one word, sheep. The village's wealth was produced, and its people's lives were defined, by an animal husbandry system dating back to pre-Roman times called the *transumanza* (Notarmuzi 2005). Sheep were valuable for wool, meat, leather, and cheese—goods that could be sold or traded for products from other regions. Each year, before the winter, Scanno's shepherds herded their sheep from the mountain pastures all the way down the Apennine mountain chain to the warmer plains of Puglia, a province that occupies the heel of the Italian boot.

For Scanno's families, the *transumanza* system meant that virtually all the able-bodied males, from the age of eight, were gone for much of the year, either up in the local mountains or down in the pastures of Puglia. The women shouldered the responsibility for a multitude of tasks (Notarmuzi 2005; Caranfa 2010). They labored from before dawn to dusk, gathering firewood, carrying water, washing clothes and wool, spinning the wool into yarn, and weaving the yarn into cloth.

With the decline of the sheep industry, in the aftermath of both World Wars, many Scannesi were forced to migrate, either temporarily or permanently. Some crossed the Atlantic, to the United States, Canada, and Latin America. Some went to northern Italy or neighboring countries. Those who remained in Scanno were determined to preserve their livelihoods and culture, waging a battle against the tide of out-migration that was emptying many mountain villages. Today, the herds of sheep in the Abruzzo territory, once numbering as many as five million animals, have shrunk to less than 200,000. Instead of being herded along the broad *transumanza* trails, these days the sheep are loaded onto trucks to travel to the winter pastures or brought into mountain barns to shelter from the snow. However, the social structure of the *transumanza* has left its mark on Abruzzo mountain culture. Today, many of Scanno's sons—and, increasingly, its daughters—still travel to nearby cities to find work, returning on weekends or holidays. While males are in the majority in Scanno's formal government structures, Scanno's self-sufficient and entrepreneurial women are still the heart of the village's social, religious, and economic life.

World War II, which was the final blow to Scanno's traditional way of life, is vividly remembered by Scanno's elders. Although Scanno escaped Allied bombardment, the town was occupied by German troops. In a bitterly resented move, the Germans commandeered all of Scanno's remaining 27,000 sheep and sent them to be slaughtered, to feed the German army. The Armistice of 1944 was followed by a period of terrible hardship. Widespread starvation gripped the mountain communities, as refugees from Rome and Naples fled these occupied cities, swelling the number of mouths to be fed. The villagers shared their bread with these refugees, as they had with escaped British and US soldiers during the German occupation (Associazione Culturale 2009).

Candido Nannarone, a mountaineer and father of two adopted children whom you will meet later in this book, likes to say that the Scannesi inherited the survival instinct from their rugged pre-Roman ancestors, a fierce people who resisted Roman domination and were never defeated. It is certainly true that the mountain people of Scanno survived multiple waves of invasion, by Roman troops, Germanic tribes, English crusaders, French troops, homegrown *Briganti* (bandits), and Spanish absentee rulers.

Through all of these changes, Scanno's villagers have retained their own distinctive dialect and traditions, while also integrating newly arrived groups through intermarriage. Despite the present national tension over immigration, during my eight seasons of watching daily life in Scanno I have observed the peaceful integration of a new wave of migrants into the town's social fabric. There are quite a few children in Scanno who have come from other countries, including Romania and Ukraine, and four of the twelve children celebrating their first communion in 2019 were biracial, with a parent born in Scanno and a parent who emigrated from Africa or Cuba. The Catholic Church has been a force in promoting integration, and the priest assisting at mass or hearing confession in Santa Maria della Valle is as likely to be from Africa or Asia as from Italy.

In the postwar years, an economy based largely on herding and agriculture has been replaced by an economy based primarily on organic farming and on ecological, cultural, and sports-oriented tourism. This shift was not an accident but a conscious plan for survival. A plaque in Via Silla honors the village leaders of the 1970s who promoted this change. Tourism has a long history in Scanno. Because of its altitude, Scanno remains cool when Rome is blistering, and families from Rome have always come to the mountains to escape the summer heat and humidity. The surroundings provide opportunities for sports like boating, fishing, biking, and mountain trekking. In the 1970s, the town built a ski lift and added a winter season for downhill skiing. While winter skiing is declining due to global warming, Scanno has become a major center for ultra sports. It now hosts a number of international events, including a mountain-biking marathon and a triathlon that combines swimming in Lago di Scanno, biking on the roads and trails, and some of the most arduous mountain running in the world. Ecotourism is another modern variation on an old theme, since visitors have been drawn to Scanno's natural setting as long as the town has existed. In addition to visits to national parks, a pastime called *agroturismo*, involving visits to traditional farms and organic food enterprises, is growing in popularity. Local craftsmen and producers have exploited growing public support for sustainable agriculture, spearheading a revival of production of local goods, including wool from Abruzzo sheep and traditional Abruzzo cheeses, meats, and sausages.

Scanno has been celebrated since the nineteenth century for its photogenic streets and the unique costumes of its women. Known as the "City of the Photographers" because of photography greats such as Henri Cartier-Bresson, who immortalized nineteenth-century Scanno, and Mario Giacomelli, whose work *Bambino di Scanno* is displayed in the Museum of Modern Art in New York, Scanno continues to be a magnet for photographers and artists from as far away as Japan (Guerra and Giacomelli 2016). Scanno is also known for its traditional crafts, including a unique style of gold filigree pendant known as the *presentosa*, a sheep's-milk cheese known as *pecorino*, and a delicious chocolate cake called *pan dell'orso* (bear's cake) (Giannantonio 2010; L'Appuntamento con La Tradizione 2018; Scanno: un borgo nel cuore d'Abruzzo 2018; Di Masso 2018). The town is also unusually rich in literary and cultural resources, including *La Foce*, a literary magazine dating to the 1940s, and the *Gazzettino della Valle del Sagittario*, which covers current events and cultural subjects. The internet has opened a new resource for sharing information, with several news blogs including one hosted by the *Gazzettino* and another called La Piazza di Scanno, hosted by former mayor Eustachio Gentile. Today, Scanno is benefiting from a renaissance in traditional crafts and foods. Visitors can taste authentic baked goods, salamis, and cheeses, visit the Museo di Lana (Museum of Wool) to see the ancient traditions of the *transumanza*, step into a replica of an antique goldsmith's shop, or observe girls and women demonstrating the ancient art of lace-making on the sausage-shaped cushion called the *tombolo* (Giannantonio 2010).

For the purposes of my research, the most meaningful Scanno traditions were those that involved children and youth. Scanno's calendar is defined by a series of religious festivals with roots in both Christian and pagan sources (Mastrogiovanni 2010). In referring to events or seasons, Scannesi commonly use the *festa* (festival) as a proxy for the month or season—"around *Sant' Antonio*" means the second week of June. "After *San Martino*" means late November. The most important *feste* all involve children. At *Natale* (Christmas) the town hosts a living nativity scene with real adults and children in costume, real animals in the stable, and the newest mothers and infants serving as the Madonna and Baby Jesus. Traditions get repurposed or supplemented as times change. The American-style Santa Claus has been added to Italian traditions, but *La Befana* (Epiphany Witch), an old lady on a flying broomstick, remains a staple, still arriving on January 5 with a stocking stuffed with sweets for children who have been good and lumps of coal for those who have been bad.

Figure 3.1. Scanno children delivering firewood during Festival of Saint Anthony. B. B. Woodhouse.

In addition to celebrations surrounding Christmas, which are child-centered in many cultures, Scanno celebrates a number of other religious festivals in which children play a central role. While the official parish church is Santa Maria della Valle, Don Carmelo presides over some four or five other churches dating from as far back as the 1400s. Many, including Madonna delle Grazie (Madonna of the Graces), Madonna del Carmine (Madonna of Mount Carmel), Sant' Eustachio (Saint Eustace, patron saint of Scanno), and Sant' Antonio (Saint Anthony of Padua), have their own confraternities, all of which join in celebrating each other's festivals. In May, a procession winds from the town down to the lakeside church of the Madonnina del Lago (Little Madonna of the Lake) to fetch a small wood statue of the saint, dressed in embroidered satin. She is especially important to children; one day during her month-long sojourn in the mother church, the children of Asilo Buon Pastore, joined by mothers pushing baby carriages, parade through town carrying Easter lilies to decorate her altar. The Festa di Sant'Antonio (Festival of Saint Anthony) occurs in June and is one of the most popular among children. In the preceding weeks, townspeople cut and gather firewood in the mountains. The high point of the festival is when the children and young people deliver the wood earmarked for sharing with those in need in a procession that leads through the town down to the piazza adjoining the church of Saint Anthony.

They come on horseback, dragging massive timbers, or leading mules laden with firewood, or riding on tractors (a modern replacement for the oxen of past centuries) decorated with yellow flowers and festooned with traditional cakes and images of the saint. Since Saint Anthony is the patron saint of children, this festival also includes a procession from the upper town to the monastery below, composed of small children and parents pushing baby carriages, to bring baskets of flowers to the Saint.

Children are an integral part of the summer feast days for the Madonna delle Grazie and the Madonna del Carmine. Each of the churches in Scanno is presided over by a statue of at least one saint, but these two beautiful life-sized and artfully painted statues of Mary are especially beloved. For these festivals, the statues are dressed in their most beautiful embroidered gowns and cloaks, dating back to the eighteenth century and carefully preserved and restored. Dressed in their communion robes and carrying flowers, the children who had their first communion that spring lead the processions. Other children, wearing white gowns and silk capes in the blue, green, or brown of their neighborhood church's confraternity, walk with flowers or banners behind a brass band and are followed by the patron saint of the day, carried on the shoulders of the strongest men. Gender roles are changing—but slowly. Little girls and women now march with their church's confraternity, wearing colored sashes. Recently, an athletic young sister from the order of Maria l'Ausiliatrice, which provides teachers for the Asilo, stepped up and took her place with the men carrying the heavy statue and was greeted with cheers and applause.

In September, the Sant' Eustachio (Saint Eustace) festival marks the end of summer. Saint Eustace, the patron saint of Scanno, was a Roman solder who converted to Christianity after an encounter in the forest with a deer bearing a glowing cross between its antlers (Notarmuzi 2010).

The most boisterous festival of the season and the favorite of young people takes place in November and is a combination of pagan and Christian rituals. Le Glorie di San Martino (the Bonfires of St. Martin's Night), assimilating various ancient pagan festivals, mark the beginning of the hard winter and have been a rite of passage for young boys for many centuries. As described to me by Enzo Gentile, an expert on the anthropology of Scanno, mothers in centuries past created psychological boundaries that limited children to safe play spaces by recounting stories of ghosts and wild beasts that would snatch children who wandered into the surrounding countryside outside the walled city. The festival of San Martino marked the first time boys approaching puberty were allowed to venture into the woods and mountains without adults. For girls, the rite of passage was marked by donning the traditional costume of a cumbersome wool skirt and carefully buttoned bodice on the day of their first communion. While few modern parents would terrify children with stories or confine them to the traditional dress, these rites of passage still exist in the communal celebration of a child's first communion and the San Martino festival.

Keeping the ancient bonfire tradition alive, young people from the three competing *contrade* (neighborhoods)—now including girls as well as boys—light towering bonfires on the three hillsides surrounding the town. In a ritual that would have an entirely different significance in the United States, where blackface signals disrespect to people of color, the children and youth smear their faces with charcoal, the equivalent of putting on a Halloween mask. They come down to the town chanting *"dolcetto o scherzetto,"* the equivalent of Americans' "trick or treat." As we shall see in chapter 4, these festivals play a key role in cementing the relationship of the children to the community and vice versa.

Although Scanno's fortunes and its traditions have been inextricably intertwined with its mountain habitat and spectacular geography, its residents know that living on a seismic fault line comes at a price. Over its long history, Scanno has been damaged repeatedly by earthquakes that strike without notice. As recently as 2009, the Mussolini-era school and two of Scanno's eleven churches were rendered "uninhabitable" by a quake centered in L'Aquila, the provincial capital, that killed over three hundred people and leveled large parts of that city (Wilson and Boehler 2016). In August 2016, tremors from the Norcia earthquake again uprooted Scanno's schoolchildren (Povoledo 2016). In January 2017 a series of quakes caused an avalanche on the Gran Sasso mountain that buried a resort hotel and killed twenty-nine people, causing renewed concern about structural safety (Smith-Spark and Messia 2017).

Despite these challenges, life goes on. The damaged churches are being restored and the school building was reinforced and repurposed as the new town hall. As of June 2018, the former town hall was being renovated to house the schoolchildren, who were too busy enjoying their summer vacation to think about school. For the children of Scanno, July brings the start of the parish's very affordable summer program (with scholarships for those in need), offering Monday, Wednesday, and Friday sports and crafts in the village, and Tuesday and Thursday all-day bus trips to the Adriatic seashore an hour away. You can see why the kids of Scanno *"stanno bene dove stanno"*—are happy right where they are.

Portrait of Cedar Key

Cedar Key may seem worlds away from Scanno—and it is. In Florida, the word "keys" signifies a chain of islands close to the mainland peninsula. The

Figure 3.2. Bird's-eye view of Cedar Key, Florida, Levy Co. 1884. Library of Congress, G3934, C 315A3 1884. 57.1884. 77–69024.

chain of islands called "the Cedar Keys" stretches about ten miles into the Gulf of Mexico from a point midway down the curving east coast of north central Florida, often called the Nature Coast for its unspoiled beauty. The Cedar Keys were named for the rich stands of juniper or red cedar that drew the earliest European settlers, who stayed to log the timber and establish factories for brooms and pencils. Early settlers occupied several offshore islands, including Atsena Otie, where pencils were manufactured, and Seahorse Key, where a lighthouse was erected.

The tiny modern city of Cedar Key is centered on the island called Way Key, but includes parts of the adjoining islands of Rye Key and Sunset Isle. Separated from the nearest population centers by thirty miles of saltwater, wetland, and sandy hammocks dense with palms and pines, Cedar Key is as geographically isolated as Scanno. Much of the surrounding territory is occupied by state or national nature preserves and wildlife refuges and is home to the Florida black bear, the panther, herds of white tailed deer and wild hogs, and the Florida alligator.

Cedar Keyans refer to leaving the "island city" by State Road 24—the only road connecting the town to the outside world—as "going to Florida." Where Scanno's streets speak of millennia of civilization, even Cedar Key's oldest building is a mere 150 years old. Cedar Key also has an ancient history of human habitation stretching back millennia, but it has left few visible marks (McCarthy 2007). The seismic change that shaped its modern history was the invasion of European migrants who brought diseases, wars, and weapons that almost wiped out the native population. When people think of the history of

Cedar Key, they usually begin with the arrival of white people, but exhibits in the Cedar Key Historical Society Museum and the Cedar Key Museum State Park document a far more ancient history. The area's first human occupants were the People of the Shell Mounds—middens of discarded shells and fibers that predated the Great Pyramids of Egypt. The First Peoples, as early as seven thousand years ago, had discovered how to reuse and recycle their civilization's debris to fortify the mud flats and make them more stable for fishing, with cast nets woven of palm fibers (Federal Wildlife Service 2015). On their way to school, Cedar Key children today pass the Indian burial ground dating back thousands of years (McCarthy 2007).

Between 200 and 1500 AD the Cedar Keys were home to settlements of the Timucua Tribe. The Timucua of Florida were the last of a culture whose way of life had remained essentially unchanged for a thousand years. With a population numbering in the tens of thousands at the time of first contact with Europeans, they were rapidly decimated by disease and forced into Catholic missions by the Spanish. Only an estimated 550 Timucua were still alive in 1698. Today there are no known Native Americans calling themselves Timucuan. In the 1700s, a band of Creek Indians from Georgia and Alabama migrated to Florida and became known as the Seminole, meaning "runaway" people. In fact, Africans fleeing enslavement became part of the Seminole Nation through affiliation and intermarriage. After 1821, when Spain ceded Florida to the fledgling US government, the Seminoles battled fiercely against military encroachment and their confinement in reservations in a series of conflicts called the Seminole Wars. Defeat was inevitable given the imbalance of power and the greed to possess and exploit Seminole lands. Levy County, where Cedar Key is situated, was created in 1845 from lands seized from the Seminoles at the end of the Second Seminole War in 1842. While a few of the remaining Seminoles escaped to the impenetrable Florida Everglades, the rest were relocated to federal reservations in distant Oklahoma (National Park Service 2017; Newcomer 2016; Federal Wildlife Service 2015). Thus ended the story of Cedar Key's ancient peoples.

Compared to St. Augustine, colonized in 1565 by the Spanish, Cedar Key was a relative latecomer to the story of Florida's colonization by Europeans. Cedar Key's short history, as chronicled through displays and objects in the Cedar Key Historical Museum, has been one of rapid change and vulnerability to destructive forces, both natural and human made (Cedar Key Historical). While the Cedar Keys showed up on Spanish explorers' maps as early as 1542, as a water stop and refuge for pirates, the first significant European settlement was a military fort on Depot Key, constructed in 1839 by US General Zachary Taylor. A Cedar Key post office was established in 1845, and

Cedar Key became an important port for shipping lumber and goods from the mainland and supplying cedar to the pencil industry.

By the start of the Civil War in 1861, only twenty years after the first settlement, the Cedar Keys had become a strategic military objective. The western terminus of the Florida Railroad, which connected the Atlantic coast at Fernandina to the Gulf coast at the Cedar Keys, had opened in 1860. Now the port was an essential link to shipping lanes coveted by both the North and South. Florida, a slave state, sided with the Confederacy. The Cedar Keys were initially held by the Confederacy but were repeatedly raided and ultimately captured by Union soldiers in 1864. During the period of Reconstruction (1868–76), when the region was under US military occupation, Cedar Key's black male residents gained the franchise and took leadership roles in city government. Incorporated as a city in 1869, as of 1873 the city of Cedar Key had sixty-one registered voters, thirty-two of whom were black and twenty-nine of whom were white. In the municipal elections of 1874, blacks won the offices of mayor and marshal and three of the five council seats. But Reconstruction was soon abandoned by the federal government. All over the South, black citizens were terrorized by white supremacists and disenfranchised through Jim Crow laws imposing racial segregation. By 1877, Cedar Key records show no blacks were active in city politics, although a small black community remained. Its heart was the Mount Pilgrim Baptist Church, which was destroyed by the 1950 hurricane (Cedar Key Historical Museum Exhibits).

During the rest of the nineteenth century, Cedar Key continued as a fishing port and home to small pencil- and fiber-brush industries, but its growth as a commercial hub was stymied by competition from the city of Tampa's port and railroad terminus a hundred miles to the south. Then, in 1896, the islands were struck by a terrible hurricane during which a ten-foot storm surge swept over the community, killing more than a hundred people. A fire later the same year destroyed what the hurricane had spared. By the start of the twentieth century, Cedar Key was still there, but the remaining industries had regrouped on Way Key, and they were small and simple—net fishing, sponge hooking, and oystering (McCarthy 2007). From the 1900s to the present day, the village has remained a quiet corner, well off the beaten track and attracting visitors who prefer its low-key style to the glamour of Orlando, Miami, and Palm Beach.

Today, the community of Cedar Key occupies a small group of islands that are connected to each other by several small bridges and it is linked to the outside world only by the State Route 24 causeway. The city's official altitude is three meters (about nine feet) above sea level. Living so close to the sea,

Figure 3.3. City of Cedar Key park and beach. B. B. Woodhouse.

Cedar Keyans are as accustomed to floods and hurricanes as *Scannesi* are to tremors and quakes. At first glance, the two villages might seem quite different in size; the population of Cedar Key hovers around 700 as compared to Scanno's 1,700. In contrast to the *Comune* of Scanno, which extends over a land area equivalent to 52 square miles, the city of Cedar Key occupies a tract of only 2.1 square miles, half of which is underwater. However, Cedar Key serves as the center of a much larger sociogeographic catchment that provides shopping, schooling, social life, and employment for many families whose homes lie outside the city's official boundaries. A better measure of the size and demographics of Cedar Key is the demographics of its postal zip code (32625). The Cedar Key Post Office, located on Second Street, the town's main street, serves an area of about 84 square miles, including the wilderness areas of the national wildlife refuges. The zip code's total population is 1,836 (United States Zip Codes n.d.). Viewed from this perspective, Cedar Key and Scanno can be seen as roughly comparable in size and function. Both "villages" are small centers of activity in a much larger, lightly populated area. While both are distinctly rural, they are both located in larger economically developed regions and have access to larger urban centers (Sulmona and Gainesville). The population density of Scanno is 13.22 persons per square kilometer while that of Cedar Key is 8.37 persons per square kilometer. This reflects different population densities in the state of Florida and in Italy. Florida, with a total area of 170,305 kilometers and a population of 21.6 million, has a population density of 136 per square kilometer, while Italy, with an area of 301,338 square kilometers and a population of 60.6 million, has a population density of 205 per square kilometer (World Bank 2018, World Population Review 2019, United States Zip Codes n.d.). Cedar Key and Scanno both fall under the category of small, isolated communities in areas that are thinly populated in comparison to statewide or national averages. Both are surrounded by large wilderness areas and have their own traditional identities.

The demographics of Cedar Key's population, whether viewed by zip code or city limits, is as homogenous as that of Scanno. Compared to the United States in general, Cedar Key has very few minorities. As will be explained later in this chapter, the low number of minority residents may have roots in local history. Over 95 percent of residents identify as Caucasian, with the remainder identifying as Native Americans, African Americans, or Hispanics. Statistics on permanent residents show that Cedar Key and the surrounding area have been losing population at a rate of 5.0 percent, while the United States has been gaining population at a rate of 2 percent (US Census Bureau 2017, for Annual Estimates of the Resident Population; US Zip Codes n.d.). Unlike so many rural communities in America that are losing population, Cedar Key's downtown remains vibrant. While some storefronts are unoccupied, there are many shops and restaurants, a well-stocked food market, a public library, a town hall, a visitor center, a waterfront park and beach, a volunteer fire station, and other signs of village life.

Resisting the pressure felt by every small community in the United States to consolidate with bigger school systems, Cedar Key has managed to preserve its own public school, serving children from pre-K (ages four to five) through high school (ages thirteen to eighteen). In 2016, there were 234 students enrolled in Cedar Key Public School. Founded as a private school in the 1800s, Cedar Key School is the smallest public school in the state of Florida. It also has the highest graduation rate and lowest school dropout rate. In 2016, there were zero dropouts and over 60 percent of Cedar Key School graduates went on to college (Florida Department of Education n.d.).

Cedar Key, like Florida generally, is a magnet for retired people who prefer its sunny weather to the snows of the Northeast and Midwest. Many older residents are "snow birds," seasonal residents who come from Canada and the colder parts of the United States. The median age of Cedar Key residents is 59.3 and the median household income is $41,316, somewhat lower than the Florida median statewide of $47,507. Children are the smallest sector of the population, with only 14 percent of households in Cedar Key proper and 22 percent of households in the 32625 zip code having children under 18 (US Census Bureau 2017, for Annual Estimates of the Resident Population; US Zip Codes n.d.). Many families headed by Cedar Key natives have relocated outside of the city limits, in rural areas on the nearby mainland or in the nearby unincorporated towns of Rosewood and Sumner, where housing costs and taxes are lower. They still shop, work, and worship in Cedar Key and send their children to the Cedar Key school. Public data on schools includes percentages of minority children as well as data on percentages of children eligible for a free or reduced-price lunch. In Cedar Key, where only 1 percent of students are black and 7 pecent are Hispanic, 71 percent of students are eligible for free lunches (Public School Review 2018–19). To qualify for a free lunch, a family of three's annual gross income must be less than $27,014. While Cedar Key children may be rich in natural resources and in the human capital of family and neighbors, most Cedar Key children are growing up in households with very modest incomes.

From a child's perspective, Cedar Key is a paradise for free play. The Cedar Keys' bays, inlets, and marshes, as well as the many remaining areas of open woodland, provide unstructured spaces for play and exploration. One mother, speaking of her ten-year-old son's free-ranging habits, told me that she could always reassure herself that he was OK by taking her binoculars out to one of the bridges on SR 24 to check on him. Even when quite far off, he was easy to spot because of his brightly colored T-shirt, and she could reassure herself that he was safely out on the shallow bay, fishing or paddling with his friends. Kids in Cedar Key learn very early how to avoid dangers such as drowning, poisonous snakes, stingrays, and sharks.

Young people in Cedar Key are very close to nature and study aquaculture and environmental sciences at school and at the University of Florida's Nature Coast Biological Station, located on the Cedar Key waterfront (University of Florida/Institute for Food and Agricultural Sciences 2018). Many are members of Levy County 4H and Future Farmers of America, raising farm animals and growing prize-winning vegetables. However, the single most unifying force among the youth—and among Cedar Keyans in general—is their identification as "Sharks." The Shark is the Cedar Key school mascot and the Shark name and image featuring the colors purple, gold, and white are on everything from the cheerleaders' pompoms and the girls' softball-team shirts to the banners on the basketball court. The letters S-H-A-R-K-S are the first thing you see when arriving in town, spelling out its allegiance on the tallest object on the skyline—a huge metal water tower, looming over the Cedar Key School building. The message on the school's website is emblematic of

Figure 3.4. View north on G Street with water tower and Cedar Key School in background.
B. B. Woodhouse.

the town's pride in its youth and its spirit of competition: "Good luck Sharks, chomp the other teams, and show off that purple, gold, and white!" (Cedar Key Sharks n.d.).

While Scanno is built of stone and terracotta tiles, Cedar Key is built of wood and metal. As the "tin roof shanty" song indicates, Cedar Keyans like it that way. None of Cedar Key's buildings has more than two stories, although tall white painted church steeples stand out above the other structures. Homes and businesses alike have metal roofs and the exteriors are naturally weathered wood or painted in faded Southern tones of pink, green, yellow, or blue. Older buildings have large second-story porches. Newer ones are built on stilts to escape storm surges. The streets are shaded by large native trees: live oaks hung with Spanish moss, long-leaf pines, sabal palms, and, of course, ancient red cedars. While it is hard to find a flat place in Scanno, in the area surrounding Cedar Key it is hard to find a hill, much less a mountainside. The experience of driving to Cedar Key is as different from driving to Scanno as one could imagine. On our way into Scanno, up the narrow, steep, and serpentine road, we peer at mirrors positioned to help us see oncoming traffic. As we approach one of the hand-hewn galleries, we see a sign stating that "cars are forbidden to pass each other in the tunnel." The sign always makes us laugh, since the tunnel is barely wide enough for a single car. By contrast, State Road 24, the two-lane asphalt road that terminates on the waterfront of Cedar Key, runs the twenty-five miles from US 98 to the Gulf of Mexico in a straight line, without a single curve, stoplight, intersection, or stop sign. This part of Florida is so monotonously flat that drivers can see oncoming vehicles from miles away. Driving to Cedar Key, we have to laugh at a sign posted where one approaches the only stretch that could be described as anything other than flat as a pancake. It states: "Caution—visibility obstructed by hill."

Cedar Key, like Scanno, draws tourists throughout the year, to visit its seafood restaurants, for family vacations, and for day sports such as kayaking and deep-sea fishing. The Cedar Key Wildlife Refuge, with its flocks of pelicans, herons, and roseate spoonbills, is a major attraction for birders. Several organized festivals in Cedar Key attract large crowds of visitors. The whimsically named "Clamerica" (Clam + America) celebrates the Fourth of July and the local clam, oyster, and fishery production. It includes patriotic parades (one with floats on wheels and one with boats on the water), cooking contests, and kayak races. Another is the Old Florida Celebration of the Arts, an April sidewalk festival featuring artists and artisans from all over Florida who come to sell their creations and compete for awards; the funds it raises support many artistic activities for both children and adults. Children and youth are not as centrally featured in these events as they are in some of Scanno's festivals, but they participate by marching in parades and staffing tents in the park, where food is sold to benefit local charities. While the clams and oysters are Cedar Key specialties, the decorated bikes, homemade parade floats, cotton candy, and hot dogs may seem more mundane to American readers than the elaborate Scanno festivals. An exception might be the annual "Pirate Invasion," during which the town is occupied by crowds of flamboyantly costumed weekend pirates and pirate wenches, coming from pirate clubs all along the east coast of the United States (Cedar Key Beacon Nov. 29, 2018). The pirate fair in the city park also draws tourists and townsfolk. But, as we shall see in chapter 4, these community events play a major role in defining Cedar Key's identity and fostering social cohesions.

Figure 3.5. View west on Second Street from Island Hotel, Cedar Key. B. B. Woodhouse.

If Scanno's theme song is "the children of Scanno are doing fine right where they are," the theme song of Cedar Key is all about the daily life on the shores dotted with those "tin-roof shanties," and especially the skills of line and net fishing, crabbing, and piloting flat-bottom skiffs called "bird dogs" (Cooper 2018). Cedar Key's identity is firmly anchored in the waters of the Gulf of Mexico. When net fishing was banned, the watermen remained and reinvented themselves as producers of clams and oysters or turned to guiding fishermen and sports and nature lovers on the waters. Even those who have nothing to do with the sea are Sharks at heart. Cedar Key's style is casual, unpretentious, and distinctly American in flavor, like the "cheeseburgers in paradise" made famous by Florida songsmith Jimmy Buffett in his anthem to America's favorite food: "Not too particular, not too precise, I'm just a cheeseburger in paradise" (YouTube 2009).

As a matter of fact, the world's best cheeseburgers (in my humble opinion) are served in the Neptune Bar at Cedar Key's Island Hotel on Second Street. As I learned on my first visit to Cedar Key, it was built in 1859 of seashell tabby, a rough-and-ready form of concrete, its roof supported by gigantic oak beams. It has been serving guests since 1884. Its Neptune Bar sports a hand-painted mural of the King of the Seas, which is famous for having been pierced by a stray bullet at one point in the bar's rowdy past. There is also an autographed picture of Jimmy Buffett, who regularly appeared there with his guitar. On Wednesday nights the Neptune Bar is always jammed with locals who come to eat good food and hear live country music. For adults, the two-block-long stretch of Second Street, with its post office, library, arts center, historical society museum, and city hall, is the closest analogue to Scanno's Piazza Santa Maria della Valle as the meeting place and hub of activity. For kids, home base could be anywhere along the half-mile bike ride from the city park and Dock Street to the Cedar Key School playground, auditorium, and gymnasium.

Beyond Description to Explicit Comparison

The comparative method tells us not to stop at describing the places to be studied; it requires a more intentional and explicit exploration of differences and similarities. To this observer, there are some obvious ways in which Cedar Key and Scanno are similar that set them apart from many other modern communities. Neither of them has even one single traffic light. Neither of them has a shopping mall. Neither has a single fast-food restaurant. Both attract visitors and residents who love their unspoiled natural environments and traditional charm and enjoy the sense of being lost in time. Below, we will explore some of their attributes that are especially relevant to the ecology of childhood.

Early Childhood Socialization and Education

The contexts in which early childhood socialization take place vary. Recall that a mesosystem is where children's microsystems overlap and early childhood is where children's microsystems begin to intersect. The two villages are quite different in their early childhood resources. In Scanno, the piazza is a place where even the youngest children encounter other members of the community. By three years of age, virtually every child is attending Asilo Buon Pastore (Good Shepherd Nursery), where church, family, and school intersect.

This is an example of a mesosystem that one could expect to be relatively free of conflict. Almost 100 percent of Scanno's families are Catholic, although not all are devout or observant. The lay and religious teachers and the chil-

Figure 3.6. Preschool-age children playing in Piazza Santa Maria della Valle with the Asilo Buon Pastore in the background. B. B. Woodhouse.

dren's parents tend to share similar goals and beliefs. The school is structured to minimize inequality and conflict and to maximize inclusion, tolerance, and solidarity. All children wear the same uniform—an easy-to-care-for and practical little track suit—to discourage competition and minimize class distinctions. There are always extra track suits or other supplies for children whose families need them. All children eat the same hot three-course meal at school and say grace before they begin. While there are downsides to systems that emphasize all the same values (e.g., excessive conformity, stifling of creativity and competition), the consistent messages from home, school, and church come together to make the Asilo a good environment for very young children.

In Cedar Key, the geography of early childhood is more individualized and dispersed. There is no equivalent to the daily gathering of families in the piazza—the playground sometimes draws parents with young children, but it is rarely crowded and often completely deserted. Children may find playmates in neighboring houses, but houses and yards are separated by backyards and front lawns, often surrounded by fences, and those communal spaces characteristic of Scanno are less evident. There is also no equivalent to Scanno's Asilo Buon Pastore. Most working parents rely on informal daycare provided in private homes at an hourly rate. Television is often used to distract the

Figure 3.7. Preschool-age boy at a Cedar Key church Easter egg hunt. B. B. Woodhouse.

child and substitute for other forms of stimulation. Religious life in Cedar Key is highly social but divided among five churches of different denominations (Methodist, Church of Christ, Baptist, Episcopal and Catholic) each with its own church or fellowship hall. Children's first contacts with the larger community often occur at church events.

Once children are old enough to be eligible for free public education, at age four or five, the microsystems of family, neighborhood, and peer group converge powerfully in the Cedar Key School. From that time forward, the school becomes the focal point for Cedar Key civil society.

Access to Free Play Spaces

The availability of spaces for free play may be the one attribute that most closely links the experience of childhood in these two villages. Parents in both communities buck the modern trend of "helicopter parenting" by allowing children wide latitude to find their own companions and engage in their own autonomously invented games and adventures. Children utilize the entire community—its streets and its sidewalks—as their "playground" and, as they get older, their play extends into the surrounding woods and waters. Bicycles, skateboards, scooters, and other wheeled gadgets are used in imaginative play and as transportation.

It would be a mistake to assume that the children are "unsupervised" because they are not accompanied by parents. The townspeople in both villages take their role as surrogate parents seriously and keep an eye on all the children. As one older man (Pasquale Caranfa) explained to me: "When I see a child I don't recognize alone on the street I call out in dialect—'Hey there, whose kid are you?' If he answers me in dialect, I know he is a local and knows his way around. If he doesn't answer, I know he is from out of town and I keep an eye on him in case he is lost." In Cedar Key, parents have a similarly high level of trust that kids can roam freely and that there will be help available should they need it. As one girl told me, "I love cross-country and I run

Figure 3.8. Children playing dancing game in Piazza dell'Olmo with older neighbors looking on. B. B. Woodhouse.

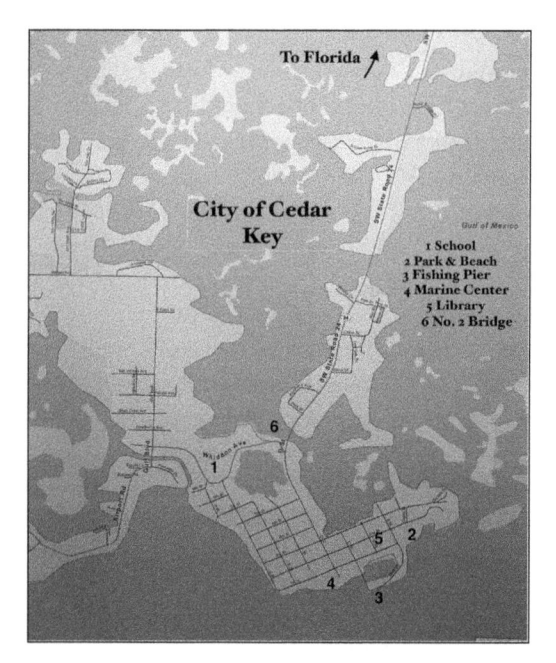

Figure 3.9. A kid's-eye view of modern Cedar Key.
B. B. Woodhouse.

anywhere I want to because everyone looks out for us kids." In both places, the advent of cell phones means parents know that kids can call for help and can be contacted if they fail to come home as expected. For once, technology enhances children's free play instead of suppressing it. Young people in both villages relish their freedom—indeed, almost take it for granted—and adults recall this freedom to roam and invent their own play environments as the most formative experience of their own childhoods.

Value Systems

If I had to distill the dominant macrosystemic values taught to children in Scanno, I would point to the themes drummed into them in Santa Maria della Valle by Don Carmelo: "Honor thy father and mother" and "Love others as God loves you." Cedar Key is also decidedly Christian but more individualistic in culture; values of patriotism and competition take a more central role than in Scanno. There would be a strong market in Cedar Key for pillows embroidered "Stars and Stripes Forever" and "God Bless Our Home Team!" While children's understanding of macrosystemic values in each community becomes more nuanced as they mature, their embrace of these values—or resistance to them—powerfully shapes their lives.

In Scanno, the school project of writing poems in dialect gave me a unique window on children's perspectives, and I have drawn on those poems in many chapters. The themes were of parents and grandparents, playmates and friendships, joys of outdoor play, favorite foods, animals, and church bells. Some poems touched on tragedies such as earthquakes or armed conflict viewed on television. In Cedar Key I had a different sort of window on how children viewed their hometown when the city hosted the opening of "Crossroads: Change in Rural America," one of a series of traveling "Museums on Main Street" created by the Smithsonian Museum in Washington, DC (Cedar Key News 2018; Museum on Main Street 2018). The project was designed to orient visitors of all ages to the challenges facing small towns, their diversity, their strengths, and their futures. The interactive exhibit included opportunities for showcasing the unique facets of each host community as well as spaces for visitors to post note cards with their own responses to questions about their community. One of them was: "If you had to leave Cedar Key today, name three things you would miss most?" On the day I visited, some of the answers written by children included: "I would miss my family, friends, school and my wonderful teachers"; "I would miss the sunset and the smallness and the teachers that taught me"; "my friends, the water, and driving my minibike"; "knowing everyone, food, friends, family"; "being on the water, the people, working on the water"; "I'd miss Miss H's food, I'd miss the horseshoe crabs, and I'd miss the beach"; and "I would miss the people around, all of the buildings to see, and the water." Perhaps the most heartfelt response was: "fishing, fishing, fishing." Some of the posted comments were political, including a card reading: "LGBT+ matters because all lives matter" and another: "Support Trump and Lock Hillary Up." It was interesting to see how bold the children were in comparison to some of the elders I interviewed. One of the docents who gave orientations to the children at the Crosssroads exhibit told me he was intrigued at how independent they seemed and how confident of their opinions. They were attentive during his structured orientation but when asked their opinions on specific questions they gave his questions short shrift and went straight to the topics that most mattered to them. "They knew what they wanted to say, and they said it," he commented with approval.

Living on the Edge

Cedar Key and Scanno are both unusually exposed to the destructive forces of nature. In Scanno, a history of devastating earthquakes reminds people of the ever-present threat of living on a seismic fault line. In 2015, Scanno celebrated the hundredth anniversary of an event that scarred the community. The schoolchildren participated by writing poems, interviewing survivors, and drawing pictures of the event. While recent earthquakes were included in my portrait of Scanno, it is worth pausing to imagine the effect of this long-ago tragedy on the children and families of today. On the night of January 13, 1915, a part of Scanno called Frattura, which then had a population of approximately 500, was leveled to the ground, killing 162 souls, 60 of whom were children age ten and under. Some 150 men and boys from Frattura were spared because they were hundreds of miles away on the *transumanza*. The tragedy suffered is almost unimaginable.

The fear of quakes is handed down from generation to generation and remains a constant. In 2009, not far away from Scanno, in the provincial capital of L'Aquila, hundreds of people were killed and many homes and churches toppled. Children living in Scanno felt the tremors from this quake. They knew that several churches and a school building in their own town had to be closed because of earthquake damage. In 2016, a deadly quake struck Norcia and shook the homes in Scanno once again, forcing closure of Scanno's school buildings as unsafe. In 2017 came another quake that buried twenty-nine people, including children, in a mountain resort much like the ones near Scanno. Even if they didn't feel the tremors, television brought news of these events into children's living rooms and kitchens.

The reality of living on the edge of disaster is mirrored in Cedar Key, but the threat comes from water, wind, and fire rather than the shifting of tectonic plates. Again, it is worth considering the effects on children. All Cedar Key children learn about the hurricane of September 29, 1896, when the town was almost destroyed by a storm surge ten feet high. They know that a large part of the population died and that many of the remaining buildings were destroyed by fire in December of the same year. In 1950, well within living memory, a hurricane destroyed two-thirds of Cedar Key's homes. One elderly man who was a boy in 1950 tells the story of how he found his own grandmother's corpse in the cleft of a tree—a story his own grandchildren must have heard. Most recently, Hurricane Hermine generated a huge storm surge that swept over the island city on Labor Day weekend of 2016, leaving behind fallen trees, mud, and debris and forcing evacuation and closure of the post office, public library, city hall, and many of the business on Second Street. Children witnessed the devastation and helped in the cleanup. Children also saw how quickly the community bounced back. A mobile post office truck parked each day in front of the shuttered post office became the new meeting place while damaged buildings and businesses were being restored and renovated. As Cedar Keyans would tell you, it is an ill wind that blows no good. By summer 2017, a sparkling city hall and library had reopened and University of Florida's spanking-new Nature Coast Biological Station rose in place of a motel that had been too badly damaged to repair. This center for marine biology research has become a major resource for Cedar Key's kids.

But despite some surface bravado, hurricanes are not taken lightly. Since the hurricane season of 2002, Florida law has required that new homes be built on 20-foot-high pilings. When a hurricane is about to strike, residents know well in advance, due to modern meteorological reports. Signs along the causeway indicate the "escape route," and in case of emergency a horn sounds to alert citizens to evacuate to the mainland. Police Chief Virgil Sandlin closes the bridges and stays behind to protect lives and property until the storm passes. Although the science of seismology is less able than meteorology to predict when disaster will strike, Scanno also has warning signals, and its teachers drill its students on what to do in the event of an earthquake. None of this is lost on children. Whether you grow up in Scanno or Cedar Key, it is impossible to harbor the illusion that humankind controls nature.

A Sense of History and Place

The two villages, although visually, topologically, and historically quite distinct, are alike in their ancient roots and strong sense of place. Although the oldest building in Cedar Key would be considered modern in Scanno, as noted earlier, both locations have been home to human settlements for a very long time. This history is still visible and present in both places. Cedar Key's schoolchildren are familiar with its indigenous people, since they study them in school. They also visit the Cedar Key Historical Museum and the Cedar Key Museum State Park, which traces the area's history from prehistoric times to the present (Florida Channel n.d.). The current generation of Cedar Key children has been exposed to the tragic history of Native Americans and taught in school to treat the First Peoples with respect. On their way to school, Cedar Key children pass the ancient Indian burial ground, crowning Cedar Key's only hill.

Children in Cedar Key also show pride in their town's maritime heritage. They grow up feeling completely at home in boats, with many opportunities to get out on the water, including fishing with lines, working with relatives on clam farms, and studying marine biology. Every Cedar Key festival includes some maritime component, not to mention food from the ocean. The annual Pirate Festival is a wild and colorful celebration of Cedar Key's past as a pirate hangout.

Figure 3.10. Girl in Scanno traditional costume hosting visiting students from another village. B. B. Woodhouse.

In Scanno, schoolchildren are similarly aware of their community's ancient roots, and on their way to school they pass by stones, incised with roman letters, that were borrowed from the remains of a Roman settlement and repurposed to build the foundations of Christian churches. A new generation of Scanno children has gotten over being embarrassed by their dialect. My anthropologist friend Enzo Gentile showed me a video, filmed around 1970, of a young Scanno woman modeling the traditional wedding costume for a newsreel. She was visibly embarrassed by the fact that the older woman sitting next to her and wearing her everyday dress of head scarf, pleated wool skirt, and apron was not able to speak Italian and could only speak dialect. When the girl was asked whether she herself would wear the traditional wedding dress when she married, she replied, blushing, "No, I will wear white." While getting married in white has become the new tradition and is unlikely to be displaced, these days many of Scanno's schoolchildren wear the traditional dress on holidays, study their traditional dialect with pride, and compete to write original poems to keep their dialect alive. On a recent school day, I encountered a contingent of students from the school in a neighboring town, who had come to visit Scanno. They were being guided by a class of Scanno middle-school students, one of whom, Clarissa, had volunteered to act as a costumed docent. Today she was wearing the traditional Scanno costume in her role as student guide for the young visitors' tour of the Museum of Wool, the Fontana Sarracco, and other important sites.

One distinctive difference between the two villages is that Cedar Key children have no experience with war that is comparable to the World War II invasion of Italy. Some of their parents have served in the military, and Cedar Key residents have died on foreign soil. But war has not visited their village since 1864. Although children in Scanno have not lived through a war, their grandparents have. World War II is still present in the community's consciousness, in stories, and whispered remembrances, even as the war generation passes into history.

Economic Trauma and Economic Resilience

Another similarity is the capacity for resilience in the face of disaster. Where hurricanes and earthquakes have destroyed and devastated, these villages have rebuilt and rejuvenated. Both communities have also suffered severe economic dislocation in recent years. Beyond the predictable pain of global and national recessions, each of them can point to moments when things looked especially dark. Much as Scanno's sheep, before they were slaughtered during the war, defined a way of life in the mountain village, in Cedar Key fishing, like herding, shaped the rhythms of family life as well as the rhythms of social and economic life. A monument next to the Cedar Key City Hall commemorates the sacrifices made by Cedar Key's fishermen. While fishing has always been a hard life, the monument memorializes a date on which many Cedar Keyans believed that their way of life had died, or had been murdered by the federal government. On July 1, 1995, a law came into effect that prohibited the use of the traditional nets that Cedar Key's fisherman had used for generations.

The future of the village fishermen was not as quite as dark as anticipated. The fishnet ban prompted a search for more sustainable methods of harvesting seafood. Cedar Key's fishermen and civil leadership, with support from the University of Florida and the State Wildlife Commission, developed a new seafood supply: commercial clam and oyster farming. Boats still go out to sea, but they come back with mesh bags full of clams harvested from Cedar Key's clam leases rather than nets filled with fish. The federal net ban had been intended to preserve various threatened species of fish and, in fact, the populations of red fish and other prized saltwater fish have bounced back in the intervening years. Today, sport-fishing boats generate revenue and attract anglers to vacation in Cedar Key. Both Scanno and Cedar Key have exhibited striking capacity for resilience in the face of change, and both are committed to developing sustainable projects, whether in ecotourism, sports, agriculture, aquaculture, or the raising of domestic animals for food and clothing.

The Menacing Legacy of Racism

While both villages have weathered many tragedies, at the beginning of my research project I had believed there was one stark difference between the two villages and the two countries under study. That difference was the menacing legacy of racism that haunts all of America, including its rural South. In my portrait of Cedar Key, I knew I would be remiss if I left out a human-made tragedy that clearly continues to affect Cedar Key—the Rosewood Massacre of 1923 (Dye 1996). Although I did not learn of it until after I moved to Cedar Key, this tragedy may partially explain the unusually low percentage of African American residents. Florida was a slave state that sided with the Confederacy in the Civil War. After the war, a community of newly emancipated African Americans settled in a wooded area about ten miles inland from Cedar Key. By 1923, the town of Rosewood was a pleasant village of African American homeowners with small businesses and farms. It was also a stop on the cross Florida railroad visible in the 1884 map (fig. 3.2). The Rosewood massacre was triggered by a false report that a white woman in the settlement of Sumner three miles nearer the coast had been raped by a black man who was believed to be hiding in Rosewood. Gangs from Sumner were joined by mobs from further inland and rampaged through Rosewood burning homes and murdering every black person they found. At least eight people died in the fighting, including two of the attackers, although survivors have since reported seeing up to twenty-seven black bodies, many of them in a mass grave in the woods. The surviving Rosewood residents fled for their lives into the swamps. Some were evacuated by local railroad conductors who hid them on trains and others fled overland to Gainesville and migrated to northern cities (Goodloe n.d.). Only one building—owned by a white merchant who sheltered many of the survivors—remained standing. No one was prosecuted and none of the black residents ever returned. Although Cedar Key residents do not seem to have been implicated in the attack, and Cedar Key history buffs told me that Cedar Key had protected its black residents, the destruction of Rosewood cast a very long shadow. Bathed in silence, or spoken of only in private, the massacre lived on in the memories of the victims and the local communities. While there were black workers in Cedar Key through the 1950s, almost all eventually moved as far as possible from Rosewood.

In 1982, Gary Moore, a St. Petersburgh journalist, began to dig into this history and published an article that drew national attention (Moore 1982). Florida lawyers and University of Florida historians set out to document this "forgotten" history; they gathered evidence from survivors and put together the legal case for reparations. After a long campaign, the Florida legislature approved "compensation" of $150,000 each to the survivors and their descendants and established a scholarship for survivors' descendants. In 2004, I attended a ceremony at which the few remaining survivors of the Rosewood Massacre spoke and were honored. Jeb Bush, then the governor of Florida, unveiled a historic marker to be placed at the site the village had once occupied, where the only physical remnant of Rosewood was a large house that had been spared because its owner was white. This history is a reminder of the ripple effect of a history of racism that has blighted so many lives in the United States. The American experience exposes the dark side of social cohesion when it takes the form of race hatred, intolerance, and fear of the "other."

Although modern Italy has generally avoided levels of racism found in countries with recent histories of apartheid, Italians are not immune from the disease. It took the form of violent anti-Semitism during the 1930s and 1940s. Beginning in 1938, Mussolini began persecution of Italy's 45,000 Jews. Jewish children were forbidden to attend public or private schools; Jewish property was confiscated and thousands of families were driven into hiding. Some 7,000 Jews managed to flee abroad, but, in the period from 1943 to 1945, when the country was controlled by the German Nazis, about 8,000 Italian Jews died in Nazi camps (Vitello 2010).

I interviewed a survivor in Florence in 2008. Doctor Pescatore, a dignified, retired educator in her eighth decade, had been a mentor to many successful Italian academics, including my close colleague from Universita' di Firenze, Doctor Elena Urso. As Doctor Pescatore showed me photographs, her childhood memories came flooding back. Born the privileged child of a powerful Italian general from an old Catholic family and his brilliant and accomplished Jewish wife, by the end of the war she had become a refugee in her own land. Hidden by nuns in a Catholic convent, she lived with the daily fear of discovery and deportation. The story of Italy's treatment of Jews during the Nazi era had bright moments and dark ones, with stories of courageous Italian civilians and clerics saving Jewish lives existing side by side with accounts of willful blindness, cupidity, and betrayal (Vitello 2010).

An Exercise in Triangulation: Pursuing Uncomfortable Conversations

In our two villages today, open manifestations of racism and sectarian conflict are only found at a very intimate level, if at all. Of course, racism is a hard thing to pin down, since race is in large part a social construct. Irish and Italian immigrants were stigmatized as "black" in nineteenth-century America and darker-complexioned Italians from Sicily and Calabria were stigmatized when they migrated to northern Italy. Both nations have constitutions that forbid discrimination based on race, religion or ethnicity. But how can I know if the changes I perceive in Scanno and Cedar Key are only skin deep?

From my wooden bench in the Scanno piazza, I watch the children sharing toys, inventing games, riding bicycles, playing bandits and police with water pistols, and dribbling soccer balls. I observe how they form little bands segregated by age and gender, and I try to understand how race and ethnicity affect their interactions. I see no sign that the biracial or ethnically diverse children are treated differently by their peers or members of the community. The children of color are not the only signs of integration; the priest celebrating mass side by side with Don Carmelo is a very dark-skinned man born in Nigeria. Digging deeper, I ask parents and neighbors about the biracial children. They report that people can be insensitive or simply uninformed. I note that those with whom I speak describe the boys as *bellissimo* (extremely handsome); what about the biracial girls? Is their beauty equally appreciated? I have my answer to this question in May 2019 when an elderly Scannese gentleman comes up to me in Santa Maria della Valle as I am admiring the photographs of the twelve children who soon will be receiving their first communion. He proudly calls my attention to the four girls of mixed racial heritage. "This girl's mother came from Cuba," he says, "and this girl's mother came from Africa. Aren't they beautiful?"

In Cedar Key, there are also signs of change. It is less easy to observe children's daily interactions in Cedar Key than in Scanno, but I see children of color in the parks and playing in the yards and streets, and I see them featured in the *Cedar Key Beacon* and Cedar Key School Facebook coverage of school events. When I bring my donations of canned and boxed foods to the Community Food Pantry, where the clients are mostly low-income whites, I am greeted by a young black volunteer wearing an orange and blue University of Florida T-shirt. When I meet Joshua Slemp, principal of the Cedar Key School, on a visit to the school in 2017, I note that he is African American. He seems extremely well liked by parents and students, and he looks completely at ease. Although his family does not reside in Cedar Key, he has enrolled his own son in the Cedar Key School.

Delving deeper, I try to open these uncomfortable conversations about race relations in Cedar Key. I know from photographs at the Cedar Key Historical Museum that black people were part of the workforce in Cedar Key at the turn of the nineteenth century and that they did not instantly disappear after Rosewood. One white old-timer, looking back at his childhood in the 1930s, describes race relations this way: "We weren't black or white; we were poor." And he adds that his best friends were all black. A young woman in her twenties, also white, recalls a large black family in Cedar Key during her school years and says they seemed to fit in just fine. I notice that the front page of the Cedar Key Beacon has the banner headline "CKS Hoops Standout Passes 1,000 Points." The star athlete pictured on the front page is Jasmine Jackson, an African American girl who has played with the Lady Sharks for all of her middle and high school years (Arnold 2018b). But does athletic prowess translate into inclusion?

As this book went to press, I came across two articles that shed a brighter, if still ambiguous, light on my inquiry into current race relations in Cedar Key. The first article, published in June 2018, reports on the groundswell of opposition from Cedar Key residents when the Levy County School Board announced that, effective July 2, 2018, it was moving the Cedar Key School principal mentioned earlier to a much larger school and more racially diverse district in Williston. Cedar Key residents were so upset that they started a petition drive to keep him in Cedar Key, but they were overruled by the school board. The news coverage never mentioned the principal's race. However, one board member made a revealing comment: "I understand what you are saying, but when you have a talent such as Mr. Slemp—and you had to look at the whole district not just one school—he's going to effect change on 1,100 some students at Williston. His talent level at that school will be spread among more students in our district than where he sat before. That's not popularity. That's not politically correct. That's not anything" (Witt 2018).

The second article, published in June 2018 in the *Tampa Bay News*, concerned the last house in Rosewood—the one that sheltered many black families and only survived because it belonged to a white store owner. A child survivor of the massacre recalled in 1983, "If it hadn't been for this house, we wouldn't be here. We wouldn't have had anywhere to hide" (DeGregory 2018, 3). In June 2018, the dwelling and its surrounding acres had just been listed for sale by its eighty-four-year-old owner. Her husband had purchased the property in 1978, without knowing anything about its history. They had first learned of the Rosewood Massacre from journalist Gary Moore in 1982. Now it had become too much for the elderly widow to keep up and she needed to sell. Her daughter wrote two different listings for it: one for buyers seeking a gracious turn-of-the-century home "surrounded by majestic oaks," and the other for the National Trust for Historic Preservation, describing a property whose "historic significance should never be forgotten" (DeGregory 2018). The owner was apprehensive that the listings would stir up trouble. She recounted that, five years earlier, in 2013, when she first thought of selling, a rumor was spread that she might sell to a group of African Americans interested in its historic value. A neighbor had dropped by with a warning: "You don't want another riot around here." Her daughter was shocked. "I thought it was over. . . . Shouldn't all that be in the past?" (DeGregory 2018, 6).

According to DeGregory's *Tampa Bay News* article, 2013 had been a year of mixed messages on race relations in Levy County and in Cedar Key. The KKK had been active in Bronson, some twenty miles to the east, wrapping rocks around racist leaflets and throwing them in the yards of prominent black residents, including a black city-council member. Meanwhile, in Cedar Key, 2013 marked the first time anyone could remember that a black student had been elected to the Cedar Key School homecoming court.

By 2019 such an event was not even cause for comment. One of the girls pictured in evening gowns as members of the Queen's Court was Jasmine Jackson, the Shark basketball star I mentioned earlier. Jasmine was also featured in a video from TV 20, a regional television station, which singled her out as a prizewinning scholar-athlete and student leader (Cedar Key School Facebook January 15, 2019; WCJB TV 2019). Judging from the Cedar Key School Facebook, diversity is the wave of the future. When the tooth fairy visited the Cedar Key School kindergarten and first grade recently, she found a rainbow of shining faces, roughly one third of them children of color (Cedar Key School Facebook May 28, 2019).

Perhaps the last word on Rosewood should go to Sherry DuPree, who runs the Rosewood Heritage Foundation. DuPree is working to raise funds to buy the Rosewood property and writing grants to the state humanities council. She says, "Every culture has its own Rosewood" (DeGregory 2018, 5). Speaking of the beautiful old house, she adds, "If those walls could talk, they would tell the story of cultures working together, a white man opening his doors to save his neighbors."

During the decade of researching this book I watched with alarm the rising levels of racial and religious tension in both the United States and Italy. Here in the United States, the Black Lives Matter movement has shone a harsh spotlight on deadly racial disparities in law enforcement. The Trump administration has been turning back the clock on African American citizens' protections against racial discrimination while simultaneously pushing for policies that exclude and discriminate against Muslim and Latin American migrants.

In Italy, the rapid influx of migrants who look, sound, and worship differently from the Italian native population has spurred the growth of anti-immigrant populism, infected by religious intolerance and racism. While racism seems not to have taken root in Scanno at this writing, hate crimes are occurring with increasing frequency all over Italy. Italian President Mattarella recently warned, using an English term borrowed from Hollywood, "We cannot allow Italy to become the 'Far West'" (Breda 2018). In Italy, as in the United States, anti-immigrant rhetoric from leaders in high places appears to have fueled an upsurge in violence against racial and ethnic minorities. When I buy my newspaper from the newsstand in Scanno's piazza, I see that the Italian coalition government is bent on blocking the flow of refugees from Africa and the Middle East. For the first time, Italian ports have been closed to NGO vessels carrying survivors rescued from the waters between Libya and Italy.

Shouldn't children, in their own small microsystems, be sheltered from these storms? Unfortunately, they are not. In late 2018 reports erupted on Italian Facebook that the town of Codroipo, in the province of Udine, located in the Friuli-Venezia region of northern Italy, had banned all references in its schools to cultural diversity or to the cultural provenance of students. According to bloggers, the ban even extended to requiring removal from the classroom of books and toys with multiracial themes and dolls with nonwhite skin colors. These rumors were partially based in fact: the town's governing right-wing coalition had amended the guidelines for its zero-to-three nursery. The original language stated a commitment to "socio-cultural diversity," which was modified to promote "nullifying social differences." Mainstream journalists tried to defuse the most shocking rumors, reporting that the town had no intention of banning dark-skinned Barbie dolls (Del Frate 2018). These tensions are not confined to Italy. In May 2019, the Tenth Annual Conference on the Rights of the Child in Geneva, Switzerland, at which I spoke, was devoted to children's religious rights and the impact of sectarian conflict on children's rights to education (Sprenger 2019).

How times have changed. Removing a school's commitment to sociocultural diversity in favor of a commitment to nullifying social differences (a euphemism for assimilation of all outsiders to the dominant white Christian culture) would have been unthinkable in the Italy of ten years ago. This and other similar controversies are evidence of an alarming resurgence of sectarian conflict and white nationalism, a trend that thoroughly contradicts Italy's antidiscrimination laws and the letter and spirit of its 1946 Constitution.

Today, in our two villages as elsewhere in the world, globalized and diffuse images of fear and distrust collide with concrete and intimate experiences of friendship and trust. Which images are our future, and which are our past?

4

The Magic of Mesosystems, Seedbeds of Solidarity

Cedar Key raised me.
There are no poor children in Scanno.
—Personal communications

The first above quotation is from a conversation that took place on Thanksgiving Day 2018 at a Cedar Key community dinner. I had approached a thirtyish man, a hard-working, entrepreneurial Cedar Keyan, sunburned and fit from working on the water, to ask what it was like growing up in Cedar Key. I had been told he had an interesting perspective on this question. He replied, simply, "Cedar Key raised me," and repeated, "Cedar Key raised me." He explained that from a very young age he had been without parents or close relatives he could rely on. When he said the town had raised him, he meant it literally. He named several local families that had taken him in over the years and treated him as one of their own. The second quotation is a statement I heard many times over, whenever I asked people in Scanno, "What about the poor children?" This sense of belonging and of responsibility is what is meant in both Cedar Key and Scanno when people say, as they invariably do, "We are all family here." What is it that makes these folks treat other people's children as if they were their own?

The Role of Social Institutions in Generating Solidarity

In the preceding chapter, I provided detailed portraits of Cedar Kay and Scanno, employing data from each village's history, demography, geography, and economic life, to draw comparisons and highlight differences. In this chapter, I will use examples from both villages to explore the role of mesosystems—those zones in the ecological model where microsystems overlap. While the ecological model of child development places an individual (the child) at the center, the model's basic insight is that the child's development occurs within a complex matrix of interpersonal relationships and social institutions. The cultures of childhood in both Scanno and Cedar Key demonstrate the pivotal role played by various social relationships and institutions formed within the mesosystem that generate a sense of shared connection with the community's children. To borrow a phrase from sociologists Norton Grubb and Marvin Lazerson, these relationships and institutions transform "other people's children" into "our children" (Grubb and Lazerson 1988, 43–45).

Human communities since before the dawn of history have spontaneously generated norms and traditions that nurture social cohesion. At a basic level, the naming of the community (not always identical to the official name on maps or census documents) operates to bind citizens together; to be a *Scannese* or a Cedar Keyan is to belong to some larger identity. A village's common identity is nurtured by shared loyalties that structure relationships, symbolize belonging, and enact membership. In studying these structures using the ecological model, I was struck by the role played by those zones where the various microsystems overlap. Where school, family, and peer group intersect is one example; the intersection of faith community, peer group and neighborhood is another. This is why I call mesosystems the seedbeds of solidarity: in understanding the magic of mesosystems, the core concepts of sociology provide a valuable methodological tool.

"Social institutions" are groups or patterns of behavior that evolve over time to satisfy social needs. For example, in order to survive, societies need a supply of new members. "Family" represents the primary social institution that evolved to satisfy this need. New members of society must be socialized, and institutions such as school and religion have evolved to meet this need, as has medicine, to meet the needs of sick members; government, law, and the military, to protect societies against invasion and to control members' harmful conduct; and markets and labor unions, for the production of goods and services and the protection of workers (McIntyre 2014, 160–61).

Sociologists also use the term "social structure" broadly, to refer to the ordered interrelationship between the different elements of a social system. While any observable "pattern" can indicate a social structure, it is typically "seen as designating the actual arrangement of individuals and groups into those larger entities that Durkheim saw as social facts" (Scott 2014, 737). The term originated as an application of ideas from biology, but it has taken on a social meaning in the science of sociology. Thus, it is no accident that family, school, faith community, market economy, and health care appear as elements in the ecological model of child development. These microsystems and exosystems affect children's lives both directly and indirectly. Since many of these social institutions or structures play a role in fostering social cohesion, it is worth pausing to identify and define them.

Family

A "family" is defined by sociologists as "an intimate domestic group made up of people related to one another by bonds of blood, sexual mating, or legal ties" (Scott 2014, 238). This rather open-ended definition, which incorporates elements of sexuality, intimacy, biological connection, and legal recognition, captures certain recurring elements of family as a structure and institution while allowing for the enormous diversity of families across cultures and over time. Different cultures or societies hold very different beliefs about family composition, divisions of labor among family members, family values, and attitudes toward child-rearing. But despite the variations in family structure, the concept of family remains a constant over millennia of social history. The Italian word for family is *famiglia*.

At the level of family relationships, many rights and duties representing expectations of social cohesion are enacted into law, such as the duty to provide for one's children or spouse. The range of legal definitions of "family" is breathtakingly broad and depends heavily on context. Who qualifies as a family member for purposes of inheritance? For insurance coverage? For prohibitions against incestuous marriages? The US Homeland Security agency ignited a firestorm of protest when it borrowed the definition of "close family" found in the Immigration and Naturalization Act of 1965 to determine who would be eligible for an exception to the executive order popularly known as the Muslim Ban (Exec. Order No. 13780, 82 Fed. Reg. 13209, March 6, 2017). The US Supreme Court had ordered an exemption for applicants with a "credible claim of a bona fide relationship with a person or entity in the United States" (*Trump v. International Refugee Assistance Project*, 582 US ___ (2017). Under the definition adopted by Homeland Security, step-siblings and parents-in-law may enter, but not grandparents, aunts, or uncles. Yet in the Middle East and North Africa, 80 percent of elderly parents live in the same household as younger relatives, and extended family often includes aunts and uncles (Torbati and Rosenberg 2017; Fischer-Baum et al. 2017). Given that the stated purpose of the restrictions was combatting terrorism, why should the fiancé of a Muslim resident in the United States be eligible to visit, but not a grandparent or grandchild? Students of family law learn very early that legal definitions of family relationships can and should vary depending on the purpose behind the law.

In addition to legal definitions, expectations regarding who counts as family may be set by religious authorities or by unwritten cultural norms. In every community a network of social facts and beliefs shapes how people envision family membership. Despite these variations, the notion of *solidarity* (a union of interests or purposes or sympathies among members of a group) is generally seen as an attribute of membership in a family. The institution of the family, while varying across cultures and centuries, has been remarkably enduring and resilient over time. Family is considered the basic unit of society and the first circle of relationships responsible for socialization of children.

Neighborhood

A "neighborhood," according to the *National Geographic Encyclopedia*, is "an area where people live and interact with one another. Neighborhoods tend to have their own identity, or 'feel' based on the people who live there and the places nearby.... When people band together in this way, it strengthens their sense of community and preserves cultural traditions" (*National Geographic Encyclopedia* n.d.). A typical dictionary definition of neighborhood is "an area within a city or town that has some distinctive features (especially one forming a community)" (*American Heritage Dictionary* 2018). As is evident from these definitions, a neighborhood, like a community, can refer to a commonality of interests as well as to a geographical location (Scott 2014, 106). I have used the term "community" in both senses, to refer to the villages under study and their identity as a community, and the term "neighborhood" to refer to geographical and social subsections of these villages. The Italian term for a town or village is *paese* but *mio paese* (my town) carries a similar meaning to "my hometown." The Italian term for a geographical and cultural neighborhood is *contrada* or *quartiere*.

Faith Community

A "faith community" is "a group of people who share a particular set of religious beliefs. In any faith community there are varying levels of commitment" (*Longman Dictionary of Contemporary English* 2018). The term "faith community" is purposefully nondenominational and encompasses all religious groups. Christian faith communities, such as those in Scanno and Cedar Key, use the term "church" to refer to their community and its governing structures as well as to their physical houses of worship. In both Scanno and Cedar Key, churches play a key role in the socialization of children and in the life of the community. The Italian word for church is *chiesa*, which can mean both the building and the larger denomination. The *parrocchia* or parish is the local administrative unit of the Roman Catholic church.

School

"School" is both an institution and a method of education. It is defined as a "process of learning and management of socially approved knowledge, involving an approved curriculum and pedagogy, paid professional educators, compulsory attendance of pupils, and school grouping" (Scott 2014, 664). "School grouping" may include grouping "by age, gender, educability or cultural factors such as religion and language" (665). "Educability" is a sociological term of art that refers to "observed variations among school pupils in their capacity to accomplish teacher-imposed intellectual tasks" (200). This dry description hardly conveys the powerful influence of schools in socializing children and creating shared identity, not to mention as sites of conflict over child-rearing practices and values. In small communities like Scanno and Cedar Key, it is hard to overestimate the importance of the school.

Schools are also an important example of how exosystems indirectly affect microsystems. In both Italy and the United States, regional and national educational systems and policies set the ground rules for local schools—for example, how and when children will be tested and when and whether children will be divided into groups according to their "educability." In the United States, despite the existence of laws requiring equal access to education, the practice of inclusion in the public-school classroom of children with disabilities, including developmental delays, mental health issues, and neurological or physical disabilities, has given rise to many court cases and conflicts. Under US law, each child with disabilities is entitled to an Individualized Education Plan (IEP), which serves as a roadmap and benchmark for the child's progress. Inclusion in the regular classroom generally assumes the child will have the capacity to advance from grade to grade. Otherwise, an alternative placement such as a special school or a special classroom is required (*Endrew v. Douglas County School District* RE-1, 580 US __, 2017). This scheme sets up a tension between a child's right to a free, appropriate education and the child's right not to be segregated.

In Italy, national laws and judicial decisions on children's rights clearly give primary place to the practice of inclusion and require integration of children with disabilities into the general primary school classroom except in extraordinary circumstances (Carnovali 2017). My observation of children with disabilities in Scanno indicates that they can and do pass from grade to grade with their peers because they are provided with an individualized path rather than judged by standardized tests. National constitutions and laws can also affect schools at the local level in aspects such as separation of church and state, sources of funding, and protections against discrimination. Even issues such as what food children eat at school and who pays for it are matters of intense local concern that can become entangled in national politics (B. and C. Woodhouse 2018). In the United States, federal funding for school meals has been a major source of support for combatting child hunger. In Cedar Key, all children receive free meals during the school year because of a federal Department of Agriculture policy allowing schools with more than a certain percentage of students who would be eligible based on family income to obtain a schoolwide waiver of individual proof of eligibility. Even while school is closed for the summer, all kids eighteen and younger can get free breakfast and lunch in the Cedar Key School cafeteria from Monday to Thursdays, under a summer program funded by the US Department of Agriculture (*Cedar Key Beacon* June 21, 2018). But federal intervention, sometimes driven by lobbyists from the food and beverage industries, is the price local schools must pay (B. and C. Woodhouse 2018). In Italy, school meals are paid for by the child's parents, with subsidies for low-income children. Local parent committees jealously guard the right to participate in designing children's school menus. At school, as at home, the quality of food is a matter of intense concern, and national law requires three-course meals with fresh fruits and vegetables and ingredients that are largely organic and locally sourced (Baldwin 2017).

US and Italian public-school systems serve roughly equivalent age groups: the only American public-school equivalent to *asilo*, the Italian nursery and daycare system that serves children from infancy to age three, is Head Start. Unlike the Italian *asilo*, which is part of the national public school system, Head Start and its offshoot, Early Start, are targeted toward low-income and at-risk families. The Italian *scuola materna* serves roughly the same age group as the US state-level pre-K and kindergarten. It is a national program that covers about 98 percent of children, while publically funded US pre-K covers only about 40 percent (US Department of Education 2015). *Scuola primaria*, like American elementary school, marks the beginning of compulsory education and serves children aged six to ten in grades first through fifth. *Scuola media* is similar to our middle school, with three grades serving ages eleven to fourteen. *Liceo* serves the same age groups as our high schools; however, students must choose among schools that focus on different subject matters and careers. In *liceo classico* students focus on subjects of a classic liberal arts education such as literature, history, philosophy, and ancient and modern languages. *Liceo scientifico* attracts students who specialize in math and the sciences as preparation for careers in medicine, science, and engineering. Other high schools are designed for training in business, sports, tourism, and other career-oriented specializations. Thus, thirteen- and fourteen-year-olds in Scanno, as compared to those in Cedar Key, face a major fork in the road as well as a rite of passage. In addition to passing the exams for graduation from middle school they are leaving the home village to study in an urban setting. The choice of stream is among the most important life choices. In Cedar Key, this choice occurs at age eighteen rather than at age thirteen. However, at the front end of the education system, Scanno children begin schooling at a much earlier age because of universal access at age three.

Peer Group

The term "peer group" refers to a "set of individuals who, sharing certain common characteristics such as age, ethnicity, or occupation, perceive themselves and are recognized by others as a distinct social collectivity. The group is seen to have its own culture, symbols, sanctions, and rituals, into which the new members must be socialized, and according to which those who fail to comply with group norms may be ostracized" (Scott 2014, 555). Obviously, under this broad definition, there are many potential peer groups in even a small community, but for purposes of studying the ecology of childhood, the most important (and observable) social groupings involve age and gender. Peer groups are generated spontaneously at the local level and defined by the relationships individuals have with others in the group. At the macro level, sociologists refer to the concept of *age sets*, meaning those "broad age-bands that define the social status, permitted roles, and activities of those belonging to them and that include all the members of the society in that particular category" (10–11).

In my observations of children in Scanno, I found myself identifying certain "age sets" such as stroller babies, toddlers, nursery schoolers, elementary schoolers, preteens, and adolescents. Over the space of nine years, I observed specific children transitioning from one age set to another. At the micro level of the piazza and neighborhood, I observed how gender identity came to dominate play that had previously been gender integrated. I saw gender-based peer groups developing within age sets—now girls walked arm in arm with girls, pestered by boys who played with other boys. A pair of female twins who had been inseparable at age six, by age ten had chosen a best friend who was not the twin. Yet the twins and their new best friends tended to walk everywhere together. By the time they turned fifteen, I was more likely to encounter the twins with a larger peer group in the city of Sulmona, where they now attended *liceo*. As preteens, they had turned very shy and stopped greeting me, but as adolescents encountering me in the city they began to greet me again.

I also observed that crossing from one age set to another is more than an individual developmental process; it is often marked by collective community rituals or rites of passage. Looking at the ecological model, these collective rites of passage are striking in that they invariably take place in the mesosystems where various microsystems meet. This coming together of family, school, church, neighborhood, and peer group holds as true in Cedar Key as it does in Scanno. What happens in the mesosystems where these social institutions and social structures come together? Whatever one calls the phenomenon, it creates a powerful social dynamic. At its best, this dynamic builds solidarity and a sense of shared commitment to the community's children. As will be discussed in part 3, it also has the potential to divide and stratify.

Mesosystemic Rituals and Relationships That Foster Solidarity

The Cedar Key School is a fine example of a social structure that thrives where the microsystemic institutions of family, neighborhood, peer group, faith community, and school intersect, and it demonstrates how social dynamics created within a mesosystem can function as symbols and as enactments of solidarity. The local newspapers, the *Cedar Key Beacon* and the online Cedar Key News, cover Shark sports and school events in great detail, and when students reach their senior year the paper publishes a personal profile and interview of each graduating senior (Arnold 2018a). During the period of this study, the Cedar Key School created its own Facebook page, which became a rich source of information. But the centrality of the school to community life in Cedar Key is evident from the moment you first set eyes on the village from the causeway: the Cedar Key water tower is the first thing you see. It announces the town's identity as home of the S-H-A-R-K-S, and, as everyone knows (or soon finds out), the Sharks are synonymous with the Cedar Key School and community identity. Community members, whether or not they have children in school, are very much engaged with the school. Its place in the town's life is symbolized by the following weekly ritual revolving around the Sharks. There is no stoplight in Cedar Key, but, for all practical purposes, the crossroads marking the center of town is where State Route 24 intersects the town's main commercial street (Second Street). For many years, on game days, a hand-lettered sign saying "Game Tonight 6:30" would appear on a pole planted in the blacktop smack in the middle of the intersection. While many schools in the United States have flashing electric notice boards on their school property, in Cedar Key the Sharks literally took over the town crossroads, and cars and pedestrians had to go around their sign to get where they were going. When the road was repaved after the 2016 hurricane, the pole disappeared, but was replaced

Figure 4.1. Cedar Key School students entertaining guests at Madrigal Dinner. B. B. Woodhouse.

by a banner stretching over the intersection. Cedar Keyans follow the various Shark teams avidly (basketball, baseball, lacrosse for both boys and girls, and now weightlifting for both sexes) and they support the school and its students. As a result, five times in the past six years Cedar Key School was selected as the Class 1A winner of a Florida High School Athletic Association award carrying a prize of $2,500 for the school "whose entire sports program best exemplifies the qualities of sportsmanship as demonstrated by coaches, players and spectators" (*Cedar Key Beacon* June 21, 2018).

The school/community intersection is also evident in other mesosystems where school, church, and family come together. Each year, the town's churches collaborate in a custom called "Baccalaureate." In this distinctly Cedar-Keyan rite of passage, each of the four churches (all Protestant denominations) takes turns hosting a sit-down dinner honoring the entire graduating class. In another tradition, students put on a Madrigal Dinner during December to raise funds for the drama club. This tradition invokes the very distant heritage of Olde England and medieval France. Dressed in medieval costumes, the student actors, musicians, singers, and tumblers bring in a stuffed boar's head (donated by a sportsman from his collection) and a gigantic bowl of wassail. A staple of the evening is participation of an adult choir of volunteers from the village churches who sing a similar menu of seasonal songs. Catered by community volunteers and held in the school auditorium, the Madrigal Dinner is always sold out. These kinds of mesosystemic structures and institutions are hardly unique to small American towns like Cedar Key; they are simply more visible to the researcher studying childhood in a petri dish.

Scanno has similar mesosystemic structures binding the members of the community in solidarity with the community's children and youth. As we discovered on our first visit to Scanno, the whole town shuts down on the day of the children's first communion. Here, family, church, and school come together, much as in the Baccalaureate in Cedar Key, for a major rite of passage. For several weeks before the big day, pictures of each of the children have been on display in the parish mother church (*chiesa madre*) of Santa Maria della Valle. Because religious education is part of the public-school curriculum, there is no sharp division between one's class in school and one's communion class. On the morning of the ceremony, the children, robed in white and carrying white flowers, assemble and march in procession, following the parish priest through the streets of town, with their parents dressed in their finest clothes walking on either side. When they arrive at the town square, the church is already packed to overflowing.

I was first invited to attend this ritual by Candido Nannarone and his wife, Angela. Their two children Massimo and Gaia (siblings whose original names had been Maxim and Galina) had been born in the Ukraine and adopted two years earlier. The children were making their first communion in May 2012. The image of these two new parents, whose children had only recently learned to speak Italian, walking hand in hand with their son and daughter in this solemn procession, remains a vivid reminder of the importance of ritual in the process of inclusion and building of identity and solidarity.

In this ritual, family, church, peer group and neighborhood came together to affirm Massimo and Gaia's belonging in and to the Scanno community.

Another Scanno ritual at the intersections of church, family, neighborhood and childhood that I pointed out in the Portrait of Scanno is a procession I witnessed one morning in May in which small children and mothers pushing strollers start from the main piazza in front of the Asilo and wind through the streets of town. Each child (and each mother pushing a stroller) is given a long-stemmed lily. The procession is led by a tiny statue of the Virgin Mary, which the older children carry on their shoulders. The statue is the children's version of the Madonnina del Lago (Madonna of the Lake), and their procession mimics that of the adults who earlier carried the Madonnina up to the mother church for the Marian weeks of May. In this mini procession, the children are practicing for their roles as adults, with the endorsement and

Figure 4.2. Massimo and Gaia and their parents in their First Communion procession. B. B. Woodhouse.

participation of the community. The town is full of parents, grandparents, and neighbors taking pictures of this procession on their smartphones. The parade ends at Santa Maria della Valle and the children place their lilies in a vase next to the Madonnina and go home early for lunch.

In a practice that reminded me of my own children's kindergarten days, the small statue of the Madonna that the children carry in procession resides in the Asilo during the month of May. Each night a different child has permission to take her home. Witnessing this ritual, I could not help but think of the kindergarten gerbil who taught my children and their peers to take care of something fragile that belonged to the whole group and to bring it back intact and happy. Every nursery schooler in Scanno, as was the case with my children's kindergarten pet, has a shared stake in the well-being of the statue and a chance to enact this relationship in their own homes.

When Communal Identity Survives Distance

Communal identity, if sufficiently strong, can become geographically diffused as populations migrate. Migrants leaving one home to settle in another often remain attached to the village of origin, even in modern times and across generations. In the United States, we see this phenomenon among African American families who settled in states like Michigan, Illinois, or New York during the Great Migration of the early 1900s but return to hold large family reunions in the Southern towns from which their grandparents migrated. Many overseas *Scannesi* return each summer from Canada, the United States, and Argentina to maintain ties with their home town. The same attachment is enacted in the annual Cedar Key Old Timers' Reunion, when people who were born or whose ancestors were born in Cedar Key gather for a weekend of picnics and festive events (Cedar Key News 2018). In another example of attachment, when the Cedar Key School was destroyed by fire in 2002, a 1944 graduate who had moved far away and founded a successful business read about the loss in the *Cedar Key Beacon* and donated $250,000 to help build a new red brick school building replicating the one he had attended (Voyles 2003).

However, one way in which Italian and US identities differ is the extent to which Italians, wherever they may live and work, tend to self-identify, as individuals, by geographic city of origin. On a typical US quiz show, the contestants commonly identify themselves by name, occupation, and place of residence; in Italy, the critical facts are name and place of origin. The most popular shows know how to play upon the audiences' regional loyalties, choosing contestants so that each region will be represented. What matters most is not what you do or where you live but where you were born. My Italian colleague, Professor Elena Urso, who has lived in Florence since age twelve and has taught for thirty years at the University of Florence, is still Elena Urso from Licata, Sicily.

The Role of Competing Social Structures and Institutions

While village mesosystems can generate a single unifying identity, they also generate subgroup loyalties that play an important role in the forging of communal identity. These social structures may be sites of conflict as well as collaboration. For our purposes, what matters most is their function as sites of collaboration. At their best, subgroups play a dual role, ratifying differences and enacting shared commitments to the community. The activities of subgroups, in addition to meeting the need for more intimate units of identity, also serve as engines of social cohesion. Their commitment to the village as a whole is enacted through engagement with other subgroups in collaborative, community-wide enterprises. These enterprises are generated in the zones where the microsystems defining the ecology of childhood intersect. Most

Figure 4.3. Cedar Key elementary school students dressed as favorite superheroes for Homecoming Spirit Week. Cedar Key School Facebook.

visible to political scientists are structures such as town councils and political parties, but for children, the more visible signs of solidarity are the festivals, parades, and holiday events that play such a large part in knitting the community together.

Of all Cedar Key's parades and festivals, the biggest event is "Homecoming Spirit Week": a week of escalating excitement that culminates in the crowning of the King and Queen of the Homecoming Court, which takes place during halftime at the Sharks' varsity basketball game. The entire town joins in the week's events, including a parade with patriotic and themed floats, a senior prom and a bonfire. At school, the week is designated "Spirit Week," when kids from the youngest to the oldest can dress as their favorite superheroes.

Studying the religious processions in Scanno made me much more attuned to these Cedar Key events—staples of the American Heartland which most Americans take for granted—and much more aware of the role played by parades in the United States. Parades are a means of celebrating membership in social structures or social groups within the larger community and of establishing cross-group connections. Parades have marked major milestones for the recognition and inclusion of groups such as Irish, Italians, and LGBTQ people. When I attended the 2015 Gay Pride Parade in Atlanta, it was heartening to see floats and participation from every community institution, from the Atlanta Fire Department to Suntrust Bank.

In small-town America, parades are how a community manifests its identity through group participation. I once took a visiting Japanese legal scholar to a Fourth of July parade in a small town in rural Maryland, and she was fascinated by the identities of the groups of marchers. The groups were as diverse as the League of Women Voters, the Veterans of Foreign Wars, and the local teenage dance troupe. Such groups, my guest explained to me, did not parade through the streets in her hometown. Most astonishing to my Japanese visitor was the custom of local municipal, county, and state court judges participating in the parade, riding in open cars, and showering the populace with handfuls of candy. As she mentally processed these novelties, she struggled to identify functional equivalents in her own, very different culture. Processions, whether religious or patriotic, have a lot to say about social structures and social institutions that reinforce group identity, group difference, and community solidarity. Parades and processions also expose the fallacy that erasure of subgroup identities will foster greater social cohesion. Subgroup identity plays a role in cementing community connection.

Faith Communities as Sites of Identity Formation

Another common site of social cohesion is the faith community. Children play a large role, as we have seen, in Scanno's religious life, but the same is true, although to a lesser and less obvious degree, in Cedar Key. Compared to big cities in Italy and America, where synagogues, mosques, and historically black churches illustrate the greater diversity of religious life in urban centers, Scanno and Cedar Key are both overwhelmingly white and overwhelmingly Christian. Yet there is surprising religious diversity within these seemingly homogenous villages in both countries.

Italian visitors to the United States often marvel at the proliferation of Christian houses of worship on Main Street, USA. Why are they so often all clustered on the same town square rather than spread out across the village? The Methodist, Baptist, Church of Christ, and Episcopal churches of Cedar Key are all located within four blocks of each other. The newest arrival, a Catholic chapel, is half a mile away. Americans take for granted that different Christian denominations coexist and compete for members in a single village or town. It is a matter of individual choice which building one enters. People can, and do, move from one church family to another, or worship in more than one. By the same token, Americans visiting Scanno often wonder why the Catholic Church (which they misperceive as monolithic) bothers to maintain five active church buildings instead of simply having one parish church and repurposing the others. Maintaining so many churches is very labor intensive. Don Carmelo, the parish priest of Scanno, holds masses on a regular basis not only in Santa Maria della Valle (twice a day, seven days a week), but in the churches of Madonna del Carmine and Sant' Antonio (every Sunday), and in San Giovanni Battista and Sant' Eustachio (special holidays and saints' days). Observing life in both Scanno and Cedar Key over the course of a year, one sees the vital role played by these different church groups. It would be almost as unthinkable for Don Carmelo to discontinue services at any of these churches as for the Baptists and Episcopalians in Cedar Key to merge their congregations.

In both Scanno and Cedar Key, the churches cherish their separate identities and compete for adherents, but they also collaborate on community-wide projects. In Cedar Key we see this in the Food Bank and Empty Bowls Soup Supper and the tradition described above, of the Baccalaureate Dinner. In Scanno, although all the churches are part of the same Catholic parish or *parrocchia* and served by the same parish priest (Don Carmelo), who reports to a single bishop or Vescovo located in Sulmona, each church has its own loyal followers and civilian administrators. Its most active members join a *confraternita'* (confraternity), often enrolling their children as toddlers. The confraternities compete to outshine each other during the festivals of their patron saints. They also collaborate on community-wide projects such as the Asilo Buon Pastore (nursery school) and a *campo estivo* (summer camp) for children, and they support each other's festivals by marching in processions, attending band concerts, and buying lottery tickets. As my husband discovered after he was invited to enroll in the confraternity of the Madonna delle Grazie and march in her procession, participation in each other's saint's day processions is not optional—it is mandatory. After his first procession in full regalia, he had returned to the role of spectator at the next festival. Signor Di Rienzo, his kindly senior mentor, took him aside and schooled him in the unwritten rules.

While the Scanno confraternities may strike US Protestants as peculiar and alien, we can find analogues or functional equivalents to these faith-based social structures in every small community. The Cedar Key Lions and Eagles Clubs, the Cedar Key Women's Club, Friends of the Library, Friends of the Wildlife Refuge, and Historical Society, as well as the faith-based institutions, are part of the fabric of social life (McCarthy 2007). As immortalized in Garrison Keillor's fictional Lake Woebegone, the various church families, fraternal lodges, and women's auxiliaries play similar roles to the Italian confraternities in the small towns of America. These public demonstrations of communal solidarity are not lost on the children who participate in these events.

Neighborhoods as Seedbeds of Solidarity

In addition to community-wide identities and religious subgroups, loyalties and identities are often grounded in microgeographies. In the United States, as noted earlier, we call these subdivisions "neighborhoods," while Italians refer to them as *contrade* (plural). Perhaps the most famous Italian *contrade* are those of the Tuscan city of Siena, home of the famous Palio horse race. The historic city center consists of seventeen wards dating back to the Middle Ages. Riders from ten of the *contrade* compete twice a year for the championship, racing wildly around the central piazza, bareback and in Renaissance dress with the brilliant colors of each *contrade* (Wikipedia, Palio di Siena).

Tiny Scanno has its own *contrade*—La Plaja, Cardella, and San Martino. Even after a family moves from one neighborhood to another, the allegiance to the family's historic *contrada* remains strong. Children tend to inherit their *contrada* from the paternal line. During the festival of San Martino, as discussed in chapter 3, youth from each *contrada* compete to build the highest and most spectacular of three bonfires, called Le Glorie di San Martino. For several weeks in November 2014, my husband and I followed the action through binoculars, as the young people of our contrada (La Plaja) gathered wood and began building a towering structure on the mountainside opposite our apartment balcony. Working on weekends and after school, young people from the other neighborhoods were building their own fires on two other mountainsides.

On the night of San Martino, after lighting the bonfires, all of the young people come down to the piazza to celebrate and share traditional foods and to demand a *scherzetto o dolcetto* (trick or treat). They bring a timber from each fire to the most recently married couple in the contrada—an omen of fertility. In a ritual that would have an entirely different and offensive meaning in the United States, before coming down to town the children and youth from all three of the *contrade* smear their faces with charcoal. This has no racial significance and, instead, is meant to render them unrecognizable as they play their pranks. Like American children on Halloween, who don masks and dress as hoboes and witches, the Scanno children are allowed for an evening to be rowdy and boisterous beyond the normal limits. This defiance of the injunction to behave and "keep your face clean" is part of the attraction for the children and youth of Scanno, as it is in the traditions of Halloween in the English-speaking world. Far from dividing the community, the robust competition between *contrade*

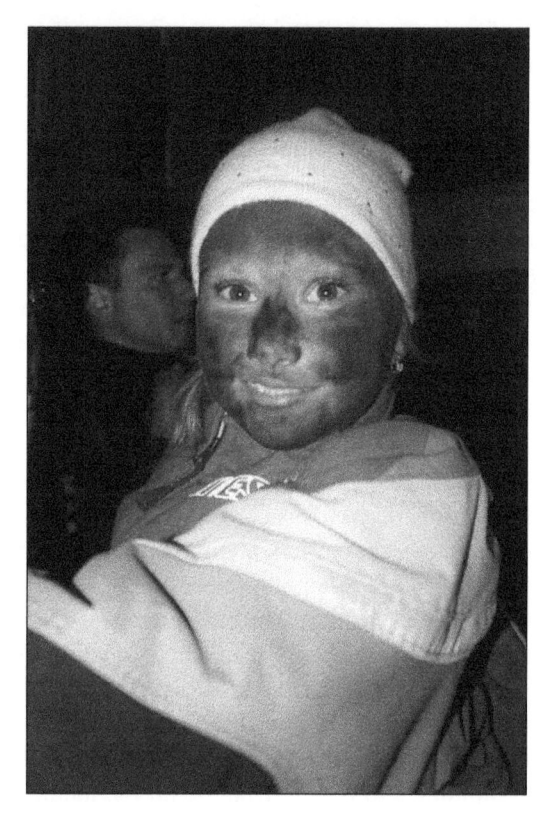

Figure 4.4. Girl from La Plaja in a mask of charcoal dust from her *contrada*'s bonfire. S. Pizzacalla.

brings it together each year in a key ritual. In interviews of school-age children, I heard them repeatedly name San Martino as one of their favorite festivals.

San Martino is an ancient rite of passage that has changed to reflect contemporary mores about gender equality. Enzo Gentile, a local expert on the anthropology of Scanno, described San Martino's origins to me, as a rite of passage for boys only. Just as men and women had different roles in Scanno—the men going away on the *transumanza* and the women tending life in the village—boys and girls followed very different paths to very different adulthoods. Part of the women's role was to create a psychological boundary around the village by telling young children stories of bears, wolves, and ghosts in the forests outside the village. At age ten, in a rite of passage, the boundary was lifted for boys when they went out into the forest to perform the ritual of building and lighting the bonfires. Girls' rite of passage came with their first communion, when they donned the traditional Scanno dress and took on the traditional roles, which also required going outside the boundaries of the village to collect firewood and get water. In recent years, girls have begun to participate with boys in the San Martino festival, "contaminating" (a technical term) the formerly strictly gendered customs and bringing them into the modern age. Look closely and you will see that the girl whose face is dirtied with charcoal dust in figure 4.4 is Clarissa, the same girl we saw earlier wearing the elegant traditional costume of Scanno (fig. 3.10, on page 66).

While Cedar Key is both too small and its dwellings too dispersed to have such formally recognized neighborhoods, a similar friendly competition between subgroups is evident at Cedar Key's Fall Seafood Festival and Old Florida Celebration of the Arts. Cedar Key's civic and church groups sponsor the best beverage stands and food stalls, while student groups host food stalls to raise funds for their activities. Churches and civic groups like the Lions Club donate the proceeds of the fair to programs for children and to CKS student groups: in 2018, the safety patrol and the cheerleading squad won cash prizes in recognition of their outstanding floats in the Seafood Festival Parade.

Gender plays a less defining role in Cedar Key than in Scanno, but gender roles have also changed over time. Girls are no longer confined to being cheerleaders and baton twirlers as they were in the past. The Sharks have

Figure 4.5. Cedar Key School Safety Patrol students selling soft drinks at grand opening of the Nature Coast Biological Research Station B. B. Woodhouse.

for many years fielded girls' basketball and track teams that regularly win regional championships. In 2018 the Lady Sharks broke another gender barrier by fielding their very first weight lifting team in a regional competition (Cedar Key Beacon December 6, 2018).

The Erosion of Village Identity

As the data in chapters 7 and 8 on the Great Recession and its aftermath will show, even in remote locations like Scanno and Cedar Key families are struggling with the fallout from current global and national policies. In Italy we see a surge in unemployment, out-migration of jobs and workers, declining opportunities for young people, rising substance abuse, and fiscal pressure to disinvest in human capital. Many of the same trends are decimating the social and financial economies of rural areas, small towns, and inner cities in America. Our environments are becoming increasingly toxic to children. This book should serve as a warning cry, calling for the innovation and courage that will be needed to restore and preserve a healthy ecology of childhood.

While my descriptions of Scanno and Cedar Key might lead you to imagine village life as a panacea to modernism's ills, that would be missing the point. They are both very real places with real problems and they exist in very real national and global contexts. Their problems are not isolated from those of the outside world but flow from and are emblematic of it. Recent events vividly illustrate the interconnectedness of communities across borders and time zones. As I will argue in chapter 9, the problems of these small communities are the world's problems. People everywhere are adjusting to rapid technological change; struggling to generate sufficient work for the able-bodied while caring for the vulnerable; racing to achieve a sustainable relationship with the natural world before it is too late; coping with the pressures of mass migration and dislocation; and striving to achieve justice, dignity, security, peace, and equality without sacrificing individual liberty. What struck me as distinctive about these two villages was the visible evidence all around me of social cohesion and solidarity. These qualities may hold the key to resolving many of the modern world's ills and to creating a healthier ecology of childhood.

It seems ironic that so many pundits have heralded the end of the welfare state at the very moment when I am arguing for strengthening social solidarity. In the wake of the economic crisis, as I noted in chapter 1, I found myself chasing a vanishing ideal: that government will provide a safety net for its most vulnerable citizens, especially children. As I write, the Trump administration is advocating further cuts to many programs that survived the Great

Recession and helped children weather the economic crisis. Entire welfare programs that have been effective at combatting hunger, reducing poverty, protecting the aged and disabled, and assuring access to medical care are on the chopping block.

The United States may be facing the dismantling of its own anemic welfare state. But the economic crisis in Italy hit harder and cut deeper than in the United States or in other European nations like Germany, France, and the United Kingdom. The Italian national debt soared along with the rates of unemployment and business failure. Under intense pressure from the EU, Italy was forced to abandon many social-welfare and pro-labor policies and to adopt austerity measures such as deregulation and drastic spending cuts. The spillover effects of austerity, even in remote and picturesque Scanno, have been devastatingly real. While Cedar Key has benefited from the stronger economy of the United States, it is steadily losing population, its children cannot find work without migrating, and the village itself is especially vulnerable to climate change. In many ways, Scanno and Cedar Key play the role of miners' canaries, giving early warning of toxic environmental and social changes as well as models for improving the ecology of childhood.

*　*　*

As this chapter illustrates, solidarity is built within mesosyems, which are the glue that hold a community together. There is no stronger glue than the realization, formed in these daily interactions, that all children are our children. It is this essential sense of solidarity between and across generations that must be nurtured and supported, from the village level to the national and international levels, if we are to surmount the challenges that lie ahead.

PART 3

Exosystems and Macrosystems

5

Falling Birth Rates and Rural Depopulation

Four houses clinging to
the top of a golden mountain.
My home village is beautiful.
You can race around on a bicycle,
you can play soccer or *rachette*.
It's only missing one thing.
There's not even a single playmate.
— Davide Nanni, "Castrovalva"

At the center of the ecological model, there is a child. We naturally assume that the child represents just one among a number of other children populating the ecosystem. The reality is different. All over the globe, populations in rural areas are shrinking and aging, and villages are dying. Young people born in small towns are leaving for cities and those that remain where they were born are delaying or forgoing having children. In addition, many of the world's developed nations are experiencing declining fertility rates. When fertility has fallen below replacement rates, it means more old people are dying than new people are being born. While Europe's low birth rate crisis is not news, the recent recession has caused it to accelerate. To ignore it is to miss a crucial factor in the ecology of childhood.

This chapter will focus on the demography of fertility, now in steep decline in developed nations. Where in the ecological model is this pending threat located? While some may say childbearing is purely a matter of personal choice—a family matter located within the microsystems of childhood—I will argue that falling birth rates are in large part a result of exosystemic factors. Choices about childbearing are influenced by labor markets, availability of child care, gender equity, cultural beliefs about parenting, and many other factors that masquerade as personal choice. In the rest of part 3, we will continue this move away from the intimate levels of micro- and mesosystems to examine the larger words of exosystems and macrosystems. Chapter 6 will look at how family-supportive policies affect people's decisions on whether to have children and how they shape those families' quality of life. Chapter 7 will refocus on the exosystems of the economics of Wall Street, examining the impact of the Great Recession on American children. Chapter 8 will follow the recession as it crosses the Atlantic, affecting the well-being of children in Italy and the rest of Europe. In chapter 9 we will turn our attention to the elephant in the playroom: globalization, which represents the dominant macrosystemic influence of our times. Its many dimensions, including economic, cultural, environmental, and ideological, shape our and our children's collective futures. Its problematic features include unrestrained capitalism, technological revolution, rising inequality, racial and ethnic division, mass migration, and the contribution of all of the above to climate change.

The Demographics of Fertility

Demography can be a boring subject until it gets personalized. The poem quoted at the beginning of this chapter was written by Davide Nanni, a nine-year-old boy who was then living in the picturesque village of Castrovalva, about ten miles down the Sagittarius Gorge from Scanno. Davide uses poetic license in saying his village is only "four houses." There are almost one hundred stone houses in Castrovalva, but only fourteen resident families, according to the most recent statistics ("The Village of Castrovalva," n.d.). Davide is not exaggerating when he uses the Italian term for "rock climbing" to describe his village's topography: Castrovalva clings precariously to a mountain ridge that overhangs the Sagittarius Gorge a thousand feet below. The road up to this village makes the road to Scanno look like a stroll down the Atlantic City Boardwalk. Castrovalva dates back to Roman times, when Italian towns were built in the most easily defended and hardest-to-reach places. It is a complete village, with a church, a fountain, several piazzas, a warren of steep streets, and stone dwellings with balconies decked out in bright flowers and washing flapping in the breeze. By the time Davide composed his poem, however, Castrovalva had lost so many young families that he was literally the last child in the village; when the summer visitors went home, he had no one to play with. "I am little and I want to play," he writes. "Alone, alone I do not want to stay." His grandmother tells him that once upon a time the village was full of children all year round. Davide says wistfully, "That's how I would like my village to be!" This is one of the most poignant poems in *Voci Antiche* (Ancient Voices), a volume of prizewinning poetry in dialect, composed by schoolchildren from the area around Scanno. Many of the poems speak of friendship and playmates, but none speaks more eloquently about loneliness than Davide's.

Being all alone is a very scary thought for a child. Here is another example of a child's perspective on demography: forty years ago, before Google Earth was even imagined, I was using our huge *National Geographic Atlas* to show our three-year-old daughter, Jessica, the place where the baby brother we were in the process of adopting was waiting for us to bring him home. The atlas included maps of population density, with each dot counting for 500,000 people. Since the island province of Newfoundland, Canada, was very sparsely populated, there was just one dot representing its entire population. Jessica pointed to it and wailed, "There's Kenny—and he's *all alone!*" She calmed down after we explained that the single dot she imagined as Kenny stood for all of the many people who lived in Newfoundland. But she clearly thought the mapmakers were very bad at drawing. And she sat down to draw her own picture, copying the island's shape and carefully populating it with many little dots.

Nowadays, parents could use the Google Earth app on their computers to conjure up almost any spot on the globe and zero in on roads, houses, forests, and lakes. Type in "Scanno, Aquila, Italy," and you will be transported from your current location across the ocean to zoom in on a detailed picture of the village. Do the same with "Cedar Key, Florida, US," and you will be lifted up and carried back across the ocean to focus in on a cluster of small islands drifting into the Gulf of Mexico. But even Google Earth provides only a static two-dimensional image of a people and their place. We need other data and other information in order to complete the picture.

Demography is not just a tool for describing a population's present; it is also a way of foretelling a population's future. Humans are no different from other animal species. All species need a reliable population supply. Too high a fertility rate exhausts food supplies and increases mortality rates. Too low a fertility rate risks extinction. Sustaining adequate birth rates is a matter of survival. In species where adults must care for vulnerable members who cannot care for themselves, replacement fertility rates are especially critical. The generations, in such species, are inherently interdependent. Some organisms can survive without a parent's care, but a mother bear or wolf who gives birth to two or three cubs must care for them over an extended period before they can survive on their own.

Looking at human societies, if the population of a nation is aging, and its supply of babies falls very far below the replacement rate, the social bargain between generations breaks down. Elders who once could count on children to support them in their old age are dependent on other resources. In modern countries with publicly funded pension systems, we have converted this bargain into a broader scheme of social insurance. The question boils down to this: If a generation of young people does not produce sufficient children, where will the workers come from to fund pensions and medical care for elders who can no longer take care of themselves? My description is clearly oversimplified and subject to many caveats, but it is a truth that is staring developed nations right in the eye. Whereas families in less developed nations often have three, four, or more children, birth rates in developed nations are shrinking. The good news is that babies in developed nations have many advantages their ancestors lacked; the bad news is that declining birth rates can become so low they precipitate a critical scarcity of human capital. Italy, like many other developed nations, is facing such a crisis. And, as we shall see, a similar fate may be overtaking the United States.

Measuring Fertility: Birth Rates and Replacement Rates

Crude Birth Rates

Over the past half-century, according to the World Bank database, rates of fertility have dropped dramatically in developed nations (World Bank, for birth rate crude per 1,000 people—1960–2016; 2018b). Italy's "crude birth rate," defined as the number of babies born per thousand residents, had already dropped by 50 percent between 1965 to 2008. In 1965 it was at 19.0, and by 2008 it was at 9.8. By 2012, after the economic crisis struck, it had dropped to 9.0. By 2016 it had dropped to 7.8. To put Italy's crude birth rate in comparative perspective, in 2016 the average crude birth rate in the EU was 10 while among OECD nations it was 12. In these latest statistics, Italy was tied with Japan and Monaco for the lowest crude birth rates on the globe. In Germany, rates seemed to have stabilized at around 8.8. Topping the EU list were Ireland with 13.9 and the UK with 11.8 per thousand. The US crude birth rate was 12.5 births per thousand residents (World Bank 2018a).

Birth rates are generally highest in the poorest countries and decrease with increasing economic development. In some sub-Saharan African countries, crude birth rates are above 40 per thousand people, while birth rates in India, once far higher, are now at about 19 per thousand (World Bank 2018a). Birth rates in developed countries also remain sensitive to economic shifts. But, ironically, instead of rising as poverty rises, they tend to fall further during economic downturns (World Bank 2018a). A slight downward shift may not cause a stir in a country with a robust birth rate, but the continuing decline has been of great concern in Italy.

Total Fertility Rates and Replacement Rate Fertility

To complete the picture we need several other key measures relating to female fertility. The "total fertility rate" is the average number of children born per woman. "Replacement rate fertility" is defined as the total fertility rate at which a population replaces itself from one generation to the next, not counting population growth from migration. While the replacement fertility rate varies slightly due to mortality rates, in most countries this replacement rate is approximately 2.1 children per woman (Searchinger et al. 2013).

Italy, with a total fertility rate of 1.32, is aging at an unsustainable pace (ISTAT 2018). In its latest reports, ISTAT concluded that what had been regarded as a recession-driven drop in birth rates has now become the new structural norm (ISTAT 2018). Italy may not be alone. Many other countries have registered total fertility rates below 1.5 (World Bank 2018b). In some cases, these low fertility rates reflect economic crisis, as with Greece and Spain, or political upheaval, as in the Middle East. But Germany, Japan, and South Korea have all experienced total fertility rates below 1.5, despite enjoying high levels of economic development and political stability. Although the causes of declining birth rates in developed nations are not fully understood, it is clear that a birth-rate crisis is overtaking childhood in these industrialized countries. With average fertility rates in the OECD countries at a historic low of 1.57, there is no escaping that affluent countries in particular are falling far below replacement rates (World Bank 2018b). But what accounts for variations in national birth rates among these OECD nations? Comparisons across peer nations of various key factors are an important step in understanding the comparative dynamics of fertility.

Five Factors Affecting Birth Rates

The first of five key factors studied by demographers is mothers' age at first birth. In modern developed nations, we are caught in a bind between reproductive maturity and the elongation of social dependency. As a matter of physiology, females now reach puberty and acquire reproductive capacity at an earlier age than prior generations. But benchmarks of social and economic maturity, such as completion of education, finding of a mate, and economic independence, arrive much later than they once did. The ideal age to begin having babies, as a matter of reproductive physiology, may be much earlier than the ideal age from the perspective of social and economic maturity. Policy-makers (and prospective parents) are balancing many different factors in assessing the implications of maternal age at first birth.

The earlier a woman starts reproducing, the longer the arc of her reproductive life, and the more likely that she will produce more children. According to data from 2016, the average age of mothers at first birth in Italy was 31.7 (ISTAT 2017). In the United States, the estimate for age at first birth for

2014 was 26.3 years, far lower than in Italy (Mathews and Hamilton 2016). In France, Canada, and many other OECD nations, the mean age at first birth has been hovering around 28 years, making the United States and Italy outliers among developed nations (Central Intelligence Agency, for the World Factbook: Mother's Mean Age at First Birth 2015, 2018). While mothers' age at first birth was on the high end in Italy, it was on the low end in the United States, when compared with peer nations.

Adolescent Fertility Rate

A second key factor is the adolescent fertility rate. When mothers give birth at a young age not only are their reproductive lives potentially longer, the time between generations is shortened, leading to an acceleration in crude birth rates. Historically, the adolescent birth rate has been far lower in Italy than in the United States. The rate in the United States in 2014 was 24.11 births per thousand adolescent girls aged 15 to 19. In Italy during the same year it was a mere 6 births per thousand girls (World Bank, for adolescent fertility rate, for the United States and Italy).

If all we cared about were increasing the numbers of babies, we would promote early childbearing. In most developed nations, the drawbacks of encouraging births by adolescents far outweigh the benefits of adding to lagging populations. Delaying pregnancy into young adulthood allows mothers to gain needed education and maturity. In societies where adolescents are sexually active, making birth control readily available is a sensible policy choice, even in nations wanting to increase their birth rates. But a society can have too much of a good thing. Social and economic forces that delay childbearing far beyond adolescence are clearly a factor in Italy's low birth-rate crisis (ISTAT 2018).

Mothers' Marital Status

Mothers' marital status represents a third key factor studied by demographers. Once again, Italy and the United States are at opposite ends of the demographic curve for developed nations. In the United States, births to unmarried mothers have been dropping; in 2016 they stood at 42.4 per thousand births. But almost 40 percent of all births in the United States were still to unmarried mothers (CDC 2018; Curtin, Ventura, and Martinez 2014). In Italy, numbers of births to unmarried women have been rising. At 25.9 percent of total births in 2013, they were still low compared to peer nations such as Germany (32.1 in 2008) and France (52.6 in 2008) (ISTAT 2014; US Census Bureau, for Table 1355, Births to

Unmarried Women by Country). By 2017, the percentage in Italy of births to unmarried mothers had risen to 30.9 (ISTAT 2018).

The overall significance of mothers' marital status is far from clear. Do mothers who are not married procreate more or less? Do children of unmarried mothers fare better or worse than other children? The rates of unmarried childbearing in the United States have been targeted by many critics as an unalloyed threat to children and society (Blankenhorn 1996; Hernstein 1994). This story is too simple. Marital status is only one of the elements affecting social stability and quality of life for children (Dowd 1997). A lot depends on other factors, such as the engagement and support of fathers and extended family, the presence or absence of social stigma, and the social supports a nation provides its families. Some of the nations in which nonmarital childbearing is most common, such as Sweden, have the most stable replacement fertility rates and rank very highly on measures of child well-being. However, marital couples' relationships may be more stable over time than those of cohabiting couples (Wilcox and DeRose 2017).

Percentage of Women in Workforce

A fourth major factor studied by demographers of fertility is the percentage of women in the wage-earning workforce. In the United States, in 2016, 70.5 percent of mothers of children under eighteen were in the paid labor force. Mothers of young children were less likely to be employed (64.7 percent) than mothers of children six to seventeen (75 percent). More single mothers were in the workforce (76 percent) than married mothers (67.9 percent) but the norm for married families has clearly shifted to the dual-income family model (Bureau of Labor Statistics 2017a). In comparison, the percentage of all Italian women age twenty-five to forty-nine with children under eighteen who were in the workforce was almost ten points lower than in the United States, at 62.2 percent. To place this in larger comparative perspective, Italy ranked in twenty-seventh place among European nations in women's workforce participation (Save the Children [Italy] 2017).

How does labor force participation affect birth rates? Some observers believe that women's participation in the workforce undercuts their desire to assume the roles of wife and mother (Stone 2018; Miller 2018). International comparisons cast doubt on this theory (Chemin 2015). Decisions about procreation are influenced by a complex mix of factors rooted in social and economic culture (Wilcox 2018). Although birth rates have declined in Europe, the preferred family size in Europe is still two children. In Europe, as in America, the two-wage earner family is increasingly necessary to economic survival. In countries with robust supports for families, such as France, Denmark, Sweden, and Holland, birth rates remain above replacement rate despite strong labor-force participation. European policy-makers in these countries have promoted women's participation in the wage economy by underlining the importance of adopting structural supports that permit more parents, especially mothers, to combine work and family (Chemin 2015; Stone 2018).

In Italy, far from promoting stay-at-home mothers as a means of increasing the population, policy-makers see increasing maternal employment as crucial to increasing fertility rates (Save the Children [Italy] 2017, 33). In July 2017, in his annual report, Tito Boeri, the head of the Italian social security and welfare agency (INPS), delivered a stark warning: balancing welfare and pension budgets will be impossible unless more women enter the labor force (INPS 2017c). If the rate of female participation stays the same, by 2040 the agency's resources will be forty-two billion euros in the red. One key component in this equation was the finding that working women are more likely, not less, to have children. In contrast with the past, when Italian women who were homemakers were more likely to have children than working women, the opposite is now true in Italy. Boeri warned the Italian Parliament that the "woman question" in Italy had passed from being a private issue or feminist discussion point to being a "national question." As he pointed out, a social protection system can only be made sustainable by increasing the base of contributors. More working women means more current contributors and more future contributors. Boeri stressed the crucial importance of expanding resources for working families and of enforcing existing protections such as family leave and pay equity (Marro 2017).

Mothers in Italy, who are increasingly taking jobs outside the home, should be heartened by US research suggesting that maternal employment does not adversely affect children and, in fact, having a mother who has a job correlates with a child's higher earnings and greater well-being in adulthood (Lucas-Thompson et al. 2010). While work is not incompatible with good parenting, most experts in child development would agree that parenting takes time and requires consistency. Infants, especially, benefit from having a full-time bonded caregiver during the first six months to a year of life (Zero to Three 2017; Zero to Three 2013; Center on the Developing Child 2007). Balancing work and family is a huge challenge in the United States, the only industrialized nation that does not have paid maternity leave (Goldberg, M. 2018). As we shall see in chapter 6, compared to working mothers in the United States Italian working mothers have greater social supports for parenting, including paid maternity leave; greater access to quality, affordable childcare; and even cash bonuses for having additional babies.

The Gendered Division of Domestic Labor

A fifth variable in the fertility equation is the gendered division of domestic labor. The data are clear that, even in highly industrialized nations, women spend significantly more time on housework and care of dependent family members than their male partners, and this continues to be true of women who do double duty as homemakers and as wage earners in the paid labor force. In Italy, according to a 2017 study by Save the Children (Italy), combining work done in the home and work done in the wage economy, the median workload of the Italian female is eleven hours and thirty-five minutes per day compared to that of males, whose workload is ten hours and thirteen minutes. In other words, an Italian woman's workday is one hour and twenty-two minutes longer than an Italian man's. For couples with children, the asymmetry in domestic workload (defined as chores around the home, acquisition of goods and services, and care of dependent family members) results in Italian women shouldering two-thirds of the domestic labor while men do one-third. Obviously, parity is still a long way off, but the gap between the proportion of domestic labor assumed by Italian women and men is closing rather dramatically. In 2013–14, women did 67.3 percent of it; in 2008–9, 74.6 percent, and, in 1998, 80.6 percent. While the levels vary from region to region, with the more traditional southern regions lagging behind the northern and central regions, the increase in men's participation is occurring in all regions of Italy (Save the Children [Italy] 2017, fig. 10).

Domestic labor is an expansive term that can cover everything from pushing a stroller to cleaning a toilet. Women have long complained that men are willing to do the more enjoyable tasks, but leave the less pleasant tasks to women. One intriguing comparative study on the gender gap in developed nations examined "core household chores," on the theory that these unpleasant tasks were the acid test of equality. The study showed that inequality, even in these unpleasant activities, plummeted across the board between 1970 and 2010 in every country studied. Scandinavian countries and the United States lead the trend with more traditional societies such as Italy and Greece lagging behind. However, the more traditional the country, the steeper the decline in inequality. In the United States, the gap in minutes spent on housework was rapidly approaching parity in the mid-1990s, but took an upward turn in the late 1990s and has since leveled out (Altintas and Sullivan 2016). In other words, the gender gap even in the least pleasant forms of work has been narrowing rapidly in all developed countries, including those with more traditional cultures, and this has been happening at the same time as birth rates have been dropping in those same countries. The gender gap in household labor surely plays a role in women's attitudes toward childbearing, but these data suggest it is not the driving force behind the drop in birth rates (Goldberg, M. 2018).

The Save the Children (Italy) study highlighted one particularly troubling dynamic of the gender gap in nations with below replacement fertility rates. The aging of a population when combined with women's traditional roles as caregivers produces an additional long-term consequence. Not only are there fewer young people in the labor force to fund the elderly population's needs; there are also greater demands on the time of the young and middle-aged adults in the so-called "sandwich generation" who must care for aging parents and grandparents at the same time as they are raising the next generation of children. In most societies, the task of caring for the elderly is overwhelmingly assigned to women. This sandwich-generation phenomenon is likely to reach a crisis level in Italy. With so many Italians living into their nineties, a woman of childbearing age may have two generations of elders to care for and fewer siblings to share the burden. If the population continues to age and birth rates continue to fall, the work of caring for a growing number of elders falls even more heavily on a shrinking number of young and middle-aged women, eroding the time and resources they have available to invest in the next generation of children (Save the Children [Italy] 2017). As this example illustrates, the five factors described above interact with each other and with other factors such as infant mortality and increasing life expectancy.

Is the United States Facing a Low-Birth-Rate Crisis of Its Own?

US birth rates have been relatively high compared to peer nations, and, according to studies of attitudes toward childbearing, parenthood remains extremely popular in the United States. About 50 percent of women aged fifteen to forty-four in a large CDC study stated they expected to have children in the future (Daugherty and Martinez 2016). The US had long seemed an exception to declining birth rates among developed nations, but birth rates dropped sharply during the recent economic crisis and, even after the country emerged from recession, the total fertility rate among US women did not return to its prior levels (Bureau of Labor Statistics 2017b; Durden 2016; Zumbrun 2016). In 2007, it was at 2.12, just slightly below replacement rate. By 2015 it had dropped to 1.84 (World Bank, for fertility rate, total, for United States).

In June 2016, alarm bells sounded in the business sector when the *Wall Street Journal* warned of a "Baby Bust" (Durden 2016; Zumbrun 2016). Economists had believed that birth rates would rise in 2015 as the economy recovered. Instead, they continued to fall. The estimated total fertility rate for 2016 had dropped further, to 1.81 births per 1,000 women. Some experts believed that the decline was no aberration and might signal a new normal. Pessimists pointed to many factors tending to depress rates of family formation among millennials, including the increased percentage of young adults living with their parents, continuing concerns about unemployment, high levels of student debt, looming responsibility for aging parents, and changing attitudes among millennials toward home ownership, debt, families, and mobility (Durden 2016). Optimists pointed to the fact that the decline in birth rates is partly due to falling birth rates among women aged fifteen to twenty-four, where policy-makers had intended to discourage teenage birth. They also stressed that the highest birth rates are in the segment of women aged twenty-five to thirty-four. In addition, women in the segment aged thirty to forty-four expressed higher expectations than previous generations of bearing children in the future (Daugherty and Martinez 2016; Cha 2017). It remained to be seen whether the decline in US birth rates was merely a blip or the beginning of a downward slope. But in May 2018, the National Vital Statistics System released a disquieting report, estimating that 2017 birth rates and fertility rates had declined another 3 percent, reaching the lowest level in thirty years, and predicting they would continue their steep decline. As of May 2019, the US fertility rate had fallen another 2 percent to 1.72, well below the replacement rate of 2.13 (National Center for Health Statistics 2018, 2019; Hamilton et al. 2018; Goldberg, M. 2018). Certainly, Americans can no longer afford to be complacent.

Further affecting the population equation in the United States are political pressures to restrict immigration, reflected in the policies of the Trump administration, such as the border wall, the Muslim ban, and the zero-tolerance policy on border crossings. Immigration is a controversial topic in Italy as well as in the United States. Major Italian political parties, inflamed by fear of the numbers of refugees arriving in Italian ports from Africa and the Middle East, have been calling for a freeze on immigration. Tito Boeri, head of the Italian social security agency INPS, has warned that, if Italy were to close its borders to immigrants, the Italian pension and social welfare systems would soon be thirty-eight billion euros in the red. He pointed out that the annual arrival of 150,000 more contributors to the tax rolls was making up for the drop in birth rates. Social media exploded with negative comments (Marro 2017). US data also illustrate the role played by immigration in population statistics. Without the arrival of immigrants and births to immigrant mothers we would be facing greater declines in birth rates. According to the Pew Foundation, any growth in annual birth rates in the United States since 1970 has been driven entirely by births to immigrant mothers (Livingston 2016).

Whether in the United States or in Europe, declining birth rates can be rebalanced by encouraging population growth through immigration as well as through procreation (Marro 2017). Unfortunately, the decline in birth rates has been exploited as a fear factor to inflame nativist and white supremacist violence. The manifesto posted online by the shooter who attacked the Mosque in New Zealand in March 2019 is titled "The Great Replacement," and it begins: "It's the birth rates. It's the birth rates. It's the birth rates" (Root 2019, 2). As demographer Leslie Root points out in an essay on these tactics of fear, demographic data has been misused to support a conspiracy theory that "white" populations are being threatened with extinction (2).

Adoption, ART, and Citizenship as Antidotes to Declining Birth Rates

Other avenues for developed nations seeking to increase the supply of babies and young workers include intercountry adoption and "assisted reproductive technology" (ART) (Cahn 2009; Sadeghi 2012). While domestic adoptions do not affect national birth rates, intercountry adoptions add to the numbers of new citizens in the receiving country. International adoption rates, however, have fallen significantly in recent years, due to a combination of advances in ART and stricter regulation of the international adoption process (Mignot 2015).

Can ART reverse declining birth rates? Experts caution women who are considering delaying conception or planning on freezing eggs for later in vitro fertilization, warning them against false optimism. While ART has increased older women's chances of conceiving, concerns remain about the effect on fertility rates of large-scale postponement of pregnancy (Specter 2017). Another development adding to the supply of children is the growing number born to LGBTQ parents through ART or surrogacy. This revolution is being felt even in conservative Italy. Laws that previously limited donation of eggs and sperm have been revised, and Italian courts are beginning to apply human-rights principles to validate gay and lesbian parenthood (Tebano 2018).

One key strategy for nations seeking to counteract low birth rates is to broaden access to citizenship and loosen restrictions on immigration. The issue of how a baby gains citizenship is an important element often left out of discussion of the low birth rate crisis. There are two major approaches to birthright citizenship: *jus soli* (the right of citizenship in the country on whose soil one is born) and *jus sanguinis* (the right of citizenship based on the nationality of one's parents). The US, in common with other "new world" countries, has both forms of birthright citizenship (Government of Canada 2018). The Fourteenth Amendment has been interpreted to establish that all persons born or naturalized in the United States are US citizens. In most circumstances, US law also recognizes the citizenship of children born to US citizens in other countries (US Citizenship and Immigration Services 2013). Thus, a child born abroad to US parents and a child born to non–US parents on US soil are both entitled to US citizenship, even when their parents are on temporary visas or undocumented. In the United States, immigration not only increases the numbers of workers contributing to the economy; it also adds to the numbers of citizens because of birthright citizenship tied to *jus soli*. The rule in Italy, as in many other European countries, is quite different (Mentzelopoulou 2018). Children's citizenship is determined by their parents' nationality. Children born in Italy do not automatically become Italian citizens and, unlike several other EU nations, Italy does not recognize any conditional forms of *jus soli*, such as conferring citizenship after a waiting period. This rule removes an incentive to immigrate to Italy, and deprives Italy of valuable human capital. From the child's perspective, it can be a cruel form of exclusion. Children born, raised, and educated in Italy remain foreigners. Children whose parents are members of the EU are less affected because they have guarantees of equal treatment with Italian citizens. Children born to *extracommunitari* (persons who are not citizens of EU nations) are excluded from citizenship and exist in a form of legal limbo. They may feel one hundred percent Italian but, as a matter of law, they are one hundred percent foreign (El Arbaoui 2018).

Italy has been deeply divided over proposals to change its laws to allow a path to citizenship for children born and educated in Italy. Many Italians have seen this as a human-rights issue, others as a threat to Italian identity and as an incentive to immigrants from developing countries who were ready to die crossing the Mediterranean from Africa and arriving in numbers so large they exceeded the capacity of Italy to absorb and integrate new arrivals. In July 2017, the Gentiloni government was pressing for a vote on this citizenship measure but, despite strong support from the majority Partita Democractica (Democratic Party) and strong support from Pope Francis and the Vatican, the vote was postponed. It had become clear that pressing this issue would result in a "no confidence" vote and risk a destabilizing change in government (Lami 2017). The role of immigration as a source of new citizens was an inflammatory issue fueling the rise of Italian populism in the 2018 elections. In December 2018 the harsh new *dicreto sicurezza* (security decree), which further restricted access to citizenship and protections for refugees, became law (Legge No. 113/2018).

Even in the US, a nation of immigrants, there have been calls to do away with birthright citizenship (Davis 2018). At this writing, the plight of young people brought to the United States illegally as children has become a political football and a bargaining chip employed by the Trump administration in battles with the Democrats over Trump's requests for funding to build a wall between the United States and Mexico. The movement to create a path to citizenship for these "Dreamers" has stalled, but the federal courts have blocked the Trump administration's efforts to repeal it (National Immigration Law Center 2018). The relationship between immigration, citizenship, the need for new blood, and the maintenance of aging populations remains a thorny issue in Europe as in the United States. These societies are deeply divided over whether births to immigrants are a threat to stability or a promise of renewal.

In the end, we may find that the low birth-rate crisis in the United States is not a crisis at all. Some researchers believe that current concerns over declining birth rates are premature and rest on myths rather than science. One 2015 study questions the received wisdom that the low birth rate crisis is cause for alarm. Hans-Peter Kohler, in *Six Myths and Truths about Fertility in the West*, challenges many of the most prevalent conclusions (2015). He argues that fertility declines will not continue to fall below replacement rates; instead he posits that, once nations reach a high level on the Human Development Index (HDI), we may see a leveling off of decreases in birth rates and even a recovery. He also challenges the notion that low fertility rates are a sign of declining desire for children. (I would agree that the indicia point to a continuing desire to have children and raise a family.) In addition, Kohler questions the belief that low fertility necessarily implies high rates of childlessness. Even in the areas where fertility rates are lowest, he argues, the "biological, social and economic incentives for children are sufficiently strong that most women (or couples) desire to have at least one child." As Kohler points out, timing of childbearing has changed and "thirty is the new twenty-five." He recognizes the reality, substantiated by research, that parenthood arrives much later than it did in prior generations. He is leery of social engineering and concludes, looking at studies on the effectiveness of tax credits and child credits, that the jury is still out as to whether social interventions affect birth rates.

However, Kohler does not dismiss all efforts by policy-makers to encourage childbearing: "A possible exception, consistent with other studies on this topic, is the expansion of high-quality day care for preschool children: It facilitated increased labor force participation among parents with small children, and had modest effects towards increasing fertility, according to evaluations." In line with the cautionary principle, I would suggest we keep trying social interventions that show some promise of counteracting the drop in birth rates in developed nations.

One thing is certain: coercive attempts by national leaders seeking to control reproduction and alter birth rates have failed spectacularly. Two examples are the Romanian pro-natalist ban on abortions, which produced a flood of abandoned children, and China's one-child policy, which severely skewed the ratios of male to female births, marginalized innocent children born in violation of the policy, and created a low birth rate problem that has been difficult for China to reverse (Odobescu 2015; Kuo 2019; Nelson et al. 2013; Woodhouse 2008a). Bitter experience has taught us that policies encouraging or discouraging procreation must tread lightly and be respectful of family culture and personal choice.

* * *

Davide, whose poem opened this chapter, personifies the sadness of the last child in the village. Demographers can study trends and they can influence policy-makers, and policymakers can play a potentially constructive or a treacherous role in shaping the demographic exosystems and macrosystems of children like Davide. What remains as a constant in our research into the ecology of childhood is that no child should be condemned to develop in a social desert, without other children to play with, whether because of geographic isolation or social exclusion. The right to play will be discussed in following chapters, but Davide's plight will resonate with any human looking back at his or her own childhood. Most of us have suffered the sting of being marginalized. But imagine the isolation of being the only child in the village, without even one playmate.

6

The Role of Family-Supportive Policies in the Decision to Have Children

Question: Do you have any children?
Answer: I have two children and they are both grown up.
Question: Did you and your husband make them?
Answer: We made our daughter, but we adopted our son.
Question: How did you and your husband make your daughter?

This conversation, which I have translated from Italian into English, occurred in the summer of 2016, when two boys about nine or ten years old approached me while I was observing daily life in Piazza Santa Maria della Valle. I was a familiar sight and always happy to chat and to answer children's questions—about my dog, Jane; about the English language they were studying in school; about life in America. One question I had not anticipated was the classic "Where do babies come from?" But it shouldn't have surprised me, since I had proven so far to be a good source of factual information. I ducked the question, acutely aware of the ethical boundaries of my role and not wanting to intrude with my own explanations or preempt the authority of their parents and teachers.

There is no single "right" answer to this question. It depends on whether you are a parent, a teacher, or a researcher, and on the age of the questioner and on the motive for asking. One mother I know, who was expecting her second child, was asked this question by her precocious three-year-old son. She began her explanation in a dreamy voice: "Our new baby began as a spark in your parents' imagination." The three-year-old interrupted her: "Mother, don't give me poetry; I want science." Both mother and child were right. In our complex modern societies, the story of where babies come from involves much more than the science of conception; it involves emotions, cultural and religious beliefs, dreams, and imagination. Increasingly, becoming a parent involves a conscious decision.

The Social Construction of Parenthood

In the decision whether and when to have children, as personal as it may seem, a host of exosystemic factors are at play, including economic markets, parents' workplace, access to housing, access to health care and child care, access to family planning, family structure, and government supports such as family benefits and income transfers. Macrosystemic values such as religion, culture, and tradition play large roles as well. In evaluating such social facts, sociologists explore how people think and feel as well as what they do. What are the beliefs and motivations behind the drop in birth rates?

One popular theory among US social critics is that millennials simply prefer to remain "child free" as a lifestyle choice. The same debate has reached Italy. Recently, I was intrigued to see the English words "free child" in an opinion piece in an Italian newspaper. The author was blaming low birth rates on the rising popularity of the "free child." As I read further, I realized the author was drawing on American and English discussions of the choice not to procreate, but, in adopting the English term, had changed "child free" to "free child." The writer's anecdotal examples of the "free child" phenomenon in Italy all involved women who had chosen to remain childless for a variety of personal reasons, including not wanting to be tied down, placing career before parenthood, or simply never having a desire for children. In Italy, as in the United States, social critics often point to such personal choices by women as the driving factors behind declining birth rates. Is opting for a "child-free" life the driving force behind Italy's lower birth rates?

Italian Perspectives on "Becoming Parents Today"

A report titled *Diventare genitori oggi* (Becoming parents today) from the Italian think tank CENSIS provides intriguing insights into how Italians think and feel about parenthood (2014). At the CENSIS workshop in Rome at which the report was introduced, Italian policy-makers in attendance seemed surprised by the results. Researchers interviewed 1,200 individuals from a representative sample of the adult Italian population. About 25 percent of respondents of all ages said they planned to have a baby in the future. When the responses were broken down by age group, interesting insights emerged. Looking at the age group most likely to bear children—the group aged thirty-four years and under—the most common reasons cited for not wanting a baby were: already having the desired number of children, not feeling ready to have a child at this time, concern that another child would cost too much, concerns about the child's future, and the impact of the economic crisis. Other issues, such as not having a suitable job, fearing damage to career, not feeling up to the task of being a parent, and not wanting the responsibility played much smaller roles. Not one respondent in the under–thirty-five age group cited risk of losing a job, damage to a relationship with a partner, loss of freedom, concern about commitment to a partner, or lack of suitable housing as a reason for not wanting a child. Contrary to popular belief, this study suggests that the current generation of young Italians is not forgoing children to preserve personal freedom, escape onerous gender roles, or avoid responsibility. Among Italians in their most fertile years, the most powerful deterrents appear to be economic issues, including fears about an uncertain economic future, the impact of the continuing crisis, and worries about the high cost of rearing a child in a modern society (table 13).

Looking at the respondents who said that they did plan to have a baby in the future, what values or beliefs contributed to their desire to become parents? The researchers asked each respondent to answer an open-ended question: "What is the meaning of being a parent?" The researchers took their spontaneous answers and analyzed and tabulated them. The most commonly expressed idea, for both men and women, was that a child makes you feel "*realizzato/a*" (complete or fulfilled). Other common ideas included: a child completes the couple's relationship, a child is a continuation of life and of one's self, a child makes you feel necessary and important, having a child makes you truly an adult, and a family cannot really call itself a family without children (CENSIS 2014, fig. 12). The researchers also posed closed-ended questions soliciting respondents' support for various value statements or propositions. Two propositions gained overwhelming approval: children are the natural complement to the person, and children are the natural complement to a couple's solid and profound relationship. Interestingly, almost nine out of ten respondents rejected the idea that a family without children is less socially accepted.

Next, the researchers explored the prevailing attitudes on women's motivations for having children. Broken down by gender, the vast majority of men (83.8 percent) and women (80.1 percent) agreed that having a child was important to a woman because it fulfilled her natural capacity to be a mother. Very few men (5.2 percent) or women (6.5 percent) agreed with the statement that a woman without children is regarded less positively from a social point of view and very few men (2.4 percent) or women (2.7 percent) agreed with the statement that a woman without children feels herself to be handicapped because of the inability to become pregnant.

Next, the researchers asked about the importance of parenthood to men. Among men, 82 percent agreed that having a child realizes a man's natural expectation to become a father. A smaller majority of women (72.5 percent) agreed with this view. Interestingly, women answering the questions were more likely than men to cite the man's ability to pass on his name (6.9 percent of men versus 7.3 percent of women) or cited parenthood as a sign of virility (3.8 percent of men versus 5.8 percent of women) as motivations for becoming a father. When asked whether having children is more important to women than to men, 88.8 percent of the males and 83.7 percent of the females responded that it had the same importance for both. The CENSIS study suggests that something other than stereotypes about self-centered Italian men and joyfully "child-free" Italian women is responsible for the country's low birth rates. The research also suggests that babies matter a great deal to both men and women in Italy. The responses about the importance of motherhood reflect what I will call "the Madonna effect"; depictions of the Madonna and child are inescapable in Italy and a culture of celebrating motherhood is deeply rooted in the Italian psyche. However, the responses relating to men and parenthood contradict many common stereotypes about Italian men. It would be a mistake to blame low birth rates on lazy Italian husbands or on the *mammone* (mama's boy) who prefers to be pampered by his doting mother rather than form a family of his own.

An Exercise in Triangulation: Testing Data against Field Observations

My field observations of families in Scanno tended to confirm the responses reported by CENSIS. What I observed tended to debunk negative stereotypes of Italian men. Men in Scanno take a very active and visible role in caring for and socializing children. Men of every age, from bachelors in their twenties to pensioners in their nineties, can be seen pushing strollers and carriages; supervising children; taking children to stores, schools, and sports; taking children to their workplaces; and playing with children in the piazza. Births of babies are celebrated by the entire community and the men are part of this celebration. Church bells ring, blue and pink ribbons are displayed on doors and shop windows, and proud fathers and grandfathers treat everyone in the café to a drink—the cultural equivalent of handing out cigars in the United States.

It is not only the younger generation of males that shares in parenting the children. Grandparents play an especially central role and it is my observation that Scanno grandfathers, more than most I have observed in the United States, seem acculturated to taking a hands-on approach. One day, as I was observing life in the piazza, I met an older man whom I recognized as an expert photographer. He proudly showed me his little grandchild in the stroller he was pushing. He apologized for not stopping to chat, but the baby had been having trouble falling asleep so Grandpa needed to keep on walking. An hour later, I met the same man in a different part of the village, still pushing the stroller. His mission had been accomplished but he kept on walking because he did not want to wake the baby. The grandfather smiled, put a finger to his lips, and walked on.

Men join women in taking babies on outings. The same day and hour I saw this grandfather, I passed a young couple, Marianna and Andrea, pushing their baby carriage. They greeted me and indicated with nods and glances that their three-month-old infant, whom they normally would have stopped to display, was sleeping. Perhaps this custom of walking babies together is an extension of the Italian custom of taking a *passeggiata*—a recreational stroll through the town to meet and greet one's neighbors and get some fresh air. Whatever its origin, the babies and parents seem to be enjoying the ride.

It took me a while to realize that babies and young children on these fresh-air outings often had a wide range of escorts in addition to their parents. In contrast to places like London or New York, there are no nannies in Scanno. So it made sense, when I first arrived, to assume that the people with strollers must be the parents or, if age appropriate, the grandparents. However, I began to notice that, during a single day, I would encounter the same baby or toddler in the same stroller, but with a different adult pushing the carriage or sitting on a bench entertaining its occupant or showing him or her off to friends and neighbors. Thinking I had been confused about which babies belonged to which adults, I started to ask more questions. I discovered that these caregivers were neither the parents nor the grandparents—they were the aunts and uncles, friends, neighbors, and older children, all of whom competed for the chance to take baby out to play. One day in June 2016, I noticed a group of four elderly men sitting on a bench in the piazza, with one toddler in a stroller between them. I stopped to admire the toddler and asked which of them was the *Nonno* (grandfather) of this beautiful child. To my surprise they said that none of them was the *Nonno*. They were an uncle and three other men who described themselves as friends and neighbors. They pointed to two little girls who looked about five and seven and were playing ball with a group of children a few yards away. This group of retired gentlemen was taking all three children out to play. I asked if the parents were away or at their jobs. No—just busy with other things. How I wish that every child had such a cadre of willing co-parents, volunteering to step in so baby could enjoy the outdoors and interact with other children, while the primary caregiver did housework, cooked, or caught up on lost sleep.

My own observations confirmed another common stereotype—the close-knit and extended Italian family. This expansive definition of "family" also contributes to the supportive network for children and youth in Scanno. *Parente* in Italian means relative, and *famiglia* is not limited to the nuclear family, but includes maternal and paternal relatives—uncles, aunts, grandparents, nieces, nephews, and cousins. The importance of these extended family networks was brought home to me one day in July 2017 when we went to have lunch at a lodge just opened by a young friend of ours named Matteo. A tall, athletic young man in his twenties, Matteo definitely has the entrepreneurial spirit. In the five years we have known him, he has matured tremendously, graduating from school and, instead of leaving Scanno where jobs are scarce, turning his passion for horses into a business. He rescued a number of horses from the butcher's knife, rehabilitated and trained them, and created a new enterprise guiding horseback expeditions into the mountains. While my husband and I waited for lunch in the lodge's dining room, I noticed a toddler peeking shyly out at us from the kitchen. I have never been able to pass up a game of peek-a-boo. When the little boy got tired of it, he turned to Matteo, who was also in the kitchen, and engaged him in a game of *dammi cinque* (slap me five). After our meal, I went to the kitchen to compliment the cook and it turned out she was Matteo's aunt. Matteo's grandmother, a white-haired, vigorous lady in an apron, also greeted me. When I remarked that Matteo was lucky to have found such gifted cooks for his restaurant, everyone laughed. They replied that it went without saying that his aunt and grandmother would help him with his new project. "We are a very close family; we look out for each other," they explained.

The happy baby boy with whom I had played peek-a-boo from a distance was introduced as Mattia, eighteen months of age. It turned out that none of the three people caring for him that day were members of what sociologists would call his "nuclear family." They were his cousin, his great-aunt, and his great-grandmother—all of whom were as captivated by him as I was. Surely the active engagement of a wide circle of family and community members is an incentive to couples deciding whether to have a baby. The message to young parents in Scanno is that babies are a source of joy and that those who produce them have accomplished a miracle that benefits the entire community. These pro-child values seem to permeate the entire ecosystem of Scanno. If we could bottle this spirit and distribute it to every community at risk of population decline, it might produce miracles. Children in Scanno are welcomed, celebrated, and shared with the community, rather than marginalized, privatized, and hidden from sight. The notion of a child-free, "seniors only" community, which is quite common in my home state of Florida, would be unthinkable in Italy.

The Role of Italian Public Policy

If Italians' desire for children and willingness to care for them is so widespread and seemingly so deeply rooted in the culture, what other barriers explain the low Italian birth rates? The CENSIS study documents the importance of public policies and access to social supports in shaping the respondents' calculus of whether to have a first or a subsequent child. Respondents cited the lack of strong family policies that might help individuals realize their desire to become parents, the difficulty of combining work and family, conflicts between the way work is organized and duties of parenthood, and the increasing barriers to counting on extended family to help with childrearing. Other factors included couples delaying rather than forgoing childbearing, and fear that children would not achieve a standard of living better than that of their parents. It is striking that almost one-third of the survey respondents cited a lack of family-supportive policies as a factor in decisions to forgo children (CENSIS 2014, fig. 18). Interestingly, middle class families were more likely than poorer families to blame the lack of government support for forgoing or limiting the number of children. Middle-class families in both the United States and Italy complain of escalating social expectations increasing the costs and complexities of childrearing. Italians are accustomed to the notion embedded in their Constitution and laws that government has an obligation to provide positive supports to the family. Article 31 states: "Through economic measures and other provisions, the Republic assists the formation of the family and the fulfilment of its duties, with particular consideration for large families. It protects maternity, infancy and youth, promoting the institutions necessary for this purpose." Article 37 states: "Working women have the same rights and, for equal work, the same wages as working men. Working conditions must allow women to carry out their essential role in the family and ensure particular and adequate protection for the mother and the child" (Casonato and Woelk 2008). Not surprisingly, Italians are more likely than middle-class Americans to look to government for family-supportive policies.

Responses to the CENSIS survey indicated widespread approval of government supports for parents. When asked whether public interventions such as monetary subsidies, daycare and nursery schools, tax breaks, scholarships, more flexible work hours, and leave from work to care for children could make a difference in encouraging couples to have babies, 60.7 percent said yes, 34.8 percent said no, and 4.5 percent did not know. Interestingly, support for these family-friendly programs remained strong across all age groups and among respondents with and without children (CENSIS 2014). When asked where government should concentrate its efforts, the most popular initiatives were tax breaks and monetary subsidies, closely followed by early childhood services such as *asilo nido* (nurseries for babies younger than three), and services for school-age children such as subsidies for school fees, meals, transportation, and books. Also high on the list were help for families of children with disabilities, more flexibility for family leave, assistance in balancing work and family, and help for young families wanting to buy a home (CENSIS 2014).

I was not surprised to see Italians calling for better family services. Italians do not live in a Scandinavian paradise. They know that Italy is average or below average when compared to other OECD countries in terms of access to the family-supportive services listed by the respondents to the survey. France, for example, is far more generous toward families than Italy. However, compared to the United States, programs in Italy are superior across several different metrics.

Comparing Family-Supportive Policies in Italy and the United States

Italian programs for child and family well-being start well before conception, with universal health care for all. The national health program has been in place since 1978. To ensure that they receive care regardless of income, all children in Italy receive health care at little or no cost throughout their childhoods. The barriers to access that play such a prominent role in the United States, even in federally funded programs like CHIP, are unthinkable in Italy. An Italian child's health-care card is not means-tested, nor does it have an expiration date. Universal access to quality health care is reflected in lower infant mortality rates, fewer low birth weight babies and greater rates of immunization. (UNICEF 2013). US infant mortality rates are approximately twice that of Italy: 3/1,000 in Italy compared to 6/1,000 in the United States (UNICEF Data, for under-five mortality rates in Italy and the United States). A parent in Italy is about half as likely to experience the death of a child under five than a parent in the United States—4/1000 in Italy compared to 7/1000 in the United States) (UNICEF Data, for under-five mortality rates in Italy and the United States). Perhaps the most shocking gap is in the likelihood of dying while giving birth. The most common measure, the Maternal Mortality Ratio (or number of maternal deaths per 100,000 live births) is more than three times higher in the United States than in Italy: 14 in the United States versus 4 in Italy (UNICEF Data, for maternal mortality; World Health Organization et al. 2015). This is not to suggest that prospective parents consult the WHO tables before conceiving a child. But these gaps are caused by real differences in affordability and access to care, and they reflect real differences in the social value placed on insuring healthy pregnancies, infancies, and childhoods. Of course, there are many confounders that affect any analysis. These disparate health-care outcomes are not explained by poverty, since Italy and the United States have similar market child poverty rates, nor are they explained by differences in dollars spent on health care—quite the opposite. Per-capita expenditures on health care in Italy, at $3258 per person, are one-third of those in the United States, where the figure is $9403 per capita (World Bank, for health expenditure per capita).

An Exercise in Triangulation: The Case of the Sulmona *Punto Nascita*

When I returned to Scanno in the spring of 2014, the village was buzzing with outrage over a new cost-cutting proposal from the bureaucrats at the Ministry of Health. Health care in Italy is provided by a network of public-health entities known by the acronym ASL (*azienda sanitaria locale*) and responsibility for operations and policies is shared at regional and national levels. In Scanno, the local office of ASL is housed in a building that also houses a walk-in clinic where residents can be seen by a doctor during scheduled hours, and a Croce Rossa (Red Cross) ambulance to provide emergency medical services and transport emergency patients to the hospital in Sulmona, forty minutes away. Helicopters are also on call for critical cases or when roads are blocked.

Women preparing for the birth of a child had been able to choose a *punto nascita* (obstetrical unit), either at the hospital in Sulmona or at any other in the surrounding area, where they would be followed by an obstetrician and give birth. Traditionally, most families had chosen Sulmona, while others preferred the hospital at Avezzano, farther away and with poorer public transportation, but on a faster road. Now the government was planning to close all but one of the area birth centers. Mothers from Scanno would no longer be able to go to Sulmona, and, for mothers in Sulmona, with a population of 25,000, the nearest birth center would be in Avezzano, an hour away. Andrea, whose wife, Marianna, had given birth a few months before, told us this news and reported that he and many others from Scanno had gone to the regional meeting of ASL to protest the plan. Marianna and Andrea had chosen to have their baby at Avezzano, partly because they felt the obstetrics department at Sulmona was becoming understaffed and underresourced. Transportation was no problem for Andrea, because he was a professional driver for his family-owned bus and limo service. But, as he told me, there were families who did not have cars and relied on the regional bus services to reach the hospital for routine visits and to visit family members.

The people in Sulmona and the surrounding towns were very angry that the regional authorities had decided to close the obstetrics department rather than improve it, as residents long had demanded. The authorities defended their decision as both economical and evidence based: they pointed to research showing a correlation between the incidence of complications at a unit and the number of procedures taking place there annually. They concluded that a birth center with fewer births was less safe than a birth center with more births, and they reasoned that consolidating all the birth centers would improve the quality of care. From the citizens' point of view, this made no sense. Had the authorities taken into account the geographical difficulties involved in travel in Abruzzo? Could it possibly be safer to force a woman in labor to travel an hour by road, especially when the mountain roads were often hard to navigate because of fog, ice, and snow? The citizens were incensed that the decline in births at Sulmona, which they attributed to bureaucratic neglect of the obstetric unit, had become an excuse for closing this key community resource. In a country experiencing a birth-rate crisis, how could it possibly make sense to reduce the services available to expectant mothers?

My own independent research suggested that the original policy had been misinformed (Maron 2017; Hanson et al. 2015; Pilkington et al. 2014; Kornelson et al. 2009). It is true, of course, that, all things being equal, a department with extensive experience in handling a particular type of procedure develops greater expertise, leading to fewer complications. However, childbirth is not like scheduling knee replacement surgery. Most of the work is done by the mother, not the doctor, and, ideally, it happens according to the baby's schedule and not the medical provider's. While the factors are complex, reducing the distance between the mother's home and the facility where she gives birth can play a role in mitigating risks, including the risk of giving birth in transit. Giving birth close to home also promotes other important values, such as avoiding unnecessary expense, maximizing involvement of supportive family members, and preserving contact between mother and her other children. Experts in public health policy have developed a range of options for providing obstetrical care at a reasonable cost in remote locations and smaller cities (Maron 2017). These include local birthing centers staffed with midwives, births in local and regional hospitals, and, if necessary, ambulance or helicopter transport to sophisticated obstetrical and neonatal units.

The battle against closure of the Sulmona *punto nascita* continued for months, but I was pleased to learn the following spring that the citizens had prevailed. The Sulmona *punto nascita* was renovated, restaffed, and reopened. The success of this grassroots rebellion demonstrated two important facts about the local community that tended once again to confirm the CENSIS conclusions about social investment in children: the community is deeply invested in ensuring access to services for families, and it has the power to affect decisions made at higher levels about the community's health care.

The "Baby Bonus" in Italy

The Italian government has adopted a number of economic incentives explicitly designed to counter the decline in birth rates. Beginning in 2015, the Italian government has offered parents with modest incomes a baby bonus of up to 1,900 euros annually called the *premio alla nascita* (prize for births). All mothers of babies born during the year are eligible and the payments continue for three years. Beginning in 2017, a bonus of 800 euros is available regardless of the family's income (INPS 2017a). In the first two months of the 2017 program, over two hundred thousand families applied for these payments. (Querzé 2017b). Mothers become eligible two months before the expected birth date. The program also applies to newly adopted children and children born to members of the EU, legal non-EU immigrants, and persons who have been granted refugee status (INPS 2017a; Losito 2016).

When I asked Scanno parents about their views on this program, they said they would happily accept the cash, but felt it was far too low to create a real incentive. As a mother of teenagers commented, "If I were in charge, I would raise the amount and lower the floor for eligibility. Better to give real help to families that really need it." Those whom I asked also wanted to see policies that take a longer view: "A baby bonus won't help with University tuition. Diapers are only the beginning of what it costs to raise a child these days." While this is all true, the Italian government is hoping for a positive result. It is too soon to determine whether the baby bonus will cause a baby boom, but it certainly sends a positive message to new parents.

In addition to the *premio alla nascita*, Italian families have for many years had a national paid leave policy or *congedo* giving new mothers twenty weeks of leave with guaranteed job security at 80 percent of their pay. Fathers are entitled to the same leave in cases where the mother is not available because of illness, death, or abandonment. If the mother takes a leave, fathers are eligible for a shorter paid paternity leave (INPS 2017b). Paid leave for the birth of a child is labeled *obbligatorio* or mandatory, to distinguish it from another form of leave, *congedo facultativo* (optional leave). Under this second program, a parent is eligible to take up to six months leave during the child's first six years at 30 percent of his or her pay. Either mother or father may take this leave, but not both. For children six to twelve years of age, parents may take unpaid leave of up to six months to deal with family emergencies or illnesses.

As of 2017, new mothers who go back to work rather than take advantage of the mandatory parental leave program are eligible for a generous *bonus babysitter* payment of 600 euros a month to cover day-care costs. (Querzé

2017b). Policy-makers hoped this assistance would encourage more mothers to remain in the workforce while adding to their families. All parents are also eligible for a *bonus nido* (day-care subsidy) of up to 1,000 euros a year, paid in eleven monthly installments, to defray costs of either public or private day care. While Italian bureaucracies can be slow, these policies are structured to put the funding where it is needed at the time it is most needed, in contrast to US-style tax deductions, which are of little use to low-income parents who pay no taxes and that require parents to spend first and collect government reimbursements later. Unfortunately, many of these crisis programs are due to lapse if funding cannot be found to continue them past 2018 (Querzé 2018).

Comparing Parental Leave and Baby Bonuses in the United States with Peer Nations

Comparison of the Italian programs for baby bonuses and similar paid leave programs in the United States begins with one striking fact. Not only is there no such thing as a cash bonus for giving birth, there is no national paid parental leave program in the United States. The US is the only OECD nation that lacks any guarantees that mothers giving birth can continue to receive a percentage of their salary for a period of time after the birth of a child. The Family and Medical Leave Act (29 USC §2601), signed by President Bill Clinton in 1993, establishes a national rule for when an employer must allow a mother to take time off after giving birth without losing her job. It provides for twelve weeks of *unpaid* job-protected leave, but is limited to larger employers and workers with at least one year of service. Some mothers may be able to take medical leave with partial or full pay under an employer's health insurance policies or under state paid leave legislation, but there is no such thing as a national paid leave program (AEI-Brookings Working Group on Paid Family Leave 2017). Italy ranks at about the midpoint among its peer nations in terms of length and percentage of wage replacement. According to a chart of OECD policies, as of 2015 every OECD country with the exception of the United States provided paid leave, with an average duration of fifty-four weeks. Most also provided paternity leave as well. Rates of wage replacement for leaves ranged from about 30 to 100 percent, depending on the length of the leave. US policy-makers on both the right and the left, pointing to research on child development and women's workforce participation, continue to press for a national paid maternity and paternity leave policy, but without success (AEI-Brookings Working Group on Paid Family Leave 2017, 16).

Comparing Access to Early Childhood Education and Care, or "Educare"

Access to early childhood education and day care is no longer a luxury in OECD nations. With the advent of the two-earner family as the new normal, and given rising awareness of the importance of children's early childhood experiences in their brain development, "educare" (my term for the continuum of nurturing and education in children's early years) has become a basic need and not a luxury (Woodhouse 2008b). As the Innocenti Researchers stated in their 2008 Report Card on early childhood care and education:

> A great change is coming over childhood in the world's richest countries. Today's rising generation is the first in which a majority are spending a large part of early childhood in some form of out-of-home child care. At the same time, neuroscientific research is demonstrating that loving, stable, secure, and stimulating relationships with caregivers in the earliest months and years of life are critical for every aspect of a child's development. Taken together, these two developments confront public and policymakers in OECD countries with urgent questions. Whether the child care transition will represent an advance or a setback—for today's children and tomorrow's world—will depend on the response. (UNICEF 2008, 1)

Children do not start learning when they reach compulsory schooling age. Nor do they stop needing care and supervision when they enter primary school. Neuroscience tells us what parents and educators have long known: that childcare and education are an integrated continuum of experiences beginning in the earliest months of life. The Innocenti Report Card 8 quoted above proposed a set of uniform standards for judging how countries are doing at supporting this transition. The table reports how well different countries did at meeting ten benchmarks: (1) parental leave of 1 year at 50 percent of salary; (2) a national plan with priority for disadvantaged children; (3) subsidized and regulated child care services for 25 percent of children under three; (4) subsidized and accredited early childhood education for 80 percent of four year-olds; (5) 80 percent of all childcare staff trained; (6) 50 percent of staff in accredited early-education services tertiary educated with relevant qualifications; (7) minimum staff-to-children ratio of one to fifteen in preschool education; (8) 1.0 percent of GDP spent on early-childhood services; (9) child poverty rate less than 10 percent; and (10) near-universal outreach of essential child health services. As these benchmarks make clear, education and day care are not isolated issues, but part of a network of systems necessary to children's learning and development (fig. 1). The table compares early-childhood services in twenty-five OECD countries in which data was collected. Italian parents justifiably complain that they are behind their EU peers. The Scandinavian countries and France score in the top quartile of the countries studied, while Italy scored at fifteen, below the Netherlands, Austria, Belgium, and the United Kingdom. The United States scored near the bottom, at twenty-two of twenty-five.

Comparing the statistics for early-childhood day care and education is a daunting project, and sometimes, despite the best efforts of the OECD or UNICEF, we end up comparing apples and oranges. The data changes year by year and so much depends on the quality of data and parameters of individual country reports. I was amazed to see, for example, in Report Card 8, that over 60 percent of four-year-olds in the United States were enrolled in early childhood education (UNICEF 2008, fig. 2b). The United States was also credited with providing 35 percent of children zero to three with subsidized and regulated child care (fig. 2a). I knew that this was not the case. Probing further in the underlying data, I found that the US response to the request for data had counted any child whose parent left them for one or more hours a week with a nonrelative caregiver as enrolled in early childhood education (Woodhouse 2008b).

Still, comparisons must be made, with a view to fixing measurement flaws and promoting best practices. Here is some comparative data on early-childhood care and education in the United States and Italy, with insights into other peer countries as well. Italian services are traditionally divided into zero to three (*asilo nido*, literally translated as shelter nest) and three to six (*scuola d'infanzia*, school of childhood). In 2012, about 14 percent of Italian children zero to three were served by the asilo nido public/private network of nurseries. By 2016, that number had grown to 20.8 percent. There remain large regional differences, with coverage ranging from a high of 34 percent in some northern and central regions to a low of 3.9 percent in some southern regions (Querzé 2017a). Fees for the zero-to-three services are computed on a sliding scale according to family income. A study of costs for a family of four with an income of 40,000 euros found that the median cost in the capital cities of the various regions was 329 euros ($376) a month, including meals, for a child to attend full time (eight hours per day) (Associazione Difesa Orientamento Consumatori 2016). This sum represents less than 10 percent of the family's monthly income. The asilo nido, with its provision of nutritious hot meals and eight or more hours of service, is designed to meet the needs of working parents. However, as a matter of constitutional law it is not considered a convenience for parents but is classified as a part of children's right to education. The Italian

Supreme Court has held that asilo nido services cannot be treated merely as a form of support for working parents but are intended to enhance the child's cognitive, affective, and relational potential and are thus an aspect of the state's responsibility for education of the young (Corte Cost. No 457/2002).

In contrast to the asilo nido system, where places are not guaranteed and there are often long waiting lists, all children aged three to six are guaranteed a place in the scuola d'infanzia. Over 95 percent of eligible children attend these schools. In addition to socializing children and providing safe places for play and learning, they prepare children to enter mandatory schooling, which begins at age six in first grade. Some of the scuola d'infanzia are religious or operated by private entities, while some like Buon Pastore in Scanno are hybrid public and religious, but all are public in the sense of being open to all and subsidized by the state. In practice, they form a national, universal, affordable, and subsidized public system of early-childhood education. In the communities I visited, the options included an extended day for working parents as well as the provision of hot meals, naps, and recreation.

In recent years, the bright line between asilo nido and scuola d'infanzia has been blurring. In spite of the fiscal crisis, the Italian government had committed to increasing places for the age group zero to three with a goal of serving 33 percent of children in that group. One mechanism, adopted as an experiment, was opening the existing scuola d'infanzia to children under three. Declining birth rates had left unfilled slots in the scuola d'infanzia and this move allowed resources to be reallocated where needed most. This option of early enrollment proved extremely popular in the southern regions, where demand for zero-to-three slots was high and supply had been low. As of 2017, the dual system of asilo nido and scuola d'infanzia was being restructured as an integrated system for all children zero to six with *poli dell'infanzia* (children's centers) in every region. While there are still not enough places for all children in the younger age group, the objective of the reform is to create an integrated system capable of serving all children three to six, plus the estimated 33 percent of the zero-to-three population whose families are expected to seek places in these centers. A final positive development is the requirement that all preschool and kindergarten teachers must have a university-level degree (Querzé 2017a). As one can see, Italy has made progress on many of the OECD benchmarks.

The US lags behind Italy as well as all the rest of the OECD nations in quality and coverage of public early-childhood services. In January 2015, Secretary of Education Arne Duncan issued a report describing the shortfall of preschool in America as "A Matter of Equity" (US Department of Education 2015). Pointing to the newest neuroscience and research on cognitive and social learning during the preschool years, the report argued that too many children in the United States begin their publicly funded education already far behind their peers. In the United States, publicly funded kindergarten, which serves five-year-olds, is offered by most school systems. However, as of 2013, only four out of ten four-year-olds attend a publicly funded preschool program. There are two major federal programs: Head Start (serving low-income children) and special education preschool services (serving children with disabilities). Some states also fund a year of "voluntary state preschool," designed to enhance children's school readiness when they enter kindergarten at age five. Only 41 percent of four-year-olds are enrolled in these programs (10 percent are enrolled in Head Start, 3 percent in special education, and 28 percent in state preschools), leaving 59 percent outside the publicly funded systems (US Department of Education 2015, table 1).

Why is this a matter of equity? If the remaining 59 percent of four-year-olds were all starting on a level playing field when they entered kindergarten, we would be looking at a shortfall in access that could be corrected. However, the missing children tend to fall into two groups: those who have attended excellent private preschools, often beginning at age two or three, while the others, if they were in any program at all, were in day care. The quality of day care ranges from adequate to abysmal.

The US Dichotomy between Early-Childhood Education and Day Care

Why is early-childhood care such slippery terrain in the United States? Here is where history and tradition play such a large role in replicating past inequalities (Woodhouse 2008b). Childcare and early-childhood education in the United States developed along two different models: one for the working classes and one for the more affluent classes. "Day care" (supervision and care while parents were at work) was considered the private responsibility of the working parent. Before child labor was regulated, children often worked for wages as soon as they were able. The United States never developed a tradition of early-childhood nurseries provided at public expense to meet the needs of working families, although some factories or businesses provided day care for their workers. Today, parents in the United States may have access to government support for day care, in the form of tax deductions and need-based subsidies to poor families, and some schools may provide after-school programs. But, generally speaking, day care (often trivialized as babysitting) is not thought of as an integral part of the public education continuum. There is a sharp difference between Italy and the United States in this regard. I noticed in my survey of attitudes in Scanno that respondents had a lot to say about what government could do to smooth the path for young couples starting a family. Front and center was improving access to early-childhood care and education and to publicly funded university education. In my admittedly small sample of Cedar Keyans, respondents seemed genuinely puzzled that I should even ask such a question as "What could government do to assist young couples starting a family?" If they answered at all, they answered "Can't think of anything" or "I don't think this is a government problem."

While day care is viewed as private, it is also true that the United States also has a long tradition of "nursery schools." While some of these schools were a response by charitable organizations to concerns about integrating immigrant children into the mainstream, they generally were regarded as enrichment experiences that would enhance children's social, motor, and cognitive skills (Woodhouse 2008b, 2009). Many of these schools are modeled after the method popularized by Italian educator Maria Montessori. While in Italy the Montessori method contributed to the development of a public system of preschools, Montessori schools in the United States remained an expensive private option. Nursery schools were used primarily by more affluent and educated parents, to give their children the advantage of early childhood exposure to peers and to an educational environment. Most nursery school programs were not adapted to the working parent because hours were short and meals were not served. Well equipped with toys and play spaces and staffed by trained early-childhood educators, most nursery schools were beyond the means of working-class and poor parents (Woodhouse 2008b). This difference in educational experiences only exacerbated the gap between poor and wealthy children. Not surprisingly, when we look at the racial and socioeconomic statistics, African American and Latino American children and children from families below the poverty line had the lowest school readiness scores while Asian and Caucasian children from families at least 200 percent above the poverty line had the highest school readiness scores (Child Trends Databank 2015).

It is no accident that the United States lacks a comprehensive publicly funded day care and early-childhood system (Cohen 2013). This gap can be traced directly to a uniquely American tradition of individualism, bias in favor of private market-based solutions, and the belief that communal approaches to education would undermine the role of the family. Looking back, it is clear that childhood in America could have been very different. In the late 1960s and early 1970s, support was gathering for expanding the Head Start program, which had been aimed at low-income children, and developing a national universal early-childhood education program. In 1971, Congress passed a sweeping bill entitled the Comprehensive Child Development Act. This was a bipartisan effort supported by the testimony of many experts in child development and education. It was vetoed in December 1971 by President Richard Nixon. While Nixon recognized the success of the Head Start program, he firmly rejected the involvement of the federal government in an area he believed was fundamentally private. He argued that the federal role should be restricted "to assisting parents in purchasing day care in the private, open market, with Federal involvement in the direct provision of such services to be kept at an absolute minimum." In his veto message he condemned the bill as a threat to "the family in its rightful position as the keystone of our civilization" and as "a long leap into the dark for the United States government and the American people." He saw the legislation as undercutting "parental authority and parental involvement with children—particularly in those decisive early years when social attitudes and a conscience are formed and religious and moral principles are first inculcated. . . . For the Federal Government to plunge headlong financially into supporting child development would commit the vast moral authority of the national Government to the side of communal approaches to child rearing over against the family-centered approach." His veto message concluded, "This President, this Government, is unwilling to take that step" (Nixon 1971; Woodhouse 2008b, note 45). Today, the same arguments are raised in opposition to government responsibility and in favor of privatized solutions, not only in proposals for day care and early-childhood education but also in in current debates over a national curriculum, the charter school movement, and vouchers for use in private schools. While both candidates in the 2016 election made campaign promises about meeting the need for day care, six months into the Trump administration nothing had yet been proposed.

According to Child Care Aware, a national network of information on childcare resources, the average cost of center-based day care for infants in the United States is $972 a month. However, costs range widely and in some cities parents must spend up to $2,000 per month for infant day care. Costs for center-based care for preschoolers are lower than for infants, at a national average of $733 a month. Day care is also offered by individuals in their homes, and the average cost for these programs is about $640 a month (BabyCenter 2016). More than half the states do not require any licensing of these facilities unless they serve more than five children. Requirements for operating such facilities vary from state to state (Child Care Aware of America 2016). According to a 2016 survey of a nationally representative sample of 1,120 parents or guardians of children five or younger, costs are a major stressor for American families. Using the Department of Health and Human Services standard classifying care that exceeds 7 percent of a two parent family's income as unaffordable, center-based care is unaffordable in 49 states plus the District of Columbia and family child care is unaffordable in 45 states plus the District of Columbia. In the state of Florida, for example, the annual cost of accredited center based care as of 2017 was $9,942 for infants and $9,158 for toddlers (Child Care Aware of America 2017). Given Florida's 2015 median household income of $49,852, accredited center-based day care is out of reach for many (Guzman 2017). Single-parent families are even worse off. Across all states, the average cost of center-based care exceeds 24 percent of the median income for single parents (Child Care Aware of America 2016, 32). As a result, many children are left at home alone or with older siblings while their mothers work. The risks are high and the consequences potentially tragic. Quality day care is a safety issue as well as an educational issue. In several US cases, children too young to be left unsupervised themselves have been tasked by desperate mothers with caring for infants or toddlers while the parent slept or worked. When the smaller child dies while in the older child's care, the older child is arrested and charged with manslaughter or felony murder (Woodhouse 2008a). A society that cares about its children will assure them access to safe places to play and learn while their parents work.

* * *

While both Italians and Americans continue to value children and look forward to becoming parents, there are still many disincentives that contribute to falling birth rates and place vulnerable families at risk. Social features such as stable family structures and support from extended family and community, combined with family-supportive public policies such as subsidies for births, access to universal health care, paid parental leave, and affordable day care can play a role in improving the environments for child-rearing.

7

Children of the Great American Recession

The United States is better than here. I call it the U-S-A [showing off his American pronunciation]. It is more developed. It is more advanced.
—Diego, age 10, personal communication, 2015

Children born today in the United States are the luckiest people in the world.
—Warren Buffett, quoted in Linette Lopez, "Poll"

The Great Recession should have served as a wake-up call for unexamined claims of American exceptionalism. Americans had become comfortable with the notion that theirs was the best system in the world, and the American myth of a land of limitless opportunity was entrenched not only in the United States but around the globe. Typical of Italian attitudes, the first claim quoted above was the unsolicited opinion of a ten-year-old boy who knew about the United States only through television and by listening to his elders. Like Diego, Italians of all ages tend to view America as a model of progress and modernity. The second claim quoted above was made by Warren Buffett, the American multibillionaire investor and philanthropist, and generated a lively internet discussion (Lopez 2012). Buffett made his statement in 2012, well after the official end of the Great Recession in America, which, according to economists, began in December 2007 and ended in June 2009 (CBPP 2016).

Most of Buffett's fellow citizens tended to agree with his claim. Those responding to one online poll voted 56 to 44 percent that he had gotten his facts right. They cited the pioneering role of the United States in building the most powerful democracy in the world and pointed to indicators of prosperity such as the US per-capita GDP of $48,100 and average life expectancy of 78.1 years (Lopez 2012). Some respondents expressed reservations. They pointed out that "luckiest" is a comparative claim and calls for comparison with other countries. Americans are often surprised by these comparisons, and they are not alone. Like Diego, quoted above, Italians of all ages with whom I spoke were convinced that children must be better off in the United States. When I cited comparative data (e.g., that the poverty rate per thousand children is far higher in the United States than in Italy) most Italian adults were incredulous. "No, no," they would insist. "That must be because there are more children in the USA than in Italy." "That must be because so many poor Italian children live in its southern regions." It was hard to move them from their preconceptions with mere statistics. American exceptionalism has a strong hold on imaginations around the world, especially in Italy, where so many generations have emigrated to America and people have grown used to viewing it as the Promised Land.

The reality is more complicated, even when it comes to classic "objective" measures like GDP cited by many respondents to the 2012 poll. Put simply, GDP is the monetary value of all goods and services produced within a nation's borders over a specific period of time, divided by the number of people living in the country. The US per-capita GDP in 2012 was surely impressive, but the United States was not number one. It trailed after nations such as Luxembourg, Qatar, and Norway, coming in in eleventh place (Knoema, for GDP per capita by country). GDP has been the classic economic measure of a nation's prosperity, but there are many other measures that capture the multitude of factors contributing to national well-being. Both sides in the debate can point to ways in which some American children are either exceptionally lucky or exceptionally unlucky.

Both ten-year-old Diego and billionaire Buffett were speaking at a time when families in the United States were still emerging from the ravages of the worst economic collapse since the Great Depression of the 1930s. With the help of researchers in government, the academy, and nonprofit sectors, it is possible to piece together a picture of how the recession and its immediate aftermath affected the ecology of childhood. In this chapter we will look at five key indices of child well-being in the United States in the period between 2008 and 2015: child poverty, food insecurity, housing stability, child health, and child maltreatment. All five of these factors affect the ecology of childhood at every level, from the microsystem of family to the macrosystem of national politics.

As noted earlier, part 3 of this book shifts its focus from the intimacy of microsystems and their interplay in mesosystems to focus on the external worlds of exosystemic factors that affect the ecology of childhood. In chapters 5 and 6 we discussed factors in the exosystems that affect the decision to have children, and exosystems that support parents and children in early childhood. Beginning in this chapter and continuing in the two that follow, we will look at children's well-being on a national and global scale. Chapter 7 examines how we measure children's well-being in the United States, and how it was affected by the Great Recession. Chapter 8 examines how children in

Italy fared when the recession crossed the Atlantic and became what Italians call *la crisi* (the crisis). Chapter 9 serves to link the exosystems to their macrosystems. It identifies six global macrosystemic forces that have contributed to destabilizing the ecology of childhood: unrestrained capitalism, technological revolution, growing inequality, mass migration, racism, and climate change. All six of these factors, grouped under the umbrella of globalization, combine to undermine and threaten the well-being of children.

Measuring Well-Being

In measuring progress, a lot depends on what is measured, who is measured, how it is measured, and when it is measured. Well-being is an expansive concept, and focusing on one measure in isolation can be highly misleading. Data crunchers have developed many different methods for measuring a nation's success and comparing one nation with others. Some compilers gather data at the national level and some at the local or regional level. Some compare data on all nations while others compare groups of similar nations, such as the modern industrialized nations of the OECD, once called "first-world" nations; others focus on developing nations, once called "third-world" nations. Some look only at statistics while others incorporate qualitative research.

Here are some examples of measurements in use as of 2012, when Buffett made his claim that children in America were the luckiest in the world. One leading indicator, the Human Development Index (HDI), looks at life expectancy, literacy, education, standards of living, and quality of life. At the time of Buffett's claim, the HDI ranked Norway, Australia, the Netherlands, the United States, and New Zealand, in that order, as the top five nations (UNDP 2011). The Global Competiveness Report, which looks at factors that make a nation a good place for investors, also ranked the United States in the top five, along with Switzerland, Singapore, Sweden, and Finland (World Economic Forum 2011). However, an economic measure called the Gini coefficient, which measures inequality, delivered bad news for American children born into lower- and middle-class families. It placed the United States ninety-fourth among the nations studied in terms of an individual's opportunity to move up the economic ladder (World Bank, for Gini Index World Bank Estimate). And the Happy Planet Index (HPI), designed to measure human well-being with a special focus on environmental impact, was even more disappointing, placing the United States at 105, trailing far behind front-runners Costa Rica, the Dominican Republic, and Vietnam (New Economics Foundation 2012).

The above rankings reflect the existing data at a point in time when the effects of recession were still visible in America, but mostly in the rearview mirror. A snapshot in time is useful, but so are studies of how rankings change over time. Booming economies of nations once stigmatized as "third world," such as China and India, are evidence of this fluidity. Countries can also fall in rankings. While Americans like to think of their country as on a continuous upward trajectory, the reality is different. Recall that, as of 2011, the Human Development Index (HDI) placed the United States among the top five nations (UNDP 2011). However, the United Nations Development Programme had already projected that by 2030 the United States would drop to nineteenth place in the HDI ranking (Asher and Daponte 2010). These predictions are coming to pass. By 2018, the United States had already fallen from fifth to thirteenth place (Human Development Index 2018). Since the HDI takes into account so many measures that affect children's well-being, a drop in the HDI should be a matter of great concern to any nation.

Changes in rankings over time can also tell a story about the relative impact of a global economic downturn on peer nations' economies. For example, Italy's 2008 GDP per capita, at $40,689, was near its all-time high. By 2017, it had dropped almost 25 percent to $31,984. The US GDP in 2008 was substantially higher than that of Italy at $48,303, placing it second on the list of major economies. Although GDP growth slowed during the recession, and even briefly dropped, by 2017 it had risen almost 12 percent above its prerecession level, to $59,501 per capita. As these statistics make clear, compared to the US economy, the Italian economy suffered a far more radical drop in productivity, accompanied by dramatically greater rises in unemployment. Another index, the Global Competitiveness Index (GCI), is commonly used by investors to measure levels of risk before investing in a given economy. The US occupied fifth place in the GCI in 2011.

But neither competitiveness nor GDP are the ultimate measure of an economy's responsiveness to its children's needs; in fact, they tell us little about the distribution of resources within a country or who benefits from the changes being measured. During the same period as its competitiveness and GDP were soaring, the US trend toward increasing inequality was also accelerating. A table from the World Bank reviewing historical data on inequality tells a troubling story. In 1979, the US Gini coefficient stood at an already high level of 34.6, but by 2016 it had risen to 41.5, placing the United States fourth from the bottom among OECD countries, ahead of only Mexico, Chile, and Turkey and behind countries like Russia and Lithuania (World Bank, for Gini Index; OECD, for Income Distribution Database). Contrary to the popular belief that America is the quintessential "land of opportunity," the Gini coefficient tells us that children born in the United States are increasingly unlikely to be better off than their parents.

A final crucial factor in shaping the ecology of childhood—one that is harder to measure but impossible to ignore—is "politics." One noted expert in political science, David Easton, describes "politics" as "the "authoritative allocation of values, or the distribution of rewards in wealth, power, and status that the system may provide" (1953). How does politics figure in our ecological diagram? Politicians and civil servants create and manage exosystems like health care and social welfare programs, but politics clearly finds its home in the macrosystem. Seismic events like the Great Recession can cause tectonic shifts in "the system" alluded to by Easton, profoundly affecting the "values" that animate it. Nowhere has this been more evident than in the United States during the decade between 2008 and 2018. The recession was bookended by two presidential elections—that of Barack Obama in 2008 and of Donald Trump in 2016. As the first black president, Obama made history. His election also caused a backlash that was most evident in the rise of the Tea Party, a far-right group that distrusted government and sought to cut spending. The Tea Party helped Republicans gain control of Congress in the midterm elections of 2010. While the Obama administration's progressive policies were often blocked by opposition from conservatives in Congress, it proposed and enacted numerous programs that benefited children and families. It is fair to say that the Trump administration, since taking power in January 2017, has been the least child-friendly administration in US history (Stark 2018).

In summary, there are many indices of national well-being, using a variety of measures, and there is no single method for ranking and comparing nations any more than there is a single way to rank and compare childhoods. Comparisons, however, can provide a valuable tool for exploding a country's illusions of superiority or countering the myth of its backwardness. We will turn next to measures that are specifically related to children's well-being. But, first, a word is needed about how we measure poverty.

Measuring Child Poverty

Measuring poverty is a complicated task, even more so when comparisons involve children and extend across national boundaries. Most children have no income of their own, so we look at the income of the household in which they are living, and we try to identify an income level where a family of a certain size crosses the line into poverty—in other words, the *poverty line*. In general, the United States has favored using an absolute measure of poverty in setting the federal poverty line, pegging it at the cost of a market basket of essentials for living (UNICEF 2005). Most other nations use a relative measure of poverty, which is more useful for comparisons, because median income and cost of living vary widely from country to country. International bodies and most European states have developed a method of measuring poverty that looks at the percent of children living in households with incomes below a certain percentage of the national median income. The OECD in its reports draws the line at 50 percent, while other expert bodies use 40 percent or 60 percent. We call this the *relative poverty line*. This method allows us to compare the percentage of children who are living at the bottom of the national heap, regardless of whether their home country is larger or smaller in size or richer or poorer in resources.

Skeptics may ask how one can say that a child in a country where virtually every child has access to a cell phone or a TV is deprived compared to a child in a country where these items are rare. True, in absolute terms, a child in one place may have more material resources than a child in another. But measuring the percentage of children below a certain percent of the median income has become the accepted international method for comparing rates of child poverty, and for good reason (UNICEF 2010).

First, this relative measure of child poverty incorporates differences in exchange rates, cost of living, and wage rates by looking at where the median family falls on the scale of resources in that particular nation. Second, it is subjective as well as objective. Poverty is experienced by children, even more than by adults, not only in absolute terms, but also in relative terms. A lot depends on the environment in which one experiences or measures poverty. My former student, Justice Yvonne Mokgoro, the first black African woman to serve on the highest court of the Republic of South Africa, explained this to a group of urban teenage girls in Philadelphia far better than I ever could. At a meeting we held at University of Pennsylvania Law School shortly after she was appointed to the South African Constitutional Court, one girl asked for advice on resisting the temptations she faced riding to school on a subway plastered with ads for electronics and luxury items she knew she could never afford unless she followed some of her peers, who engaged in drug trafficking and other illegal acts. Justice Mokgoro responded very sympathetically, saying that her own life had been far *easier* than that of this African American girl. As a child growing up in a segregated South African township where she lived with her laundress mother and streetcar-driver father, Yvonne had only one pair of shoes and two dresses. But all the other girls she knew only had one pair of shoes and two dresses.

It was only when Justice Mokgoro grew older and traveled into affluent white enclaves that she saw how deprived she had been of equality of possessions and, more important, of equality of education. By that time, as she explained to these wide-eyed girls who hung on every word, her character already had been formed by a strong family, strong church, and close-knit community, and she was able to take a longer view of how to redress inequality. With the help of Rotary Club scholarships, she studied law in segregated universities in South Africa and then with me, at the University of Pennsylvania in the United States. When Nelson Mandela was released and apartheid ended, she was one among a cadre of highly educated black South Africans who were poised to take leadership roles. Unlike Justice Mokgoro, for better or for worse, poor youth growing up in today's global societies are subjected to tremendous stress when bombarded with advertisements and dramas depicting a world of luxuries and compare it with their own lives. Poverty is intrinsically comparative as well as objective.

Another criticism of comparative measures of poverty goes like this: a large and diverse country like the United States may simply have more poor families and more poor children than a small and wealthy country like Norway. They cannot be compared because they start from a different benchmark. This is true, but it poses new questions. What does a nation do about child poverty within its borders? What percentage of its resources does it spend to combat child poverty? Are its interventions effective? One country may act aggressively to reduce child poverty while another does little. For example, based on statistics from 2007 to 2009, the United States and Canada had equivalent child-poverty rates (25.1 percent) before benefits from government policies such as taxes and income transfers were factored in. We call this the "market child-poverty rate" to distinguish it from the poverty rate after government acts to mitigate child poverty. After counting taxes and transfers, Canada typically cut its market rate of child poverty to 13.3 percent while the US rate, at 23.1 percent, budged by only two points. France, in the same period, started with a market poverty rate of 19.4 percent and cut that to 8.8 percent, while Spain's market poverty rate started at 18.8 percent and, even after government transfers, it remained at 17.1 percent (UNICEF 2012, Fig. 8a).

Insights can be gained as well by comparing poverty rates for children with *overall poverty* rates. In the United States, the overall poverty rate in 2012, at about 18 percent, was substantially lower than the poverty rate of about 23 percent among children. In other words, children were far more likely to suffer poverty than members of the general population. In Italy, looking at data from 2012, both child poverty and overall poverty were lower than in the United States, at about 17 and 12 percent, respectively (UNICEF 2012, Fig. 9). There are nations where the old are poorer than the young, but, thanks to social security and pension systems, the United States and Italy are not among them. In the United States, however, the gap between overall and child-poverty rates was almost double that of Italy. These statistics help us compare how effectively nations respond or fail to respond to existing income inequalities between children and other groups.

A different challenge in measuring child poverty in rich countries is that poverty in rich countries may be less visible. Relatively few children in rich countries are actually seen starving or begging on the streets. But even in these countries, some children lack basic resources. Unpacking the statistics, one can ask how far a country allows its children to fall below the relative child-poverty line. We call this the "poverty gap." As a 2012 study by UNICEF shows, Finland had a very low child-poverty gap, with only 10.9 percent below the poverty line. Italy's poverty gap, based on statistics from 2009, was 29.8 percent. Italy's poor children fell almost three times as far into poverty as those of Finland. In the United States, poor children on average fell even further than in Italy, to 37.5 percent below the poverty line (UNICEF 2012, fig. 7). A child in a family with income below 25 percent of the poverty line is defined as living in "extreme poverty." To translate "extreme poverty" into more concrete terms of dollars and cents, as of 2009, even before the recession really hit home, almost 40 percent of poor children in the United States were living in households with income of less than $979 per month for a family of four (Children's Defense Fund 2014, 4).

In the United States, children of color, including black, Native American, and Hispanic children, have been disproportionately likely to grow up in poverty. As reported by the Children's Defense Fund in 2014, one in three children of color lived in poverty. In six states, half or more black children were poor and nearly half the states had black child-poverty rates of 40 percent or more. One statistic from 2012 stands out starkly: over one-third of children of color were poor during their first two years of life, the period of most rapid brain development and greatest vulnerability (Children's Defense Fund 2014, 22).

Poverty in America is also influenced by regional factors and tied to family demographics. Everyone who watches American TV is familiar with images of the urban ghetto, where rates of child poverty hover at about 29 percent, but few realize that rural areas and small towns have poverty rates averaging about 26.7 percent. Surprisingly, nearly two in five poor children now live in the suburbs (Children's Defense Fund 2014, 4, 44). In contrast with many European cities, the US suburbs have been seen as a haven of peace and affluence, but this no longer holds true. Comparing regions of the US in 2014, the Children's Defense Fund found that the South had the highest poverty rate, with one in every four children living under the poverty line, while in the rest of the country the ratio was one in five. Children of single parents were nearly four times as likely to live in poverty than children of married couples. Race and ethnicity play a role here as well. While 70 percent of all children lived with two parents, more than half of black children and more than one-third of Hispanic children lived with a single parent (Children's Defense Fund 2014, 44–8). Thus, many factors, including race, region, demographics, and family form, combine to affect rates of child poverty in the United States.

How Did Children in the United States Fare in the Wake of the Great Recession?

There is a saying common among statisticians that "every person is a statistic of one" (Kells 1997). Any graph charting the rising, falling, or stagnating rates of child poverty, homelessness, or hunger is the aggregate of many individual children's stories. As developing organisms, children are especially vulnerable to the sequelae of episodic as well as chronic deprivation. This is why it is important to examine the course of the recession over time and its continuing impact on children. Although experts disagree on precise timelines, it is generally accepted that the recession began in the United States in December 2007 and officially ended in June 2009 (CBPP 2016). Almost five years later, American children were still suffering its aftereffects. A January 2015 study by the PolicyLab of the Children's Hospital of Philadelphia painted a grim picture. Among the measures examined were rates of hunger, homelessness, and stressors such as domestic violence, job loss, eviction, and mortgage foreclosure precipitated by the economic crisis (Meadows et al. 2015). It would be impossible to describe all of the measures of child well-being, but the recession has prompted study of a number of areas important to children. Those that follow are a sampling of these measures as of 2015. They paint a disturbing picture in which children seemed still to be losing ground.

Poverty

Child poverty in the United States has been rightly called a national disgrace (Children's Defense Fund 2015, 3). As the prior discussion of measuring poverty illustrates, this should not be news to anyone who researches or works with children. Despite living in the world's most powerful economy, children in the United States have not shared in its wealth. Long before the recession struck, the first Innocenti Report Card published in 2000 reported relative child poverty rates in the United States of 22.4 percent, placing it twenty-second out of twenty-three countries. For comparison, in the same study, Italy placed twenty-first, with a rate of 20.5 percent. Sweden was first, with only 2.6 percent of children in poverty (UNICEF 2000, fig. 1). Instead of shrinking in the first decade of the twenty-first century, the percentages of US children in poverty increased. The US also maintained its record of placing near the bottom among its peer nations. As of 2014, the United States had the second highest child poverty rate among thirty-five industrialized nations (Children's Defense Fund 2015, 7). In 2012, looking at twenty of the most affluent industrialized nations, the Innocenti study ranked the USA dead last in combatting child poverty (UNICEF 2012, fig. 4).

During the recession the absolute number of children living in poverty in the United States rose from 12.8 million to 14.7 million (Meadows et al. 2015, 3). According to Innocenti Report Card 12, published in 2014, the rate of child poverty in the United States grew from 30.1 in 2008 to 32.2 percent in 2012 (UNICEF 2014b, table 1). As of 2017, the highest rates of child poverty in the United States were occurring during the period from birth to age five, during the time of greatest brain development, with one in five children living in poverty and one in ten in extreme poverty (Children's Defense Fund 2018). In both absolute and relative terms, whether looking at US statistics generated by the federal government or international statistics generated for comparative studies, too many children in the United States are poor and they are remaining poor long after the recession has ended.

Poverty is only one measure. The other measures discussed below do not compare the United States with other countries but simply report on the effects domestically of the recession as measured in studies published near the end of the Obama administration.

Food Security

To measure what we used to call hunger, the United States Department of Agriculture (USDA) has adopted a metric called *food insecurity*, defined as limited or uncertain access to adequate food (ERS 2015). It examines whether and how often a household unit is unable to acquire adequate food for active, healthy living for all household members as a result of its having insufficient money and other resources to obtain food. A national chart of hunger/food insecurity in the United States over the past decades generally shows numbers rising in times of financial crisis and falling in times of financial gain, but the correlation is imperfect. While economists debate whether prosperity on Wall Street trickles down to Main Street, the effects on children of a financial crisis are all too clear and immediate. In 2005, the percent of US children under eighteen living in food-insecure households had declined to about 17 percent and remained fairly steady until 2008. In the first year of the recession, the percentage rose sharply, from 16.9 to 23.2 percent. Recovery in food security lagged far behind recovery in the stock market. By 2013, the percent of families with children suffering food insecurity remained high, at 21.4 percent (Child Trends Databank 2014, appendix 1).

Children are especially likely to be hungry compared to the general population. In 2014, the rate of food insecurity among families with children was 19 percent, much higher than the national average of 12 percent among all households (Feeding America n.d.). In raw numbers, this means that 15.3 million American children were living in food-insecure households five years after the recession had officially ended (Feeding America 2014). Measuring hunger is a political as well as a statistical enterprise. No one likes to think of children going hungry in a rich nation, but the fact remains that too many American children do not know where their next meal is coming from or whether they will get enough to eat. In 2006, with uncanny timing, the USDA relabeled the category previously called "food insecure with hunger among children" with the euphemistic label of "very low food security" (Child Trends Databank 2014; ERS 2015). Between 2006 and 2008, the rates of children living in families with very low food security more than doubled, rising 0.6 to 1.5 percent. By 2013, the rates had declined but remained at 1 percent—higher than at any time since 1999 (Child Trends Databank 2014, appendix 2). In raw numbers, at the height of the recession over a million children were suffering hunger in the United States, and five years later 740,000 children were still going hungry. Remember that food insecurity measures all sources for accessing food. Many more children would have gone hungry had it not been for charitable programs such as soup kitchens, food banks, and government-funded nutrition programs.

The rise in food insecurity during the recession was accompanied by a steep rise in families receiving federal nutrition assistance. Once known as food stamps, the largest federal nutrition program is now formally known as SNAP (Supplemental Nutrition Assistance Program). It distributes electronic debit cards instead of the old-fashioned paper stamps, to be exchanged for food, but the term "food stamps" lingers on. Recipients can use their cards to shop in supermarkets or grocery stores for an approved list of foods. SNAP is a "means-tested" program, meaning that to qualify for benefits, recipients must show that they lack the financial means to buy adequate food. The amounts of aid depend on where household incomes rank with relation to the poverty line and the numbers of persons in the household. Single adults are generally not eligible, and families with children must be very low-income and without significant assets and must document their eligibility every six months to a year or be dropped from the program.

Charts from 2015 tracing the numbers of food-stamp recipients tell the story of a recession followed by a jobless recovery, with severe hardships for families with children. The numbers of SNAP participants shot up from 26.3 million in 2007 to 40.3 million in 2010. Half of these recipients were children. While SNAP enrollment declined slightly after 2013, the numbers of children living in food-insecure households remained far higher than before the recession, with one in three children as of 2015 receiving supplemental nutrition assistance and others left out because of lack of funding (Meadows et al. 2015, 17–18).

It is difficult to overestimate the importance of federal nutrition programs in surviving the recession. At the height of the crisis, the Obama administration's stimulus spending package, the American Recovery and Reinvestment Act of 2009 (ARRA), played a crucial role in alleviating child poverty and child hunger. However, the ARRA provided only a temporary increase in funding and a temporary relaxation of the strict limits on duration and eligibility. With Congress in gridlock, and austerity hawks facing off against supporters of stimulus spending, the ARRA nutrition benefits were not reauthorized as scheduled, and the ARRA expired in 2013. The result was a $5-billion cut to SNAP benefits nationwide, despite the fact that food insecurity remained high (Dean and Rosenbaum 2013). A family of three needed a gross monthly income of no more than $2,144 in order to be eligible for a monthly average benefit of $378 (USDA 2014a). This income level may seem high by European standards, but it was barely enough to survive in the United States, where costs of living are much higher, especially for health care, childcare, housing, and education.

Although SNAP is federally funded, each of the fifty US states administers the SNAP programs and have great latitude in setting the criteria for eligibility. Benefits vary drastically, and there are also significant barriers to participation. State reports suggest that the decrease in participation rates after the ARRA lapsed should not be taken as a sign that the food crisis is over. Prior to the decrease in participation, many states had reduced benefits compared to those offered at the height of the recession, and they had also erected greater barriers to participation. In many states, advocates for the hungry report that longer delays in reviewing applications, higher criteria for eligibility, and burdensome, repetitive paperwork are discouraging people in need from applying. As of 2015 about 15 percent of those households eligible for SNAP did not participate (Cunnyngham 2016).

Other programs serving children's nutrition needs showed similar spikes in demand and had not returned to prerecession levels long after the official end of the recession. Participation in the Special Supplemental Nutrition Program for Women, Infants, and Children, commonly known as WIC, increased from 8.2 million to 9.1 million between 2007 and 2010 (Meadows et al. 2015, 18).

This program is intended to reduce the impact of poverty on nutrition during pregnancy and in children's earliest years. The National School Lunch Program (NSLP) provides free and reduced-price meals at school to children from families below a certain income level. Quality of nutrition and spending levels improved under the Healthy and Hunger-Free Kids Act of 2010. However, the numbers of children in the school-lunch program receiving reduced price or free meals rose from 59 percent in 2007 to 65 percent in 2010, and as of 2013 it was at an all-time high of 70 percent (Meadows et al. 2015, 19). Gross expenditures had grown to record levels because so many more children had become poor enough to qualify for free meals.

These are the government statistics. But what does food insecurity mean in terms of the ecology of childhood? We now know that even "marginal" food insecurity is associated with poor health and poor developmental outcomes (Cook et al. 2013). Some of its effects are obvious, while others are more subtle. Inadequate food intake during childhood is associated with more illnesses, poorer school performance, impaired cognitive development, and heightened rates of anxiety, depression, and behavior problems. Hunger in the United States does not fit the image from less developed countries of skinny children with big eyes and swollen bellies. Paradoxically, food insecurity in the United States is closely related to being overweight and high levels of obesity. Poor families are often trapped in urban or rural "food deserts" that lack access to healthy foods. When money is scarce, families tend to stretch their budgets by substituting cheaper mass-produced foods, which are often lower in important nutrients and higher in fat, sugar, and empty carbohydrates. While nutrition is a complex field, it is now clear that food insecurity during pregnancy and lack of access to healthy, nutritious foods during childhood are partly to blame for record levels of childhood obesity (Woodhouse and Woodhouse 2018).

In the microsystem of the family, food insecurity is keenly felt by children too young to know why their parents are stressed or why there is not enough food to go around. If my own experience as a child is any measure, food insecurity is keenly felt even by children old enough to understand the dynamics of surviving on a low income. When I was growing up in the 1950s, my father was the primary breadwinner in our family. He was a classical musician and composer whose bread-and-butter job was playing the bass fiddle in dance bands. His income varied from week to week, and he had to compete for a limited supply of jobs that grew smaller whenever money got tight. I do not remember ever actually going hungry, but I do remember sometimes having to scrape the bottom of the barrel. My parents made a game of it when there was nothing for dinner but oatmeal or that can of plum pudding lurking in the very back of the cupboard, where a small child could help out by crawling in to reach it. It can be scary, even to a very secure child with caring and responsive parents, to experience the stress that goes along with what the USDA calls "food insecurity." It is especially harmful to experience the actual hunger of "very low food security."

Housing Instability

Housing instability is another measure of the impact on children of an economic downturn. Housing was at the center of the recession in the United States. Many homeowners had borrowed more than their houses were worth in order to own their piece of the American dream. When the US housing bubble burst, its youngest victims were the 2.3 million children whose families lost their homes to foreclosure (Isaacs 2012). Although the housing markets as of 2015 were slowly recovering, the housing crisis continued to unfold. As of 2015, in addition to the children who had already lost their homes, another 6 million remained at risk of their homes being foreclosed (Isaacs 2012). While federal rental-assistance programs had helped families avoid homelessness during the worst of the recession, cuts to these programs forced by deficit hawks have placed many children at risk and unprotected from homelessness in the event of a future downturn.

Homelessness affects children profoundly. Along with the security of a roof over their heads and a place to call home, their connections with family, community, schools, and health care are often disrupted. Homeless children are more likely to lack adequate health care, suffer from developmental or mental health issues, and are more than twice as likely as those with homes to fall behind a grade or more in school. Numbers of homeless children rose sharply in 2007–8 and continued to rise (Children's Defense Fund 2014, 27). Factors such as job loss, foreclosure, and increasing domestic violence in economically stressed families were blamed. Infusions of federal funding from the ARRA, combined with existing McKinney Vento Act funds, were not enough, as they were able to reach only one in five school districts (NAEHCY and First Focus 2010, 2). During the school year 2013–14 public schools in the United States listed 1,360,747 students enrolled in schools as "homeless" (NAEHCY n.d.). These statistics underestimate the numbers of homeless children, since they do not count infants and preschoolers or children who fall between the cracks and do not attend school. As the recession ended, Republican lawmakers were unresponsive to their needs; the 2015 budget from the Republican House as proposed by Representative Paul Ryan included steep cuts to funding of services to these homeless children (Litvinov 2014). While these cuts were defeated, and McKinney Vento funding was held constant or increased, according to the latest federal report the number of homeless students, which had doubled between 2005 and 2015, continues to rise (National Center for Homelss Education 2019, table 2).

Child Health

The one bright spot for US children in the aftermath of the recession was access to health care. Unlike many developed nations, the United States has never had a universal national health-care system. Traditionally, children have relied on private insurance purchased by their parents to cover costs of seeing a doctor, receiving immunizations, and being treated in hospitals. Private insurance has been augmented by some government programs; the most important is Medicaid, aimed at very poor children and children with special medical needs. Another is the Children's Health Insurance Program (CHIP), aimed at providing affordable care to children from working-class families whose parents were unable to afford or obtain insurance for the entire family (Rudowitz et al. 2014). CHIP gives less affluent parents the option of buying affordable health insurance for their children even if the parent remains uninsured.

At the start of the recession, because of gaps in these programs, more than one in ten children in the United States lacked health insurance. With so many children insured through the policies provided through their parents' workplace, health officials predicted a steep rise in uninsured children as unemployment figures rose and parents lost their jobs. Despite the economic crisis, the number of children without health insurance actually decreased during and directly following the recession. As of 2014, the percentage of children without health insurance had fallen from over 10 percent to 7 percent. Much of this decrease can be traced to programs that had already been enacted before the economic crisis, such as increases in CHIP funding (Kenney et al. 2014). In addition, the ARRA provided federal funding to increase children's access to care as part of its stimulus package (Meadows et al. 2015, 3,10).

One of President Obama's main campaign promises had been the enactment of a comprehensive health-care system that would provide health care at affordable rates to all Americans. Models exist in many peer nations, but opposition to single-payer systems such as those in Italy and the UK had long been demonized in the United States as "socialized medicine." The complicated system enacted in 2009 called the Affordable Care Act (ACA) attempts to provide affordable access to care through a partnership of federal, state, and private programs. US citizens knew, and either loved or hated, the ACA by its nickname, "Obamacare." The name was first used by opponents of universal health care but was embraced by President Obama, who pushed the plan through against fierce opposition by the Republican Party. Although its primary goal was expanding adult insurance coverage, the ACA was a giant step forward for children. One of its provisions eliminated the right of insurers to refuse to insure patients who had a "preexisting condition." Before the ACA, insurers routinely denied coverage to infants born with congenital or birth-related health challenges, even when their parents had been insured at the time of the child's birth. Children who developed chronic illnesses before obtaining insurance could be denied coverage, and lifetime caps on benefits meant that families with sick children were bankrupted by health-care costs (Brief of Child Advocacy Organizations 2012).

During the Obama administration, the ACA was challenged twice before the Supreme Court. It survived the first challenge but not without damage. In *National Federation of Independent Business v. Sebelius* (2012), it lost a key component: extension of health insurance at the state level through the means-tested program called Medicaid (Liptak 2012). Medicaid is a federal program enacted in 1965 during the Lyndon Johnson administration to serve the poor at the same time as Medicare was created to serve the elderly. Medicaid is funded primarily with federal dollars but is implemented by the states. The state governments are not compelled to participate but every state has done so, some extending more generous benefits than others. Medicaid eligibility has varied from state to state but was always limited to families with very low incomes. In order to reach more people, the Affordable Care Act conditioned the states' continued receipt of Medicaid funding on their extension of benefits to more of the states' low-income citizens. The federal government in the ACA promised to fund from 90 to 100 percent of the costs.

As soon as it was enacted, Republicans challenged the ACA as exceeding the limited powers of Congress under the US Constitution. The Supreme Court in its 2012 decision rejected this argument, holding that the requirement that citizens must pay a penalty if they failed to buy insurance on one of the private or newly created government insurance markets was a tax and not a penalty. However, the court overruled the portion of the ACA that conditioned existing funding for Medicaid on extension by the states of new Medicaid eligibility. As a result, many families and individuals too poor to afford insurance and but not poor enough to qualify for benefits have been left without access to affordable insurance. In 2015, the Supreme Court, in *King v. Burwell*, rejected a second challenge to the ACA, which claimed that the federal government could not offer a federal plan to states that did not create their own state-level plans. An adverse decision could have wreaked havoc with the remaining structure of the ACA.

Despite the ACA's improvements in health coverage, at the end of the Obama administration children's health care remained extremely vulnerable to shifts in economic prosperity. There is no right to health care in the US Constitution, and programs like CHIP must be reauthorized periodically in order to survive. In April 2015, after an extended battle in Congress, CHIP was reauthorized for another two years, providing coverage to some six million children. But when these two years were up, a gridlocked Congress allowed CHIP to lapse for an astonishing 114 days, creating turmoil and uncertainty for millions of children. In Januuary 2018 Congress finally reauthorized it, but only through fiscal year 2023 (Brooks 2018). Children's access to health care remains precarious in many ways, dependent not only on the balance of power in Congress and cuts to Medicaid but hampered by regulations designed to contain costs by discouraging enrollment, imposing high deductibles (out of pocket payments not covered by insurance), and requiring recertification of eligibility.

To qualify for programs, parents must overcome barriers such as burdensome paperwork and complex regulations. To retain coverage for children they have to cope with a pernicious practice called "churning": the requirement in many states that children redocument their eligibility as often as every three months in order to remain covered. Each year, hundreds of thousands of children fall out of coverage because of churning or fluctuations in family income. Children covered for only a part of a year are still counted by the US Census Bureau as insured; thus the statistics on coverage do not tell the whole insurance story. Studies show that when children lack continuous coverage they are less likely to get preventive care, more likely to develop chronic conditions such as asthma, and more likely to delay care (Meadows et al. 2015, 13, 14).

Children's health insurance is only one piece of the story of the recession's impact on US children's health. A graph showing percentages of children covered by health insurance fails to capture whether families actually utilize the coverage (DeNavas-Walt et al. 2013). Access to health-insurance coverage does not equate with access to affordable care. Even insured children may face barriers such as out-of-pocket costs for medications, co-pays for doctor's visits, and high annual deductibles. A study from 2013 showed that as family incomes dropped during the recession, utilization of health care also dropped (Karaca-Mandic et al. 2013). Parents had to choose between buying food and shelter and buying health care. The broad spectrum of risks associated with high rates of poverty and with lack of care for pregnant mothers continued to affect children's health even as the economy recovered. These risks include high rates of infant mortality, low birth weight, and increased rates of chronic disease, especially asthma (Meadows et al. 2015, 15). More difficult to measure are the effects of family stress, disruption, and uncertainty about the future that characterized this period for children and families. The American Academy of Pediatrics 2017–2018 Agenda for Child Health identifies reducing child poverty and combatting health inequity as crucial to improving the health of America's children (American Academy of Pediatrics 2018; American Academy of Pediatrics 2016).

Child Maltreatment

Researchers are still trying to unravel the connections between child maltreatment and the recession. One source of data is the number of reports to the child protective agencies of child abuse or neglect. Child maltreatment reports tended to decrease in the decade between 2005 and 2015. However, there are many confounders that make it difficult to judge whether the drop in reports mirrors a drop in actual cases of abuse (Meadows et al. 2015, 31). The decade saw significant decreases in Child welfare budgets and downsizing and privatization of child protection programs, complicating the task of drawing firm conclusions.

Changing policies toward state intervention also make it hard to evaluate changes in levels of reported maltreatment. In the 1970s, the United States began to develop an elaborate system, through laws at both the state and federal level, for responding to maltreatment reports from citizens and professionals who work with children. Large numbers of children were removed from their families, taken into state custody, and placed in foster homes. Family prevention and preservation services were intended to make these stays temporary and to reunify children with their families. The systems did not work as planned. During the 1980s and 1990s, more children entered than exited foster care, and by 1998 there were 560,000 children living in foster care (US Department of Health and Human Services 2000). Frustration grew as children continued to be injured and to die. In the period preceding the recession, the emphasis shifted away from prevention and family preservation toward the speedy terminations of parents' rights as a means of preventing abuse and moving children out of foster care into adoptive homes (Woodhouse 2002). Meanwhile, as the recession deepened, budgets for child protection services were also put on the chopping block.

These changes in child protection policies make it difficult to isolate the effects of the recession from other changes in the system. We know that, in past recessions, reported rates of child maltreatment tended to increase. It does not take an expert to understand that stressed-out parents coping with fear of unemployment and homelessness are more likely to lash out at their equally stressed-out kids. Some data suggested that there was a link between rising unemployment and maltreatment cases in pediatric hospitals during and in the wake of the recession (Meadows et al. 2015, 31). Poverty and lack of social support exacerbate the risks of child maltreatment. Therefore, data on aggregate child-welfare expenditures and the reach of supportive programs can help to shed light on the connections between the recession and child maltreatment. The US child-welfare system is a patchwork of federal, state, and local initiatives. The most important pieces are the federal Title IV-E of the Social Security Act, which funds foster-care programs, and Temporary Assistance to Needy Families (TANF), which funds time-limited income support and social service programs for the poor through federal block grants to states. About half of child-welfare funding comes from the federal government, which tries to encourage some level of uniformity by conditioning its funding on compliance with certain basic standards to insure that children's basic needs are met. States and localities are still left with a great deal of latitude in designing, funding, and operating their programs to combat child maltreatment. TANF is the program touted during President Bill Clinton's administration as ending "welfare as we know it" by replacing Aid to Families with Dependent Children (AFDC) with less generous and more limited support. While AFDC had succeeded in lifting 62 percent of children out of deep poverty, TANF could do the same for only 21 percent. When it was initiated in 1996, TANF funding was sufficient to provide assistance to sixty-eight out of one hundred poor families. By 2010, it was providing aid to only 27 percent of families in poverty (Trisi and Pavetti 2012).

At the beginning of the recession, reported rates of child maltreatment were already declining and the rate appeared to have stabilized at 9.2 per 1000 children in 2011 and 2012 (Finkelhor et al. 2015). Numbers of children in foster care, either voluntarily placed or involuntarily removed from their families, were also declining, and the recession did not affect this trend. In 2009, there were about 424,000 children living in out-of-home placements (Sell et al. 2010). It was difficult to trace a connection between the recession and increases in maltreatment of children using data from foster care, but longitudinal studies and studies of hospital admissions may tell a more detailed story. Based on these measures, rates of serious child maltreatment appeared to correlate with changes in rates of unemployment (Meadows et al. 2015, 35). In one study, every one-percent increase in unemployment appeared to correspond to a .50 per 1000 increase in confirmed maltreatment reports during the following year (Zagorsky et al. 2010). Other studies found connections between rising rates of home foreclosure, unemployment, and delinquency in paying bills with increases in admissions to hospitals of children with traumatic brain injury and serious physical abuse. Studies also showed an increase in the use of spanking to discipline children (Meadows et al. 2015, 35).

The one constant in postrecession studies was an increase in incidence of child neglect (Meadows et al. 2015, 34). A finding of child neglect may be based on a parent's failure to act as opposed to the parent's intentional infliction of harm. Defined as the failure to provide adequate care and subsistence to a child, neglect is closely tied to poverty. As we know from the field of neuroscience, maltreatment and neglect both exert a powerful influence on a child's cognitive and emotional development (Perry 2006). Child neglect is by far the most common reason for removal of children from their families by state child protective agencies, responsible for 74.8 percent of maltreatment cases and 74.6 percent of child fatalities (Child Welfare Information Gateway 2018). In the period between 2007 and 2009, reports of child neglect spiked by an alarming 21.9 percent (Wiltz 2015). It is no secret that neglect correlates with poverty and poverty correlates with homelessness, drug addiction, domestic violence, food insecurity, and infant mortality. This is the reason that we treat widespread child poverty as the key indicator of an affluent nation's neglect of its children. Failure to reduce child poverty creates a vicious circle that condemns huge numbers of children to a bleak future or no future at all.

* * *

As we have seen in this chapter, there are many competing and sometimes complementary ways to measure a nation's well-being, rank its standing among peer nations, and determine whether the trajectory of the particular measure suggests progress or decline. Among these various measures are GNP (gross national product), Gini Index (inequality), and HDI (human development), to name a few. Which measure or combinations of measures you choose depends on what you are trying to measure and why. If we examine the factors that experts deem especially important to children—poverty, housing stability, child health, food security, and child maltreatment—one can see that the recession may be over for some segments of US society, but that it continues to harm many vulnerable American children. As will be discussed in chapter 8, the recession also created a populist backlash that poses further challenges to the future of child supportive policies such as those discussed in chapter 6.

8

The Great Recession Crosses the Atlantic

Until recently, some economists had thought that Europe might suffer less from the recession, which started in the United States before spreading to most of the rest of the world. . . . But instead, European industry has been walloped as businesses around the world, and particularly in the United States, cut back on new orders to bring down their inventories.
—Eric Pfanner, "Europe's Economic Slump Deeper than Expected"

Unemployment rates not seen since the Great Depression of the 1930s have left many families unable to provide the care, protection and opportunities to which children are entitled. Most importantly, the Great Recession is about to trap a generation of educated and capable youth in a limbo of unmet expectations and lasting vulnerability.
—UNICEF Innocenti Research Center, "Children of the Recession"

Travel between the "new" and "old" worlds was once a slow and arduous process. Crosscurrents between Europe and the United States have grown faster and more powerful as technology has shortened distances and revolutionized trade, travel, and communications. Today, even middle-class youth in Europe and the United States have visited each other's continents. Florence–*Firenze* in Italian—is an obligatory stop on any student's European tour. Many tourists and college students have visited the Piazza della Santissima Grazia, often without appreciating its place in the history of childhood. My first impression of this beautiful square was formed at age eighteen, as an art student. I did not know its place in children's history, but I was delighted to discover that the stone gargoyles decorating the piazza's two fountains must have been some Hollywood artist's models for the Wicked Witch's flying monkeys in *The Wizard of Oz*. Each time I visit the piazza I am reminded of the ebb and flow of influences between our cultures. As I researched this book, images of Elsa and

Anna and their songs from Disney's incredibly popular movie *Frozen*, based on an old Scandinavian fairy tale, were everywhere in Italy—but with Italian lyrics. Americans continue to draw on European culture to entertain their children, even as they export American culture to Europe.

The Ospedale degli Innocenti (Hospital of the Innocents), which runs along one side of the piazza, was the first orphanage in Europe long before the one in London memorialized by Charles Dickens in *Oliver Twist*. It is a beautiful stone building designed by famous Renaissance master Brunelleschi, its façade decorated with roundels of blue and white ceramic from the studio of the Della Robbia family, depicting the baby Jesus in swaddling clothes. Its museum has preserved the ancient *ruota* (wheel), a hand-hewn wooden revolving door, just big enough for a baby, that rotated outside to inside, allowing desperate mothers to "abandon" infants in anonymity, knowing they would be raised by the nuns inside. Today, the Ospedale degli Innocenti houses a day nursery, an Italian center for statistical analysis, and a group of UNICEF researchers who have been tracking the well-being of children since 1988. Formally named the UNICEF Office of Research, it is still referred to as the Innocenti Centre. As a researcher of children's issues, I have been a frequent consumer of its output. During my trips to Italy, I often visited its library and attended its seminars, and its research, as readers will have noted, has been a cornerstone of my own.

While we tend to associate UNICEF with outreach to developing countries, the Innocenti Centre also gathers and analyzes knowledge about children in developed nations. In the past decade and a half, it has issued a series of report cards examining the well-being of children in rich countries. A report card is inherently comparative: it provides advocates and policy-makers with a useful tool for drawing attention to strengths and weaknesses by grading or ranking individuals, regions, or nations based on their levels of progress toward a stated goal. Fourteen Innocenti Report Cards on children in developed countries have been issued since 2000, many of which have already been cited to in this book.

In 2014, the Innocenti Centre released its twelfth report card: *Children of the Recession: The Impact of the Economic Crisis on Child Well-being in Rich Countries*. It analyzes data from forty-one countries and examines changes in children's lives since the recession struck in 2008. As the authors emphasize, the effects on children of this unprecedented economic crisis have differed from country to country, depending on the "depth of the recession, pre-existing economic conditions, the strength of the social safety net and, most importantly, policy responses" (UNICEF 2014b, 2). Report Card Twelve measures the effects of the crisis on children and families along a number of vectors. Child poverty is one key measure. In twenty-three of the forty-one countries, child poverty has increased; in eighteen countries child poverty has fallen (UNICEF 2014b, league table 1). In round numbers, there were 2.6 million more children in rich countries living in poverty in 2014 than in 2008. A total of 76.5 million children were living in poverty in these forty-one most affluent countries (UNICEF 2014b, 9). Report Card Twelve also examines a number of other measures, utilizing data gathered from sources such as EUROSTAT and the OECD, augmented by data and self-perception indicators drawn from surveys. In addition to poverty, the vectors include youth unemployment, levels of stress, access to food and housing, satisfaction in life, and severe material deprivation. It also documents the effects of cuts or increases in public expenditures and charts changes in rates of inequality.

I was especially struck by one statistic. The median income in households with children has decreased in almost half of the countries with available data (UNICEF 2014b, 16). In other words, in absolute terms of available funding for a family's survival, the baseline for determining whether a child lives in poverty relative to his peers has been sinking. Poor children in rich countries have been getting poorer. A rising tide may lift some boats but a falling tide can sink those who are already struggling to keep their leaky craft afloat.

Report Card Twelve tells a disturbing story. Families in the countries most affected have seen a rise in joblessness, an erosion of income through declining wages and underemployment, and a downturn in public services. Numbers of working poor (families where parents are employed but still falling below the poverty line) have risen during the recession. Having a child in the household increases the risk of poverty from 7 percent to 11 percent (UNICEF 2014b, 17). Since 2008, the percentage of households with children that are unable to afford to eat meat, chicken, or fish every second day has doubled in Estonia, Greece, Iceland, and Italy (UNICEF 2014b, 19). Numbers of children living in "severe material deprivation" in thirty of the thirty-one European countries studied (twenty-eight from the EU, plus Iceland, Norway, and Switzerland) rose from 9.5 million to 11.1 million (UNICEF 2014b, 3). As in the United States, children have suffered more from the crisis than other groups. In twenty-four of the thirty-one European countries, poverty levels of the elderly have decreased. During the same period, in twenty of these countries, poverty levels of children have increased. Data show that the safety net for children has not been as effective as the safety net for elders, and it has been less effective during this recession than during past recessions (UNICEF 2014b, 23, 24).

Child poverty rates in Europe since 2008 have ranged from a decrease of 7.9 percent in Poland and 4.8 percent in Switzerland to an increase of 20.4 percent in Iceland and 17.5 percent in Greece. Italy falls in the bottom quartile, with an increase of 5.7 percent in child poverty. For comparison within the North American continent, in Canada the rate has fallen by 2.44 percent; in the United States it has *risen* by 2.06 percent (UNICEF 2014b, league table 1). The tables and charts in Report Card Twelve speak volumes. One can argue about methodology or dispute the importance of one or another measure of well-being, but it is impossible to ignore the differences that emerge when a coherent and consistent set of methods and measures is applied to determining poverty rates in the forty-one richest nations and the thirty-one European jurisdictions. We see the data displayed side by side, presented in absolute measures and in relative measures.

Looking at Italy and the United States, we can see where children stood before the recession and how much damage the recession has inflicted. One chart ranks the nations by how much child poverty has increased in the years between 2008 and 2012. This measure is especially telling, since it uses each nation's standing in 2008 as an anchor.

The relative poverty line commonly used in international comparisons can obscure the effect of overall decline in incomes. For example, relative child poverty in the United Kingdom decreased from 24 percent in 2008 to 18.6 percent in 2012 (UNICEF 2014b, 9). The decrease was not due to more families becoming richer, but to a sharp drop in median incomes, resulting in lowering of the relative poverty line. The anchored indicator used in table 1 of the report shows that the UK poverty rate actually increased from 24.0 percent to 25.6 percent (UNICEF 2014b, league table 1).

According to this table, measuring how much child poverty has increased between 2008 and 2012, the United States ranks twenty-seventh, with an increase of 2.06 points and Italy ranks thirty-third, with an increase of 5.70 points. Chile ranks first, with a *decrease* in child poverty of 8.67 percent. Looking at percentages of children in poverty, the United States began with a child poverty rate of 30.1 percent and ended with a rate of 32.2. Italy began with a child poverty rate of 24.7 and ended with a rate of 30.4 percent. In other words, Italian children fell faster during the first four years of the recession, yet they did not fall further than US children. In 2012, the Italian child poverty rate was still almost two points lower than that of children in the United States. According to Report Card Twelve, Greece, Latvia, and Spain ended 2012 with child poverty rates above 36 percent. However, child poverty in Greece had skyrocketed by a devastating 17.5 points, while Spain and Lithuania saw increases of 8.1 and 8.3 percent, respectively. In sum, US children were poorer to start with and lost two points, but the worst-hit European nations suffered spikes in child poverty greater than in any economic or political crisis since World War II (UNICEF 2014b, league table 1).

Other tables display anchored rankings for changes in different measures of child well-being side by side with the raw numerical percentages. Table 2, displaying rates of NEET—the acronym for youth aged fifteen to twenty-four who are "Not in Education, Employment or Training"—shows that NEET rates have increased between 2008 and 2012 by 5.6 percent in Italy, placing it thirty-seventh out of forty-one; in the United States, NEET rates have grown by 3.0 percent, placing it thirty-first. The United States began with a NEET rate of 12 percent and ended with a rate of 15 percent, an increase of 3. Italy began with a rate of 16.6 percent in 2008 and ended with a rate of 22.2 percent in 2012, an increase of 5.6. The NEET rate in 2012 was greater in Italy than all but two other countries, Israel (30.7) and Turkey (25.5). Israel's rate had barely budged, rising from 29.8 to 30.7. Many disparate factors play a role in the rates of youth employment, education, and training, but these comparisons clearly show that Italy, Romania, Croatia, Greece, and Cyprus were hurting badly, with increases of over 5 percent (UNICEF 2014b, league table 2). Imagine what it means to a country and its demographics when so many youth are unable to transition from school to work. Careers are delayed or lost, new families are not formed, and human resources are wasted. The Great Recession has delayed or destroyed the prospects of many young people in the United States, but its impact has been far greater on youth in many European countries.

Table 3 of Report Card Twelve displays changes in self-reports of child well-being between 2007 and 2013. Surveys in each country asked four questions of a matched sample of the population: 1) Have there been times in the past twelve months when you did not have enough money to buy food that you or your family needed?; 2) Did you experience stress today?; 3) What is your overall satisfaction with life?; and, 4) Do most children in your country have the opportunity to learn and grow every day, or not? In Italy, three indicators had worsened. Italy ranked thirteenth on access to food, twenty-first on stress, eighth on whether all children had opportunities to learn and grow, but a dismal thirty-sixth on overall satisfaction with life. In the United States, the answers to all four of these questions showed a decline in well-being. Lack of access to food in the United States had risen dramatically, ranking it at thirty-seventh place out of forty-one. Overall satisfaction had dropped dramatically, ranking the United States at thirty-third. For purposes of comparison, Germany was at the top of the overall rankings with zero worsening markers and rankings of 4, 9, 3 and 6, respectively, on the four questions. Switzerland came in second, with rankings of 3, 12, 8, and 11 in how much the answers had changed between 2007 and 2013. Rather than decelerating, the children's crisis in the countries most affected seemed to accelerate. The countries at the bottom of the list showed rapidly worsening conditions between 2011 and 2013, suggesting that the recession continued to play a large role in subjective measures of well-being (UNICEF 2014b, league table 3).

How did a financial crisis that began in the United States turn into a crisis for so many nations' children? A great deal has been written about the recession from the viewpoint of the mighty. Terms like "one percenters" were coined by those left behind to describe the chasm separating those benefiting from the rising markets and the man and woman in the street. Some blamed deregulation and the bursting of the bubble on Wall Street, while others blamed borrowers who took on unrealistic levels of debt to buy houses and lost everything when they lost their jobs (Reich 2015; Stiglitz 2013; Krugman 2012). There has been plenty of blame to spread around, but very little has been written from the point of view of children.

A research paper from the UNICEF Office of Research attempted to fill this gap, by charting how children and youth became the hardest-hit group and why this happened in some countries more than in others (Natali et al. 2014). The researchers began by sorting nations into categories of most affected, moderately affected, and least affected. Nations most sharply affected fell into two categories. The first category was countries relying on the International Monetary Fund (IMF) and/or the European Central Bank (ECB). These nations were quickly forced to implement "fiscal adjustments" (a euphemism for drastic cuts in spending that, in Italian, are called *manovra*). This category included countries from the former Soviet sphere, such as Hungary, Latvia, and Lithuania. Another category of severe impact included various more established economies that began the crisis with fiscal problems and quickly experienced severe market pressures (defined as a credit default swap over five hundred in 2012). These included Greece, Ireland, Italy, Portugal, and Spain (Natali et al. 2014, 10, 11).

As a noneconomist experiencing the crisis in Italy, I watched in disbelief as "the market" seemed to target and take down, one by one, each nation that was perceived to be weakened and next in line for attack. Because the Italian government had accumulated a high debt ratio for its GDP, the costs to Italy of borrowing to keep its ship afloat rose to punishing and then unsustainable levels. The common wisdom in northern Europe seemed to track the European fairy tale "The Three Little Pigs." At one point, talking heads even referred to the most vulnerable countries as Europe's PIGS (Portugal, Italy, Greece, and Spain). These nations, all sharing a Mediterranean culture and geography, were typecast as the first of the three pigs who foolishly built his house of straw so he could enjoy *la dolce vita*. When the wolf of recession began to blow, this lazy little pig's house fell down because it was not built with sturdy bricks, like those built by the Germans. Ironically, data show that

Italian families are notoriously oriented toward saving rather than spending. They often build their houses out of stone and over a span of years, paying for the building materials with cash. The same cannot be said of their leaders. While the Italian people had one of the highest levels of personal savings and lowest levels of consumer and housing debt among developed nations, their leaders had been busy spending on themselves (OECD, for Household Savings indicator). There had been little or no bank speculation in Italy, since banks are highly regulated, but this mattered less to the market than Italy's apparent weakness in debt to GDP ratio.

It might surprise many Americans, but the United States is classified in this study as only "moderately affected," along with fifteen other nations, including the UK, Canada, France, Germany, Austria, and Belgium. These countries were struck because they were either highly indebted at the time of the recession (more than 60 percent of GDP) or experienced a rapid rise in indebtedness. But, while they suffered notable losses, they were not as hard hit as many of their peers (Natali et al. 2014, 10, 11).

Charting the Impact on Children of the Economic Crisis

The Natali research paper and Report Card Twelve consider many variables contributing to the fierce impact of the recession on children. They identify two factors as particularly important to children: "the position of parents in the labor market and the depleted capacity of states to protect families" (UNICEF 2014b, 14). But how did the crisis get from the global level to the microsystems where children live? Figure 1 of the Natali research paper is a flow chart titled "How did the financial crisis turn into a crisis for children?" (Natali et al. 2014, fig. 1). The crisis originated in the housing and banking sectors in the United States and spread to other parts of the world, quickly evolving from a financial crisis to an economic crisis. In some Eurozone countries, like Italy, it took the form of a sovereign-debt crisis. The flow chart begins with the "global financial crisis" and shows how "transmission channels," including labor markets, financial markets, and the public sector, allowed the crisis to flood downstream, creating "household impact," which flowed into "direct impact on children and youth." A decrease in demand for goods led to fewer jobs and a drop in household income, while the deterioration in financial markets resulted in a loss of private wealth and restricted both business and consumers from accessing credit. In the public sector, rapid deterioration of public finances prompted aggressive austerity programs and higher taxes or lower spending on public services (UNICEF 2014b, 15; Natali et al. 2014, fig. 1).

You may recognize these as the very same impacts that produced the effects we noted in describing how the recession harmed American children. The dominoes continued to fall. Family asset depletion meant that families lost their homes and savings. Reduced consumption meant that more children were skipping meals and wearing shoes that were too small. Stress and domestic violence meant more children in emergency rooms and missing school and skipping immunizations. And social exclusion meant that children were increasingly consigned to the bottom of the heap by their race, ethnic origin, or family structure. In the flow chart, we see a box at the bottom of the chart titled "Direct impact on children and youth." The list includes material deprivation, food insecurity, lack of capital investment in child health and child education, poor mental health, and inadequate child protection. Youth employment and dropping fertility rates are also classified as direct effects of the crisis. This chart is unique: because the authors began by asking "the child question" (What did all of this mean to children?) they are unsparing in examining what happened, down to the very last domino in the row (UNICEF 2014b, 15; Natali et al. 2014, fig. 1).

Was all of this inevitable? Were the dominoes already in place, making it unavoidable that the bursting of a Wall Street bubble would be so harmful to so many children in all of these nations? Not necessarily. The flow chart includes a box along the left side titled "Policies to contain the negative consequences of the macroeconomic shock." It represents policy responses that could flow laterally into the mix, to mitigate the impact of the crisis at various levels. These include monetary policies, fiscal policies, and social protection system responses. As the arrows pointing horizontally suggest, these policies could be introduced at various levels of the social economy—including financial markets, labor markets, and the public sector—to protect the household in time to prevent or mitigate direct harms to children (UNICEF 2014b, 15; Natali et al. 2014, fig. 1). This did not happen.

In the majority of cases, according to the researchers, monetary policy was "accommodating but inadequate, since policy interest rates were close to zero" (UNICEF 2014b, 15; Natali et al. 2014, fig. 1). In other words, as recession loomed, countries did not or could not combat it by cutting interest rates and spurring investment. Many countries depreciated their national currencies to help climb out of recession, but the Eurozone countries could not do this. Unlike the United States, where our Federal Reserve Bank controls the supply of dollars, those EU countries that adopted the euro were unable to mobilize monetary policy without the support of the EU's most powerful members. Countries like Germany, the Netherlands, Austria, and Belgium, content in their houses of brick, rejected the path of depreciating the euro to respond to the crisis of their Mediterranean neighbors. Instead, deep cuts and harsh austerity policies were demanded as the price of help from the ECB to the countries that were in deepest trouble (Krugman 2015).

For children's households, social protection systems could have been the dike that held back the flood. Policies such as robust unemployment insurance and a guaranteed minimum income can provide stabilizers that directly affect families. Various discretionary policies, such as cash payments mobilized early in the crisis and increases in public spending in the second period, were also potential tools for mitigating the impact of the crisis on the most vulnerable. Who got these income supports, insurance protections, and cash payments, and who suffered the deepest cuts? How different nations answered these questions had a very clear and direct impact on children (UNICEF 2014b, 15; Natali et al. 2014, fig. 1). Throughout Report Card Twelve, in order to provide real-world illustrations to accompany their analysis, the authors select different countries for focused, in-depth exploration. These case studies illustrate the effects on children of the crisis and how different nations coped with the challenge of protecting children from the spillover effects. One section explains the US method of calculating poverty (discussed in chapter 7) and provides a state-by-state comparison of changes in child poverty between 2006 and 2013. It also explores what the authors call "social safety, American-style" and discusses how the American approach to the social safety net affected outcomes for children (UNICEF 2014b, 37–39).

Of all the newly poor children in the OECD and/or the EU, about a third were in the United States. To counter the recession's effect on children and families, the United States adopted a number of programs, including expansion of the Earned Income Tax Credit (EITC), extension of unemployment benefits, and increases in SNAP funding. The term "after-tax and transfer income" (ATTI) used by the report refers to the income available to a family after government transfers are added to its own earnings. In order to get a picture of various resources available to families at or below the poverty line, the report breaks ATTI into five categories: 1) income earned by the family; 2) welfare payments from AFDC/TANF; 3) the EITC (Earned Income Tax Credit); 4) nutrition support through Food Stamps/SNAP; and 5) other programs such as veterans benefits, unemployment insurance, and workmen's compensation for injuries. One table in the Innocenti Report Card shows the relative contributions of these categories to a family's ATTI in 1982—a prior period of recession in the United States—and 2010 and looks at families below the poverty line (the poor) and families below 50 percent of the poverty line (the extreme poor). The contribution to reduction of poverty of TANF, the successor to AFDC, fell from almost 20 percent to less than 5 percent. In

2010, at the height of the crisis, TANF reached only two million families compared with five million receiving AFDC in 1994 and accounted for a much lower percentage of the income available to poor families in 2010 than in 1982. Unemployment insurance and EITC were significant sources for families at the poverty line, but those below 50 percent of the poverty line often did not qualify for these programs, which depend on a working parent earning income or having recently become unemployed. Overall, the safety net for children has weakened in the years between 1982 and 2010, and, at present, it favors children whose parents are employed or who recently lost their jobs, which leaves the most vulnerable children unprotected. Not surprisingly, extreme child-poverty rates rose more rapidly in the United States during the recession than during previous economic downturns (UNICEF 2014b, 39).

In summary, the depth of the recession varied according to many factors, including how much debt a nation had accumulated during the boom years, how robust a safety net existed prior to the crisis, and how aggressively public spending was utilized to turn the economy around. At the time the United States emerged from the recession, much of Europe was still struggling to escape its grip. Nobel Prize–winning economist Paul Krugman blames Europe's poor recovery on politics, ideology, and adherence to flawed economic theories that predicted recovery would be hastened by austerity and spending cuts. Many of these ideas were made in America. The powerful European nations that controlled the euro, foremost among them Germany, insisted that the Eurozone countries that were suffering the most must cut their spending the most. Children in Greece, Spain, and Italy were among those most affected. As Krugman explains,

> While European policy makers may have imagined that they were showing a praiseworthy openness to new economic ideas, the economists they chose to listen to were those telling them what they wanted to hear. They sought justifications for the harsh policies they were determined, for political and ideological reasons, to impose on debtor nations; they lionized economists like Harvard's Alberto Alesina, Carmen Reinhart, and Kenneth Rogoff, who seemed to offer that justification. As it turned out, however, all that exciting new research was deeply flawed, one way or another. (2015)

While there are still those such as Wolfgang Schäuble (2015) who disagree, I am convinced that Krugman (2012, 2015) and his colleagues are right (Warren 2017; Reich 2015; Stiglitz 2015, 2016; Piketty 2014). The old-fashioned notion that a recession calls for deficit spending helped the United States recover from the recession that began in America. In Italy, Berlusconi seemed to fiddle, caught up in his own legal problems. Mario Monti, who replaced him, shared the views of elitist economists about the need for austerity and reforms. Matteo Renzi, the young and vigorous president of the council who was asked to form a new government in 2014, tried to push back against pressure from the EU to continue the austerity policies that had brought his country down; instead, he looked to the American example. In a meeting with President Obama in April 2015, he explicitly embraced the Keynesian path advocated by the Obama administration involving public investments in infrastructure and education (Ciancio 2015). But neither Renzi nor his Democratic Party successor, Gentiloni, were able to turn back the tide of austerity.

As the recession receded in the rearview mirror, I have continued to wonder whether the US economic model would be a good fit for the Italian crisis. It places great emphasis on efficiency, individual autonomy, and privatization—an approach which seems to conflict with core values of Italian culture and history and undercuts the nation's unique strengths, such as social solidarity, strong families, attachment to the land, deep roots in one's community, and the Italian network of small businesses and local and regional agriculture. As we saw in prior chapters, many of these strengths are integral to the fabric of Italian childhood and cannot be ripped out without harming children.

One thing is certain: the impact of the crisis will be felt far into the future, not least in the next generation of young families. Europeans speak of a lost generation of youth who have been sacrificed to balance national budgets and bolster financial markets. The NEET rate (percentage of youth aged fifteen to twenty-four not in employment, education, or training) is at an all-time high, having gone up everywhere and tripled in the countries most affected. Young people cannot plan on careers, marriage, and children. Even when they find employment, youth are often underemployed and in highly precarious positions. These lost years of earning cannot be recovered. It is fair to say that the transition from childhood to adulthood has stalled for even larger percentages of young people in Europe than in the United States.

The recession has also exacerbated the Italian "baby bust" discussed in chapter 5 and stunted the progress of women in the workforce. The birth rate has continued its downslide from its high point of 1.46 in 2010 to 1.34 in 2017 and shows no signs of recovering. One gloomy headline from July 2018 laments: "This is no country for mothers: For women it is ever more difficult to combine work and motherhood and many of the measures designed to help those who try are about to lapse for lack of funding" (Querzé 2018). With the costs of daycare in the asilo nido out of reach for many working women, the percentage of mothers of young children in the workforce has been dropping instead of rising as policy-makers had hoped it would (Querzé 2018). As one thirty-six-year-old mother who works in a clothing store explained: "If I hadn't had the help of my parents I could never have had a baby. I wouldn't have been able to afford the daycare fees, especially because my husband was unemployed when my daughter was small" (Pivas 2018). Any country that is no country for mothers is, by definition, no country for children.

The Aftermath of Recession: A Story of Backlash, Isolation and Denial

In chapter 7, we saw the impact of a Wall Street crisis trickling down to the small worlds in which US children live. In this chapter we have seen how the crisis metastasized in Italy and Europe. One thing has been clear: economic meltdowns hurt children even more than they hurt adults. Hunger and malnutrition, while temporary stressors to the adult organism, cause permanent damage to the growing body and brain of a child. While homelessness, domestic violence, and poverty are traumas that harm adults, they cut far deeper in children for whom stability and security are essential to the formation of a neurological foundation of trust and resilience that occurs in early childhood. Children who routinely miss meals, school, or health care can be expected to feel the consequences not for a month or a year but for their entire lives.

As data on the effects of the recession on children accumulated, experts proposed numerous ways in which government policies could be improved to alleviate the harms already suffered and prevent new risks. In the United States, increased funding for SNAP and CHIP, debt relief for homeowners, affordable housing for renters, expansion of early-childhood programs, staffing of preventive services, and affordable childcare—the list goes on of the ways in which we could have mitigated harms to our children while at the same time prodding a recovering economy back to life.

As noted in chapter 7, the Obama administration found its progressive child-friendly policies blocked at many turns by opposition from right-wing Republicans. While Obama scored some victories, he suffered many defeats in his attempts to combat child poverty, food insecurity, access to housing and health care, and protection against maltreatment (Stuckler and Basu 2013; Woodhouse and Woodhouse 2018). But in 2016, with the polls predicting a win by Hillary Clinton, a long-time supporter of children's rights, advocates for children were cautiously optimistic that the next administration would continue the gradual improvements in child well-being and the progressive family policies of the Obama administration. The shock of Clinton's unexpected defeat was followed by the even greater shock of the Trump administration's open hostility toward children.

This hostility is consistent with the larger themes of backlash, isolationism, and denialism that characterize the Trump administration. Backlash against the immigrants and elites whom Trump has demonized as the villains who are to blame for middle- and working-class Americans' woes. Isolation from the rest of the world community through an escalation of "America First" policies, fueled by imaginary grievances. And denialism as the response to documented threats—such as global warming, carcinogenic toxins, and growing inequality—that scientific evidence indicates are all too real. As this book goes to press, the prospects for poor and middle-class children in the United States have worsened dramatically. Instead of acting to remedy the damage to children caused by the recession, the Trump administration has embraced none of the options listed above. Instead it has imposed drastic cuts on programs for poor children while cutting taxes for the richest Americans.

Perhaps the most stinging indictment of these policies came on May 4, 2018, when the secretariat of the United Nations (UN) issued the "Report of the Special Rapporteur on extreme poverty and human rights on his mission to the United States of America" (UN General Assembly 2018). The report was authored by Philip G. Alston, the John Norton Pomeroy Professor of Law at New York University and co-chair of its Center for Human Rights and Global Justice. In his role as special rapporteur for the UN Human Rights Council, he had been tasked with evaluating the extent to which the US government's programs for addressing extreme poverty were consistent with the nation's human-rights obligations. Such visits are a routine part of accountability mechanisms that apply to all members of the UN. The visit was at the invitation of and facilitated by the Trump administration, and his report was based on meetings with federal, state, and local officials; a variety of stakeholders; and a wealth of statistics from the US Census Bureau, as well as other respected sources of research and data. His report, which produced a firestorm, is worth quoting at length; it paints a very alarming picture.

Here are some of the key points from the report's "Overview" (paragraph numbers and footnotes omitted):

> The United States is a land of stark contrasts. It is one of the world's wealthiest societies, a global leader in many areas, and a land of unsurpassed technological and other forms of innovation. Its corporations are global trendsetters, its civil society is vibrant and sophisticated and its higher education system leads the world. But its immense wealth and expertise stand in shocking contrast with the conditions in which vast numbers of its citizens live. About 40 million live in poverty, 18.5 million in extreme poverty, and 5.3 million live in Third World conditions of absolute poverty. It has the highest youth poverty rate in

the OECD and the highest infant mortality rate among comparable OECD States. Its citizens live shorter, sicker lives compared to those living in all other rich democracies, eradicable tropical diseases are increasingly prevalent, and it has the world's highest incarceration rate, one of the lowest levels of voter registration among OECD countries and the highest obesity levels in the developed world.

The United States has the highest rate of income inequality among Western countries. The 1.5 trillion in tax cuts in December 2017 overwhelmingly benefited the wealthy and worsened inequality. The consequences of neglecting poverty and promoting inequality are clear. The United States has one of the highest poverty and inequality levels among OECD countries, and the Stanford Center on Inequality and Poverty ranks it 18th out of 21 wealthy countries in terms of labor markets, poverty rates, safety nets, wealth inequality and economic mobility. But in 2018 the United States had over 25 per cent of the world's 2,208 billionaires. There is thus a dramatic contrast between the immense wealth of the few and the squalor and deprivation in which vast numbers of Americans exist. For almost five decades the overall policy response has been neglectful at best, but the policies pursued over the past year seem deliberately designed to remove basic protections from the poorest, punish those who are not in employment and make even basic health care into a privilege to be earned rather than a right of citizenship. (UN General Assembly 2018)

Although the data points contained in the report's "Overview" are depressingly familiar to academic researchers, rarely if ever have the American people been presented with the stark reality of poverty in the United States in such brutal and unflinching language. The report is "political" only in the sense that it highlights particular factors that were identified as contributing to the nation's high rates of poverty. These included racism, cuts to welfare programs beginning in the Clinton administration, high rates of inequality, disenfranchisement of the poor through gerrymandering and barriers to voting, failure to set a livable minimum wage, reliance on criminalization rather than prevention of crime, privatization of public functions, and deployment by political leaders of myths about fraud and the unworthiness of the poor as a strategy to undercut public support for antipoverty initiatives.

Alston explicitly singled out the Trump administration for criticism, noting that his report came at a time of radical changes in the direction of US policies. The report highlights a list of newly implemented policies that were sure to worsen the current situation, including: providing unprecedented financial windfalls to the very wealthy; paying for these tax cuts by cutting benefits to the poor; embarking on destructive deregulation in financial, environmental, health, and safety programs; neglecting health care by reducing twenty million poor and middle-class persons to the ranks of the uninsured; unduly restricting and erecting spurious obstacles to safety-net coverage; increasing spending on defense while refusing to improve veterans benefits; failing to address the opiate crisis; and making no effort to tackle the structural racism that keeps a large percentage of non-whites in or near poverty.

The Trump administration reacted as might be expected. The ambassador to the UN, Nikki Haley, launched a scathing attack on Alston, stating, "I am deeply disappointed that the Special Rapporteur used his platform to make misleading and politically motivated statements about American domestic policy issues." She charged that Alston had "categorically misstated the progress the United States has made in addressing poverty . . . in [his] biased reporting." She rejected the entire premise of the visit: "It is patently ridiculous for the United Nations to examine poverty in America. . . . The special rapporteur wasted the UN's time and resources, deflecting attention from the world's worst human rights abusers and focusing instead on the wealthiest and freest country in the world" (Pilkington 2018). One UK newspaper, employing the British gift for understatement, observed that Haley's comments "prompted puzzlement as Alston had carried out his investigation at the formal invitation of the Trump administration" (Pilkington 2018).

The report had come at an awkward time for the Trump administration, as it was under intensive criticism because of the outcry over its policy forcibly separating young children from their parents as they attempted to cross into the United States from Mexico. The Trump administration had been signaling its displeasure with the UN Human Rights Council for many months because of the council's criticism of Israel. In the midst of the outcry over family separations, and just two days before Haley issued her attack on the poverty report, the United States formally announced its resignation from the council (Borger 2018). This marked the first time any state had withdrawn from it since its inception in 2006 (Pilkington 2018). Reports surfaced after the resignation that Trump officials had warned the rapporteur that, in his report on poverty, he would be wise to avoid damaging US support for the UN. The Trump administration appeared to be making good on its threats.

The report specifically addresses child poverty in the United States in sections 37 through 41, titled "Social protection for children." It notes that 18 percent of US children (13.3 million) were living in poverty in 2016 as defined by US official measures. About 20 per cent of children were living in "relative income poverty" (the international metric) compared to an OECD average of 13 per cent. It noted that the United States ranked 25th out of 29 industrialized nations in investing in early-childhood education. On any given night in 2017, about 21 per cent of individuals in homeless shelters were children (a total of 114,829 children). In 2015–16, over 1,304,800 school children experienced homelessness. The infant mortality rate was 5.8 deaths per 1,000 live births—almost 50 percent higher than the OECD average of 3.9. While noting that expansion of CHIP and Medicaid had extended access to health care to a historic high of 95 percent, it warned that these programs were under threat from Trump administration policies. While crediting the Supplemental Nutrition Assistance Program (SNAP) and the Earned Income Tax Credit with lifting many children out of poverty, it noted that Temporary Assistance to Needy Families (TANF), the primary social welfare program for extremely poor families, only reached 23 percent of poor families and in some states as few as 10 percent.

While some might quibble over various approaches and methods of calculation, there is simply no escaping the fact that the US record on child welfare is abysmal, not only when compared to other nations but when examined at national and state levels. Study after study confirms the take-home message of the UN Poverty Report: America can and should do much better on many measures of child well-being.

Tracking the Five Childhood Enders

In recognition of the magnitude of the economic crisis within children's small worlds, Save the Children in 2017 began utilizing a new index called "Childhood Enders." The goal of the index is to identify when a child is not merely "impacted" by a toxic ecology but actually missing out on childhood itself (Save the Children 2017a). The five "Enders" identified in this index are: (1) when a child dies; (2) when a child is malnourished; (3) when a child drops out of school; (4) when a child is a victim of violence; and (5) when a child has a child. The study was comparative and global. The End of Childhood Index Results ranked the United States in 36th place out of 118 nations studied. Obviously, nations such as Bolivia, Rwanda, and Colombia (ranking 116, 117, and 118, respectively) have much further to go than the United States in assuring a fair start for all of their children. But childhood poverty in the United States is hardly "fake news," despite the Trump administration's protestations.

A companion publication focusing on the United States titled "Stolen Childhoods" provides a more detailed study of why too many childhoods are ending too soon in a rich country like the United States (Save the Children 2017b). In 2018, it was followed by a study focusing on the plight of rural children in the United States titled *Growing up Rural in America*. It calculates that 14.1 million US children are growing up in poverty (Save the Children 2018b, 4). Contrary to stereotypes about urban poverty, the study found that rural rates of child poverty, at 23.5 percent, are higher than urban rates, at 18.8 percent, and rural children had suffered more from the recession than their urban counterparts. In some counties, 41 percent of children were living in poverty. A state-by-state analysis also confirmed that the most severe levels of poverty are in states commonly identified as Trump country, including Nevada, New Mexico, Oklahoma, Arkansas, Louisiana, Mississippi, Alabama, Georgia, and South Carolina, with as many as one in four children living in poverty (Save the Children 2018b, 6). Looking at other Childhood Enders, the data from an often overlooked segment—rural America—was especially alarming.

Infant Mortality

Rural rates of infant mortality, at 6.5 percent per 1,000 live births, were higher than urban rates, at 5.44. In both settings, minority race and ethnicity as well as poverty were associated with higher mortality rates. In Alabama and Mississippi, rates of infant mortality were 9.1 and 8.6, respectively—higher than rates in nations such as Malaysia and Romania (Save the Children 2018b, 12; World Bank, for mortality rate, infant, per 1,000 live births).

Malnutrition

The study found that food insecurity, which had soared during the height of the recession, still remained very high, with 14 percent of children (12.9 million children) in food-insecure households and 703,000 children living in households with severe food insecurity, regularly going hungry or missing a meal (Save the Children 2018b, 13).

Leaving School

In 2016, 707,000 US teenagers aged sixteen to nineteen were not in school and had not graduated from high school. The national dropout rate was 15.9 percent, and in more than ten states dropout rates exceeded 20 percent and peaked at 29 percent. For too many youth, high-school graduation marks an end of education and not a new beginning. Again, rural youth fared worse than their urban counterparts. Only 29 percent of rural youth were enrolled in higher education, compared to 48 percent in urban areas (Save the Children 2018b, 14).

Violence

The rate of deaths by homicide and suicide during childhood, at 6.5 per 100,000, are higher in the United States than in any other developed country. Variations from state to state are large, ranging from a low of 2.8 in Connecticut to a high of 14.2 in Montana. Accidents with cars and firearms exacted a heavy toll. Once again defying stereotypes, the risk of violent death was 20 to 30 percent higher in rural than in urban areas (Save the Children 2018b, 15).

Children Having Children

While adolescent birth rates have been dropping nationwide, they have been dropping more slowly in rural areas. In 2016, teenaged girls gave birth to 209,809 babies, with the highest rates in Southern states. A huge gap has opened between white girls in urban and rural environments: white rural girls are 250 times more likely than white urban girls to become teenaged mothers (Save the Children 2018b, 16).

If American children are looking for a champion in the White House, as the UN Report on Poverty suggests, they will have to wait for a new election cycle. Documenting all the ways in which the Trump administration, even during its first year in power, has harmed the nation's children would require a volume of its own. In fact, the *Family Court Review* in April 2018 published a special issue documenting the Trump administration's violations of children's rights (Stark 2018). Together with my husband, an expert on food law, I researched and published an article in this special issue, focusing on Trump's policies toward children's nutrition (Woodhouse and Woodhouse 2018). These policies include deregulation of carcinogenic pesticides, cuts to SNAP and school-lunch programs, rollbacks on regulations promoting nutrition labeling, rollbacks on programs to reduce obesity, and even cutbacks on funding for the Women, Infants and Children's food programs. These policies are characterized by a combination of greed, fear, isolationism, and science denialism.

The deterioration of US support for children's well-being has had repercussions around the world as well as in the United States, through Trump administration cutbacks of foreign-aid funding. External policies have also been tainted by pressure from global corporations and heavy doses of anti–science denialism. One small example of the global reach of US policies occurred in July 2018. Experts around the globe have agreed for forty years that the breastfeeding of infants is a key element in reducing infant mortality; an estimated 823,000 babies' lives could be saved each year by implementing policies that promote maternal lactation whenever possible and discourage marketing of artificial substitutes for breast milk. In a move that stunned world health officials, the Trump administration came close to defeating a UN resolution encouraging breast feeding. It forced Ecuador, the sponsoring nation, to withdraw the amendment by threatening it with punishing trade measures. Officials from other poor UN member countries in Africa and Latin America were so fearful of retaliation that they would not agree to take up sponsorship. The administration even threatened to withdraw funding from the World Health Organization (Jacobs 2018).

The policy director of the British group Baby Milk Action expressed the revulsion of the world health community when she commented: "We were astonished, appalled and also saddened. What happened was tantamount to blackmail. With the United States holding the world hostage and trying to overturn nearly 40 years of consensus on the best way to protect infant and young child health." Only when Russia agreed to sponsor the measure did the United States back off (Jacobs 2018). It is unclear how much of the Trump administration's opposition was prompted by lobbying from the infant formula industry. But Trump was already on record for his hostility to breast feeding, which he views as "disgusting," and his failure to support sound lactation policies in the United States (Woodhouse and Woodhouse 2018). In common with many of the Trump administration's policies, this policy flew in the face of an overwhelming scientific consensus. It is no exaggeration to say that the Trump administration has blasted a hole in the myth of American family values. It is difficult to predict what may lie ahead.

The isolationist sentiment was also rising on both sides of the Atlantic. While it had been brewing in many EU nations, Brexit was the first big shock wave. The advocates favoring Brexit won by a small margin, but, as of this writing, Brexit represents the new reality. Backlash, denialism, and isolationism in the wake of the recession reverberated in other parts of the EU, and especially strongly in Italy. Italy's recovery, as we have noted, was much slower than that of the United States, which could print dollars and use deficit spending to jump-start its economic recovery. The EU, by contrast, kept a tight rein on the euro, blocking deficit spending by its constituent nations. It refused to consider investments in infrastructure and social programs until Italy had reduced its deficit.

In chapter 7, we compared the economies of Italy and the United States and the pace of recovery in each country, using various measures of well-being, from GDP to Gini coefficient and GCI. Italy's marked improvement in the GCI (Global Competitiveness Index) was achieved at the cost of severe austerity measures imposed by the EU that cut deeply into Italian social welfare programs and raised taxes on already struggling families and businesses. Those cuts and taxes, compounding the ill effects of the prolonged economic crisis, fed the discontent that led to the Italian backlash against immigrants and political elites. In the summer of 2019, the Italian coalition government, an uneasy partnership of the nativist League and the antiestablishment Five Star Movement, fell victim to overreach by Matteo Salvini, leader of the League, and was replaced by a more moderate but still uneasy coalition of the Five Star Movement and the center left Democrats, with Giuseppe Conte remaining as Prime Minister. Elsewhere in Europe, signs point to a strengthening of the nativist and isolationist elements, with the closing of borders and rising rates of hate crime fueled by some leaders' open expressions of racism and ethnic hostility. The latest flare-up is occurring in France, where the "Yellow Jackets" are rebelling against Macron's reforms, which are intended to make France leaner and more competitive globally but further erode the quality of life for working- and middle-class citizens. In this movement, as in the coalition government in Italy, we may be seeing the emergence of a new and troubling left-right populism (Zakaria 2018).

In the next chapter I will argue that these exosystemic developments in Europe and the United States are symptoms of a much larger macrosystemic reality—the ever-sharper and more corrosive discontents of globalization.

9

Globalization

The Elephant in the Playroom

Globalisation is a multi-dimensional process characterized by:

The acceptance of a set of economic rules for the entire world designed to maximize profits and productivity by universalizing markets and production, and to obtain the support of the state with a view to making the national economy more productive and competitive;

technological innovation and organisational change centred on flexibilisation and adaptability;

the expansion of a specific form of social organisation based on information as the main source of productivity and power;

the reduction of the welfare state, privatization of social services, flexibilization of labor relations and weaker trade unions;

de facto transfer to trans-national organizations of the control of national economic policy instruments, such as monetary policy, interest rates and fiscal policy;

the dissemination of common cultural values, but also the re-emergence of nationalism, cultural conflict and social movements.

—UNESCO, "Globalisation"

This definition from the UNESCO glossary illustrates the many dimensions of what must be acknowledged as the dominant macrosystemic force of our time. The definition of "globalization" is contested terrain. A specialist in labor relations might define it with reference to its effects on labor markets, while a business scholar in defining it might focus exclusively on its economic dimensions. Globalization can be defined in both of these ways and more. As Manfred B. Steger points out in his book *Globalization: A Very Short Introduction*, defining globalization is a lot like the fable of the blind sages attempting to describe an elephant (2017). One sage grasps the tail and says the elephant is like a brush; another starts at the leg and declares that the elephant is like a tree trunk. As I researched the ecology of childhood, I found myself, like the sages of the story, grasping at various elements of the macrosystem and trying to understand what I had encountered. Various factors seemed to pose existential threats to children's small worlds, and on a very large scale. These overarching elements that emerged from my research included unrestrained capitalism, technological revolution, rising inequality, mass migration, growing racial and ethnic division, and the global threat of climate change. Each of these phenomena seemed distinct, yet interconnected. When I put them all together, I realized I had come face to face with the elephant in the playroom.

Globalization, for all its promise and benefits, poses an apocalyptic threat to the small worlds of children. An apocalypse is a day of reckoning. Environmentalists looking at climate change on a global scale have long feared that the day of reckoning is already upon us (Solomon et al. 2009). In studying the ecology of children, we have seen the effects of the economic crisis, both in the United States and in Europe. Many of the factors I have identified seemed to play a role in making the recession more profound and the recovery slower than at any time since the Great Depression. In fields including science, international law, ethics, and liberal democracy, the dynamic they created has placed at risk a host of values we thought were secure. The various dimensions of globalization overlap and intertwine to produce rapid and destabilizing changes in the way people work and live, and in how they think about their lives and those of their children (Light 2017; Poushter 2016). It is clear that globalization has contributed to altering children's social and natural environments. While entire books have been written on globalization and its dimensions, my focus here is upon its implications for the ecology of childhood. To introduce each factor, I will provide a quotation from a global sage I have quoted before—Pope Francis.

Globalization

> I recognize that globalization has helped many people to lift themselves out of poverty, but it has condemned many others to starve. It is true that in absolute terms the world's wealth has grown, but inequality has also increased and new [forms of] poverty have arisen. (Vatican Radio 2015)

Globalization as a concept first captured public attention as an international buzzword in the 1990s (Steger 2017). As the metaphor of the elephant illustrated, it has been difficult to pin down a precise description. Professor Steger, in his book *Globalization: A Very Short Introduction*, identifies six dimensions of globalization—historical, economic, political, cultural, ecological, and ideological. As he states in his preface to the new, fourth edition, "The transformative powers of globalization reach deeply into *all* aspects of contemporary social life.... It is best thought of as a multidimensional set of objective and subjective processes that resists confinement to any thematic framework" (Steger 2017, xv). Steger argues that globalization, in all its complexity, is implicated in a vast range of pressing global problems including social inequality, the rise of global terrorism, the escalating climate crisis, growing streams of refugees, and the electoral victories of populist candidates.

As Pope Francis recognized, globalization has certainly enriched our lives in many ways. Wealth, in absolute terms, has grown. Diseases have been tamed and eradicated and across the globe more people are living longer. Countries that once seemed distant can be reached in a few hours. Goods and people from other parts of the globe that once took months in transit arrive in days or hours. Ideas and images appear in seconds via the worldwide web. Many books have been written in defense of globalization, exploring the ways in which humanity has been enriched by the breaking down of barriers between national economies (Bhagwati 2007; Easterbrook 2018). But globalization has also resulted in rapid and destabilizing change, and critics are concerned about the effects of these changes in each of the dimensions identified above (Steger 2017; Rodrik 2011; Stiglitz 2002, 2018).

Looking at children's ecology, globalization is shaping virtually all of the exosystems that combine to create their social and physical environments. Their parents' workplace is a striking example. In both Italy and the United States, the effects of globalization—including erosions of labor unions, competition from cheap labor in other countries, the high premium placed on flexibility, and the centrality of the profit motive—have destabilized old patterns of employment, made workers redundant, and threatened many formerly secure middle- and working-class jobs (Brainard and Litan 2004; Holger 2011). Jobs in manufacturing, once a ladder to a secure lifestyle, have been hit especially hard. One can still find items that are genuinely "Made in Italy" or "Made in the USA," but even in supposedly domestic corporations, a large proportion of production in these countries (as well as services such as customer relations, marketing, and research and development, once believed immune to international outsourcing) is characterized by fragmentation and mechanization or has been off-shored (Brainard and Litan 2004; Holger 2011; Stiglitz 2012).

Pope Francis spoke of globalization as a source of new forms of poverty and rising inequality, both of which are toxic to children, but globalization hurts children in other ways. We are all familiar with the plight of children in poor countries where globalization can lead to their exploitation as sex workers, low-wage laborers, and servants. Although less dramatic, the harm to children in wealthier nations is also becoming more apparent; we see it, for example, in the plight of young people who cannot afford to marry or start a family. As Pope Francis noted in an interview with the authors of a book profiling the social teaching of the Church under his leadership,

> When money, instead of man, is at the centre of the system, when money becomes an idol, men and women are reduced to simple instruments of a social and economic system, which is characterised, better yet dominated, by profound inequalities. So we discard whatever is not useful to this logic; it is this attitude that discards children and older people, and is now affecting the young. I was shocked to learn that, in developed countries, there are many millions of young people under 25 who are jobless. I have dubbed them the 'neither-nor' youth, because they neither study nor work. They do not study because they do not have the opportunity to do so, they do not work because there are no jobs. (2015a)

The Pope's "neither-nor" youth are the NEETS of the UNICEF Report Cards discussed in previous chapters. Pope Francis's observations touch on several dimensions of globalization: the economic, the cultural, and the profit motive as a driving force crowding out other concerns. A global economy that allows its old people to die of exposure, and does not produce jobs for its young, is an economy that kills, by inches and by generations.

Not enough attention has been paid to the psychological harms to children of a particular dimension of globalization: the presumption of a taste for mobility that people with young children do not necessarily share. The prevailing economic theories are simple: if a job can be done more cheaply in country X than in country Y, then the job should go to country X. Workers can follow the jobs within their country or emigrate if they need work and cannot find it. This economic model presumes a rootlessness and nonchalance toward the human costs of mobility that appears to be peculiarly American.

When Alexis de Tocqueville visited the United States in 1831, he was struck by the American attitude toward pulling up stakes and moving on: "In the United States a man will carefully construct a home in which to spend his old age and sell it before the roof is on. . . . He will settle in one place only to go off elsewhere afterwards with a new set of desires" (2003, 623). As a nation of immigrants, it is not surprising that Americans embrace change as a positive good. Relocation is just part of the job.

By contrast, Italians have a far more ambivalent relationship to geographic mobility. As I mentioned earlier, the most popular Italian quiz shows treat where you were born as much more significant even to modern-day Italians than where you live today. Italian hosts (*presentatori*) always ask the contestants to introduce themselves; name and place are the sine qua non of Italian self-introductions. "I am Marcello Bruno and I come from Scilla in Calabria"; "I am Maria Bianca and I come from Assisi in Umbria." Italian women have never had the tradition of abandoning their birth surname and taking their husband's. They retain their surnames from cradle to grave. Also, one's birthplace seems to matter far more than one's profession. I soon noticed that, long after they have left their birthplace for jobs in other regions and cities, Italians tend to self-identify as coming from the region of their birth and not their current place of residence, or they provide the city where they currently live and work but quickly add that this was not their real home and they had come from elsewhere ("I live in Torino but I come from Calabria").

Sometimes it seems as if the mainstream economists and scientific researchers who study child development inhabit different universes. While economists advocate breaking down barriers to movement, psychologists document the harms inflicted on children by an increasingly mobile economy. For experts in child development, stability and continuity rank near the top in the hierarchy of children's basic emotional needs, right behind the number-one requirement: attachment to a loving parental figure. Movement of people and jobs is not cost free to children. Studies show that a move can be as traumatic to some children as the death of a loved one or parents' separation and divorce (Oishi and Schimmack 2010). A parent's decision to stay in a lower-paying job rather than move to follow the market can be a rational choice from the perspective of children's welfare. When families are forced to migrate, especially internationally, children lose ties with extended family members and supportive communities (Batista-Pinto Wiese 2010).

In my teaching, I use a case study from a psychiatrist's caseload to illustrate these costs. In their book *The Boy Who Was Raised as a Dog and Other Stories from a Child Psychiatrist's Notebook: What Traumatized Children Can Teach Us About Loss, Love, and Healing*, psychiatrist Bruce D. Perry and journalist Maia Szalavitz tell the story of a young family, a homemaker mother and a wage-earner father, forced to move away from the city where they had grown up, married, and started their family in order for the father to find work. The young mother, who had mild developmental disabilities, had been doing well raising her young son. Deprived of the support of her extended family and parenting a new infant in a strange place, she was unable to cope, with tragic consequences. Overwhelmed by the conflicting demands of a toddler and a fussy infant, she simply left the infant to cry in his crib and spent her days out of the house with the toddler. This case came to Dr. Perry's attention more than twenty years later when he was trying to untangle why the older son had grown into a responsible adult while the younger son, seeming to lack any sense of empathy, was a convicted murderer on death row (Perry and Szalavitz 2006).

Employment statistics do not convey these human costs. Nor do they convey the trauma to a child of the departure of a parent who must leave home in order to find work to sustain the family. Relocations are often compounded by other traumatic circumstances, such as a parent's loss of employment or escape from violence. As studies show, the children left behind, especially when the departing parent is a mother, may suffer disruption and neglect (Yanovich 2015). These costs are difficult to figure into economic calculations, yet they are very real to children and have continuing implications for society.

Unrestrained Capitalism

> Just as the commandment "Thou shalt not kill" sets a clear limit in order to safeguard the value of human life, today we also have to say "thou shalt not" to an economy of exclusion and inequality. Such an economy kills. . . . Some people continue to defend trickle-down theories which assume that economic growth, encouraged by a free market will inevitably succeed in bringing about greater justice and inclusiveness in the world. This opinion, which has never been confirmed by the facts, expresses a crude and naïve trust in the goodness of those wielding economic power and in the sacralized workings of the prevailing economic system. (Pope Francis 2013, 53, 54)

Pope Francis caused quite a stir in his 2013 apostolic exhortation, coauthored with Pope Emeritus Benedetto XVI, when he dubbed unrestrained capitalism "the economy that kills" (53). They are not alone in harboring doubts about our current models of capitalism. Since the recession, even in the United States economists and public leaders have been calling attention to the evils of a system that worships profit and efficiency and treats human beings as fungible and dispensable. Critics in the United States blame the outsize power of big banks and big business for decades of deregulation, the loosening of government controls and relaxation of consumer protections that precipitated the economic crisis. The recession produced many changes but, according to experts such as Paul Krugman, Robert Reich, Jospeh Stiglitz, and Elizabeth Warren, it has not changed the balance of power between Wall Street and Main Street (Reich 2015, 2018; Krugman 2017; Warren 2017; Stiglitz 2012,

2017). Even in the aftermath of the economic crisis, Congress failed to enact controls sufficient to prevent a future crisis.

Why is the United States so admiring of big business and wary of big government? It seems to have been baked into our culture from the start. Perhaps because the Europeans who settled the United States were often fleeing oppression and looking for freedom and opportunity, the United States has a long tradition of celebrating rugged individualism and freedom from government restraints. A strong strand of libertarian philosophy is very much alive today in the Tea Party movement. Consider the phrase "right to work": in the United States, "right-to-work" laws, popular in many so-called red states, refer to laws that undercut the ability of labor to organize and to unionize a workplace. In Italy, the color charts on TV and in printed media during elections use red and blue as shorthand, just as we do in the United States— except that, in Italy, the color red is used to identify parties on the left of the political spectrum while the color blue stands for those on the right. Likewise, the term "right to work" carries a very different meaning for the two nations. In the United States it denotes a legislation that is antiunion; in Italy, the right to work is understood as a right to a government that fosters full employment, provides workplace protections against arbitrary termination, and facilitates union representation to protect workers from overreaching by employers. Italy has more union members than any other EU country (Fulton 2015). By comparison, union membership in the United States as of 2014 was at its lowest level since the Great Depression, with only 13 percent of workers belonging to a union, down from a peak of 34.8 percent in 1954 (Desilver 2014). According to Ana Swanson, writing about NPR's Planet Money study of the decline of unions, "Unions remain deeply contentious in America. Neoclassical economics considers a union a monopoly on the supply of labor, and thus a kind of market inefficiency. Yet other economic studies suggest that the decline of unions has led to changing realities for workers that are not so pretty—including stagnating wages for men, and even a decline in marriage" (Swanson 2015).

Another difference between the two nations lies in their philosophies of wealth creation. In the United States during recent decades, the intellectual elite and politicians in Republican and often even Democratic camps were deeply influenced by the Chicago school of economics, which is the source of what Pope Francis refers to as "trickle-down theories." These economists saw regulation as an unnecessary barrier to the free functioning of economic markets and believed that markets were inherently self-correcting and that prosperity at the top would trickle down to lift up the working classes. Take care of the job creators, and the jobs will take care of themselves. The recession has changed the minds of some free-market economists, most prominently Judge Richard Posner, who acknowledged that "his one-time support for deregulating the financial industry was based on a 'basic misunderstanding'" (HuffPost Business 2012). However, the notion that government regulation is inherently bad remains a bedrock principle for many Americans.

Capitalism in its most unrestrained form is alien to modern Italian history and culture. The Italian Constitution opens with the words "Italy is a democratic republic, founded on work" (Art. 1 Costituzione). The principles of social and economic solidarity are repeated again and again in this document. The Italian labor movement played a key role in founding of the Republic in 1946 and has remained strong until very recent times. While there are many Italians who support strong labor and government regulation to protect jobs and strengthen the safety net, free-market economics exported from the USA has influenced many Italian elites and policy-makers. In Italy, the 1960s, 1970s, and 1980s are thought of as the years of the "Italian miracle." Still recovering from the devastation of World War II, Italy's economy took off and manufacturing flourished. A robust labor movement protected Italian workers from wage exploitation and "Made in Italy" became a major selling point for many products. In the years after Italy switched from the lira to the euro, the economy slowed, and Italy suffered from a number of stubborn problems. Corruption that was spread by crime "families" such as the Mafia, Camorra, and 'Ndrangheta, and exploitation by an entrenched political class were two of the most damaging. When the recession struck, Italy was floundering under the leadership of Silvio Berlusconi, who was famous for evading taxes and consorting with underage prostitutes. His successor, Mario Monti, provided more sober leadership, but his response to the crisis was shaped by his past as a student of the Chicago school and an economist at an elite Italian university. The EU had been demanding deep cuts in spending as a price for EU support and got them. "Austerity" is the name Europeans give to the budget balancing policies that, in the United States, stunted the effectiveness of the American Recovery Act and persisted throughout the Obama administration in the sequester. Although the US recession is over, under pressure from deficit hawks the Trump administration has continued to cut spending on essential social services while also cutting tax rates on the wealthiest Americans under the doubtful theory that the deficits will be erased by economic growth resulting from the tax cuts. In Italy, in response to EU pressure in 2011, and lacking the option of printing more euros to invest in infrastructure, Mario Monti's "technical government" raised taxes, cut services, and sought to increase productivity by increasing competitiveness (*Economist* 2012). The wisdom of the Chicago school held that Italian global competition was being hampered by too much regulation and too many protections for workers. As we have seen in prior chapters, in the countries hardest hit by recession such as Greece, Spain and Italy, many longstanding protections for workers and their families have been gutted and the safety net for the poor and unemployed is now badly frayed.

Why is it that policies that have been discredited in the United States continue to exert such a pull on Italian policy-makers? I know that everywhere I go in Italy, Italians seem to assume that systems and conditions in the United States must be superior. Like the population of the United States, most Italians have not internalized what we see in international comparisons. To this day, "finding America" is a popular Italian slang expression for good luck, especially if it involves a sudden boost in one's socioeconomic status. *Hai trovato l'America!* (you found America!) is what one says, with a tinge of envy, to a friend who lands a great new job or wins big in the lottery. It remains to be seen whether finding American-style capitalism is something for Italians to celebrate or approach with caution. The voters clearly favored a return to the more traditional welfare state. The coalition government formed in May of 2018 has promised to reinstitute many of the traditional job protections for workers that had been abolished by the Monti government and have proposed a new *reddito di cittadinanza* (citizens' income), a payment that would guarantee all citizens a minimum income.

An Exercise in Triangulation: The Meaning of Money

In 2014, I interviewed a seventy-year-old woman, still quite beautiful and widely traveled, who had been born in Anversa degli Abruzzi, a small mountain town located twelve kilometers north and three thousand feet below Scanno. Describing her childhood, she spoke of the freedom to play and the sense of safety and belonging. The town sits above a ravine cut by a swiftly flowing river, and as we walked together through a wooded valley that once had been filled with intensively cultivated farms, she recalled how, in summer months, her mother would give her a sandwich of bread and cheese and she would run down to the valley and spend the day playing with the other children while the women washed laundry on the rocks by the river. But it was not this idyllic memory of an Italian childhood that stuck with me after our talk. I had heard this theme from adults of all ages and even teenagers reflecting on current childhoods in Abruzzo. What struck me was the woman's observation that money had changed everything. "Before the war, no one needed money. If your family grew crops and my family made ceramic pots, or your family had sheep and my family wanted cheese, we traded with each other. After the war, you could not survive without money. People began leaving in order to find jobs that paid money. Some went to Milano or Bologna, but they might as well have gone to America. Everyone left. The fields were abandoned. Now nobody here makes anything and we use money to buy everything. And there is no way to make money except by going somewhere else." I think of this town, which is now a shadow of its former self, when I hear Pope Francis speak of the economy that kills. There are towns like this all over America. They may be less picturesque, with their cracked cement sidewalks and their boarded-up storefronts, but they were once home to generations of children.

Technological Revolution

> The media can be a hindrance if they become a way to avoid listening to others, to evade physical contact, to fill up every moment of silence and rest, so that we forget that "silence is an integral element of communication; in its absence, words rich in content cannot exist." (Pope Francis 2015b)

Technology, like globalization, is a mixed blessing. At every turn, we see machines doing the work once done by people and doing it more cheaply and more quickly. Technology costs jobs. Technology saves lives. Technology has given human beings the tools to unlock the secrets of biology, astronomy, and physics and to decode the language of DNA, the basis for all life on Earth. Technology is everywhere, even in the microsystems of childhood. Compare the environment in which my father grew up with the environment surrounding my grandchildren. My father was born in Saskatchewan, Canada in 1905, when it was still a territory. As a child, he saw the first automobile in town, the first telephone, the first airplane, the first electric light. When I was four, he brought home a new technological miracle—a television that weighed a ton and had a bulky cathode-ray tube screen. Each of these technologies, at first greeted as novelties, caused a revolution in family life and in the patterns of childhood. Technology separates humans, as Pope Francis points out, and it also brings them together. My grandchildren use iPhones, watch streaming video on a gigantic flat screen, and engage with a Grandma who lives a thousand miles away via FaceTime.

While parental alarm is usually focused on children's overuse of mobile devices, use by adults may have even more insidious effects on children's lives. In *The Big Disconnect*, Catherine Steiner-Adair and Teresa H. Barker provide vivid examples of how children experience their parents' absorption with technology (2013). Toddlers stop their play to gaze longingly at a parent totally absorbed in communicating with a tablet. A seven-year-old complains:

> My parents are always on their computers and cell phones. It is very, very frustrating and I get lonely inside. When my Dad is on the phone I have this conversation in my head: 'Hello! Remember me? Remember who I am? I am your *daughter*! You had me cuz you wanted me. Only it doesn't feel like that right now. Right now it feels like all—you—care—about—is your phone!' But I don't say that because they'll get mad at me. It doesn't help. It feels worse. So it's just a conversation I have with myself. (13)

Psychologists long ago documented the adverse effects on children of growing up with an unavailable, disconnected, or narcissistic parent. A "secure attachment" is one of the most important predictors of children's emotional and cognitive health. According to the authors of this study, "at some point, distracted, tech-centered parenting can look and feel to a child like having a narcissistic parent or an emotionally absent, psychologically neglectful one" (16). Parents have coped with distractions from the time parenting began. Technology makes it easier to work at home but harder to share undivided time with children.

Technology has changed how children experience and relate to the world. In developed countries, it is routine for children to have multiple gadgets: smartphones, iPads, laptops, game consoles. American children aged eight to eighteen spend an average of seven and a half hours a day, seven days a week, on electronic devices. Multitasking multiplies screen time, as kids pile device upon device: watching TV while texting while checking Facebook while doing homework on a computer. Screen time is starting earlier. According to a 2006 study by the Kaiser Family Foundation, an astonishing 61 percent of children under age one used screen media, for an average of one hour and twenty minutes a day, while 90 percent of children aged four to six used screen media, for an average of more than two hours a day. Thirty-three percent of children under six had a TV in their bedroom (Rideout and Hamel 2006, tables 2, 3, 8). While TV was still the most widely used platform, mobile devices were rapidly catching up. Ownership of mobile devices in the zero-to-eight crowd, including smartphones, tablets, and touchscreens, has become the new norm. In 2011, 52 percent of children owned a mobile device. By 2013, that figure had shot up to 75 percent. Between 2011 and 2013, the time children spent using mobile devices tripled, with typical users in this age group spending over an hour a day on their mobile devices (Common Sense Media 2013, tables 9 and 13). By 2017, the time children zero to eight spent on mobile devices had tripled, from fifteen minutes in 2013 to forty-eight minutes in 2017. Children's tablet ownership had soared; the percentage of children zero to eight who owned their own tablet had shot from 7 percent to 42 percent (Common Sense Media 2017, figs. A and B).

Technology can level the playing field, but lack of access to technology can also widen the divide between poorer and wealthier children. With the advent of mobile devices, the "digital divide" has now been joined by an "app gap." As with measures of poverty, the gap is relative. While 20 percent of lower-income children in the United States had a tablet in the home as of 2013, the figure for higher-income children was 63 percent (Common Sense Media 2013, table 26). While 35 percent of lower-income parents had downloaded an educational app for their children, the figure for higher-income families was 75 percent. By 2017, the digital divide and the app gap appeared to be narrowing, but the screen time of children from low income families had risen by 50 percent to 3.5 hours a day, while exposure of high income families to screens had remained stable, at less than two hours a day (Common Sense Media 2017, figs. C and E), suggesting that the closing of the digital divide may be problematic for the most vulnerable children. It bears noting that this media explosion has happened in the face of dire warnings from the American Academy of Pediatrics (AAP) about the cognitive damage caused by early, inappropriate, or chronic exposure to electronic media. The AAP recommends that children younger than eighteen months be exposed to *zero* screen time other than supervised video chatting (a boon to faraway grandparents), and older children be allowed access only to high-quality content and limited to no more than one or two hours a day (American Academy of Pediatrics 2016). How many parents, rich or poor, can claim to have followed these guidelines?

Technology has changed the way children play. We used to worry about kids watching too much TV. Here is how Suzannah, a thirteen-year-old expert, described the impact of mobile electronics in 2013 and compared today's childhood to her own, simpler childhood, when TV was the great time waster:

> Kids are so obsessed with sitting inside and playing with their iPod Touch and it's so useless. I watch my cousin, who's six, and she sits on the couch and plays Scooby Doo with her friends on the iPad, and I'm like, jeez, when I was six years old I was figuring out how to tie teddy bears to gate posts or flinging them over the banisters. I just think of all the fun things my sisters and I would do, all these fun memories that I have and my cousins won't because they are sitting on the couch and video-chatting. My cousins aren't having any childhood. (Steiner-Adair and Barker 2013, 130)

In the United States, I had become inured to seeing kids tethered to earbuds and staring into space or playing solitary games alone with their consoles. I was accustomed to seeing other diners at restaurants transacting business on their cell phones, checking their tablets, and carrying on a conversation with everyone except the family members sitting beside them. It was refreshing to see the children of Scanno playing out of doors, with bikes and soccer balls and dolls and water pistols and with *each other*. And it was refreshing not to see parents and grandparents hunched over mobile devices instead of watching and enjoying their children and grandchildren as they played. As I sat on a bench in the piazza and recorded data about children's play, I was the only person of any age hunched over an iPad. Over the eight years I have been observing Scanno's children, mobile devices have become increasingly common. At first it was only the adults and young people who had access to them. By 2014 some school-age children owned them. By 2018 I began to see very small children playing with their parents' devices. However, I have yet to see a child in Scanno sitting alone and playing with a handheld device. Most often, they are sharing the device with a group of other children, passing it hand to hand or playing a game together. I can only hope this difference in the culture of play continues to prevail.

According to the Italian government's statistical agency, the Italian National Institute of Statistics (ISTAT), cellular technologies represent the area of swiftest change in the daily lives of Italian children and teens. The use of cell phones almost doubled among eleven-to-seventeen-year olds (from 55.6 percent in 2000 to 92.7 percent in 2011). In 2011 the cell phone was already being utilized as a multimedia device: the percentage of eleven-to-seventeen-year-olds who use their cell phones only to make phone calls had dropped from 20.3 to 3.9 percent in the period between 2000 and 2011. There also had been a notable growth in the use of the internet: for the six-to-seventeen-year-old age group, it had gone from 34.3 percent in 2001 to 64.3 percent in 2011; among eleven-to-seventeen-year-olds, it had grown from 47 to 82.7 percent in the same period (ISTAT 2011). By 2016, almost 24.4 percent of children aged three to five, 52.9 percent of children aged six to ten, 78.4 percent of children eleven to fourteen, and 83.2 percent of children aged fifteen to seventeen were using a personal computer. In the same year, 48.2 percent of children aged six to ten, 82.9 percent of children aged eleven to fourteen, and 91.6 percent of children aged fifteen to twenty-seven were using the internet (ISTAT 2016). In 2011, 45 percent of six-year-olds and 55 percent of ten-year-olds were using graphics on electronic devices. In 2015 the rate for the same age groups had risen to 72 percent of six-year-olds and 82 percent of ten-year-olds.

Figure 9.1. Scanno schoolchildren clowning around after perfectly executed earthquake drill. B. B. Woodhouse.

An Exercise in Triangulation: Comparing Statistics to Observation

Scanno is probably behind the typical Northern Italian town in the ubiquity of iPhones and other sophisticated smartphones (Italians use the English term). One day in 2014, when I was visiting a primary-school class in Scanno, I was so impressed with the maturity of the children, who had just executed a surprise earthquake drill with seriousness, quiet order, and precision and were now clowning around in the safe space of the nearest piazza, that I took out my iPhone to take a photograph.

They immediately swarmed over me, asking what model of iPhone I had, how much it had cost, and where I had gotten it. Feeling oddly embarrassed, I told them I did not know how much it cost because my boss in America had bought it for me, as I needed it for my research work. My fib did not make me feel any less uneasy with the luxury item I held in my hands. Today, five years later, I doubt if my iPhone would cause such excitement, although it would still be a coveted object.

It is far too soon, in an evolutionary sense, to predict the impact of electronic devices on developing brains and social connections, not to mention epigenetics. But it is clear that children today, in both Italy and the United States, are trading time spent in active, outdoor, free-form play for time spent staring at a screen. While the United States may once have been in the lead as a consumer of mobile devices and electronic media, other developed and developing nations are rapidly catching up and even surpassing us.

Let me be clear. With the exception of use by very young children, it is not these technologically sophisticated devices themselves that pose a threat to children. It is how much they are used and the images they convey. The images they transmit can be educational and developmentally appropriate or they can be damaging to healthy cognitive and emotional development. A broad consensus has developed that exposure to violence is harmful to children (American Academy of Pediatrics 2009; American Psychological Association 2015; Ferrario 2018). Entire books have been written discussing the effects of violent media and debating whether regulators can or should intervene to protect children from exposure to violent media content (Dowd et al. 2006; Anderson et al 2007). Researchers continue to document the effects on growing brains of witnessing violent content on television and especially in enacting violent content through high-tech gaming platforms. While the debate continues, the primary authorities on child and adolescent health have concluded that exposure to this form of violence poses risks of psychological harm and contributes to aggressive behavior in youth (American Academy of Pediatrics 2009; American Psychological Association 2015).

When compared to European countries, the US has been eager to regulate children's exposure to content depicting nudity or sexual intimacy, the harms of which are far less documented by evidence-based research. It has been much less successful in regulating children's exposure to violent media content. Despite growing evidence from researchers who study its effects, especially those of violent video games, regulations protecting children have been struck down by the Supreme Court as violating constitutional rights to freedom of expression. The landmark 2011 case of *Brown v. Entertainment Merchants Association* specifically addressed regulation of sales of violent video games to minors. Justice Antonin Scalia, writing for the majority, held that a California law limiting sales to minors and requiring age-appropriate labeling violated First Amendment protections of free expression. In this realm, as in many others, there are inescapable tensions between rights to individual liberty and children's rights to protection from harm. Children are caught in the middle as these tensions are played out in Hollywood and Silicon Valley, as well as on big screens and handheld devices in children's homes and communities.

One troubling new statistic from Italy relating to social media: between 2010 and 2017, the percentage of children who report negative experiences associated with the internet—from cyberbullying to pornography—has doubled, reaching 13 percent of all minor online users (Ferrario 2018; Mascheroni and Ólafsson 2018). The situation is even worse in the United States, where an estimated 20 percent of youth aged ten to seventeen report having received a sexual solicitation or having been approached online, and 65 percent of children aged eight to fourteen report having been involved in a cyberbullying incident (Child Guard n.d.).

Rising Inequality

> The worship of the ancient golden calf has returned in a new and ruthless guise in the idolatry of money and the dictatorship of an impersonal economy lacking a truly human purpose. The worldwide crisis affecting finance and the economy lays bare their imbalances and, above all, their lack of real concern for human beings. (Pope Francis 2013, 55)

> How can it be that it is not a news item when an elderly homeless person dies of exposure, but it is news when the stock market loses two points? This is a case of exclusion. Can we continue to stand by when food is thrown away while people are starving? This is a case of inequality. (53)

Both quotes are from Pope Francis' apostolic exhortation issued in November 2013. As the Pulitzer Prize–winning UK newspaper the *Guardian* remarked in its coverage of the Pope's apostolic exhortation, "Inequality is the biggest economic issue of our time. It's only surprising it took so long for a globally prominent figure to say it" (Moore 2013). The title of the piece was: "Pope Francis Understands Economics Better than Most Politicians." As must be clear by now, inequality is harnessed to and feeds upon globalization, technology, and capitalism. It may be one of our biggest threats, but it may also be the hardest to pin down and examine. Without a shared understanding of the meaning of "equality," it is difficult to confront inequality.

Equality and inequality are inherently comparative terms. They are also heavily context dependent and culturally constructed. There are differences between how Italians and Americans talk about them. Pope Francis uses a synonym for inequality that is more common in Europe than in the United States: *exclusion* (2013, 53). Exclusion is what happens when some members of the community are kept from sharing in the community's prosperity or welcomed as valid members of the community. Its opposite, *inclusion*, is the word used for policies that break down barriers between the community and its members. Exclusion is a form of discrimination and inclusion is the antidote.

While researching equality and inequality, I have been struck by the outsize role that a particular measure of equality—equality of opportunity—plays in American culture and policy. We seem more concerned about social mobility than about gaps between rich and poor. In his influential essay for the Brookings Institution, Richard Reeves argues that the crucial challenge faced by the United States is not inequality but achieving greater equality of opportunity (2014). According to Reeves, it is not feasible or consistent with the American character to emulate European-style policies that aim to increase equality of resources. He argues that meritocracy is the value most highly prized by Americans. Instead of trying to achieve equality, we should restore the level playing field that opens the door to opportunity.

Reeves, although an Englishman by birth, is channeling the "American dream"—the notion that any one of us, with enough grit and determination, can reach the highest rungs of the economic and social ladder, regardless of where we started in life. Unfortunately, research suggests that Americans grossly overestimate their rates of upward mobility. In one study, more than three thousand respondents were asked to estimate the likelihood that a randomly selected person born in the bottom quintile would move to other income quintiles during his lifetime (Davidai and Gilovich 2015). Data from the Pew Research Center show that on average only 30 percent of individuals make such a move. Respondents overestimated the likelihood by fifteen percentage points (Kraus et al. 2015). These survey results should come as no surprise. The myth of upward mobility remains difficult to challenge because it serves rich and poor alike: it helps the rich justify their wealth and it provides the poor with hope for a brighter future. Another myth that persists in spite of the evidence is the myth that the United States is uniquely a land of social mobility. In fact, as research has shown, it lags behind its peers. A son's earnings are more closely tied to his father's earnings in the United States than in Canada and most countries in Europe. Italy, the United States, and the UK appear to be among the least mobile of the OECD countries (Isaacs 2008). What distinguishes the United States from other countries is not its upward mobility but its citizens' faith in the possibility of upward mobility. Hand in hand with this comes a widespread if uncritical rejection of the notion that government has a responsibility to reduce inequality. This partially explains why mobility is especially low for US children born at the bottom of the economic ladder (Isaacs 2008).

Income mobility, whether reality or mirage, should not be confused with income equality. The myth of economic mobility may have distracted US voters and policy-makers from grappling with the reality of income inequality. Eduardo Porter, writing in the *New York Times*, argues that income inequality, not lack of opportunity, is our key challenge and shows how it has been exacting high costs from our society (2015). According to Porter, inequality has been made worse by the unraveling of the US safety net and the loss of a shared sense of solidarity. For Porter, solidarity is the missing ingredient. As he points out, globalization happened everywhere, creating challenges for working-class families in Europe as well as the United States. However, many European nations took advantage of the boom to strengthen their safety nets, while the United States has let its already flimsy one fray even further.

Is poverty something to be alleviated or something to be escaped? This question exposes the different roles of mobility and solidarity. Solidarity is that sense of relationship to others that makes us want to help our neighbor in distress instead of turning away or blaming him for his condition of dependency. How we define our family and our neighborhood and how we draw boundaries of solidarity have profound effects on the ecology of childhood. The more we view our "neighbor" as the "other," the harder it is to muster feelings of solidarity. Perhaps because of the Catholic tradition of outreach to the poor and vulnerable, Italians have tended to support social solidarity, and social and economic supports are entrenched as "rights" under the Italian Constitution and the international treaties their country has ratified. Italy entered the recession as a welfare state committed to the socioeconomic welfare of its citizens with a constitution guaranteeing positive rights to health care, education, unemployment compensation, and other forms of government support. When Italians feel social welfare entitlements are threatened, they not only threaten mass protests but actually do *scendere in piazza* (go down into the piazza in large numbers) to protest. Italians practiced the Occupy strategy long before it came to Wall Street.

Contrast this focus on supports for workers and families with a bold experiment in individual mobility launched by the US Congress in the wake of the Los Angeles race riots more than twenty years ago. Called "Moving to Opportunity," it gave vouchers to help poor, predominately African American and Hispanic families relocate to homes in better neighborhoods. The vouchers were awarded on a random basis so researchers could study their effects. After twenty years, the results of this antipoverty experiment were deeply disappointing. As described by Pulitzer Prize–winning journalist David Leonhardt and his *New York Times* coauthors, "Parents who received vouchers did not seem to earn more in later years than otherwise similar adults, and children did not seem to do better in school. The program's apparent failure has haunted social scientists and policy-makers, making poverty seem all the more intractable" (Leonhardt, Cox and Miller 2015). Recently, a group of researchers reexamined the data using new formulas and ran some experiments of their own (Chetty and Hendren 2015, 2018). These new studies exploded on the scene like a bombshell. The lead researcher stated: "The data show that we can do something about upward mobility. Every extra year of a childhood spent in a better neighborhood seems to matter" (Chetty as quoted in Leonhardt, Cox, and Miller 2015).

The *New York Times*'s coverage of this research includes an interactive "Atlas of Upward Mobility" that allows readers to identify which counties near which metropolitan areas produce the greatest effects when children move to them from less prosperous places. As was noted in chapter 2, poverty in Italy tends to be concentrated in the southern geographic and political regions, such as Sicilia, Puglia, and Calabria, with the northern regions of Lombardy and Emiglia Romagna far more affluent than their southern counterparts. But because of its geography, law, and history, Italy is characterized by mixed-income residential neighborhoods. In the United States, geography, law, and history have produced a different result. A major factor in permitting income segregation was the Supreme Court's 1926 decision in *Euclid v. Ambler*, which permitted zoning designed to preserve upper-income enclaves and exclude smaller or commercial lots. This means that although poverty may be greater in some states or regions such as the Deep South, the Appalachian Mountains, or states like Mississippi and Alabama, there are also stark differences in every town or city between adjacent racially and economically segregated neighborhoods. US researchers, looking for fine-grained data on neighborhoods, have started to identify pockets of poverty with reference to counties, zoning codes, or postal zip codes rather than larger metropolitan areas or states.

This is why the studies of mobility in the United States cited above compared movement between smaller units (counties) rather than larger units (states or metropolitan areas). According to David Grusky, director of the Center on Poverty and Inequality at Stanford University, "This [new Chetty and Hendren study] delivers the most compelling evidence yet that neighborhoods matter in a really big way" (Leonhardt, Cox, and Miller 2015). What traits do these neighborhoods share that make them "better"? They have schools with higher test scores, a higher share of two-parent families, greater involvement in civic and religious groups, and more residential integration of affluent, middle-class, and poor families.

While Chetty and Hendrens's research is impressive and pathbreaking, I worry that it points us down the wrong road. In my view, the American obsession with physical and social mobility as an engine of equality is at best a distraction and at worst a formidable barrier to building a more just society. It masks the underlying inequalities that make a particular neighborhood "good" and another "bad." Can any society achieve true equality of opportunity without a redistribution of resources from the affluent grown-ups at the top to the poor children at the bottom? Or from the rich regions of the North to the poor regions of the South? To ask this question is to answer it. As long as children who are born into the lowest economic strata lack the basics all children need in order to grasp the opportunity for self-realization, equality is an empty promise. A nation's commitment to meritocracy finds expression in its fostering of fair and transparent competition, as its commitment to solidarity finds expression in its dedication to leveling the playing field by ensuring that every child has a decent start in life (Woodhouse and Woodhouse 2018). International human-rights documents such as the CRC, the focus of chapter 10, establish a collective obligation, lodged in government and the institutions it supports, to make equality possible. Progressive taxation and robust social, educational, and health systems are means of accomplishing these ends.

The recession and its aftermath have threatened to unbalance the delicate equilibrium between concern for the individual and concern for the general welfare that has been the hallmark of welfare democracies in the EU zone. As seen in chapters 7 and 8, these are the very nations that have been most successful at creating healthy environments for raising children. In addition to exporting the American financial crisis to Europe, followers of the Chicago school of economics have been exporting to Europe its excessive individualism and misplaced faith in deregulation and the invisible hand of the market. Myths that have been discredited in the United States are still accepted as gospel among many European elites. Struggling economies in countries such as Italy are being told to increase competition through deregulation, rollback of labor laws, and privatization of public-sector services. In succeeding chapters, especially chapter 12, which describes experiments in Naples' *Rione La Sanità* and Harlem Children's Zone, we will see how people in the United States and people in Italy often differ in the value they attribute to class mobility and equality and in how they imagine and construct remedies for poverty and inequality.

Mass Migration

> You shall treat the stranger who sojourns with you as the native among you, and you shall love him as yourself, for you were strangers in the land of Egypt. (Leviticus 19:34).

> The Lord entrusts to the Church's motherly love every person forced to leave their homeland in search of a better future. This solidarity must be concretely expressed at every stage of the migratory experience—from departure through

journey to arrival and return. This is a great responsibility which the Church intends to share with all believers and all men and women of good will, who are called to respond to the many challenges of contemporary migration with generosity, promptness, wisdom and foresight, each according to their own abilities. (Pope Francis 2018)

When migrants arrive to a country, "you have to receive them, help them, look after them, accompany them and then see where to put them, but throughout all of Europe," he said, noting that "some governments are working on it, and people have to be settled in the best possible way, but creating psychosis is not the cure" (Catholic World Report 2018)

Migration is as old as humankind and as new as yesterday. Pope Francis' invocation in the first quotation above of an Old Testament Bible passage is one indication of migration's ancient lineage. In the other quotations, Pope Francis is responding to the Trump administration's "immoral" policy adopted in 2018 of separating migrant children from their parents to punish them for crossing into the United States. Twenty-first century migration continues to pose moral and political challenges.

We now know that the first migrations began not long after Homo sapiens first appeared in Africa, during a period of dramatic climate change some 300,000 years ago. Homo sapiens spread gradually across the globe, until they reached every continent (Galway-Witham 2018). Today, with the advent of low-cost DNA technology, you can send a sample of your saliva to a service that will tell you where your ancestors came from. According to Helix, the *National Geographic*-sponsored service, my ancestors migrated via the Middle East to northern Europe. I have a touch of eastern and southern Europe and a smidgen of Neanderthal, but, like every other living human, my origins are in Africa. Interestingly, recent research suggests that Homo sapiens, rather than exterminating other hominid species, was interbreeding with species that later became extinct (Galway-Witham 2018). Our collective history is a history of migratory movement and adaptive evolution. In discussing globalization, I have been critical of economists who treat migration in search of employment as a morally neutral and cost-free means to improve efficiency and lower labor costs. But voluntary migration has long served an essential purpose: as a safety valve releasing pressure in times of famine or natural disaster, and as an escape from persecution, violence and war.

A popular meme on American Facebook goes like this: "I am: 1) Native American, 2) an Immigrant. Check one or two. There are no other choices." Unlike Americans, Italians have all too recently experienced both sides of the migration experience—the leaving and the being left behind. Many regions of Italy and many Italian families have experienced out-migration as a tragedy rather than an opportunity. As Italians continue to move to urban areas within Italy or to other countries, those who leave as well as those left behind experience a sense of loss. In the villages of Abruzzo, it is not unusual to see a monument dedicated to those who emigrated during times of hardship, recognizing the sacrifices made by those who moved away in order to preserve resources for those who remained and promising never to forget them. Ties to the family birthplace and regret at leaving are celebrated in song and story and can endure for generations, even traveling with the migrants into a second new land.

In 2017, a "cover" of the heartbreaking Abruzzo folk song "Amara Terra Mia," recorded in 1971 by Domenico Modugno, was wildly popular at the Italian San Remo song festival, a televised spectacle second in popularity only to the soccer World Cup. The song's popularity should be no surprise, at a time when Italians are again leaving their homes because they cannot find work. Its words are simple and its melody is heartbreaking. In common with American folk songs, its history is far older than the first recorded performance. Brought to Abruzzo in the 1400s by a wave of Slavic refugees, it entered into the folklore and language of Abruzzo and Italian immigrants, who carried it to other lands as they were forced to migrate. As one Italian historian of music commented, "Along with their miserable belongings, the migrants brought their cultural baggage, made of songs they sang on their voyage. To sing in their language, their own songs, was a sign—as it is today—of the umbilical cord that forever ties a people to their origins" (Salera 2017, English translation by B. Woodhouse). The song describes a relentless sun searing the hills and valleys, fields and towns emptied of life, the moon rising among the olives, a baby crying at its malnourished mother's breast. The refrain expresses the singer's love for a bitter but beautiful homeland. The song speaks to generations of migrants and refugees from every corner of the world: "Addio, addio amore, io vado via. Amara terra mia, amara e bella" (Farewell, farewell, my love. I must go away. My bitter land, bitter and beautiful). Scanno, where families who left long ago come back year after year from Canada, South America, and the United States, provides a contemporary example of the importance of rootedness and the social costs, as well as the benefits of pulling up roots in order to participate in the global labor economy. Ermal Meta, the young singer who won the San Remo Festival prize, himself had emigrated to Italy from Albania. In introducing the song he reminds his listeners that the *terra amara*—the bitter land—is not necessarily the old one you left behind. It can be the new one in which you now struggle to survive (YouTube 2017).

All of these truths are expressed in Pope Francis's statements, quoted above, about the moral challenges of contemporary migration. The pope, of course, grounds his theology in a quotation from Leviticus. But this belief in a moral duty to shelter refugees is not only a part of the Old and New Testaments; it is revered by numerous religions and is grounded in international law (UN Convention on Refugees 1951; UN Protocol on Refugees 1967).

Mass migrations such as we have seen in the past decade are inherently destabilizing and can produce crisis and backlash. We see this manifested in the rising intolerance toward migrants and refugees from ethnicities and cultures viewed as alien to the majority's way of life. We also see it in the rising tide of nationalist sentiment resulting in elections of political leaders who gained popular support by demonizing minority groups, foreigners, and liberal elites, and by promising to close their physical and economic borders to these invasive elements. Both Italy and the United States have been caught up in this turmoil. As a result of the wars in Iraq and Afghanistan, the unraveling of the so-called Arab Spring and continuing fighting and unrest in Africa, Italians have had to bear the brunt of an unprecedented wave of refugees seeking asylum in Europe. Italy is only 290 miles by boat from Libya, its former colony. With the fall of dictator Muammar Al Gaddafi, Libya became a battleground for warring factions and a breeding ground for smugglers of human beings (Kirkpatrick 2015).

As of June 2018 over 690,000 migrants had arrived in Italy by boat since 2013, when the migration crisis began. In 2017, 120,000 arrived by sea, costing the Italian government 4.2 billion euros. In 2013, there were 22,000 people in asylum centers, and in January 2018 that number had swelled to 182,000 (The Local.it 2018; Amnesty International 2016). Many had been rescued from drowning in the Strait of Sicily. A horrifying 2800 souls drowned or died of thirst and hunger on the sea in 2017 alone. Initially, Italians had responded to the crisis with extraordinary compassion. But the flow was putting a huge strain on Italy's resources.

When the exodus from the Middle East and Africa began, Italy had adopted a policy called *Mare Nostrum* (Latin for "Our Sea") and its coastguard and navy were able to rescue an overwhelming majority of the refugees and migrants and bring them to Italy for processing and integration (Amnesty International 2016). As the influx continued, tensions developed between the instinct for solidarity with those in need and fear of being overwhelmed by the sheer numbers of migrants. The fact that these migrants were of a different color and often a different religion from the majority of Italians heightened these tensions. Italians felt abandoned by their EU neighbors who closed their doors and reneged on promises to share the burden. Italians also felt abandoned by the United States. Not only had the United States initiated the endless war in Iraq, destabilizing the entire region, it had joined with Italy in supporting the militias that overthrew Gaddafi. The objective of this intervention had been to promote a new democracy in a country with continuing ties to Italy, but the result was to unleash total chaos in Libya. Italians saw the connections between US policies and their own dilemma. One cartoon posted on Italian Facebook, referencing the flotillas of refugees from Libya and Turkey, has a picture of an Italian family watching then–presidential candidate Hillary Clinton on their TV screen, with the father saying: "Why doesn't the country that caused this mess take the refugees?"

While the tensions within Italy are high, and its response has not always been ideal, it must be recognized that Italians have historically responded to the migration crisis with compassion. Pope Francis has played a key role in advocating for the human rights of refugees in Italy, as in other parts of the world. Italy's leaders, while sharply critical of prior governmental policies, continued to receive refugees and asylum seekers at their ports. Then, in June 2018, making good on a campaign promise, the interior minister Matteo Salvini, leader of the party formerly called Lega del Nord (League of the North) and now simply Lega (The League), ordered closure of all Italian ports to rescue vessels. Human-rights leaders and Italian liberals charged the government with holding innocent people hostage as a means to strong-arm the EU into changing the ground rules for handling refugees. The battle that ensured between the Italian president, the prime minister, and the powerful minister of the interior reveals the high levels of conflict within the coalition government over the rights of refugees and pressure from its base to stem immigration (Messagero 2018). Meanwhile, Italy called on the EU to revise the policy (the Dublin Regulations) that assigned responsibility for processing applications for entry into the EU to the first EU country where a migrant set foot on land (Smyth 2018).

Ironically, Italy's hard-line policy came at a time when the numbers of refugees reaching Italy by sea were already in decline. But inside Italy, a different reality prevails, fed by social networks like Facebook and Twitter, that the anti-immigrant forces have used very effectively. Large numbers of Italians are convinced that their country is being overwhelmed by a surging tidal wave of illegal immigrants that dwarfs the numbers of migrants in other EU nations. In fact, the percentage of immigrants in Italy's population is quite low in comparison with other EU countries. As of January 1, 2017, there were only five immigrants for every thousand inhabitants, less than half the number of immigrants per thousand inhabitants present in Netherlands (11.1), Belgium (10.9), Germany (12.5), Denmark (13), and Sweden (16.4) (Eurostat 2017). The anti-immigrant backlash. although based on misperceptions, had become all too real.

In the United States, the backlash against mass migration played a central role in the election of Donald Trump. He famously used frightening and unfounded narratives of Mexican rapists and Muslim terrorists to whip up support. If there had been any doubt about his willingness to carry through with his plans to build a wall across the southern border and to close US ports of entry to Muslims, it was dissipated almost immediately. Trump's Muslim ban wreaked havoc in American airports and had severe repercussions for Muslims seeking to come to the United States and for US employers and academic institutions seeking to recruit them. The hostility to migrants from Latin America reached a sorry low point in the spring of 2018, when Trump and his then–Attorney General Jeff Sessions instituted a "zero-tolerance" policy against any unlawful entry into the United States. Under this policy, parents who attempted to enter the United States without documentation were arrested as criminals, so that their children could be reclassified as "unaccompanied minors" and placed in detention centers or sent to foster homes in distant states and cities. It took a month for the media to catch on, but by June 2018 they were publishing stories of parents desperately seeking their children and even of being deported without having found them. The media were filled with images of children kept in cage-like enclosures in former commercial warehouses. UN spokespersons, not to mention the heads of state of many nations, issued statements condemning this practice, while US citizens marched in the hundreds of thousands. It seemed that visible evidence of children's suffering had awakened a sleeping public to the damaging effects of Trump's policies. Faced with overwhelming opposition even from within his own party, Trump backed down and discontinued the policy. But the federal agencies handling the removals had made no plans for reunification. They had failed to keep records of the relationships between parents and children and in many cases had destroyed the records linking the child to its parents. According to the administration. roughly three thousand children had been removed, reclassified, and warehoused in empty Walmart stores and military bases, or sent to private foster-care agencies in distant states. Ordered by a federal judge to reunify all the children under five within two weeks, and the remaining children within thirty days, lawyers for the Trump administration were unable to comply (Sacchetti 2018). In January 2019, the administration finally admitted that it had no idea how many children had been separated from their families because it had not kept track; estimates ranged in the thousands (Jordan 2019). It was to be hoped that this debacle represented the low point in American immigration policy. But, once again, as with Italy and the EU, the prospects do not look good.

Racial and Ethnic Discrimination

> We must overcome all forms of racism, of intolerance and of the instrumentalisation of the human person. (ADNKronos 2017)

Pope Francis, the most modern of prelates, tweets almost daily. His tweets are part of the official Vatican record and are both shorter and sweeter than those of many other leaders. "Racism" and "intolerance" are familiar terms describing aspects of discrimination. The term "instrumentalization" is less familiar to American readers. Drawn from Kantian moral philosophy, this principle recognizes that the concept of "human dignity" prohibits using a person merely as a means to an end (Kaufmann 2011). The notion of human dignity plays a central role in international human rights and it is no surprise that Pope Francis would include this in his trinity of violations. These scourges of racism, intolerance, and the instrumentalization of the human person are a global scourge, the context in which Pope Francis is tweeting. But their roots are planted at the most intimate and local levels. They are the polar opposite of inclusion, tolerance, and respect. In both Italy and the United States, these evils have been heightened as economic insecurity has exacerbated already existing tensions arising from differences of class, religion, ethnicity, gender, sexual identity, and disability.

Regional bias is another form of discrimination that has played a large role in the response of the EU to the struggles of its Mediterranean members, primarily Spain, Italy, and Greece. This bias is a subtle form of racism. Many people in the northern EU nations regard the citizens of the southern nations as lazy, backward, and corrupt. No amount of contradictory data can shake this conviction, that the peoples of the Mediterranean nations are inherently inferior and need to be whipped into shape and join the civilized world. A similar north/south divide with racist overtones exists within Italy. Rooted in history, economics, and ethnic differences, it is understood by all within the popular culture (Bullaro 2010). In the 1960s, when I lived with a working-class family in Umbria, *Meridionali* (southerners) were held in deep distrust, and it was clear that anything south of Rome was considered a foreign country.

This history of discrimination provides the plotline of a popular *"fiction"* (Italians have borrowed the English word) titled "Questo Nostro Amore" (This Love of Ours) consisting of thirty-six episodes airing on *Rai Uno* (the flagship state TV channel) in 2012, 2014, and 2018. Set in the rapidly changing Italy of the sixties, seventies, and eighties, it tells the story of two Italian families, neighbors in an apartment building in Torino, capitol of the northern region of Piedmont. One family had migrated north from Sicily, and the other family was from a small town near Torino. With artfully scripted characters portrayed by convincing actors, every north/south stereotype gets full dramatic and comedic play, but the most compelling feature of the first season's plots was the implicit bias and overt hostility encountered by the family from Sicily. The racist epithets hurled at the intruders by their coworkers at the factory, as well as the tensions around the teenagers' dating across class and ethnic color lines, were all-too-familiar themes to an observer from the United States. I learned more directly about the effects of northern/southern racism in conversations with a colleague at a major university, whose family of distinguished teachers, doctors, and lawyers moved to Tuscany from Sicily half a century ago. Having lived and studied in Florence since childhood, she has been hampered in her career as a result of subtle ethnic cues such as her southern accent, hair texture, dusky skin color and just being so . . . Sicilian.

Northern Italians have been fond of pointing out that, if one were to divide the Italian economy into northern, central, and southern regions, the north would outperform Germany on many measures of economic success. In the prosperous northern regions, resentment of southern Italians and separatist sentiments gave birth in 1991 to the political party called Lega del Nord, or the Northern League. At times it has advocated for the creation of an independent nation, *Padania*, the boundaries of which are disputed but are generally agreed to encompass the industrialized regions of Lombardy, Piedmont, Veneto, Liguria, Emiglia Romagna, Tuscany, and perhaps Umbria. Abruzzo, where Scanno is located, is considered part of the central or southern region, depending on whom you ask. *Lega del Nord*, now calling itself simply *Lega*, has gone nationwide. *Lega* continues to oppose redistribution of resources to poorer regions and instead favors devolution of responsibility from Rome to the regional governments. The rhetoric of the Lega reflects the sentiments of many Italians who are convinced of the superiority of northern populations and blame rising unemployment on competition from immigrants from southern Italy as well as from less-developed foreign nations. Primary targets of hostility are "extra-communitarians" coming from non-EU countries. Even immigrants from the poorer EU nations such as Romania experience stigma and hostility. The Roma, a group that in the United States is known as "gypsies" and in England as "travelers," is also subject to discrimination based on many centuries of distrust and separation from society. These populations are overrepresented in Italian prison and child-welfare systems, much as people of color are overrepresented in these systems in the United States (Bapat and Woodhouse 2016).

In the United States, as in Italy, tensions of religion, region, culture, and class also play a role in fomenting discrimination, but race is the devil that continues most tragically to divide us. Sadly, the impact of racial and ethnic discrimination on *children* of color in America is greater than for any other age group. During the recession, we have seen a widening of the already existing gaps between the well-being of children of the majority white race and minority races including blacks, Latino/as, Native Americans, and people of Asian and Pacific descent. Black Americans are still suffering from the legacy of a legal system of racialized slavery. While de jure slavery was abolished only 150 years ago—about the same time Italy became a unified nation—and Jim Crow racial-segregation laws were outlawed in the 1960s, de facto segregation and systemic discrimination continue to this day. While slavery has existed in many societies over the millennia, the mass importation of black people from Africa to work the plantations of the American South stands out as uniquely horrible. It has been called America's original sin.

The continuing consequences of racism for children and their families have been the topics of multiple works of research and theory. Dorothy Roberts exposed the harms to children and families perpetuated by racism in our child-welfare system in her *Shattered Bonds: The Color of Child Welfare* (2002). Michelle Alexander, in her book *The New Jim Crow*, traces how the zero-tolerance policies of the 1990s resulted in mass incarceration of black men, women, boys, and girls, creating a new chapter in our history of oppression of black people (2009). Nancy E. Dowd, in her newest book, *Reimagining Equality: A New Deal for Children of Color*, uses a developmental perspective to trace the effects of racism on black boys from birth to age eighteen, exploring this group as an exemplar of the damage inflicted by entrenched racism and inequality, and proposes adopting a policy initiative grounded in a developmental equality model (2018). These contemporary scholars give eloquent voice to the tragedies of racism as it affects children and youth and point the way to attacking it at its roots.

Europeans are well aware of the racial situation in the United States, which has been covered extensively by both national and international mass media. It is crystal clear that racial discrimination continues to this day, compounded by local zoning laws and mechanisms of school funding that facilitate segregation by neighborhood, zip code, and school district. The Supreme Court, once a leading force in combatting racism as mandated by the Equal Protection Clauses of our Constitution, now seems increasingly hostile to laws and policies that attempt to combat de facto segregation (Parents Involved in Community Schools 2017). Racism in the United States is impossible to overlook in Europe: images from the United States of police shootings and beatings of black youth and footage of neighborhoods in flames are a staple of Italian television news programs, for example. As we have seen, even peaceful Cedar Key has been affected by the regional legacy of racial violence.

In an example of how inequality, market capitalism, and racism intersect, it strikes me as no accident that mobility—in the form of projects to get minority kids out of toxic neighborhoods before they become angry young men and women—emerged as a response to uprisings in Baltimore in 2015, just as it did to riots in Los Angeles in 1992. In both cities, the conflicts were triggered by a history of police brutality against black men and boys. The mobility solution–move children away from the neighborhood and let the problem continue to fester—is part of the American dream that upward mobility is equally available to all. It has also been part of the American nightmare for the marginalized poor and people of color. It was tried as a large-scale solution in the Orphan Train Movement that took "black" Irish kids out of New York City slums in the 1870s, in the busing of black kids to white neighborhoods during the school-desegregation efforts of the 1980s, and in the policy of removing children from black communities for placement in foster care, which continues today (Roberts 2002; Woodhouse 2008a).

The relocation solution was also proposed in 1996 as essential to winning the war against drugs and crime in a book by William Bennett, John Diullio, and John Walters, titled *Body Count: Moral Poverty* (1996). This book warned of a new generation of superpredator teens growing up in neighborhoods that were criminogenic because the adults lacked basic moral values. The neighborhoods were toxic, but the kids could be saved. If we could move those "innocent children" out of those "bad neighborhoods" before they become corrupted by their toxic neighbors, we could get a grip on discrimination and crime and achieve social mobility for all. The black superpredator myth was discredited, but not before it resulted in a brutal and unnecessary wave of incarceration of children and youth and removals of children from black families (Roberts 2002; Dowd 2018). The fiction of criminogenic neighborhoods lives on in our child-welfare policy.

The strategy of removing children from "bad" neighborhoods to promote upward mobility is not a solution to racism or to inequality. Inequality, which fuels discrimination and racial conflict, is on the rise and our schools are more segregated by race and class than ever. I will put my money instead on investing in all of our children, wherever they and their families need our support. I strongly support policies such as affordable housing in diverse neighborhoods. Growing up in a mixed-income, integrated neighborhood is a far healthier ecological environment for children's maturation than either the gated communities of the affluent that are so common in Florida or the zones of concentrated poverty that so often surround our richest urban neighborhoods. But the holy grail of upward social mobility is based on an inherently unjust philosophy, one that discriminates between "winners" and "losers," rewarding those lucky enough to get ahead and condemning the rest of humanity to the shame of being left behind. Combatting racism, intolerance, and assaults on human dignity must begin as early as possible in the life of each of our children, utilizing every weapon at our disposal, including the powers of education, trauma-informed practices, and especially the kind of developmentally grounded policies proposed by Dowd and other thinkers whose ideas we will examine in our closing chapter.

The Ultimate Global Apocalypse: Climate Change

Bill McKibben, an expert on climate change, had this to say about Pope Francis's positions on global warming:

> You kind of expect popes to talk about spiritual stuff, kind of the way you expect chefs to discuss spices or tree surgeons to make small talk about overhanging limbs. Which is why it was so interesting to hear Pope Francis break down the climate change debate in very practical and very canny terms, displaying far more mathematical insight than your average world leader and far more strategic canniness than your average journalist. . . .
>
> In fact, with a few deft sentences, he laid bare the hypocrisy that dominates much of the climate debate. The occasion was the gathering of fossil fuel executives at the Vatican, one of a series of meetings to mark the third anniversary of *Laudato Si*, his majestic encyclical on global warming. Francis graciously thanked the oil executives for attending and for "developing more careful approaches to assessment of climate risk." But then he got down to business. "Is it enough?" he asked. "Will we turn the corner in time? . . . No one can answer that with certainty, but with each month that passes, the challenge of energy transition becomes more pressing. . . . What's really worrying, though, is the continued search for new fossil fuel reserves, whereas the Paris agreement clearly urged keeping most fossil fuels underground. . . . . Decisive progress cannot be made without an increased awareness that we are all part of one human family, united by bonds of fraternity and solidarity. Only by thinking and acting with constant concern for this underlying unity that overrides all differences, only by cultivating a sense of universal intergenerational solidarity, can we set out really and resolutely on the road ahead." . . .
>
> But Francis also understands that our current approach must make mathematical sense. We must solve the problem of energy access for the poor by using renewables, not fossil fuel, because "our desire to ensure energy for all must not lead to the undesired effect of a spiral of extreme climate changes due to

catastrophic rise in global temperatures, harsher environments and increased levels of poverty. Civilization requires energy, but energy use must not destroy civilization!" (2018)

In the passage quoted above, the words of Pope Francis are embedded in an opinion piece penned by an expert interpreter of the science of global warming, Bill McKibben, Schumann Distinguished Scholar at Middlebury College and founder of the climate campaign 350.org. In prior sections we have discussed the economic, political, technological, and cultural dimensions of globalization, and we have touched on the ideological dimensions of globalization, including market globalism, justice globalism, and religious globalism (Steger 2017). Climate change represents the ecological dimension of globalization—the ultimate in apocalyptic threats, placing the future of the planet and of human civilization as we know it at risk. We can predict with even more certainty than usual that the most catastrophic effects on humans will be felt by generations of vulnerable infants and children.

This book is not the place in which to debate whether the threat is real or when it will become irreversible. It is clear beyond discussion that, with the coming of the industrial revolution, our use of fossil fuels and our abuse of chemicals have transformed previously limited degradations of the environment into a global threat. Some of globalization's benefits (e.g., longer life expectancies, higher-yield crops, and lower infant mortality) have alleviated suffering and expanded the planet's capacities, while globalization's costs (e.g., overconsumption by industrialized economies, diversion of food production to wasteful and nonnutritive uses, accumulations of toxic and nonbiodegradable wastes, and the reduction of biodiversity) have combined to escalate the pace of ecological degradation. There are inescapable tensions, referred to by Pope Francis, between providing justice to the large percentage of the world's population that has not reaped the benefits of globalization and satisfying the demands of the smaller sector of the world's population that has created most of the damage. Compare the 2012 figures on the USA's annual per-capita consumption of oil (3,504 liters); automobiles per 1,000 people (808); annual per-capita consumption of meat (123 kilos); and per-capita use of fresh water (1,518 cubic meters) with that of Indonesia (oil 302, 79 automobiles, 11 meat and 356 water); and that of the Democratic Republic of the Congo (10 oil, 5 automobiles, 5 meat, and 5 water). Other industrialized nations consume more than their fair share, but the United States is among the worst offenders (Steger 2017, table K, 94).

How does the ecology of childhood figure in this equation? Steger's book includes a chart illustrating the major manifestations and consequences of global environmental degradation that incorporates the following broad categories: Patterns of Consumption, Population Growth, Loss of Biodiversity, Hazardous Waste, Industrial Accidents and Warfare, GMOs, Global Warming, Food Insecurity, Disease, Transboundary Pollution (2017, chart L). Each of these manifestations and consequences—and the list is only a representative sample, not an encyclopedia—has obvious and profound effects on children's growth and development. Simply superimpose the chart of manifestations and consequences on the ecological diagram and begin to list the ways in which every microsystem, mesosystem, and exosystem of children's small worlds is potentially affected, from birth and even before, by globalization.

It is also patently evident that we cannot simply reject globalism as evil and retreat from the international community, since the problems of climate change and ecological degradation are not confined by national boundaries, and their solutions will depend on cooperation at a global level. They will also depend on action in every one of the dimensions of globalism—economic, political, technological, and cultural. Finally, our ideologies of globalism must be examined and reformed. Market globalism, justice globalism, and religious globalism are examples, but they do not cover the field of ways in which macrosystemic forces either impede or aid us in finding solutions. Among the worst current manifestations of macrosystemic failure are the spread of science denialism and the rejection of what former Vice President Al Gore famously identified as "an inconvenient truth." The rejection of uncomfortable truths in favor of divisive rhetoric and escalating isolationism is rapidly reaching the scale of an environmental crisis of its own. We cannot hope for civilization to survive in a fact-free zone, much less live on a diet of empty untruths.

These macrosystemic forces, seemingly so far above and abstracted from the small worlds of children, are present in every minute of every microsystem of their lives. The destinies of children the world over are shaped by macrosystemic forces, even in the absence of daily entanglement with globalization. In developed nations, the connections between childhood and the cultural, economic, ideological, and environmental dimensions of globalization are right before our eyes. Consider the children of our two villages: separated by an ocean, they are increasingly bound together and their lives are increasingly being reshaped by globalization. The children of Scanno and the children of Cedar Key consume its messages and feel its physical effects in the food they eat, the images they see on television, the games they play, and the temperature of the air they breathe. The very definition of what constitutes a "good" life is shaped by these forces. As these children approach the end of childhood, their rites of passage to adulthood are hollow and leave them in limbo. Consider the generation of NEETS in both countries who are neither in school, in education, in training, or in employment. Will they be able to start families of their own?

Part 4 of this book, comprising the final three chapters, will explore various concepts and approaches to healing the ecology of childhood that may seem very small in relation to the magnitude of the threats. One such concept is an ideological shift—the adoption of a children's-rights frame for thinking about justice globalism. A children's-rights frame helps us to answer the question of what we, as individuals, nations, and societies, owe to children. The second concept is a radical shift in market globalism that is already in process: the shift from mass consumption towards an ideology that "small is beautiful." This shift toward sustainability and a circular economy would have to occur at every level of globalism, but it begins in the small worlds of children, families, and neighborhoods, where the solidarity Pope Francis calls for is nurtured. A third shift involves activism by individuals and groups at the local level, replacing words with concrete actions.

* * *

Pope Francis stated an obvious truth, one that depends not in the slightest on a direct connection with the voice of a Creator: "Decisive progress cannot be made without an increased awareness that we are all part of one human family, united by bonds of fraternity and solidarity. Only by thinking and acting with constant concern for this underlying unity that overrides all differences, only by cultivating a sense of universal intergenerational solidarity, can we set out really and resolutely on the road ahead" (McKibben 2018, quoting Pope Francis). The value of solidarity, although fundamental to the religious teachings of many different faiths, is not confined to religious ideology. With every passing day, its moral and ethical dimensions are becoming less vague and abstract, and the pragmatic, common-sense dimensions of solidarity—including strategies such as mutual support, collaboration, problem-solving, mutual respect, and nurturing of a common purpose—are becoming more concrete. But solidarity begins in the home, the school, the neighborhood, the village: not in the abstract realms of policy, but in the small worlds of children.

PART 4

Transforming the Ecology of Childhood

10

The Role of Children's Rights

Where do human rights begin? In small places, close to home—so close and so small that they cannot be seen on any map of the world. Yet they are the world of the individual person: The neighborhood he lives in; the school or college he attends; the factory, farm, or office where he works. Such are the places where every man, woman, and child seeks equal justice, equal opportunity, equal dignity without discrimination. Unless these rights have meaning there, they have little meaning anywhere.
—Eleanor Roosevelt, "Where Do Human Rights Begin?"

It was Eleanor Roosevelt, speaking to the United Nations about the 1948 Universal Declaration on Human Rights, who posed what has come to be known as the "Great Question" of human rights. Rather than pointing to some vast abstract external source, she traced the beginnings of human rights to the everyday lives of men, women, and children, in small places, close to home. In part 4 of this book, I will argue that the overarching principles of universal human rights, far from being distant abstractions, can serve as a blueprint for preserving and protecting the small worlds of children.

The preceding sections of this book have focused less on the law than on social-science data, using an ecological model drawn from the social and developmental sciences to investigate the environments of childhood. In part 1, we focused on the microsystems (e.g., family, school, faith community) where children live. In part 2 we examined the mesosystems where their worlds intersect, and the role of these zones as seedbeds of solidarity or sites of alienation. In part 3, which examined the influence of systems where children rarely go, we saw how the exosystems such as parent's workplace, health care systems, social welfare systems, and the market economy sometimes directly but more often indirectly affect children and often determine whether their needs are met and their voices heard. The macrosystem, by contrast to the other levels of the ecological model, is a broad array of ideas that infiltrate all levels of the ecology. In chapter 9, under the umbrella of "globalization," we examined various threats in the contemporary macrosystem. The cultural macrosystem has been defined as "the patterning by history, power, and ideas" of the broader society in which an ecology is embedded. The macrosystem is not just "big," as its name implies. It is everywhere. Perhaps the closest analogies in the natural sciences for the macrosystem would be concepts like atmosphere, weather, and climate. We take these elements for granted, because they are all around us and seemingly beyond our control. But when the ozone layer deteriorates, we feel the heat and thus all pay the price for irresponsible policy choices.

Just as global warming is forcing a reckoning with our natural environment, the macrosystemic threats of unrestrained capitalism, technological revolution, rising inequality, mass migration, discrimination, and climate change are forcing a reckoning in our social worlds. Children are our canary in the coal mine: they exhibit the effects of a toxic environment long before it harms the workers or the bosses. Just as climate change is forcing us to take responsibility for harms inflicted on the natural world, these factors are forcing us to take account of the damage we are doing to the social environment and the threat this poses to the future generations on which our survival depends. The cultural macrosystem, far more than the physical atmosphere or climate, is clearly within human control. Indeed, it is created and replicated by humans. Even more than in our relationship with the natural world, human societies have the capacity to reshape their macrosystems and to change the patterning of human societies.

In the remaining pages of this book, I call for a transformation of the macrosystems that shape and channel our policies affecting children—a transformation that must begin by putting children's needs and rights at the center rather than on the margins. Before embarking on this process, several preliminary tasks remain. The first is setting a goal. If we do not have a clear goal in our sights, and if we lack clarity over who is responsible for the work of getting from here to there, it will be difficult or impossible to move forward. Ecogenerist theory, described in chapter 2, posits that our shared goal must be to protect and enhance a healthy and supportive social and natural environment for future generations. Current reality demands that we identify sustainable goals and reach them through sustainable means, and we can mobilize objective, evidence-based science to take us part of the way in charting our course. But how do we define what constitutes a healthy environment? Generating a definition of a "good childhood" and deciding who should share in the responsibility for achieving it is an inherently value-laden enterprise (Wall 2010). In my work, I have proposed that we adopt a theory of children's rights as our value system in moving forward. A children's-rights perspective emphasizes the needs of children and establishes a shared responsibility for meeting these needs (Woodhouse 2008).

In the world of law-making, the work of reaching consensus on universalizing principles that accommodate a wide range of values is the realm of human rights law. Generating a theory of children's rights and adults' responsibility toward children is no easy or simple task, but we do not have to start from scratch. As we shall see, a basic framework already exists and has been ratified on a global scale by virtually every nation but the United States. Formally titled the United Nations Convention on the Rights of the Child, this charter introduced in 1989 is also known as the Children's Rights Convention, or CRC (Wall 2016). In every other country but the United States, any analysis of systems serving children or affecting their lives would begin with citations of the CRC's principles. More important, by ratifying this treaty every other nation has agreed to periodically examine its policies affecting children, in order to identify areas where improvement is needed. Since the CRC entered into force, the African Union, a regional group, has adopted a regional charter on children's rights to supplement and reinforce the global charter, placing it within a distinctly African context (African Charter on the Rights and Welfare of the Child 1990). Other treaties, such as the Additional Protocol to the American Convention on Human Rights in the Area of Economic, Social and Cultural Rights (Protocol of San Salvador) as well as the ASEAN Human Rights Declaration (AHDR) have specific provisions that cover the specific rights of children and youth in specific geographic and cultural contexts. Another important source for children's rights is the United Nations Declaration on the Rights of Indigenous Peoples (UNDRIP), which was adopted by majority vote of the UN General Assembly on September 13, 2007 (United Nations 2008). It contains a number of provisions that deal with the rights of indigenous children in contexts that mirror the actual injustices they have suffered at the hands of settler-colonial governments. For example, Article 7 declares that children are not to be taken from their parents, a practice that harmed indigenous children not only in the United States but in many other developed nations. While the United States, together with Australia, New Zealand, and Canada, voted in opposition to this resolution, all other nations have subsequently adopted it. In this chapter, I will highlight the children's-rights principles outlined in international law, with a special focus on the CRC, to show how concepts of children's essential needs and inalienable rights have gained global recognition and how they can shape and drive the project of ecological reform.

Comparing Constitutional Rights and Human Rights

It is important at the outset to distinguish between human rights and constitutional rights. Americans tend to think of rights in terms of those protections embodied in the US Constitution. However, the concept that certain rights preexisted and justified the American Revolution played a crucial role in the framers' thinking. The Declaration of Independence speaks of the "inalienable rights" to life, liberty and happiness, and the preamble to the Constitution defines among its purposes "preserving the blessings of liberty to ourselves and our posterity." But the framers did not fully trust government. Even as they sought to establish a new nation, they were worried about government overreaching. They added the Bill of Rights to the Constitution to define what the federal government could *not* do *to* its people rather than what it *must* do *for* them. This type of protection is referred to as "negative rights" or "civil and political rights," while the affirmative duties of a government toward its people are called "positive rights" or "economic and social rights."

The US Constitution, which dates back to 1789, is terse and streamlined compared to many modern constitutions. It is silent regarding positive or economic and social rights such as health care, education, housing, a basic standard of living, or income supports for persons in need because of job loss, age, and disability. The Italian Constitution, drafted in the aftermath of World War II, explicitly recognizes these economic and social rights as part of government's responsibility to its citizens. In the United States, social welfare programs such as Social Security, Medicaid, and Medicare are not guaranteed by the Constitution. We often call them a form of "entitlement," which sounds and functions a lot like a right. But since these programs were enacted by Congress, they can be repealed by or defunded by Congress and crippled by executive action or inaction. If government offers them to anyone, eligibility must conform to constitutional principles of nondiscrimination and fair application. But these entitlements exist at the will of Congress.

The news that there is no federal constitutional right to education comes as a shock to many Americans. My students often insist that I must be mistaken. Of course education is a constitutional right, they say, pointing to the 1954 landmark desegregation case *Brown v. Board of Education*. But *Brown* was an antidiscrimination case, applying Fourteenth Amendment guarantees of equal protection of the law. It held only that, if government provides a public good such as public education, it may not restrict access or dole out the benefit based on race. If state, local, or federal governments are not willing to provide a good on a nondiscriminatory basis, they may cut the Gordian knot by simply eliminating these public resources. This is exactly what many municipalities did during the civil rights movement, closing down public schools and public pools to evade Supreme Court desegregation orders. Although many state constitutions include a right to free public education, the Supreme

Court has refused to recognize a federal constitutional right to education (*San Antonio Independent School District v. Rodriquez* 1973).

Other landmark cases that we think of as children's-rights cases, such as 1967's *In re Gault*, rest on Fourteenth-Amendment guarantees of due process. *In re Gault* involved a boy who was sent to a juvenile correctional facility without a fair trial; he was deprived of the basic protections of due process, such as notice of the charges against him, the right to be heard, or access to an attorney. The court commented: "Under our Constitution, the condition of being a boy does not justify a kangaroo court (*In re Gault* 1967, 28)." These cases and others like them recognized that existing constitutional doctrines of equal protection and due process applied to children and youth as well as adults. But these cases are not based on protections of children as children. Unlike more modern constitutions, such as that of the Republic of South Africa, the US Constitution lacks any explicit discussion of the rights of children or of families. Because the US Constitution is a living document that changes with changing times, modern concepts of rights can gradually become incorporated into constitutional law. Rights to gender equality, family integrity, and marriage are examples of such changes (Woodhouse 1999). However, when it comes to children, the process of incorporation has been halting and piecemeal. At this writing, US constitutional law provides no comprehensive vision of the rights of children.

Human Rights as the Ozone Layer of the Global Ecological Model

Children were also largely neglected by international human rights law until the late twentieth century. The League of Nations had introduced a nonbinding Declaration on the Rights of the Child in 1925. And in the 1947 UN Declaration on Human Rights, Article 28 explicitly recognized children's rights to special protections. But the development of a comprehensive document defining the human rights of children and youth dates to 1979, when, in recognition of the International Year of the Child, the United Nations convened an ad hoc working group to draft a treaty on children's rights. After ten years of discussions and drafts, the CRC was opened for signature in November 1989. The treaty gathered sufficient signatories to enter into force in record time, in September 1990, and has become the most rapidly and universally accepted human rights document in history.

Human rights treaties are similar in some respects to constitutions: they transcend laws passed by parliaments or legislatures, drawing boundaries around politics as usual. Even when passed by a majority vote of a congress or parliament, a law that conflicts with a national constitution can be attacked in a court of law and invalidated. Human rights treaties play a similar role at the international level, placing limits on the international legal and moral authority of nations to transgress certain values. However, treaties and conventions, in comparison to national laws, do not necessarily provide a clear-cut path to court. Most constitutions allow an individual to bring a lawsuit and obtain a remedy for the wrong suffered. In the United States, especially, we assume that every right, by definition, must have a remedy. Human rights documents often operate at a more atmospheric level; they create a global layer of protection against injustices, in the form of a document that represents the global consensus among nations on how people should be treated. This is why I call them the "ozone layer" of the law (Woodhouse 2008a). In describing the role of law in the ecological model, I have analogized laws and policies to water in the natural ecosystem—an essential element that permeates everything, infusing macrosystemic values throughout the system. Human rights can be seen as the ozone layer of global law. The integrity and effectiveness of this layer are essential to protecting children from the harsh effects of selfish, destructive, and abusive policies. The CRC has been a powerful force in shaping macrosystemic values at national, regional, and international levels (Stalford and Drywood 2011).

Admittedly, the CRC is not the only way to conceptualize the human rights of children. Many other variations and theories on the theme of rights for children and youth coexist with the CRC. For example, the Church of England recently published guidelines for diocesan schools to use in ensuring that children who identify, or are coming to identify, as gay, lesbian, bisexual, or transgender are not discriminated against and that their right to express themselves, particularly in the domain of human sexuality, is protected (Church of England Education Office 2017). Elsewhere, foster-care bills of rights establish standards for the protection of children in foster families (NCSL 2016).

One of the variations on the theme of rights for children is my own innovation. In *Hidden in Plain Sight: The Tragedy of Children's Rights from Ben Franklin to Lionel Tate*, my objective was persuading US readers that, despite our refusal to ratify the CRC, children's rights are not alien to the American way but rather are deeply rooted in our own history and traditions (Woodhouse 2008a). As mentioned earlier, I proposed an "ecogenerist" theory of children's rights, combining the "eco" in ecology with the concept of "generativity." This term was inspired by the environmental sciences and Eric Erikson's theories of human development. I suggested that the special nature of childhood, as a time of inherent dependency and also of evolving capacity, gives rise to another way of classifying children's rights—as "needs-based" and "capacity-based" rights. I identified five core principles that should inform our thinking about children's rights: Privacy, Agency, Equality, Dignity, and Protection. Using stories from the American experience, I showed how rights to privacy and autonomy, and rights to protection and assistance, function as complementary elements in a larger theory of children's rights. Ecogenerism was not presented as a replacement for the CRC, nor is it inconsistent with it. The concept of indivisibility is as central to ecogenerism as it is to other human rights schemes. However, in the current project, where we are dealing with comparisons at the international level, the CRC rightfully takes center stage as the global standard.

The Basic Principles of the Convention on the Rights of the Child

Entire books have been dedicated to the CRC. It is also easily available on the internet (Todres et al. 2006; Detrick 1999; Invernizzi and Williams 2011). Therefore, my goal in this section is to introduce its basic concepts as they unfold in the small worlds of children. The CRC is essentially a litany of basic human rights, but it also adds provisions that recognize factors unique to childhood, such as the immaturity and evolving capacities of children, the rights of parents to guide children's upbringing, and children's special vulnerability and needs for protection. The treaty's preamble states that it will augment, not displace, children's human rights, by adding specific rights for the protection of children *in addition* to the general rights they enjoy as human beings.

Although it does not set forth operative provisions, the preamble provides valuable context for interpreting the CRC. It situates children's rights within the larger scheme of human rights and emphasizes the role of family, broadly defined, as the fundamental unit of society and as the natural environment for children's growth. The core of the treaty consists of forty-one articles, some discussing overarching principles, others various specific rights. The term "States Parties" as used in the CRC text refers to all the nations that have ratified the treaty and are bound by it. It is important to note that States Parties are free to and often do register reservations that limit agreement to specific articles or explain their positions on a particular provision. It is also important to note that huge gaps remain between the lofty aspirations of the CRC and the global reality of children's lives.

The CRC in Child-Friendly Language

What you see printed below is not the official UN text but rather its operative articles translated into child-friendly language. The UNICEF website presents several brightly illustrated versions in many languages, including Italian and

Ukrainian. I give the child-friendly text as a handout to students in my children's law classes to remind them that the CRC may have been drafted and is interpreted by lawyers, but it was written for children. I can think of no more powerful way to convey the spirit of the CRC than to present it in the plain language designed to make it accessible to young people and their families.

UN Convention on the Rights of the Child, Child-Friendly Version, New York: UNICEF 2012

Preamble: "Rights" are things every child should have or be able to do. All children have the same rights. These rights are listed in the UN Convention on the Rights of the Child. Almost every country has agreed to these rights. All the rights are connected to each other, and all are equally important. Sometimes, we have to think about rights in terms of what is the best for children in a situation, and what is critical to life and protection from harm. As you grow, you have more responsibility to make choices and exercise your rights.

Article 1 Everyone under 18 has these rights.

Article 2 All children have these rights, no matter who they are, where they live, what their parents do, what language they speak, what their religion is, whether they are a boy or girl, what their culture is, whether they have a disability, whether they are rich or poor. No child should be treated unfairly on any basis.

Article 3 All adults should do what is best for you. When adults make decisions, they should think about how their decisions will affect children.

Article 4 The government has a responsibility to make sure your rights are protected. They must help your family to protect your rights and create an environment where you can grow and reach your potential.

Article 5 Your family has the responsibility to help you learn to exercise your rights, and to ensure that your rights are protected.

Article 6 You have the right to be alive.

Article 7 You have the right to a name, and this should be officially recognized by the government. You have the right to a nationality (to belong to a country).

Article 8 You have the right to an identity—an official record of who you are. No one should take this away from you.

Article 9 You have the right to live with your parent(s), unless it is bad for you. You have the right to live with a family who cares for you.

Article 10 If you live in a different country than your parents do, you have the right to be together in the same place.

Article 11 You have the right to be protected from kidnapping.

Article 12 You have the right to give your opinion, and for adults to listen and take it seriously.

Article 13 You have the right to find out things and share what you think with others, by talking, drawing, writing or in any other way unless it harms or offends other people.

Article 14 You have the right to choose your own religion and beliefs. Your parents should help you decide what is right and wrong, and what is best for you.

Article 15 You have the right to choose your own friends and join or set up groups, as long as it isn't harmful to others.

Article 16 You have the right to privacy.

Article 17 You have the right to get information that is important to your well-being, from radio, news-paper, books, computers and other sources. Adults should make sure that the information you are getting is not harmful, and help you find and understand the information you need.

Article 18 You have the right to be raised by your parent(s) if possible.

Article 19 You have the right to be protected from being hurt and mistreated, in body or mind.

Article 20 You have the right to special care and help if you cannot live with your parents.

Article 21 You have the right to care and protection if you are adopted or in foster care.

Article 22 You have the right to special protection and help if you are a refugee (if you have been forced to leave your home and live in another country), as well as all the rights in this Convention.

Article 23 You have the right to special education and care if you have a disability, as well as all the rights in this Convention, so that you can live a full life.

Article 24 You have the right to the best health care possible, safe water to drink, nutritious food, a clean and safe environment, and information to help you stay well.

Article 25 If you live in care or in other situations away from home, you have the right to have these living arrangements looked at regularly to see if they are the most appropriate.

Article 26 You have the right to help from the government if you are poor or in need.

Article 27 You have the right to food, clothing, a safe place to live and to have your basic needs met. You should not be disadvantaged so that you can't do many of the things other kids can do.

Article 28 You have the right to a good quality education. You should be encouraged to go to school to the highest level you can.

Article 29 Your education should help you use and develop your talents and abilities. It should also help you learn to live peacefully, protect the environment and respect other people.

Article 30 You have the right to practice your own culture, language and religion—or any you choose. Minority and indigenous groups need special protection of this right.

Article 31 You have the right to play and rest.

Article 32 You have the right to protection from work that harms you, and is bad for your health and education. If you work, you have the right to be safe and paid fairly.

Article 33 You have the right to protection from harmful drugs and from the drug trade.

Article 34 You have the right to be free from sexual abuse.

Article 35 No one is allowed to kidnap or sell you.

Article 36 You have the right to protection from any kind of exploitation (being taken advantage of).

Article 37 No one is allowed to punish you in a cruel or harmful way.

Article 38 You have the right to protection and freedom from war. Children under 15 cannot be forced to go into the army or take part in war.

Article 39 You have the right to help if you've been hurt, neglected or badly treated.

Article 40 You have the right to legal help and fair treatment in the justice system that respects your rights.

Article 41 If the laws of your country provide better protection of your rights than the articles in this Convention, those laws should apply.

Article 42 You have the right to know your rights! Adults should know about these rights and help you learn about them, too.

Overarching Principles of the CRC in Both Simple and Complex Terms

The first five articles of the CRC set out its overarching principles. Article 1 defines who is covered. For children, the straightforward statement that "everyone under 18 has these rights" is clear and simple. This is the child's perspective. For judges charged with defining legal terms, there are nuances behind the drafters' choice of words. For example, Article 1 in the official text defines "child" as "every human being below the age of 18 years." This wording was the result of compromise, to avoid the divisive and ultimately unanswerable question of when life begins.

Article 2 states a broad nondiscrimination principle. The child-friendly version is very direct and personalized ("All children have these rights, no matter who they are, where they live, what their parents do") and uses the language of fairness and unfairness ("No child should be treated unfairly on any basis"). Fairness is among the earliest moral values children understand and is central to the development of the CRC (Freeman 1997; Coles 1986). The official text provides a list of terms commonly used in legal documents (race; color; sex; language; religion; political or other opinion; national, ethnic, or social origin; property; disability; birth). But it also adds an important catch-all phrase: "any other status." Under rules of legal interpretation this phrase establishes that the list is not exclusive. Examples of groups not specifically listed that have been targeted for discrimination because of their status include HIV-positive children, transgender children, and children created through new reproductive technologies. These nuances are important to the adults charged with protecting children's rights.

Article 3 invokes a legal doctrine known as "the best interest of the child." While it appears in many legal systems, the "best interest" standard is often criticized as vague, subjective, and malleable. The child-friendly language cuts through this debate by couching the principle in subjective terms: "All adults should do what is best for you. When adults make decisions, they should think about how their decisions will affect children." In both versions, however, the transformative innovation is that *all* adult decision-makers, not just parents and judges, should make children's well-being central to their actions.

Article 4 commits signatory states to implement the rights set forth in the convention, not just by passing laws but by actually assisting families in realizing their children's social, cultural, and economic rights. This concept of positive rights to support is largely absent from systems based on negative rights. However, even the child-friendly version of the CRC is crystal clear on this point: "Government must help your family to protect your rights and to create an environment where you can grow and reach your potential." How should we measure the extent of government's duty of support? The children's version is silent on this question. But the more formal language of the CRC explains, "With regard to economic, social and cultural rights, States Parties shall undertake such measures to the maximum extent of their available resources and, where needed, within the framework of international co-operation." This principle is familiar from family law. We recognize the injustice of leaving children of divorced or unmarried parents "peering through the windows" at the affluent lifestyle of a rich parent who refuses to share. Rich nations, like wealthy parents, have an obligation to support their children in a manner appropriate to their economic resources. According to Article 24 (4), developing countries, like poor parents, should do their best given their resources, but should also receive international assistance and support.

Article 5 establishes an overarching principle of respect for the rights, responsibilities, and duties of parents and also articulates the parents' duty to respect the "evolving capacities" of the child. Are these rights and responsibilities restricted to the nuclear family? The child-friendly version of Article 5 lets the child define the family unit: "Your family has the responsibility to help you learn to exercise your rights." The official text is more elaborate; it refers to "the rights and duties of parents." But it also reaches, "where applicable, members of the extended family or community as provided by local custom." This structure leaves room for local customs and variations in defining the family—elements that, not incidentally, are constitutive of the child's own definition of family.

The rest of Part 1, from Article 6 to Article 42, is a list of specific rights. Each is expressed from the children's perspective in the child-friendly version, but elaborated in the official text aimed at adults. Many of the specific provisions describe rights attributed to all human beings; others are tailored to children's special situation. In the remainder of this chapter, rather than focusing on specific rights, we will examine the CRC's structures for implementation and consider how the overarching values of the CRC can inform and reshape the ecology of childhood.

CRC Part 2: Implementing Children's Rights

Part 2 of the CRC (Articles 43 to 54) outlines procedures for ratification, future implementation, and international cooperation. The first article is a commitment of the States Parties to make the provisions of the CRC widely known to adults and to children alike. The right to know your rights is integral to the

CRC, which views children both as active agents as well as passive recipients of care. Because of the CRC, children's rights of participation have blossomed in recent years and have become a staple of national and international policymaking (Baraldi and Maggioni 2003; Bellotti 2011; Rossi and Tagliaventi 2011; Woodhouse 2014a).

Another article outlines procedures for formation of a Committee on the Rights of the Child, to be composed of ten experts, nominated and elected by States Parties, to serve staggered four-year terms. Perhaps the most significant strategy for encouraging concrete steps toward realization of children's rights is the commitment of all States Parties to submit periodic country reports. These reports describe the nation's progress in realizing the goals of the CRC and identifying barriers to their achievement. The goal of the reporting provision is to make sure that children's issues appear regularly on the policy agenda of each State Party. In addition to government officials and agencies, nongovernmental organizations (NGOs) have opportunities to contribute. States Parties must lodge these reports with the General Assembly and make them widely available to the public in their own countries. The committee provides feedback on these reports, although its comments and suggestions are purely advisory.

This process of self-examination and international dialogue, when it works as intended, helps to place children's rights in their cultural, social, and historical context and encourages the setting of priorities that are meaningful and responsive to local needs. I have observed this process in action. In 1999, I was invited by Jaap Doek, then serving as chair of the Committee on the Rights of the Child, to observe a hearing at the Japanese Diet in Tokyo, where the committee presented its comments on the Japanese country report submitted a year earlier. I was surprised to learn that among the most pressing challenges identified by the Japanese was an epidemic of children refusing to go to school and becoming recluses in their own homes. Children were even committing suicide in alarming numbers because of school anxiety. At the time, in the United States, we would have pointed to school shootings and the black/white achievement gap as among our most troubling educational challenges. As this example illustrates, no two national contexts are identical, and often the challenges and barriers to the full realization of a specific right are unique and call for unique solutions. In many developing nations, access to education is simply not available because of lack of resources. In other countries, gender discrimination presents the most serious threat to the right to education.

The CRC has evolved since 1989 with the addition of several Optional Protocols. The United States has actually joined two Optional Protocols, one on child trafficking and one on child soldiers, which forbids using children under eighteen in armed conflict, while still declining to ratify the treaty itself. At the time it came into force, the CRC did not include any mechanism for bringing specific violations of children's rights before any international tribunal. In 2011, an Optional Protocol was opened for signature that would allow individuals to bring their claims to the Committee on the Rights of the Child. As of December 2018, this third Optional Protocol had been signed by fifty-two countries and ratified by forty-one (Optional Protocol 2011).

How the CRC Can Inform and Reshape the Ecology of Childhood

The overarching principles of the CRC should inform and reshape our approach to the ecology of childhood. Among the innovations in these overarching principles are: (1) a holistic approach to best interests; (2) a commitment that unites public and private spheres; (3) a focus on systems and systemic change; and (4) a developmentally informed approach to children's participation. Together they have great potential for renewing the ecology of childhood.

Viewing Best Interests through the Lens of Indivisibility

A basic principle of human rights is that human rights are "interdependent and indivisible" (Nickel 2008, 985). Experts on human rights have written thousands of pages debating and discussing the exact meaning and application of this principle (Nickel 1993; Whelan 2010). As the UNICEF web page explains, "Although human rights are often divided into categories—civil and political rights, and economic, social and cultural rights—rights cannot be treated separately or in distinct categories because the enjoyment of one right usually depends on the fulfillment of other rights" (2014a). Advocates for children were reminded of this truth when it was discovered that a campaign from American and European advocates to boycott oriental-rug factories that employed children had the unintended consequence of forcing girls who lost their weaving jobs into prostitution (Todres 2006). Clearly the rights to leisure, to protection from abuse, or to an education are meaningless to a child who is starving or living on the streets. For this reason, especially when it comes to children, we cannot treat rights as separate and independent. Children's rights must be regarded as a fabric of interwoven elements that stabilize and strengthen the whole.

One important way in which the CRC and other charters of children's rights contribute to our understanding of the ecology of childhood is their insistence that the best interests of children must be a primary consideration in all of our actions, whether public or private, that affect children's welfare. This obligation is much broader than the cramped notion of "best interests of the child" as it is generally applied in Anglo-American family law. The best-interests standard appears in numerous family law statutes, from adoption to child custody to child protection, and instructs the decision-maker to ask which decision among the available choices will be in the best interests of this child. As noted earlier, it has been criticized for vagueness and subjectivity. It can often be reductive, focusing on just one aspect of the child's life; misapplied and misunderstood, it can lead the decision-maker to substitute personal views and cultural biases for an evidence-based, developmentally informed, and child-centered analysis of the child's interests. When included in a human rights charter such as the CRC, the concept of best interests incorporates the child's interests not just in material terms but in *the full panoply of rights.*

History provides many glaring examples of the misuse of best interests to rob children of their rights. Children of indigenous peoples were routinely separated from their families on the grounds that it would be in their best interests to be saved from backward cultures by forcible integration in the dominant culture (Niezen 2013). Vagrant children in Victorian England and the United States were swept up in raids and placed in workhouses or exported to other states and nations on the ground that it would be in their best interests to put them to useful work in a wholesome environment (Woodhouse 2008a). At the close of the Civil War, many thousands of black children in Southern states were reenslaved, under the theory that it would be in their best interests to be in the custody of their white former owners instead of their parents (Holt 1994). As recently as the 1980s, a custody judge in Texas removed a white child from her mother, who had married a black man, on the grounds that it would be in the child's best interests to protect her from social stigma (*Palmore v. Sidotti*, 466 US 429, 1984). In the classroom, after highlighting these cases, I ask my students to go to the list of CRC Articles and identify other rights that were ignored or trampled upon by this shallow conception of children's "best interests." The exercise is eye-opening.

Building a Bridge across the Public Private Divide

The CRC's application of the best-interest principle to all actors, public and private, and to governments as well as parents, is also a major breakthrough. The best-interests principle, in US law, has generally been applied to the actions of those who have or who seek legal custody of a child. While parents and guardians have a duty to protect the children in their care, there is no general duty on the part of other private actors to protect children or consider their best interests. When it comes to state agencies, the "state action" doctrine developed by our Supreme Court places strict limits on the positive obligations of government to act as opposed to its negative obligations to refrain from acting. Even when a child is under the supervision of a state child protection agency, the Supreme Court has held that our Constitution does not impose a duty to protect, unless the child is actually in state custody (*DeShaney v. Winnebago County Department of Social Services*, 489 US 189, 1989). But pressure has been mounting to expand the concept of state responsibility for children beyond these limits.

Variations on a Bill of Rights for Children have been adopted by many state and local governments, and courts have issued regulations and handbooks establishing duties of care. Borrowing from the environmental movement, advocates for children have called for children's impact statements, modeled on environmental impact statements (Hanna, Hassall & Davies 2006). They argue that before any policy is enacted or major change is undertaken, we should examine how it will impact the environment for children. By bridging the divide between private and public responsibility, the CRC advances a more ecological understanding of children's rights. It gives support to the argument that children's interests are not marginal to the discussion of policy and *must* be considered as a primary element in our individual and collective actions affecting them.

But the CRC goes far beyond the best-interest principle. By recognizing positive as well as negative rights, the CRC responds to the irrefutable needs of children for support and protection as well as for liberty and autonomy. And it makes clear the public stake in supporting the private family. States Parties have the responsibility of not only recognizing these rights, but also of ensuring that steps are taken to make them a reality in the lives of children. States Parties must do more than refrain from interfering in the privacy of the family; they must provide support and assistance. As in the ecological model, children are seen in social context, in relationship to their families, and to the surrounding culture and community, as they are embedded in intimate microsystems and are dependent on the external exosystems that can either sustain or fail them. The CRC, like the ecological model, recognizes that many other influences besides the family play a role in determining whether an environment is fit for or harmful to children.

Integrating Child Development into a Rights Framework

Historically, the common law excluded minors from asserting their own legal rights. On reaching the age of majority, they instantly passed from childhood to adulthood and became fully autonomous individuals able to enter into contracts and make their own decisions. Obviously, this was a "legal fiction"—a legal concept that does not reflect reality. Common sense and developmental science tell us that maturation does not happen in an instant: maturation is a process. In recent years, US law has begun to integrate this reality into its laws, but it has taken a piecemeal and ad hoc approach. It is not uncommon now to see references to child development in judicial opinions and statutes, as well as increasing attention to children's evolving maturity in laws that require family court judges to take children's views into account in adoption and custody cases. We see neuroscience influencing rulings under the Eighth Amendment, holding that it is cruel and unusual punishment to subject adolescents who commit crimes to the same standards and penalties as adults. We see respect for adolescents' evolving capacities reflected in the "mature minor doctrine," which recognizes the rights of sufficiently mature pregnant minors to make decisions about childbearing. We also see a shift toward the assumption that effective parenting involves respect for the individual child's evolving capacities.

The CRC makes clear that children's rights and parents' rights are interwoven. Many of a child's rights pertain to protection of family privacy, family relationships, and family-support services (Article 18). Parents function as the natural guardians of their children's well-being. As noted earlier, Article 5 of the CRC recognizes the rights and duties of parents to guide and direct children in the exercise of their rights "in a manner consistent with their evolving capacities": the right belongs to the child, but parents hold these rights in trust for the child. The CRC goes beyond recognizing parental rights and commits States Parties to respect and support parents in this role of trustee. Critics have claimed that the CRC somehow diminishes the rights of parents, but human rights are not a zero-sum game (Woodhouse 2006b). Children's rights add to and do not subtract from the totality of rights enjoyed by members of a family. Recognition that children have rights of their own empowers parents to assert not only their own rights to parental control and custody but the child's rights to equal protection of the law. This is what Linda Brown's father did in *Brown v. Board of Education*. The notion of "evolving capacities" is familiar to every parent. Children start out entirely dependent and gradually achieve greater levels of autonomy. The CRC asks parents to take account of the child's progression toward autonomy as they go about the role of guiding and directing their child.

An important vehicle for implementing children's evolving capacities is in Article 12, which figures importantly in chapter 11 in this book. Article 12 recognizes children's right to voice an opinion and to be heard in court cases, administrative proceedings, or other matters affecting the child: "States Parties shall assure to the child who is capable of forming his or her own views the right to express those views freely in all matters affecting the child, the views of the child being given due weight in accordance with the age and maturity of the child" (Article 12, para. 1). While the fully autonomous adult rights-holder is entitled to make his or her own choice, the child is given the more limited right to a voice. The right to a voice—to be heard—is fundamental even when the child is not empowered to make the ultimate decision (*In re Gault*, 387 US 1, 1967). Decision-makers are instructed not merely to hear the opinions of children who have sufficient maturity to express them, but actually to consider and give due weight to the child's opinion.

Earlier in this chapter, I set out certain preliminary steps necessary to the process of transforming children's ecologies. The first was setting a goal: to protect and enhance a healthy and supportive social and natural environment for future generations. While scientific evidence could take us part of the way, charting the way forward would require defining a values metric for evaluating a healthy environment—or, if you will, a "good" childhood. It was also necessary to determine who would be responsible for providing the means to this end. The CRC provides answers to both these questions.

* * *

In this chapter we have explored how the CRC, reflecting the wisdom of the ecological model, can advance our goals. Children are not the independent autonomous individuals of classic liberal theory. They begin in total dependency and are nourished by intimate relationships and embedded in communities and in cultures. In order to meet children's needs, we must respect children's evolving capacities. Room for children's progress toward maturity must be integrated across the ecological environment, in the microsystems of families, schools, and neighborhoods, as well as at every other level. In the United States, even more than in other peer nations, this will require a revolution of the dominant macrosystems.

11

How the CRC Affects Actual Children's Lives

Some adults these days don't listen to what us kids say. Am I right or wrong?
Maybe they need to be trained to understand our views.
—Council of Europe, "Challenges to Children's Rights Today"

In the preceding chapter, I examined the role of human rights in defining our individual and collective obligations to children, and I proposed the CRC as a value system and source of norms for healing the ecology of childhood. In this chapter, I will respond to the claim—voiced by critics on both the left and the right—that the CRC has no impact in the real world. What follows is a demonstration, illustrated with stories from my fieldwork, of how the static articles of the CRC actually play out for children and their families in the intimate environments of home, school, neighborhood, and community. The actualization of human rights, for children as for all persons, requires a dynamic and complex performance and takes place in a real world in real time.

It is no easy task translating words into lived experience. I have struggled to find a proper metaphor to describe the dynamic interplay of specific CRC rights and children's environments. Suppose we imagine these rights as musical notes, and the children and young people, supported by their families and communities, as the creators and performers of the music; the ecological setting in which they are situated is the musical score that shapes and colors the performance and brings the voices of the various performers together, or fails to perform these crucial harmonizing functions. The specific rights discussed below are merely examples—selected passages of this music. The principle of indivisibility of human rights should remind us that no individual right can be fully performed in isolation and all must be harmonized.

The discussion that follows draws on cases I encountered in my research in Italy. This is not to suggest that children's rights are absent from the US context. They are everywhere. In their book *Human Rights in Children's Literature: Imagination and the Narrative of Law*, Jonathan Todres and Sarah Higinbotham show how the books Americans read to children bring human rights principles to life (Todres and Higinbotham 2016). Classic children's books, such as Dr. Seuss's *Yertle the Turtle* and *Horton Hears a Who*, are powerful expressions of human rights. They teach that all creatures, no matter how small, situated at the top or the bottom of the heap, have voices that must be heard and rights to be protected. These themes of justice for children are universal, crossing language and cultural barriers. As Todres and Higinbotham show, the fairy tale of Cinderella is the European version of a narrative that exists in almost every culture: a universal story about a girl who is forced into servitude and denied her own heritage. Children's literature is even powerful enough to frighten dictators. Munro Leaf's *The Story of Ferdinand*, about a young bull who prefers smelling the flowers to fighting in the bull ring, was written in 1936 and banned in Nazi Germany. Stories like *Ferdinand* and Cinderella are all about the rights to own one's identity and to be protected from exploitation. As academics like Philip Veerman, John Wall, and Michael Freeman have shown, as a moral and ethical matter children's rights are undeniably human rights (Veerman 1992; Freeman 2017; Wall 2017, 2010). But the discourse of children's human rights has been so marginalized in the United States that it takes gifted authors like Todres and Higinbotham to show us that we actually do teach human rights to children, and that we began to do so long before the CRC was written.

Here is how some of the rights articulated in the CRC can and have changed the lives of real children in a country where the CRC has gained acceptance and been integrated into the fabric of the law and of life.

The Right to Play

> CRC Article 31 (1) States Parties recognize the right of the child to rest and leisure, to engage in play and recreational activities appropriate to the age of the child and to participate freely in cultural life and the arts.
> —United Nations Convention on the Child (CRC), 1990

FRIENDSHIPS
At our desks in school
We study and we play
We do classwork together
And beautiful friendships are born.
Our hearts laugh
At the sound of the school bell,
And we get together again in the *Ciambella*
Where we always find so many companions.
And, later, when it gets dark

Mamma, who has
the patience of a saint,
prepares a bath and supper.
—Filippo Di Rienzo, "Amicizie"

Filippo's Story: Playing in the Ciambella

Play is one of the most fundamental rights of children. Experts know how important it is for their development. According to the American Academy of Pediatrics (AAP), "Play is not frivolous: it enhances brain structure and function and promotes executive function (i.e., the process of learning, rather than the content), which allow us to pursue goals and ignore distractions." When play is missing from a child's life, "toxic stress can disrupt the development of executive function and the learning of prosocial behavior" (Yogman et al. 2018, 1). Yet unstructured play has become so marginalized in the United States that the AAP actually advises pediatricians to write prescriptions for play at children's well visits. Children couldn't agree more. Play is often the first thing they mention when asked about their environment. Play, friends, and family compete for the place of honor. The right to play has a spatial dimension (places in which to play), a relational dimension (people with whom to play), and a cultural dimension (games and rules of play). In fifth grader Filippo's poem, written in dialect and translated by this author, we can identify all of these facets of the right to play. We can hear the rhythm of his day—school as a place for didactic learning and forming friendships; the transition from structured school to free-form play; the importance of spaces in which to assemble for play; and the role of the mother as home base and nurturer at the end of the day. Filippo's poem also traces the rhythm of the adults' day in Scanno: at eight o'clock in the evening the town center grows suddenly quiet when all creatures but a few stray dogs go home to supper.

In translating Filippo's poem, I was stumped by his reference to the *Ciambella*, although I recognized everything else in his narrative. The context of the poem indicated it must be a place name, but *Ciambella* was nowhere on any map of Scanno. The Italian dictionary translated *Ciambella* (pronounced *cham BEH' la*) as "a ring-shaped cake or doughnut." No help there. So I decided to go to the poem's source. Filippo Di Rienzo, who had written his prize-winning dialect poem in fifth grade as part of an annual school competition, was now a tall young fellow of about twenty. I had chatted with him several times at his family's shop, where he helped out between semesters at university.

228 | HOW THE CRC AFFECTS ACTUAL CHILDREN'S LIVES

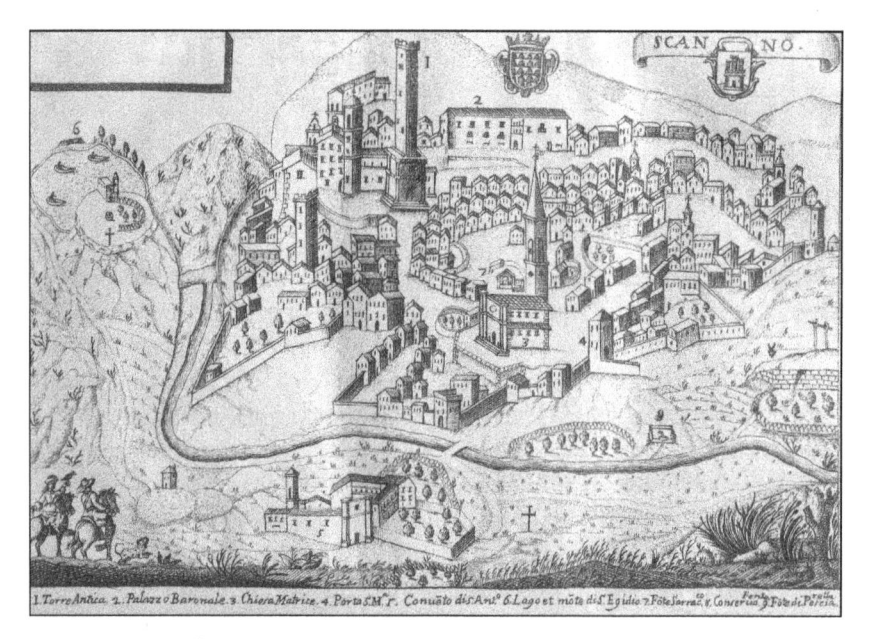

Figure 11.1. Map of Scanno in Abruzzo, Italy, seventeenth Century. DEA/A DE GREGORIO/De Agostini Editore/agefotostock.

It turned out that the Ciambella of Filippo's poem was right outside my door, and I had walked it hundreds of times unaware. As Filippo explained, *Ciambella* is the local nickname for a centuries-old loop of streets, many of them impassable to cars, that circle the heart of the historic center.

Today, although cars now travel single file along a few sections of the route, the Ciambella remains much as it was it was in the seventeenth century (fig. 11.1). You can walk the route in ten minutes, clockwise or counterclockwise, and you will see almost everyone you know. You can start anywhere along the loop, but let's take as our starting point Santa Maria della Valle, the tall, steepled church in the center of the map. Proceeding clockwise, pass the sacristy door of the church, follow the curve around the church façade overlooking the ravine below, and turn down a steep slope on Via Abrami. Continue downhill past the Fontana Sarracco. Climb uphill on Via Vincenzo Tanturri to reach Piazza Vecchia (the old piazza) in front of the tall tower. Although the tall tower rising above it was torn down centuries ago, the piazza remains a popular gathering place. There are always children biking, playing soccer, or filling their water pistols from its fountain, while old folks watch from benches. Where the tower used to be, the Ciambella route takes a sharp turn to the right and goes steeply uphill on Via Silla, passing the pocket-sized Piazza dell'Olmo (Piazza of the Elm), shaded by large elm trees, which have grown there since this map was made. My own tiny apartment in Scanno is tucked in Vico dell'Olmo (Alley of the Elm), hidden behind the Palazzo Baronale (Baronial Palace). Continuing around the Ciambella loop, proceed beyond the Palazzo Baronale along Via Silla, the uppermost street on the map, as it curves past the tiny church of San Giovanni Battista. Opposite the church is a mini piazza, just big enough for kids to practice soccer moves, play tag, and jump rope. Up ahead, a bit further along Via Silla, is another favorite destination for children, Grazia's toy store. At Grazia's store, the Ciambella route takes a sharp turn to the right and threads back toward the center of town through Via dei Angelis, a dark and narrow pedestrian passage several blocks long but only wide enough for three people walking abreast, and too narrow to appear on the seventeenth-century map. The Ciambella route emerges into the open right in front of the Di Rienzo jewelry workshop where I found Filippo, located at the top end of sunny Via Roma (recently renamed Via Henry Mancini after the American composer, one of Scanno's favorite sons). The Ciambella's final lap is a pleasant pedestrian street with a butcher shop, pizza parlor, cheese shop, and several jewelry and clothing stores. It slopes downhill to the corner of the piazza, where today stands the bronze statue of the Donna di Scanno. The map shows a tower beside one of the gates to the walled city; today, the gate is gone, and instead cars and buses pass by on a two-lane state road that connects Scanno to Naples, a few hours drive to the south. Here, we arrive back where we started, in Piazza Santa Maria della Valle, with the church to our right and the Asilo Buon Pastore, built in the 1930s, to our left, overlooking the piazza. Near the bottom of the map, downhill from the town, is the Convento di Sant' Antonio where the children of today still deliver their offerings of firewood for the festival of St. Anthony.

All along the route, in addition to churches and stores, there are alleyways and steps leading down to stone dwellings and small entryways tucked out of sight. There are myriad small public spaces that provide impromptu playgrounds for children and convenient gathering spots. The route is also well supplied with benches where parents and grandparents can rest, as well as wrought-iron handrails for icy weather. The Ciambella represents the site of children's earliest social encounters with the community. From traveling in strollers to learning to walk and run, this is where they find friends and concoct games.

Mapping children's play always presents a challenge. As observers, it is hard to process what we see without some context telling us what happens in the home, just as it is difficult to know how children think about their worlds. In exploring Scanno, I had the great good luck to have Dr. Angelo Di Gennaro as my guide and teacher. An expert on human psychology and child development, Dr. Di Gennaro is a white-haired man of about seventy with a cherubic face and an enormous store of knowledge and insights into Scanno's people and past. He presented me with a copy of *Scannismo* (Scannism), a study of the relationship between personality and environment that he had done on the children of Scanno forty years before we met (Di Gennaro 1981). It had originally been designed to explore issues of class—specifically, whether children from upper-class families developed larger vocabularies than those from lower-class families. The researchers asked 112 children in grades 1 through 5 to report, on three specific days (in February 1975, March 1975, and February 1976, respectively), what they did during the hours when they were not in school. As so often happens in designing such research projects, the expectation that the vocabulary the children used in their reports would reveal insights about class was not borne out. In fact, the reports showed very little difference between the vocabularies of Scanno children from different social classes. The researchers concluded that Scanno was an unusually class-free environment.

The finding that jumped out of the data—both qualitative and quantitative—was that the experience of growing up in Scanno seemed to shape the town's collective identity. The "*Scannismo*" of the published study's title stands for a particular culture, cemented in childhood, that bound together all who had grown up in Scanno, and that Dr. Di Gennaro believed accounted for their resilience and sense of solidarity. For me, as a student of childhood, the book was a treasure trove. In addition to learning about the social context of the village in the 1970s, I could compare the children's verbatim reports from forty years ago with my own observations of where, what, how, and with whom children played today.

Some differences between the two time periods were obvious—the advent of the smart phone, for example, and the declining numbers of children per family unit. The fact that many families from the historic town center had relocated to more modern homes on the surrounding hillsides also diluted the percentage of Scanno's children who not only played but resided in the center of town. But I soon realized that children in the 1970s and the 2010s seemed to favor many of the same play spaces and many of the same games. Self-segregation by gender was diminishing but still quite strong. Girls in the 1970s played dolls, kitchen, mother and baby, school and storekeeper, as

Figure 11.2. Girls playing *bancarella*.
B. B. Woodhouse.

well as jump rope and singing and clapping games that remained off-limits for boys. In the 2010s, groups of children of both sexes aged four to ten still played hide-and-seek and tag, now sometimes in coed groups. Older boys' favorite game was still soccer, with girls sometimes joining in. Scanno children managed to play soccer anywhere and everywhere, even in very small piazzas and narrow streets, where passing cars interrupted their game. I observed some conflict with elders over noise, but less than I might have expected. I also observed that Scanno children had invented games of their own that took advantage of the peculiarities of their play spaces. For example, I saw them playing a game in a narrow pedestrian passage of stone steps in which the challenge was to follow instructions from the leader at the top in order to be permitted to ascend the next step or risk being sent back down to the bottom. It looked a lot like a vertical version of "Mother, May I?"

Figure 11.3. Boys playing *bancarella*. B. B. Woodhouse.

I used the children's reports from the 1970s to map specific places where children played back then and observe where they played now. Some of the names children gave to their play spaces were not on any map, but I was able to locate them by asking adults who had been children in the 1970s or children who were playing there now. Scanno is unbelievably rich in nooks and crannies, hidden courtyards, narrow passages, and stairways connecting with other passages and other stairways and connecting back to the Ciambella. Children took advantage of all these spaces, in 1975 as in 2015, both to play and to find a quiet nook in which to chat. Some games required more public settings—for example, a popular place for girls to play *bancarella* (a cross between a garage sale and flea market) was on the foundation stone supporting the statue of the Donna di Scanno, perfectly situated in the path of people passing through the central piazza and up Via Roma on foot.

In another part of town, I encountered two brothers who had set up a *bancarella* with a friend on some steps near their mother's cheese shop, located in Via Tanturri. Their display of wares from their collections of toys—cars, trucks, dinosaur models, and other small play figures—was quite different from the picture frames, writing paper, and dolls on the girls' stand.

Play is a serious form of hands-on learning. When one child responded to my offer to buy an item for one euro by offering to sell it to me for two euros, she learned that bargaining the buyer up from the item's marked price is even harder than bargaining the seller down.

In present-day Scanno, the Ciambella continues its ancient role as a meeting place, where early encounters between girls and boys are monitored by the community. Now, as in the 1970s, single-sex groups of teenage boys and girls were using the Ciambella as a place to be noticed by members of the opposite sex. I even found a reference from elementary school-age girls in 1975 to "playing Ciambella" (i.e., pretending to be older girls engaging in courtship rituals). During the evenings after supper, teens still gather in mixed groups on steps and stairways along the Ciambella while adults stroll or sit on benches. On our walks, we often encounter Filippo there with a group of his twentysomething friends, and they always say *buona sera* (good evening).

But even in Scanno, globalization in its many dimensions has changed the context of children's play. We see this influence in every dimension, including shrinking pools of playmates, loss of access to wild spaces, diminished opportunities for the kind of free and imaginative play that is essential to brain development, loss of play space to what Italians call *cementificazione* (the process of covering the earth with concrete), degradation of the environment, and contamination by toxic chemicals, not to mention the impact on play of both real and metaphorical war zones created by armed conflict and concentrated poverty. As noted in chapter 9, in affluent countries the ideology of play is changing in an especially insidious way, in being co-opted by ideologies of materialism and competition.

Note that Article 31 of the CRC explicitly includes under the heading of play the right "to participate freely in cultural life and the arts." In the 1950s, when I was growing up in a small village not far from New York City, I spent a lot of time at my parents' workplace, the Bennett Conservatory of Music, which had been founded by my father and his siblings. Most students walked there on their own after school to take music, dance, and art lessons, and they often stayed an extra hour to sit around the table in the waiting room doing their homework. Today, for many American children and families, there is no more walking or wasting of an extra hour. Every minute is tightly scheduled and supervised. In this respect, Cedar Key is an outlier in the United States. In much of the country, including the safest suburbs, walking from school to lessons or just "hanging out" on the block are a thing of the past. For many families caught in the education rat race, playing a musical instrument in the school orchestra is just another box to check when building a college resume. Recapturing the right to play—be it a game of tag, rambling around town on bikes, or learning a musical instrument—is just one way in which the CRC can make a difference in actual children's lives. An important tool in this process is asking children to express their needs and likes and identify their own priorities. The following section on participation rights illustrates how careful listening can mitigate adults' tendency to undervalue the needs of a community's children and help us to appreciate how important play spaces are to children themselves.

The Right to Participation

> States Parties shall assure to the child who is capable of forming his or her own views the right to express those views freely in all matters affecting the child, the views of the child being given due weight in accordance with the age and maturity of the child. (CRC, Article 12, 1990)

Genny's Story: Youth Mayor of Scanno

At the ripe old age of twelve, Genny was the youngest member of the Scanno town council, which had adopted an ordinance that provided for election of a *Sindaco dei Ragazzi* (mayor of kids) whose role was to serve as representative of the town's school-age children. Genny looked like a future leader: tall for her age and athletic, with a serious demeanor, she glowed with good health and a warm smile. She was also already an accomplished skier. As she explained when I interviewed her, the road to youth mayor began with running for office prior to the final year of middle school, competing for votes from the entire student body. Once elected, the youth mayor became eligible to attend town council meetings. Genny met regularly with the school's student council, which was composed of representatives elected by each class.

In consultation with her constituency, she developed a platform for action that included two major initiatives. The first was pushing to get the Palazzetto dello Sport (Sports Center) brought up to code so it could be reopened to the public. A covered arena suitable for many sports activities, it had been declared in violation of a fire code, and the kids were really missing it. Second was pushing the council to restore a small grassy park that had fallen into disrepair. It had been a favorite place for kids to gather, just a little bit removed from the prying eyes of the piazza. Genny was realistic about her level of influence. She felt her advocacy had been at least fifty percent successful: the park renovation had stalled due to political infighting over funding priorities. but, by the end of her term, the sports center had been reopened. Genny counted this as a major accomplishment.

I first interviewed Genny when she was in her last year of middle school. I asked whether she thought growing up in a small village was a good or bad experience. First she listed the plusses—the close bonds that developed

Figure 11.4. Genny, youth mayor of Scanno. B. B. Woodhouse.

with classmates, the freedom to play and socialize in a safe natural environment. Among the downsides was the looming prospect of leaving the tight-knit community to attend school each day in the city of Sulmona 40 minutes away. But Genny saw the benefits of starting school in a small town and then moving to high school in a bigger city; Sulmona offered the chance to choose between several types of schools and the opportunity to meet new people. She had chosen a *liceo classico* while others chose science or vocational schools. One thing she was sure of: kids from Scanno would never feel alone or be bullied in Sulmona. As she told me, "Scanno kids always have each other's backs."

In 2018, I touched base with Genny, now in her senior year, to catch up. Some aspects of her life have changed. Global warming has made snow, once abundant in Scanno, less predictable. Genny is still athletic and a nature lover. She is passionate about horses and she goes on long trail rides in the mountains with her friends. She is an ardent supporter of action to combat climate change. Asked how she feels about her stint as youth mayor she replies that "it seems so long ago" and then adds, "Besides, there haven't been any more elections for youth mayor." It seems the leaders in Scanno may have violated a basic best practice for mobilizing youth participation—gaining and retaining young people's trust. But Genny and her classmates added a powerful voice as schoolchildren to the discussion about priorities and as young adults active in *Pro Loco* Scanno they continue to speak out on matters of local and global concern.

In hindsight, the choice of renovating the sports center was even more prescient than the students realized. The next building to fall victim to seismic events was the 1970s-era school building itself, which the children had to vacate. Because of their advocacy, the sports center was available as an alternative space to hold classes. The sports center has also been a magnet for recreation, and it hosts the national roller-skating championship, mountain-biking race, and Scanno triathlon that bring tourists to Scanno's hotels. Clearly, tending to youths' priorities also benefits the community as a whole. Apparently, the youth of Scanno are gaining traction in the town council. In 2018, one of the first acts of the newly elected (adult) mayor was to convene a forum of young adults, ranging in age from eighteen to twenty-five, to discuss the formation of an Assemblea dei Giovani (Young People's Assembly). Youth advocacy also kept the school building at the top of the priority list. As noted earlier, for almost a decade Scanno's primary- and middle-school students had begun each school year in a state of emergency: they were repeatedly relocated to different provisional sites because of concerns about the earthquake resistance of the old school building (Lavilloti 2018). Finally, in September 2018, all the students from first to eighth grades were reunited in a large building in the center of town, just up the street from the nursery schoolers in the Asilo Buon Pastore. Formerly used as the city hall, the building had been renovated, enlarged, and reinforced to meet strict new anti-earthquake requirements (*La Foce* 2018). As the headline in *La Foce* exclaimed, "Together at last!"

What does the CRC have to do with this Scanno story of youth engagement? Actually, quite a lot. There is a direct line between CRC Article 12 and Genny's stint as the youth mayor of Scanno. The CRC in 1989 formalized the notion that children's insights into their own needs and priorities could enhance sound decision-making by adults charged with acting on their behalf. But despite the explicit requirements of CRC Article 12 (1), during the early years of the CRC even advocates for children's rights often gave lip service to children's rights to participate in all decisions affecting their welfare. The UN Special Session on Children, which took place at the UN's New York City headquarters in 2002, marked a turning point. As the leader of the American Bar Association (ABA) delegation, I witnessed this myself. I was leading a group of four adults, all of whom were lawyers or professors of law like myself, but there were also over three hundred youth delegates from nations around the world. All under the age of eighteen (hence the nickname "U-18s"), they had traveled to New York City from many countries and actively participated in the proceedings. In the year prior to the special session, youth delegates had been meeting in national and regional gatherings. The U-18 delegates brought life and action to the normally quiet halls of the UN. They held a congress of their own in the days before the special session, and during the special session they networked with each other, staffed a cluster of computer terminals connected to the internet, had representatives on every panel, and presented their own report to the General Assembly. These young people played a crucial role, and they felt the sea change that had occurred as the notion of children's participation rights had matured. As I heard one young participant remark, "Last time around we were holding the pen for the adults at the signing ceremony. This time we are writing and presenting our own report." Since 2002, a wealth of guidelines and studies on youth participation have been published, driving home the value of youth engagement, and the importance of asking children what they think about matters of significance to them and to society (Garbarino 1989; Daly et al. 2015).

Comparing Italy and the United States, we can see the difference that a robust theory of children's participation rights has made. In the United States, where children's right to be heard has been largely confined to judicial contexts, the Italian approach has been far more inclusive and more systematic. Italy is not the most advanced nation in terms of children's participation rights; that honor would have to go to Wales. But Italy is fairly representative of the differences between US approaches and those of the nations of Europe (Woodhouse 2014a). Italian law now recognizes children's rights to several forms of participation, including *participazione sociale* (social participation). The Italian Parliament's passage in 1997 of Law 285/1997, titled "Provisions for Promotion of the Rights and Opportunities of Children and Adolescents," paved the way for Genny's election. It established a fund for promotion of participation initiatives, defined types of initiatives to be supported, and required periodic evaluations. Law 285/1997, citing the CRC, calls for "positive actions to promote the rights of children and adolescents, for exercise of their fundamental civil rights, for improvement of the enjoyment of natural and urban environments by minors, for the improvement of well-being and quality of life for minors, for respect of gender, cultural and ethnic diversity" (Art.3.1.d; Mittica 2003a). At the local level of government, many cities and towns have responded to Law 285/1997 and Article 12 of the CRC by creating a position like Scanno's youth mayor. Others have established a Consiglio Communale dei Ragazzi, or CCR (Children's City Council).

A significant literature has grown up around children's participation rights. Children's participation is conceptualized as active and public, as opposed to passive and private (Baraldi and Maggioni 2003). Beyond merely educating and entertaining children, activities should enable them to make their collective voices heard and to exercise autonomy and agency in the public sphere. To qualify under Italian law, initiatives must include children in design and implementation as well as execution, and priorities must be based on children's own views (Baraldi and Maggioni 2003). There are three distinct forms of social participation: 1) play/recreation and expression; 2) participation in "projects"; and 3) participation in civic organizations, youth councils, and forums (Mittica 2003b). In all of these settings, children's views must be solicited in age-appropriate ways. Focus groups can be used to determine what rights of participation mean to different age groups, and role plays can help children understand the functions of prosecutors, defense attorneys, and judges in order to provide informed insights into improving systems. Italian law recognizes that access to public and private spaces, both built and natural, is fundamental to the right to play, and participation rights engage children in advocating for their play environments. Youth centers, playgrounds, museums, day camps, community centers, and parks are all venues to be supported where they exist and created where they are lacking, so that children may freely aggregate and engage with each other.

The second category of social participation, known as "projects," includes national initiatives such as Citta' dei Bambini (Children's Cities) and Citta' Sostenibili (Sustainable Cities). But many projects are local and focus on issues of specific importance to children in a particular neighborhood or village, such as preserving public spaces for children and youth. For example, in a project called Partecipiamo (Let's Participate), high school students in earthquake-affected communities in the region of Abruzzo were asked to evaluate the impact of the 2009 disaster on their lives and to brainstorm solutions that would be responsive to their needs. Interviews confirmed that *terramotati* (earthquake-affected children) experienced the relocation of their families and the dispersion of their communities as a form of social exclusion and loss of peer support. While rebuilding old neighborhoods would be a slow process, the Partecipiamo project demonstrated the immediate need for action to mitigate the harms from loss of youth-friendly spaces like local streets, piazzas, and parks. Partecipiamo mobilized students to collaborate with local government, schools, and private entities to imagine, build, and operate easily accessible, child- and youth-friendly public spaces to replace those that had been destroyed (Rossi and Tagliaventi 2011).

The third type of initiative, political participation, takes many forms. But, from a comparative perspective, its most striking feature is the entrenchment in law of legal structures for inclusion of youth in institutional policymaking. We saw a small-scale example in Genny's story. It was not an isolated event, nor was its connection with the microsystem of the school an accident. The law governing public-school students (Law 249/1988, modified by Law

235/2007), cites both the Italian Constitution and the CRC in recognizing students' rights of freedom of expression, thought, conscience, religion, and mutual respect for the dignity of all persons, regardless of age or social condition. Participation rights are explicitly addressed in Articles 2 (4) and (5) of this law, which states that students have a right to participate in the life of educational institutions and must have the opportunity to express their views in decision-making.

Legal structures also support youth participation in the national policy arena. The Forum Nazionale delle Associazioni Studentesche (National Forum of Student Organizations; Law 79/2002) mobilizes independent student organizations to provide representation and to engage with the ministry of education (Forum Nazionale 2002). Each secondary-school student body elects two representatives to the Consulte Provinciali degli Studenti (CPS; Provincial Student Councils). The councils are required to meet on a regular basis with the ministry of education to discuss matters of educational policy and express the views of their constituencies. Young people serving as council members are also available to assist students who have grievances, suggestions, or questions. These initiatives utilize attractive internet sites and interactive web technology to facilitate youth engagement as opposed to passively conveying information. For example, Spazioconsulte, the portal for the provincial student councils, includes a news site with both textual and streaming video productions created by youth for youth. In a recent visit, I found content on laws relating to youth, antibullying initiatives, materials on rule of law, debates about social media, and many other issues affecting young people (Spazioconsulte n.d.). By accessing this site, youth can move seamlessly across national borders to access EU and UNICEF materials and initiatives.

The economic crisis and its aftermath have been a spur to action for Italian youth, who have weighed in forcefully on the impact of fierce austerity policies pushed by the European Central Bank as a condition of monetary support to struggling EU economies. Young people's educations, daily lives, and hope for their futures have fallen under the knife while politicians continued to resist long-overdue cuts to their lavish lifestyles. Italian university-age students have a long history of social activism and protest, but today younger students are also engaging in organized advocacy. For example, in 2008, several unions of middle-school students came together in the Rete degli Studenti Medi (Middle-School Students Network) in reaction to the effects of the economic crisis, and they have continued to agitate against cuts to educational resources and lack of opportunity for youth, utilizing street protests, communiqués to government, and strikes (Rete degli Studenti 2010).

The story of youth speaking truth to power is not a novel product of the CRC. It is a story as old as David and Goliath, and as new as Malala and the Taliban. In the United States, young people also have a long history of social justice activism, especially during times of war or economic turmoil (Woodhouse 2009a). Consider the role of school-age children in the civil rights movement, and the Vietnam War protests by young adults between the ages of eighteen and twenty-one, subject to the draft but not entitled to vote. More recent examples include the Dreamers (undocumented youth who were brought to the United States as children), the Black Lives Matter movement, and the student-led March for Our Lives advocating for gun safety in schools. The most significant difference between youth engagement in Italy and the United States is that Italy has structures in place for formal recognition and integration of youth voices into the social and political fabric. In the United States, youth too young to vote often have no recognized avenue to voice their opposition. They engage in school boycotts and walkouts, march in spontaneous demonstrations, and engage in civil disobedience, but they run the risk of arrest, expulsion from school, deportation, and incarceration (Woodhouse 2014a; 2009b). Even courts, which were created to provide legal redress for wrongful acts, are traditionally closed to minors unless the case is filed on their behalf by an adult. Pressure is mounting for change in this area as well. In 2018, a major breakthrough came in the case of *Juliana v. United States*, brought by young people seeking a declaration that the US government's actions exacerbating climate change violate their constitutional rights to life, liberty, and property. A lower court's decision refusing to dismiss the case was upheld unanimously by the Supreme Court (Conca 2018). To say that the CRC is toothless is to ignore the steady progress in nations in which it has been accepted and is being implemented, as well as its spillover effects in the United States.

The Right to Be Heard in Judicial and Administrative Proceedings

> 2. For this purpose, the child shall in particular be provided the opportunity to be heard in any judicial and administrative proceedings affecting the child, either directly or through a representative or an appropriate body, in a manner consistent with the procedural rules of national law. (CRC, Article 12, 1990)

A CRC Story: The Channeling Function of Human Rights

As noted previously, in both Italy and the United States recognition of the rights of children to be heard in civil and administrative cases have lagged behind their rights to be heard when accused of criminal violation

(Woodhouse 2014a; Bapat and Woodhouse 2016). While the practice of considering children's views in custody and child protection cases has become the norm in US family law, it has not been viewed through the lens of children's rights. Marriage and divorce in the United States are governed by state law, and rules differ from state to state. In most states, children are not formally treated as parties to their custody cases and the Supreme Court has never held that the practice of obtaining children's preferences is a constitutional right of the child. While federal laws enacted since the 1970s conditioning federal funding of state child protection services on compliance with certain criteria have brought some measure of uniformity to state child protection laws, the Supreme Court has not yet recognized children's participation in civil cases as a constitutional right.

Italy's experience has been distinctly different, in large part because of the CRC. The rapid change in Italy has resulted from what family-law scholar Carl Schnieder has identified as "the channeling function of the law" (1992). As part of the EU, Italy is also bound by rulings from the European Court of Human Rights and guidance from the Council of Europe. These bodies, in addition to the CRC, have motivated reforms of Italian family-court procedures. For its part, the Italian Corte Costituzionale (Constitutional Court) interprets the CRC, including Article 12, as a self-executing treaty under Italian law (Corte Const. 2002a). Thus, ratification placed a duty on the Italian government to implement the right to be heard in a manner consistent with Italy's procedural rules. In February 2006, the Italian Parliament enacted a law requiring that children's views be listened to in parental custody determinations (Pazé 2011). Another impetus for change has been the Council of Europe document "Guidelines for Child-Friendly Justice" (2010). These guidelines promote inclusion of children's voices and protection of their dignity in legal proceedings, but, like the CRC, they leave room for tailoring best practices to fit the legal and social culture of the particular nation. Italian family court judges and lawyers now meet with and observe children in the courthouse playroom or in chambers. Children's rights of *ascolto* (right to be listened to) recognize that sometimes an interpreter is called for. In certain cases, the child's right to expression can best be implemented by having skilled professionals translate the very young, preverbal, or traumatized child's needs and feelings to the decision-makers.

Rights of Children Accused of Crimes

1. States Parties recognize the right of every child alleged as, accused of, or recognized as having infringed the penal law to be treated in a manner consistent with the promotion of the child's sense of dignity and worth, which reinforces

the child's respect for human rights and fundamental freedoms of others and which takes into account the child's age and the desirability of promoting the child's reintegration and the child's assuming a constructive role in society.
3. States Parties shall seek to promote the establishment of laws, procedures, authorities and institutions specifically applicable to children alleged as, accused of, or recognized as having infringed the penal law, and in particular:
    (a) the establishment of a minimum age below which children shall be presumed not to have the capacity to infringe the penal law;
    (b) whenever appropriate and desirable, measures for dealing with children without resorting to judicial proceedings, providing that human rights and legal safeguards are respected.
4. A variety of dispositions, such as care, guidance and supervision orders; counselling; probation; foster care; education and vocational training programmes and other alternatives to institutional care shall be available to ensure that children are dealt with in a manner appropriate to their well-being and proportionate both to their circumstances and the offence. (CRC, Article 40, 1990)

Angelo's Story: Stumbling and Learning to Fly

The boy I will call Angelo lived with his single mother in the city of Lecce, located in Puglia, an economically challenged region occupying the heel of the Italian boot-shaped peninsula. He was caught committing a nonviolent but serious criminal act. Italy sets the minimum age of criminal responsibility at fourteen; before then, conflict with the law is seen as a psychological or social issue and both child and family are referred for supportive services. Because Angelo had turned fourteen a few days before the crime, his case came under the statutes applying to juvenile offenders. As part of my research, I interviewed the juvenile prosecutor based in the Lecce Family Court, housed in a restored seventeenth-century convent, amazingly peaceful and glowing with light. She explained that each of Italy's twenty-seven juridical regions has a designated team composed of a lawyer and a social worker who are employed by the national government. The team is required to respond to the scene of any crime involving a juvenile, and their job is to ensure that the child's rights are protected. They also have the responsibility of assembling a support team, based on their interviews with the child, his teachers, and family members. The support team is to be composed of people who are committed to helping the child in each of the key realms of daily life—school, sports, family life, health, and community engagement. When Angelo was arrested, a team was mobilized to work with him. He was entitled to legal representation as well as to have a trusted adult accompany him, but Italian lawyers for juveniles do not automatically instruct their clients to remain silent, as is routine in the United States. So Angelo had ample opportunity to communicate directly with the investigator, the judge, and the support team. Here is what they learned from him, some of it conveyed in words, some in body language and some in his actions and reactions to events.

Angelo hated school. In fact, he was failing in every subject. He was not slow or stupid—quite the opposite. If anything, his brain and body were moving too fast. Angelo loathed being made to stay indoors as well as being told what to do and where he was to go. He was affectionate with his rather overwhelmed working mother and younger sibling, but when his mother was not at home, he got to roaming around the neighborhood getting into trouble. Angelo's body language was revealing. He simply could not sit still: squirming and fidgeting, reaching for objects on the psychologist's desk, tipping so far back in his chair he nearly fell over. With his every move, he told a story of undiagnosed ADHD, possibly complicated by dyslexia and dysgraphia.

Angelo and his team decided to take advantage of an option provided in Italian juvenile justice laws called *messa alla prova* (put to the test). Charges would be suspended while the team, working with Angelo, designed and implemented a plan for addressing the issues that had brought him into conflict with the law. Angelo could continue to live at home and attend his public school, but he would be picked up every day by a counselor to spend the afternoon at a farmhouse on the city's outskirts that had been converted into an after-school youth center. Keeping Angelo busy after school was a large part of the solution. He related well to his counselor and therapist, enjoyed the vigorous outdoor activities, and liked being around kids of all ages. But the hours at school were still a problem. Angelo saw no point in much of the didactic learning tasks. What did these letters and numbers that he found so alien and hard to grasp have to do with him and his life?

Understanding his frustration and the disconnect between how Angelo learned and how he was being taught, Angelo's counselor arranged for him to be "*home-schooled*" (Italians have borrowed from English for the concept) by the staff at the youth center. The breakthrough came when he was given responsibility for the farm's small herd of horses. It was a physically and an intellectually demanding job, dealing gently and calmly with very large and powerful animals, measuring and weighing grain and feed, maintaining logs, and reading manuals on the care and feeding of horses. It suited him and challenged him. Suddenly, Angelo was associating numbers and letters with something that mattered—he needed them in his work with the horses. The key had been found and the door to his potential was now opened wide.

On the day I met Angelo, some four years after his arrest, he was visiting the youth center to show off his high school diploma. The psychologist who directed the youth center described his case to me as an example of how *messa alla prova* could work to turn a child's life around. Angelo had passed his school leaving examinations and his *messa alla prova* had been declared a success. For his final review, he had demonstrated to the education board supervising his home schooling progress how he had learned mathematics from measuring feed and administering medicines to the horses and how he learned to read fluently by devouring books about raising and training them. During my visit, I observed another impressive skill he had mastered. A volunteer had come to the center to teach tumbling classes, and Angelo was instantly hooked. Between his work with the horses and his training in acrobatics, he was no longer the gangly adolescent who had been unable to concentrate or sit still. In the impromptu acrobatics show the kids put on for me, Angelo, tall and steady, was the stable anchorman, supporting a pyramid three layers high of progressively smaller kids. I watched him catching and tossing his teammates with gusto and precision and encouraging them when they made mistakes. With help from his team he had harnessed his own restlessness, impulsivity, and excess energy and tuned them into assets.

That evening, I learned another secret to the city's success in dealing with juvenile crime. As I strolled in the streets, which were crowded with young people, I encountered several elderly couples wearing reflective vests, identifying them as volunteer *Nonni di Strada* (street grandparents). When I asked about their role, they explained that they were there to discourage bullying or disorderly behavior; they find that a gentle reminder is quite effective.

As we see in Angelo's case, Italy draws a sharp line protecting children below a certain age from criminal responsibility. In addition to CRC Article 12, which covers all judicial and administrative proceedings, Article 40 singles out criminal proceedings for in-depth treatment. It provides a comprehensive set of rights applying to "every child accused of or recognized as having infringed the penal law" (CRC Art 40 [1]). In compliance with the requirements of Article 40, Italian law sets a minimum age for criminal responsibility and has chosen age fourteen as its threshold. Special rules apply to juvenile defendants; for example, juvenile justice hearings for youths under eighteen are not public, but are held in the privacy of the judges' chambers, to minimize trauma and stigma. There are no orange jumpsuits or shackles on children such as I observed in the juvenile courts of Florida. In Angelo's case, Italy's embrace of children's rights made all the difference. With its emphasis on rehabilitation and reintegration to society, and its attitude that incarceration should be the last and not the first response, his story turned out very differently than it would have in most US jurisdictions. Not surprisingly, a minor growing up in Italy is thirty times less likely to end up in jail than a child growing up in the United States.

There are many reasons for this disparity. It is not because US children are monsters and Italian children are angels. When I described Angelo's case to my colleague Professor Randee Waldman, who directs the Juvenile Defender Clinic at the Emory University School of Law, she recognized him instantly. He is like so many of her young clients in Atlanta, Georgia, who were not bad kids but have learning disabilities or poor home situations. As she explained to me in an email,

> They often get funneled into what we call "the school-to-prison pipeline" and, depending on the severity of the charges, can even be tried in adult courts in states like Georgia and Florida. While diversion programs providing alternatives to incarceration are gaining in popularity, they are often unavailable when the charges involve serious felonies. Moreover, the diversion programs that exist generally consist of some minor consequences and monitoring for a short period of time, rather than intensive intervention. The most likely outcome for a first time offender would be to place him on probation. School attendance without suspensions and passing grades are standard conditions of most probation orders, and most probation officers are not adept at providing services to students with disabilities in the school system. As a result, rather than helping the young person succeed in school, the probation officer becomes one more set of eyes to document school-based failures.

Italian lawyers for children can point to several remaining concerns and breakdowns between the law on the books and the law in practice. Many worry that the informality of juvenile proceedings undercuts the minor's due-process rights by allowing excessive freedom of communication and too much judicial discretion over admission of evidence (Cesari 2007). In addition, the family-centered approaches that work for many Italians may fail to meet the needs of socially marginalized youth from Roma, North African, and Eastern European communities (Gatti and Verde 2002). However, Italy has made significant progress toward avoiding unnecessary involvement in the juvenile justice system. And, as Angelo's case illustrates, when the structures work as they should, the child's voice is not confined to speaking (or remaining silent) in the courtroom, but becomes part of a team-based decision-making process.

Children's Rights to Education

States parties agree that the education of the child shall be directed to:

a. The development of the child's personality, talents, and mental and physical abilities to their fullest potential;
b. The development of respect for human rights and fundamental freedoms, and for the principles enshrined in the Charter of the United Nations;
c. The development of respect for the child's parents, his or her own cultural identity, language and values, for the national values of the country in which the child is living, the country from which he or she may originate, and for civilizations different from his or her own;
d. The preparation of the child for responsible life in a free society, in a spirit of understanding, peace, tolerance, equality of sexes, and friendship among peoples, ethnic, national and religious groups and persons of indigenous origin;
e. Development of respect for the natural environment. (CRC, Article 29:1, 1990)

Rita's Story: Teaching the Arts of Peace and Resilience

Rita is not a child, but an adult who understands the hearts of children and respects their perspectives, whether spoken or communicated through their art. I was introduced to art teacher Rita Quaranta by my friends at the Bar Centrale, home of the best gelato and croissants in town and one of the hubs of Scanno social life. On learning of my research, Rita invited me to visit the primary and middle school to see the fruits of some projects she had given to her students. Art and art history are a very important part of the Italian school curriculum; her middle-school students had worked for several weeks during their daily art periods, creating posters on the theme of world peace. The impetus was a competition sponsored by the international Lions' Club. When they showed me their work, each child told me what had motivated them and what their picture symbolized. One scientifically minded boy had used a colorful drawing of spiraling chains of DNA to illustrate how all people are bound together and should learn to live in peace. A girl whose family had fled armed conflict in the Balkans had drawn a very powerful scene much too old for her years, depicting a wounded woman being carried to safety by a helmeted soldier and another soldier shooting at them. Executed with great skill and realism, it may have been an image from her own store of memories.

Another group art project, of the fifth graders, was a competition to create a logo for the centennial of the 1915 earthquake that destroyed the nearby

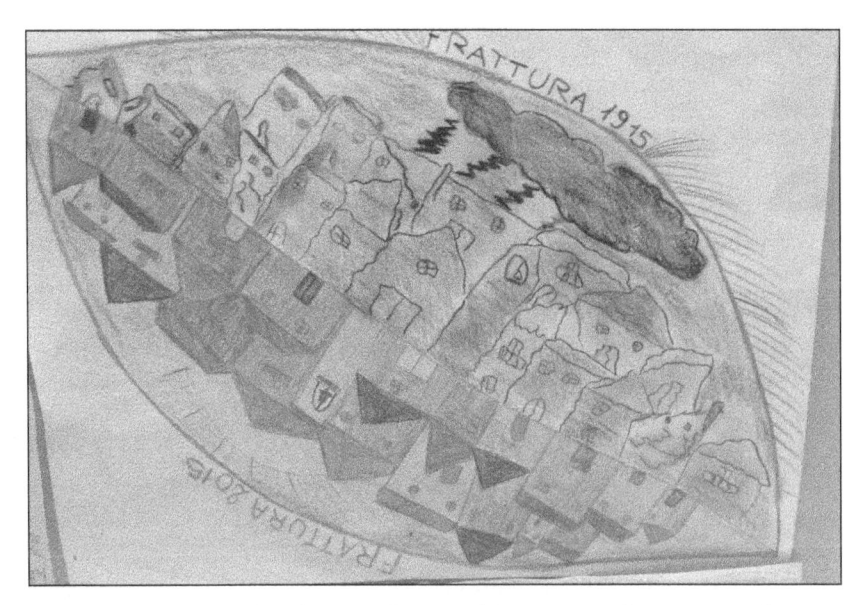

Figure 11.5. Frattura earthquake logo. Photograph by B. B. Woodhouse. Design by Scanno fifth graders.

hamlet of Old Frattura. In their entry for the contest, the students had placed images of ruined buildings under dark skies with jagged thunderbolts within the same eye-shaped frame as images of the rebuilt town of New Frattura, a sturdy stone village basking in a healing sunshine.

In an accompanying essay titled "The Frattura Earthquake through our Eyes," the students explained, "We wanted to create an eye that like our eyes could see both the past and the present, both the destruction and death and the reconstruction and return to life." Pause for a moment and consider their carefully chosen words, and how the children understand their role as "eyes" able to see both past and present while looking toward the future.

It is not surprising that these images of war and of nature's destructive powers figured in the Scanno children's imagery, along with pastel imagery of doves and rainbows worthy of a Disney animated film. Their darker drawings reflected not only news seen on television but Scanno's own history, including occupation by the Germans during World War II, which the children had not experienced but had learned about from their grandparents. I was blown away by the quality of the children's artwork. Their teacher explained that she always asked students to do multiple drafts in succeeding weeks because she wanted them to spend as long as it took to perfect their visions. Through art and story, students were engaging deeply with the concepts of peace and resilience, developing their fullest potential, and expressing their connections to family and community, realizing the spirit of CRC Article 29.

A statement of educational values such as we see in Article 29 would be dead on arrival in the overheated culture wars of the US public school system. Rather than imagining Article 29 as a potential battlefield for adults, it is worthwhile examining what it means to children in a place where the CRC has become the guiding norm. In Angelo's story, we have already seen many of the values in Article 29 implemented. He was able to develop his talents and mental and physical abilities to their fullest potential. He developed a life-saving respect for the natural environment. And he was prepared for a responsible life in a free society, instead of being drawn into a school-to-prison pipeline.

On my visits to Italian classrooms, in Scanno and in many other cities, I did not have to search for evidence of the influence of Article 29; it was everywhere I looked. My first visit to a public nursery school took place in 2007 in San Sisto in the province of Perugia, region of Umbria. I noticed a colorful poster on children's rights in the hallway. When I expressed surprise, given the age of the children (zero to three), the teacher showed me an entire segment devoted to children's rights in the teacher's handbook. The materials for the youngest group focused on children's right to be included and not excluded because of their differences. As the teacher explained to me, "We try to present rights in a way that is meaningful to each age group. Even the littlest children appreciate the importance of being included and the pain of being left out or ignored." Like the poster on the wall, the curricular materials showed children in wheelchairs on the school playground and children of different colors playing together.

The CRC's impact on the Italian culture of childhood is reflected not only in schools but also in public and private discourse. References to children's rights are common on television and in other media and in informal discussions with parents and teachers. For example, the host of a children's TV show inviting young guests to join a game will comment, "Play is one of the most important rights of the child." Imagine a US television host making such a statement without a flurry of calls complaining that she was politicizing a children's show. While "children's rights" are fighting words in the United States, in Italy it is accepted that all children have "rights" and that these include not only negative rights to freedom from government intrusion and discrimination but positive rights to health care, to education, to a basic standard of living, to good nutrition, safe places to play and live, to family life, and to protection from abuse. I cannot count the number of times I have heard a parent or grandparent—in discussions about everything from school lunches to repairing playground equipment—begin a sentence with the phrase "all children have the right": to play, to eat healthy food, to go to school.

The Rights to Identity and to Family

> States parties undertake to respect the right of the child to preserve his or her identity, including nationality, name and family relations as recognized by law without unlawful interference. (CRC, Article 8:1)

> States Parties shall ensure that a child shall not be separated from his or her parents against their will, except when competent authorities subject to judicial review determine, in accordance with applicable law and procedures, that such separation is necessary for the best interests of the child. Such determination may be necessary in a particular case such as one involving abuse or neglect of the child by the parents, or one where the parents are living separately and a decision must be made as to the child's place of residence. (CRC, Article 9:1, 1990)

Stefano's Story: Mothers Are Not Fungible

What initially drew me to San Patrignano in May 2012 was the furor over a case that would seem unremarkable in the United States. A child welfare case brought by the social services in Florence was winding its way through a family court. A little boy whom I shall call Stefano had been placed in foster care when his mother entered a drug treatment facility. The Florence court held that the drug-addicted mother had constructively abandoned her child and issued an order declaring that Stefano, now three years old, was eligible for adoption. Meanwhile, in the confusion that seems endemic to child protection cases everywhere, Stefano's mother had voluntarily entered the *comunita'* (therapeutic community) of San Patrignano, where she was reunited with her child, who had been placed temporarily in the legal custody of San Patrignano (Sirianni 2012). At the time, about three hundred children were residing with their parents in family housing and going to school while the parents worked toward recovery. San Patrignano's inclusion of children in a therapeutic community was not some ad hoc experiment. A team of sociologists and psychologists from the University of Urbino had recently published an exhaustive study of the philosophy, structure, and outcomes of the family reunification program (Baraldi 1998). The study concluded that, especially for young children, the risks of growing up in the San Patrignano community were minimal and the psychological and social benefits for both children and parents were substantial.

Undeterred by the change in circumstances and the documented quality of the family reunification program, the court in Firenze dug in its heels. It insisted that it retained proper jurisdiction and that its decree must be enforced. While some commentators viewed the community experience with suspicion and placed greater trust in the judges and court psychologists, the general public reaction to this case was one of outrage. Termination of parental rights leading to stranger adoption is rare in Italy, but Italians were especially appalled that a court would order a three-year-old permanently removed from his mother and placed with strangers when mother and child were settled in a secure environment where the child was attending preschool, recovering from the trauma of separation, and appeared to be doing well.

At San Patrignano I learned another detail about the case that I had not known. Stefano had been the older of two siblings, both of whom were removed from their mother by the state and placed in a center for children. Stefano and his little sister were inseparable. While the siblings were in care together, the little girl died suddenly. It is difficult even to imagine the trauma of a three-year-old separated from his mother and then experiencing the death of a baby sister. Knowing this tragic history, the people at San Patrignano were determined to fight against yet another traumatic separation. On my visit to San Patrignano I learned more about the structure of the community and its policies toward children and families. By law, juveniles are housed separately from adults, so youths below age eighteen had a residential cluster of buildings of their own with access to appropriate public schools in the vicinity. There was also an accredited preschool and afterschool program that served all of the community's children, whether their parents were residents or staff. The two preschool teachers with whom I spoke reported that the little boy whose case had been making headlines was thriving. He was very attached to his mother, who was now in recovery and making good progress in acquiring skills and building relationships. The community was determined to fight hard to keep the family together. Shortly after my visit, the family court finally agreed to leave the child with his mother in the legal custody of San Patrignano.

In Italy, as I learned early on, the word *comunita'* (community) has a special significance when used in the context of addiction treatment. A *comunita'* is a therapeutic residential community, ideally located far from the addict's hometown. It is organized around two key goals: supporting and sustaining recovery from addiction and preparing the individual for reentry into society. The addicted person must be willing to join the community voluntarily and is expected to remain for as long as necessary. Historically, the word *comunita'* was associated with closed religious institutions such as monasteries and convents. Most of the current drug treatment communities have a religious affiliation, and they are similar to the traditional religious community in providing an all-enveloping environment where work, study, and daily life revolve around a common core of spiritual, social, and cognitive practices. As scientific evidence confirms, it takes years for the brain to recover from the effects of addiction. In Italy, the expectation is that those who enter a *comunita'* will remain for as long as it takes—usually at least two years and often more.

You may be wondering what addiction treatment has to do with children's rights. One statistic from the United States tells the story. In 2017, 92,000 children were removed from home and placed in foster care because of a parent's addiction (Curry 2017). The dominant US policy response to parental neglect due to addiction has been removal of children from their parents' custody. If the addiction persists, in order to continue receiving federal funds state agencies must move to terminate parental rights and place the children in permanent adoptive or foster homes (Woodhouse 2002). This practice of treating family as fungible and disposable is shocking to most Italians. San Patrignano welcomes family units, a policy that enables families to remain together in a supportive community environment during a parent's treatment and recovery from addiction and reintegration into society. When I visited San Patrignano again in June 2018, I met again with outreach director Monica Barzanti, who had been my guide in my 2012 visit. I mentioned the case that had brought me to San Patrignano six years earlier, and she smiled with delight. "As a matter of fact, his mother called me on the telephone just yesterday," she told me. "She graduated from San Patrignano a few years ago and is living and working in Milano. Stefano, who is now in middle school, is doing very well."

The Right to Adoption

> [States parties shall] recognize that inter-country adoption may be considered as an alternative means of child's care, if the child cannot be placed in a foster or adoptive family or cannot in any suitable manner be cared for in the child's country of origin. (CRC, Article 21:b, 1990)

The Story of Gaia and Massimo: Preserving Identity and Finding Family

Gaia and Massimo, whom you met in chapter 4, are not the names these siblings were born with. Their original names were Galina and Maxim. They came to Italy from an orphanage in the Ukraine through Italian procedures for intercountry adoption. As an older sibling pair (sister age six and brother age seven) who had been affected by early traumatic experiences, they must have faced special challenges in finding a suitable placement. They came to Italy speaking no Italian. Their adoptive parents, Candido and Angela, chose names that would be easy to say and spell and as close as possible to their Ukrainian names. Such is the balancing act of adoption, especially apparent in intercountry or transracial adoption, of claiming a new identity without erasing or sacrificing the old. My husband and I first learned their story during a stop for coffee at the Rifugio lo Scoiattolo (Lodge of the Squirrel), a rustic mountain lodge and restaurant in the Abruzzo and Molise National Park. Situated in Passo Godi, a high mountain pass about half an hour's drive from Scanno, it has an amazing view, great food, lots of animals—including dogs, sheep, chickens and horses—and a cozy wood fire burning even in summer.

When Candido, the owner of the lodge, learned that I was a professor specializing in children's law, he pulled out his cell phone to show us pictures of his adopted children. Out came our cell phones with pictures of our son, Ken, adopted as a seven-month-old and now a forty-six-year-old independent owner operator of an eighteen-wheeler long-haul truck. As parents of children through intercountry adoption, our common experiences bridged the differences of age and nationality between us. As I recounted in chapter 4, the photograph I took of Massimo and Gaia and their parents walking hand in hand in the procession at their first communion is my favorite image of this annual rite of passage (fig. 4.2). For these adopted siblings, it was an especially significant benchmark. Having made an enormous transition to a new country and a new family, they now spoke fluent Italian and seemed very much at home. Just like all the other Scanno children, they were now marking the passage from childhood to adolescence, accompanied by their parents and welcomed by the community in an age-old ritual. But their story of origin, far from being a secret, was a source of family and community pride.

In the six years since that day, I have watched Massimo and Gaia grow up. I noticed that their parents sought out and nurtured connections with Ukrainian families and families who had adopted Ukrainian children. In 2018, Massimo turned eighteen. He is handsome and fit, still with the bluest eyes, and on weekends and holidays he works side by side with his father at the lodge. He was about to graduate from high school in Sulmona. Gaia is a gentle, brown-eyed seventeen-year-old with a shy smile, but she is tougher than she looks. She was part of the four-person team from Enrico Fermi Science High School that won the silver medal at the 2018 National Student Championship in Precision Orienteering. So close as small children, the siblings remain close as teenagers, but I have observed them over the years as they made their own friends and sought out their own places in the world. Growing up in the busy lodge at the mountain pass, thirty minutes'

Figure 11.6. Gaia cradling baby lamb. C. Nannarone.

drive and many hairpin turns above Scanno, they are straddling two worlds in more ways than one. My photo gallery of Scanno's children includes pictures of Massimo riding his horse (his father attributes his riding skills to his Cossack roots) and herding sheep, and of Gaia in front of the lodge cradling a baby lamb in her arms.

My gallery also includes scenes of their life in Scanno, with Massimo and Gaia joining their Scanno friends in participating in religious festivals and rehearsing songs and poems in dialect. A favorite image shows Gaia with another girl at a dialect poetry competition. She is wearing Scanno's traditional wedding costume, with its distinctive blue silk cap adorned with braided silk cords, its dress with black bodice, light-colored apron, and full, dark green woolen skirt.

After finishing middle school, first Massimo then Gaia made the transition along with their peers to attending high school in Sulmona. Gaia made the same journey as her classmates; her special educational needs were met without

254 | HOW THE CRC AFFECTS ACTUAL CHILDREN'S LIVES

Figure 11.7. Massimo herding sheep. C. Nannarone.

excluding her from this rite of passage. It was a transition for their parents as well—Angela had to set up a home base for the family down in the village, since the distance between home and school was now too great, especially in snowy weather. With a strong family supported by a strong community, it seems clear that Massimo and Gaia have found that crucial balance that preserves adopted children's access to their pasts while opening the door to their bright futures. They and their family are pleased to have me share their story and to be identified by name in this book.

The CRC shaped this story as it has each story I have told here. Italian adoption law, in contrast to US law, is grounded in the CRC, which Italy's legislature treats as the authoritative source for modern adoption reforms. The CRC balances children's interest in being adopted with their interests in connection to their family and culture of origin and in preserving their identity. What this means, in legal terms, is that children must be certified as free for adoption *before* a match can be made; any match must be made purely on the best interest of the child. For example, parents seeking to adopt are not permitted to discriminate based on race or ethnicity—a common practice in the United States, where the law says that would-be parents may not be denied a child based on race, but where they are free to discriminate as they see fit in choosing a child.

There is no such thing in Italy as a private placement, where the birth parents and adoptive parents find each other through advertisements or an intermediary and finalize their adoption in family court. All adoptions, including intercountry adoptions, must be handled through approved regional agencies in both the receiving and sending countries. Intercountry adoption programs are judged not by how many children they place but how many children they help. The Italian philosophy behind intercountry adoption in Italy was explained to me by Anna Maria Colella on a visit to the nonprofit

Figure 11.8. Gaia and friend at a regional dialect poetry competition. B. B. Woodhouse.

agency she founded, ARAI-Piemonte (the acronym for the Piedmont regional agency for international adoptions), which is located in Torino. Dr. Colella was a pioneer in developing Italy's CRC-inspired policies and practices. Each international program must include a component for prospective adoptive parents and agencies to volunteer in the sending country, building domestic capacity for at-risk children and families. The dual purpose is for adoptive parents to become familiar with the heritage and culture of their adopted children and to ensure that as few children as possible have to leave their country of origin to find a family (Woodhouse 2014b; ARAI-Piemonte 2018). The CRC has shaped the adoption law in Italy to recognize that families are not fungible commodities and that children are people with rights to identity as well as rights to a family of their own.

The Right to Inclusion of Children with Disabilities

> States parties recognize that a mentally or physically disabled child should enjoy a full and decent life, in conditions which ensure dignity, promote self-reliance, and facilitate the child's active participation the community. (CRC, Article 23:1, 1990)

A Story about Creating a Culture of Inclusion

The teacher of students nine to ten years old had just finished a social studies class when one child erupted in piercing screams. Without missing a beat, the other students clustered around her, making soothing noises. By the time her teacher reached her side she was already much calmer. The teacher spent a few minutes reassuring the child and then thanked the class for being such good friends to their classmate. The child, who had obviously been in great distress, was able to move on to the next activity with her peers. After the children had left the classroom, the teacher explained to me that this child had a disability on the autism spectrum. The other children knew her triggers and also knew how to soothe her when she panicked. They had learned this by watching their teacher and a teacher's aide who sometimes helped the child. I asked whether there had been objections from parents of children without disabilities to her inclusion and the teacher was puzzled by my question. There had been some grumbling aimed at the government when austerity measures had led to cuts in the funding for the teacher's aides assigned to assist teachers whose class included a child with special needs, but no one had ever suggested that the children with disabilities should not be included in the regular class or complained that their own child was cheated or harmed by classroom time spent helping an autistic or developmentally delayed child.

As this example from Scanno illustrates, Italian law takes a strong stand favoring inclusion of children with special needs in the same classrooms with their age mates (Carnovali 2017). An integral part of the scheme of inclusion is provision of teacher's assistants for disabled children. While resources and implementation vary from region to region, the Italian Constitutional Court has safeguarded inclusion as a right of the child, not a mere government benefit. For example, the court struck down an across-the-board austerity cutback on teacher's assistants for children with disabilities, holding that decisions about the education of children with disabilities could not be driven by fiscal priorities, but must be individualized and tailored to the particular child's needs (Corte Const. 2010). It is my impression that Italians' heightened consciousness regarding children's rights has served to mitigate some of the tensions that are common in the United States around the inclusion in the regular classroom of children who do not speak the English language or children with disabilities who may demand more of a teacher's time. When I probed parents in Scanno to see if they were concerned that inclusion of immigrant children or children with disabilities into their own child's classes would have a negative impact on their own child's schooling, they were firm on the principle that "all children have a right to go to school."

In Scanno, children of different language groups and abilities were all being taught together. Having myself, as a parent, faced the choice between special-education services as provided in public schools and a private school exclusively for children with learning disabilities, I was curious to see how total inclusion in the regular public classroom might work in practice. I observed that teachers seemed to adjust for the differences between students—for example, finding creative ways for children with physical or mental limitations to join in sports or projects rather than sit on the sidelines. A lot of peer-to-peer teaching was happening as well, as classmates absorbed the lessons of inclusion and adaptation. Over the course of six years, I was able to follow the progress of various children with developmental delays and autism, as well as children like Massimo and Gaia who arrived in Scanno speaking no Italian. I was also able to observe how practices of inclusion learned in school were reinforced and mirrored in the experiences of children in the community at large, and vice versa.

People with disabilities, young and old, are highly visible in Scanno. Motorized wheelchairs and scooters are a common sight in the piazza. Ramps lead into churches and buildings and, where there are obstacles, people come forward eagerly to help. Children with developmental disabilities march in parades and play drums in the marching bands. One popular youth with cerebral palsy serves as a traffic guard from his motorized scooter. Children with Down syndrome wait on customers in stores, chat with people of all ages, and generally enjoy free access to the life of a community where everyone knows and accepts them. One Down syndrome youth assists Don Carmelo at almost every mass wearing a T-shirt and jeans and humming out of tune. He and a Downs syndrome girl of similar age often lead the marching bands that are part of every festival, gesturing in time with the music like drum majors. Although the bands come from many different towns, they always welcome these young people.

In the August 2018 reenactment of the *Ju' Catenace* (traditional marriage procession), it was a beautiful sight to see a pair of Down syndrome young people walking arm in arm in their handsome traditional costumes. It seems that children generally, and Down syndrome or developmentally disabled individuals in particular, enjoy a special status. Like VIP travelers, they are accommodated most quickly, listened to most attentively, and get the warmest smiles. I love this aspect of life in Scanno. I remember vividly how I felt as a seven-year-old when my favorite grown-up cousin was married to a beautiful girl whom he had known in grade school. She had vanished from the school after she lost her sight but they were reunited as young adults. It was my first wedding, and I watched entranced as the bride entered the church. But grown-up invitees were explicitly told that children were not welcome at either the ceremony or the reception, so I had to wait in the car while my parents were in the church, and we left for home before the reception. It would be unimaginable in Scanno to exclude children, especially differently abled children, from events like a wedding, let alone from attending school with their peers.

* * *

The stories highlighted in this chapter only begin to scratch the surface of the ways in which the rights protected by the CRC can and do play out in the context of children's daily lives. The stories have implicated a wide range of children's rights; sometimes several were implicated in a single story. However, my sample was driven by the children's stories, not by an analytical structure imposed from outside or dictated from above. Unpacking these children's experiences, one can identify specific rights—the right to have your voice heard; to participate in your community; to enjoy free play and free expression; to a value-rich education; to inclusion as opposed to exclusion; to grow up in your own family; and to know and preserve your identity and cultural heritage. Other researchers in other times and places might have observed different rights at work in different children's lives. But, for the purposes of our study, these children have been offered as living evidence of what we see in this particular Petri dish. I can assert, based on the evidence, that a culture of respect for children's rights, given a favorable climate, can take root and grow. These examples show how a truly rights-regarding macrosystem can change the ecology of childhood from the bottom up as well as from the top down.

12

Building Small Worlds in Urban Spaces

We cannot and will not accept any speed limit on America's economic growth, It is the task of economic policy to grow the economy as rapidly, sustainably, and inclusively as possible. Statement of Larry Summers when he served as Treasury Secretary under President Bill Clinton.
—Larry Summers, quoted in E. F. Schumacher, *Small Is Beautiful*

The market . . . represents only the surface of society and its significance relates only to the momentary situation there and then. There is no probing into the depths of things, into the natural or social facts that lie behind them. In a sense, the market is the institutionalization of individualism and non-responsibility. Neither buyer nor seller is responsible for anything but himself.
—Schumacher, *Small Is Beautiful*

Be afraid of "Bigness." Be very afraid. In the 1930s it contributed to the rise of fascism. Alarmingly, we are experimenting again with a monopolized economy.
—Tim Wu, "Be Afraid of Bigness"

The quotations above represent threads in a long-running debate about the limits of speed and size as the measure of success and freedom. The first quote comes from Larry Summers, secretary of the treasury under President Bill Clinton and a proponent of the power of large-scale and rapid growth. The second is from E. F. Schumacher, a 1970s economist who advocated in favor of sustainable growth at a human scale and was an early pioneer in the small-is-beautiful movement. The third quotation comes from Tim Wu, a professor of law at Columbia University, who warns that concentrations of power in huge corporations facilitated the rise of fascist dictators and fears that history may be repeating itself.

In this chapter we will look at the role played by "bigness" in shaping social and political environments and explore recent calls for a renewal of a "small is beautiful" movement. How could opting to mobilize the power of "smallness" play out in children's worlds? Far from descending from the lofty into the mundane, we will be going to where the real action is taking place. Just as Scanno and Cedar Key informed our sense of how small worlds support children, we will see how smallness can be used to revitalize urban spaces. We have already encountered initiatives that create small therapeutic communities to tackle specific threats to children's flourishing—for example, the story of Angelo, surrounded by his supportive team in Lecce, and of Stefano, reunified with his mother in the supportive setting of San Patrignano.

Smallness has been a theme throughout this book. In the first chapters we started small, examining the ecology of childhood at the village level in two different cultural, political, and sociological environments. We then expanded our view, to examine how major national and global forces and macrosystemic values shape children's small worlds. We identified the universalizing principles of the CRC as a framework that can guide policy-makers and citizens in creating an environment conducive to children's growth. In common with the ecological model, the CRC starts small: by placing the child at the center and recognizing the importance to children of circles of intimate relationships within positive, supportive environments. It makes explicit the critical importance of social solidarity and a sense of commitment to the next generation.

In chapter 11 we addressed a common concern undercutting support for the CRC: Given its lack of enforcement mechanisms, is it actually having an impact at the national and local level? In the three decades since the CRC came into being, we have been accumulating the kind of evidence needed to answer that question. A growing body of research is documenting the CRC's effects at the political level of legislatures, agencies, and courts. Fewer studies are like this one, focused on documenting the CRC's effects at the microlevel of children's lives. But we can see from the accumulating studies that the CRC is being "implemented" in the experiences of individual children like Genny, Angelo, Stefano, Massimo, and Gaia. We can also show its impact on groups of children whose microsystemic environment has grown and changed as CRC rights permeated to the grassroots level. The children playing in the Ciambella, the Scanno schoolchildren participating in policy-making, the art students in Rita Quaranta's class, and the Scanno children who "implemented" their autistic classmate's right to inclusion have all been touched by the CRC. To plant the seeds of a rights-regarding culture, all it takes is a favorable climate.

But what are the crucial elements for creating that favorable climate? As I studied childhood in Scanno and Cedar Key, I found myself puzzling over what it is about these two villages that makes them a good place for children to grow. It struck me that a quality they both share—one that is missing from so much of contemporary society—is a strong sense of intergenerational solidarity. This sense of solidarity, linking every adult in the community to every child, reaches across generations, institutional affiliations, and boundaries of family loyalty. None of these boundaries is erased, but concern for the well-being of children seems able to transcend social divisions. While each of these villages is relatively homogenous racially and linguistically when compared to neighboring urban centers, both Scanno and Cedar Key have their own social stratifications. In each village there are sophisticated people and unpretentious people, families just scraping by and families that are more affluent, professionals and farmers or service workers, newly arrived and native-born residents, and voters of every political stripe. Why are these communities different? Is it simply that they are small? Is smallness the missing element in building solidarity?

In recent years, "small," "local," "slow," and "simple," once seen as pejoratives, have emerged as catchwords representing a different set of values and a different way of life. As globalization erodes a shared sense of rootedness and of social and economic connection, many people seem to be experiencing a yearning to recapture the values of a simpler time. In Italy and in the United States, more and more people are drawn to movements like "slow food," organic farming, local markets—all qualities we associate with the old-fashioned hometown, whether it is in small-town Italy or small-town USA. Of course, the hometown or the *paese* of memory and tradition are inevitably seen through a haze of sentimentality. Even if we could magically repopulate all the empty main streets of Rust Belt America and the deserted mountain villages of Italy and restore their economic prosperity, these small communities would still have their own shortcomings and limitations. Moreover, imagining a world in which small towns dominate and cities become obsolete is not a viable or even a theoretically appealing goal. Modern societies will continue to need urban centers even as we succeed in revitalizing small towns. The point of this chapter about "small is beautiful" is not to celebrate an imagined past but to envision ways in which the benefits of growing up in a small community can be integrated into larger policies about children's environments. In this chapter, after a discussion of the work of Schumacher, a pioneer of the "small is beautiful" movement, we will examine two "small is beautiful" projects: one in Naples, Italy, and the other in New York City. Each of these projects aims to improve the lives of children by nurturing the ecology of childhood—not on a nationwide or even citywide scale, but in a single small neighborhood.

A Question of Size: Economics as If People Mattered

The idea that "small is beautiful" is not new. In many ways, it is hardwired into the human spirit and essential to human development (Center on the Developing Child 2007; National Research Council and Institute of Medicine 2000). It is no accident that the ecological model is a set of concentric and intersecting circles representing the child's connection to others, starting at the most intimate level of the family. We know from developmental science that human infants, without the intimacy of emotional attachment to a caring adult, will fail to thrive even if all their material needs are met. Yet economists and political scientists can lose sight of this basic truth as they scale up from the realm of human development to the realms of political science and economics.

One early and influential critic of classical economics and its obsession with growth was economist E. F. Schumacher (1911–1977). His 1973 book *Small Is Beautiful: Economics as if People Mattered* challenged the notion that growth measured by GNP should or could be an end in itself. His theories found a sympathetic ear in President Jimmy Carter, who was also one of the first world leaders to recognize the environmental threat posed by unrestrained and unsustainable growth. Carter warned against unrestrained materialism and heedless exploitation of natural resources. His message of scarcity and restraint failed to resonate with his fellow Americans, however, and he was swept from office after only one term by Ronald Reagan, whose message of "morning in America" and whose vision of a nation of limitless possibilities, growing ever-greater and ever-richer, was more to their liking. In the decades that followed, growth for its own sake seemed to dominate the field of economics.

After the recession, Schumacher became newly popular, with a 2010 edition of his book making the *New York Times* bestseller list. Environmentalist Bill McKibben, in his foreword to the new edition, points to fossil fuels and their limits, the financial crisis, and climate change as Exhibits A, B, and C for why Schumacher's moment has returned. Like Schumacher, many of us were brought up to see civilization as a progression from units like the family and tribe to greater and more perfect ones like the unions of states and nations. We accepted that "bigger is better" and believed in the power of "economies of scale." Yet observation tells us that, once bigness has been achieved, "there is often a strenuous attempt to attain smallness within bigness" (Schumacher 2010, 68). For different purposes, humans need many different structures, some large and some small, some exclusive and some inclusive. According to Schumacher, this duality is intrinsically human, and part of the continuing search for a balance between human needs for both order and freedom. In reaction to what he called an almost universal "idolatry of giantism," Schumacher called his contemporaries' attention to the virtues of smallness.

Almost half a century ago, Schumacher warned of all the global forces that I have identified as posing singularly dangerous threats to the small worlds of children. Among these destabilizing elements were technology and mass migration. Schmuacher believed that rapid transportation and communication had made people "footloose" and too prone to migrate (2010, 72). In the past, when people were relatively immobile, social and geographical structures were simply a given; people who wanted to stay put stayed put. Only in times of crisis were ordinary people driven to leave their homes in mass migrations, flocking to cities or crossing national boundaries in order to survive. But, Schumacher warned, when people move but cannot find a new place in society they can easily become rootless and vulnerable. Here is how Schumacher described the effects of mobility in 1973: "Now, a great deal of structure has collapsed, and a country is like a big cargo ship in which the load is in no way secured, It tilts, and all the load slips over, and the ship founders" (73).

In rich countries the tilt results in sprawling, environmentally damaging megalopoli and the emptying out of once-vibrant cities, towns, and villages. In poor countries, it results in mass migrations, mass unemployment, and starvation, as the vitality is drained out of rural areas. While people may believe that rapid transport and instantaneous communication open up new freedoms, as Schumacher cautioned they can also "destroy freedom by making everything extremely vulnerable and extremely insecure, unless conscious policies are developed and conscious action is taken to mitigate the destructive effects of these technological developments" (74). Today, his warnings seem prescient: the notion that has dominated the past half-century of economic theory—that workers left behind by the demands of efficiency should stop complaining and simply retrain for skills that are marketable or move to wherever the goods are produced—has proved damaging to the fabric of society and is ecologically and logically flawed.

Schumacher also identified the dilemmas of "regionalism" and the geographic distribution of population, advocating a commitment to developing all the regions within each country. If this effort is not made, he argued, the only choice for those left behind is to remain in misery or to migrate: "An entirely new system of thought is needed based on attention to people, and not primarily attention to goods. . . . It could be summed up by the phrase, 'production by the masses, rather than mass production' (169). Surprisingly, Schumacher looked to innovations in technology and science as the keys to a new "economics as if people mattered" built on a human scale: "What was impossible, however, in the nineteenth century, is possible now. That is the conscious utilization of technological and scientific potential for the fight against misery and human degradation—a fight in intimate contact with actual people, with individuals, families and small groups, rather than states and other anonymous abstractions. And this presupposes a political and economic structure that can provide this intimacy" (79).

Schumacher called for an articulated structure that could cope with a multiplicity of small-scale units. He pulled no punches in stating his bottom line: "If economic thinking cannot grasp this it is useless. If it cannot get beyond its vast abstractions, the national income, the rate of growth, capital/output ratio, input-output analysis, labour mobility, capital accumulation; if it cannot get beyond all this and connect with the human realities of poverty, frustration, alienation, despair, breakdown, crime, escapism, congestion, ugliness, and spiritual death, then let us scrap economics and start afresh" (80).

Particularly relevant to the ecology of childhood are Schumacher's insights on the importance and fragility of social structures: "The life, work, and happiness of all societies depend on certain 'psychological structures' which are infinitely precious and highly vulnerable. Social cohesion, cooperation, mutual respect and above all self-respect, courage in the face of adversity, and the ability to bear hardship—all this and much else disintegrates when these social structures are badly damaged" (204). His criteria for creating smallness in big organizations are valuable in thinking about creating small communities within big communities and small worlds within big worlds. He posits five principles:

1) The Principle of Subsidiary Function, which rests on the belief that "it is an injustice and at the same time a grave evil and disturbance of right order to assign to a greater and higher association what lesser and subordinate associations can do, For every social activity ought of its very nature to furnish help to the members of the body social and never destroy or absorb them."
2) The Principle of Vindication, which holds that, except for exceptional cases, deference must be given to subsidiary units and subsidiary units must be defended. This does not mean that all must be treated the same because not every unit contributes in the same manner. Using the language of economics, Schumacher argues that if a unit enjoys special advantages it must pay an appropriate *rent*. If it must cope with inescapable disadvantages, it must be entitled to a *subsidy*.
3) The Principle of Identification, which in the context of economics deals with accountability via a balance sheet. For our purposes of looking at social structures, it boils down to taking sufficient data to reward successes and identify and correct failures.

4) The Principle of Motivation relates to the rewards of individual effort. Those at the top have plenty of motivation as they strive to make those at the bottom redundant, in service of profit and efficiency. Schumacher exposes the incoherence of policy makers who preach the virtues of hard work and restraint while painting utopian pictures of unlimited consumption without either work or restraint. What is required is genuine respect for and preservation of the dignity of work.
5) The Principle of the Middle Axiom is aimed at creating a proper balance between order and freedom within subsidiary units. Subsidiary units must have the freedom to engage in assessing and implementing policies and not simply enduring orders from above (260–70).

Some of Schumacher's principles for humanizing large-scale organizations seem more useful in thinking about "firms" than in thinking about other social structures, but many of them are easily recognizable to lawyers, political scientists, and sociologists of the twenty-first century as principles associated with justice and good government. "Subsidiarity," for example, is a well known principle of Catholic social justice theology—in fact, Schumacher is quoting verbatim from section 79 of Pope Pius XI's 1931 encyclical on "Reconstruction of the Social Order" (Pope Pius 1931, section 79). The principle of subsidiarity is also a fundamental principle of international law and of many national systems that vest authority over local affairs at the local level. The principle of "vindication" sounds a lot like a defense of federalism or a call for policies of solidarity and mutual support among regions within a nation or among constituent nations within a union or commonwealth. The importance of "motivation" for those who do the work needs no explanation in a time when rewards for those at the top are skyrocketing while workers are seeing their jobs downsized, exported, or replaced by robots and AIs in the name of efficiency.

In a chapter titled "New Patterns of Ownership," Schumacher asks the very question with which I began this ten year long research project. Citing John Kenneth Galbraith's description of the United States as a nation of enormous private affluence existing side by side with the deepest levels of public squalor, Schumacher asks: "How could there be public squalor in the richest country, and, in fact, much more of it than in many other countries whose Gross National Product, adjusted for the size of the population, is markedly smaller?" (290). He lays the blame on the belief, common among US conservatives, that taxation of profits earned through "private enterprise" is an unjust taking of an individual's or a firm's hard-earned property. He also points out that supposedly "private" enterprise relies upon public infrastructure and taxpayer supports of every kind and advocates for a restructuring of business law so that profits of private enterprise are shared with the public in proper proportion to the firm's use of public resources. His storyline made me think of Senator Elizabeth Warren's speech arguing that there is no such thing as a self-made man—every one of us got where we are with inputs from the public educational, physical, and social infrastructure paid for by others' sweat, sacrifices, and tax dollars. Her speech hit a nerve in 2012 and went viral on YouTube (Smerconish 2012).

Schumacher ends his book by reminding readers that the virtue of smallness and the evils of materialism are not his invention—sages and teachers through the ages have preached these evils and the importance of community. But looking at the world around him in 1973 he saw a new urgency: "Today, however, the message reaches us not only from saints and sages but from the actual course of physical events. It speaks to us in the language of terrorism, genocide, breakdown, pollution, exhaustion" (Schumacher 2010, 314). Instead of limitless growth he urges us to seek sustainable equilibrium. This call was urgent forty-five years ago; today, we know that the future of human civilization on planet Earth hangs in the balance. Schumacher's book examines the principle of smallness in the context of subsidiary units of a larger whole; he operates at the macrolevel of the economist and policymaker. As we saw in chapter 7, a number of contemporary economists have been advocating for a more nuanced approach to measuring value at the macrolevel. Another focus of the contemporary small is beautiful movement has been sustainability, which now plays a role in every area of policy design. This is partially a reaction to the looming threat of climate change: unlimited consumption of fossil fuels and the throwaway culture of consumerism that depletes natural resources have been major drivers of this crisis. Economists and political leaders as well as environmentalists are rediscovering the virtues of the "circular economy" as an alternative to the wasteful and dangerous "linear economy" that gained dominance in the industrial and modern eras. For those unfamiliar with the terms, here is a thumbnail sketch of the concept of the circular economy from the website of the Ellen MacArthur Foundation: "Looking beyond the current 'take, make and dispose' extractive industrial model, the circular economy is restorative and regenerative by design. Relying on system-wide innovation, it aims to redefine products and services to design waste out, while minimizing negative impacts. Underpinned by a transition to renewable energy sources, the circular model builds economic, natural and social capital" (2018). Concepts like sustainability and the circular economy can also be useful models in thinking about the ecology of childhood. Suppose we focus on strategies that are restorative and regenerative and search for strategies that build social capital at the local level; the inescapable reality is that large numbers of children—especially poor minority children—are growing up not in small towns but in child-unfriendly urban wastelands. Are there strategies to nurture or recreate the solidarity of a village-sized community within these anonymous urban spaces? In the following pages we will examine two initiatives for enhancing the ecology of childhood in large urban spaces. In each case, building or rebuilding a local community—creating a village-sized space inside an urban environment—was seen as the first step in improving children's lives. Both initiatives are located in large, economically challenged cities. In the city of Napoli (Naples) we will visit the quarter called La Sanità, where a network of youth cooperatives, under the guidance of an inspired parish priest, has tapped the human, cultural, and artistic capital of a decaying low-income neighborhood to create jobs and resources for the community's youth. In the United States, we will visit the Harlem Children's Zone (HCZ), named after the historically black New York City neighborhood where it is located. The brainchild of a gifted black educator, this project was designed to prove that, given the proper education, social skills, and resources, poor children of color have the capacity to move up the educational ladder and escape from a cycle of poverty into the middle class.

La Sanità: Utilizing the Power of Youth to Transform Human, Cultural, and Artistic Capital into a Sustainable Collaborative Community

At age forty-two, Don Antonio Loffredo suddenly found himself responsible for four inner-city parishes with beautiful but crumbling churches serving several thousand poor Neapolitan families. In the eighteenth century, La Sanità was a prosperous and peaceful, almost rural enclave. Nestled in a valley between the three hills that overlook the Bay of Napoli, the zone was known for its beautiful homes, fresh air, and pleasant environment. Then in 1809—in a stroke of disastrous urban planning that many inner-city Americans would recognize—La Sanità was literally buried alive. The French Army, pushing the Napoleonic Empire further and further south, had conquered Napoli. Wanting a nice wide and level causeway to facilitate travel between the harbor and their fortifications on the hill Capodimonte, they constructed a broad avenue cutting across the city and connecting the port to the fortifications. Its most ambitious feature was a massive stone bridge patterned after the Roman aqueducts, slicing across, over, and through La Sanità. The bridge, taller than the tallest steeples and wider than the widest streets below, dwarfed everything beneath it. The neighborhood, now marginalized both geographically and economically, was left to deteriorate.

Fast forward a hundred and fifty years, to about 1965, and we see little Antonio Loffredo, firstborn son of an affluent Neapolitan businessman, enjoying an outing with his grandfather. One of their favorite walks was across the bridge over La Sanità to the elegant park in Capodimonte. Antonio's earliest memory of La Sanità was of a procession celebrating the neighborhood's patron saint: "I watched from above, peering through the wrought iron railings of the viaduct, as this festive and colorful crowd of people surged by, feeling fascinated and wanting nothing more than to lose myself in the crowd, and explore the novelty of this loud and rowdy festival" (Loffredo 2013, 13). When he was older and had more freedom to roam, the young Loffredo made many visits to this exciting place, descending via the elevator that linked the bridge to the streets below. The people of La Sanità were indeed a group apart, deeply attached to their heroes and saints and fierce guardians of their local traditions. But by 2001, when Don Loffredo took charge of the four parishes, the social fabric of La Sanità had been ravaged by chronic unemployment, domestic violence, organized crime, and government neglect. Even the elevator connecting La Sanità with the city above had long been out of service,

Infrastructure was crumbling and public services were breaking down. Crime families had perverted the virtue of solidarity into the vice of *omerta'* (the Mafia's code of silence). Parents feared losing their children to a stray bullet, as rival factions of the Camorra battled for dominance. It seemed as if people had given up hope. Loffredo tells how he discovered a secret weapon in the young people of the parish: shortly after his arrival, the security system that protected the Basilica of Santa Maria della Sanità from thieves and vandals went down along with the rest of the power grid in the neighborhood, and a group of adolescents took it upon themselves to move into the church and occupy it around the clock, ostensibly to guard its artistic treasures. Don Loffredo figured that no one steals that which already fully belongs to him, and so he not only welcomed the youths as protectors of the sacred spaces; he joined their vigil. During those long nights he earned the young people's trust, and they began to share their frustrations and their dreams.

Young people are not stupid. Coming of age in this marginalized neighborhood, they understood the barriers they were facing. Realistically, they had only two options. They could leave their homes and families behind and go "find America" (whether in a Northern Italian city or in a foreign country), or, if they wanted to remain in La Sanità, they would have to affiliate with one of the organized crime families that controlled the local economy. With Don Loffredo as a bridge to the wider world, the young people were able to chart a third way—creating a sustainable community right there in the neighborhood where they were born and where many of them wanted nothing more than to settle down and raise children of their own in peace (Loffredo 2013).

In the period between 2001 and 2013, as Don Loffredo recounts in *Noi del Rione della Sanità* (We of the Sanità), the young people of his parish were able to transform their own small world. A major element in his program of transformation was exposing them to travel—at first, he took groups of kids on day trips to the seashore, only a few kilometers away. For many of the kids, this was their first time they had ventured out of the neighborhood. Eventually, they went as a group to places like Palestine, Malta, Paris, and Germany. These trips opened the kids' horizons and motivated them to take risks and break down psychological barriers. Within ten years, the small group of teens who had hung out at the Basilica of Santa Maria della Sanità had matured, grown in numbers, and become a central asset to their community. The Fondazione San Gennaro, a licensed nonprofit dedicated to development of the community's resources, was formed to support their work. With help from private donors, community members willing to share their skills, and their own sweat equity, they reclaimed the crumbling convents and churches. The empty spaces were now repurposed as day nurseries, after-school programs, a bed-and-breakfast, and a full-fledged performing arts center.

To accomplish all of this the young people had to do more than simply repurpose the physical spaces. They had to retool their own skill sets in order to contribute their own sweat equity to the project. They learned by doing, with guidance from skilled neighborhood volunteers, and they passed on what they learned to the next cadre of youth. In the process, they built a network of cooperatives, capable of offering services at a fair price to the community. Created and managed by the young people, these co-ops grew to include hundreds of local youth. What began as a project to staff preschool and after-school programs, had eventually expanded to include training caterers, ironworkers, stonemasons, builders, electricians, and specialists in hospitality and tourism.

Perhaps the most impressive achievement of Don Loffredo and his team of young people was persuading the Vatican to give them permission to restore the vast pre-Christian catacombs, clogged with centuries of junk, that honeycombed the area beneath the Basilica of Santa Maria della Sanità. The soft *tuffa* (volcanic stone) of Napoli is much easier to excavate and carve than the stones beneath Rome. For those who have visited the claustrophobic Roman catacombs, the vaulted ceilings of the Neapolitan catacombs are a revelation. Having cleaned and installed illumination in these amazing spaces, some as lofty as cathedrals, the young people obtained permission to open this treasure to the public. Employing members of the group who had studied foreign languages to act as docents and actors, they created a dramatic guided tour, where (for a fee) visitors could relive the colorful history of the city.

As soon as I learned of this project, I was determined to visit it. In the summer of 2013, I traveled to Napoli (located on the Mediterranean coast about a day's drive southwest of Scanno) to see if I could connect with the young people who had accomplished this miracle. The city of Napoli is definitely a whole-body experience; coming from tidy and peaceful Scanno, I felt almost physically assaulted by the chaos—stunned by the noise and the dirt and the heat and the crowds as I picked my way across sidewalks littered with garbage and broken chunks of pavement, dodging motorbikes as they mounted the curbs to avoid the choking traffic. Yet the crazy, messy scene was brimming with vitality—neighbors calling out to each other from balconies, music spilling from doorways, brightly colored washing flapping overhead, good smells of home cooking filling the alleys, and boisterous children everywhere I looked.

Hoping to make contact with the young people of La Sanità, I took a taxi to the entrance to the San Gaudio Catacombs, where I was greeted by Susi, who turned out to be one of the leaders of the tourism and hospitality cooperative. I recognized Susi from her picture on the dust cover of Loffredo's book: the image of a young woman with long light brown hair and an open smile, pointing the way through the catacombs. Susi told me the story of her own involvement in La Sanità, beginning from when she was in her early teens. As she began to find her voice and identity, she discovered a passion for languages and for cross-cultural communication. By the time I met her, she was a young mother and married to a young man named Salvatore, one of the original group of boys.

Here is how Don Loffredo introduces Susi and Salvatore in his narrative:

And then there was Susi, who more than any of them believed in the dream., In addition to studying languages, earning her degree from the local University and enrolling in courses at the Goethe Institute sponsored by the German Consulate of Napoli, she married Salvatore and they are awaiting the birth of a baby girl, their future and ours. (Loffredo 2013, 57, translation mine)

Susi and Salvatore, as the project's first young family, symbolized the beginning of a new generation. Salvatore first appears in Loffredo's narrative as a scared little kid standing up for his buddies when they got into trouble on a trip to Israel. Like so many of his peers, Salvatore had to drop out of school as an adolescent in order to earn his bread and help support his siblings.

Although working full time, with Don Loffredo's encouragement and the support of his peers, he finished high school at night. He learned a skilled trade during the renovations and became a mainstay of one of the cooperatives.

At the time of my visit, Susi was back at work doing public relations for the Catacombs, after a year as a stay at home mother. The baby was enrolled in day care at one of the project's centers. As I listened to Susi's description of her childhood, her career, and her dreams for the future, it was absolutely clear that she knew she had the talent and capacity to succeed anywhere. But her roots and those of Salvatore were in La Sanità. They wanted the same sense of rootedness for their child. It was also clear, from her description of their interactions, that Don Loffredo was not simply being modest or self-effacing in describing himself as mentor and facilitator while crediting the young people as the real architects and agents of change. They were the decision makers. The gift he gave them was encouraging them to believe in a different future. His style is captured by the story of his encounter with a boy named Lello.

Lello had to leave school to work in a local store and, before he was fourteen, he was already bringing home the groceries for his family. He worked from eight in the morning until nine at night and was hardly ever at home, preferring to spend any precious spare time hanging out on the streets with his buddies. His story was not unusual. As Loffredo writes,

> When you are born in La Sanità, you enter into a framed painting, a scene, a journey already charted, with very little room for freedom. If it is true that money does not provide happiness, it nevertheless determines the course of an existence, sometimes down to the smallest details. (Loffredo 2013, 52, translation mine)

Turning to his pivotal encounter with fourteen-year-old Lello, Loffredo writes:

> One day I asked him something that perhaps I should never have dared to ask him. "You, what do you want to do with your life?" He looked at me. His expression was one of bewilderment, but there was a spark of curiosity. It passed like lightening, but I had seen it. He responded with his own demand, "So, what *can* I do?" The abyss contained in those few words nearly knocked me down, but I kept my balance. I suggested that he come to the church. There, together, maybe we could find something. He came the same evening. I told him about the various projects we were involved in and those we were planning for the future. (Loffredo 2013, 53, translation mine)

Even though he was cautioned that he could not count on a large or even a regular paycheck, Lello threw himself into the projects, making the rounds of all the skill groups. By the time he was through he had trained as a blacksmith, stonemason, electrician, maintenance operator, and hotelier. He loved it all. Lello was the first to go abroad (to Malta and London), to study English, and to work as a volunteer in the favelas of Brazil. But he always returned to home base, where his passion was working with the little kids. As Loffredo says of the grown up Lello, that original spark of curiosity now shines brightly, and its beauty is profound, because it is "rooted in the ransom he paid for his own liberation, which makes him feel both happy and fortunate. Lello carved out a space in the world with his own hands, and began to build his own future, thanks in part to the strong relationships that bound him to his friends in the neighborhood, his companions in adventure" (54).

At the close of our first meeting, Susi gave me two tickets to a benefit gala scheduled for that weekend. I brought my husband as my guest and it turned out to be one of the great experiences of our lives. It began with a tour of the catacombs at night, with the young people as docents and costumed actors. When we finally arrived in the huge old church at the far end of the underground route, it was packed with people from the neighborhood, side by side with affluent patrons. There, we were treated to a wonderful concert, the highlight of which was the performance of the Sanitensemble, an enormous youth orchestra composed of children of all ages, playing every kind of instrument. I have never heard "O Sole Mio" rendered with such joy and such conviction.

We returned to La Sanità in November 2014 and stayed for a week at the Casa del Monacone, a delightful bed-and-breakfast in the heart of the neighborhood, created and operated by the young people in part of the former convent. We celebrated our forty-third wedding anniversary La Sanità–style, at a legendary pizza parlor called I Tre Santi (The Three Saints), just a block away from the Casa del Monacone. Each day, I visited a day nursery, a foster home, or an after-school program. Many of these programs were housed in improvised spaces intended for other uses, and many lacked the modern equipment that might be standard in a more affluent environment. But the staff was young and eager, and the children were noisy, active, happy, and learning how to play together as well as how to count and read. What stood out for me was the level of commitment to the children, which held steady even in the face of government budget cuts forced on Italy by the EU's demand for austerity. One young couple operating an extremely well-run foster home for six very young children reported that their funding had been frozen for over a year.

Determined to avoid trauma to these fragile children, they were maxing out their personal credit cards to put food on the table and buy diapers.

I also spent time talking with the young people of La Sanità and walking around the neighborhood with Don Loffredo. This time, we *Americani* had learned the ropes and accordingly came and went via the elevator that carries pedestrians from the top of the bridge down to the valley below, leaving our car safely parked. In a few seconds we could travel from bustling modern Napoli to the smaller world below, where we now felt completely at home. Before we left, I had coffee at the local bar with Don Loffredo. As we said goodbye, he reached over and patted me gently on the cheek. It felt like a blessing.

The Harlem Children's Zone: Doing "Whatever It Takes" to Give Poor Black Children a Fair Chance at the American Dream

Around the time that Don Loffredo began his projects in La Sanità, another inspired leader was launching a much larger project in Harlem, a historically black neighborhood occupying the northern sector of the borough of Manhattan in New York City. The area became famous as the cradle of "the Harlem Renaissance" of the 1930s, when some of the greatest African American writers, artists, and thinkers made it the cultural capital of black intellectuals. It was also one of the era's great hubs for jazz artists. My father, a bass player in big bands during the 1930s, recalled finishing his sets around 2 a.m. at the Waldorf Astoria Hotel and walking uptown through Central Park to jam until dawn with buddies at the Cotton Club.

In the decades that followed the Supreme Court's 1954 holding in *Brown v. Board of Education* striking down laws that segregated people by race, de facto segregation still exerted a powerful influence in Northern as well as Southern states. It persisted in practices such as single-family residential zoning codes—which enable the affluent to segregate themselves by dictating the size of lots and prohibiting multifamily dwellings—and in redlining, a banking practice of refusing to write mortgages for homes in minority districts that survives today although it has been illegal for fifty years (Grabar 2018; Jan 2018). These practices meant that poor minority citizens were unable to move up and out of ghettos, while more affluent blacks could and often did migrate to more stable and affluent communities nearby. As a result, Harlem lost many of its prominent citizens and became synonymous with high crime rates, concentrated poverty, drugs. and violence. Its schools failed and its buildings deteriorated. By 1990, the life expectancy of a young man in Harlem was lower than that of a young man in Bangladesh (Tough 2009, 21).

I first met Geoffrey Canada, the leader of the Harlem Children's Zone, when we invited him to deliver the keynote speech at a conference at the University of Florida on Children, Culture, and Violence cosponsored by the Colleges of Law, Arts and Sciences, Medicine, and Education, We already knew of Canada through his powerful autobiography, *Fist, Stick, Knife, Gun: A Personal History of Violence in America*. In this book he describes how he had witnessed the carnage resulting from young people's access to ever-more-efficient tools of violence; what had once been fistfights between teenagers were now deadly gunfights and drive-by shootings. Canada knew about his topic from personal experience: born in 1952 to a single mother in the South Bronx, one of the poorest and most violent sectors of New York City, he knew what it was like to run the gauntlet of gang violence just to get from home to school each day. He was able to get a foothold on the ladder to higher education and used it to escape the violence and poverty of his childhood. Having earned a master's degree in education from Harvard University, he became a teacher in Boston and eventually returned to New York to work with inner city youth in Harlem (Tough 2009).

One March evening in 2003, at our conference in Florida, Canada, dressed in khaki pants and a golf shirt, mesmerized his audience as he demonstrated his secret weapon for reaching kids—his training as a black belt in karate. He showed us how he had been able to convince the kids in Harlem that they could find true strength and validation as men and women by meeting violence with nonviolence. We academics were hooked. His charisma also made him successful at persuading policy-makers and funders to buy into his vision. Like Don Loffredo, Geoffrey Canada possessed unique powers of connecting with the young. I could well imagine the impact he had on groups of adolescent males, many of whom were growing up without father figures. This towering, muscular, athletic, graceful, and confident black man, demonstrating his martial arts techniques, speaking softly and moving as smoothly as a panther, was showing them a third option besides victimization or an early, violent death.

By the time he spoke to us in Florida, Canada was boiling over with frustration. He was tired of hearing "we have to save for a rainy day" when he knew full well that a rainy day would only bring bigger budget cuts. He was sick of going to teenagers' funerals, and he wanted to break through the inertia, to find a way to intervene early, before kids fell behind, became involved with gangs, and lost hope. His real endgame was to create a blueprint that could be used to support other communities so that poor black children would have a fighting chance at following the same path he had followed, using the merit system of access to higher education to escape poverty and enter the middle class (Tough 2009).

My primary source in telling the story of the Harlem Children's Zone (HCZ) is a wonderful book, *Whatever It Takes: Geoffrey Canada's Quest to Change Harlem and America*, written by journalist Paul Tough, who provides a detailed account of the early years of HCZ from its first beginnings in about 2000 to the book's publication in 2008. Tough had obtained Canada's permission to embed himself in the HCZ working group. Already an expert on poverty in the United States, Tough was able to provide a mix of first-person observations, compelling narratives, and social science context, showing how the project was a response to the heated debates in the 1980s and 1990s about the causes and cures of poverty. Canada rebelled at theories by academics such as Charles Murray, who, in his 1994 book, *The Bell Curve*, argued that the gaps in academic achievement of white and black children could be traced to their inherently different intellectual capacities (Hernstein and Murray 1994). Murray and his coauthor used data from IQ tests and standardized testing to argue that biology and not politics could explain why black children consistently lagged behind their white peers. Canada, along with many others, was outraged. In common with William Julius Wilson, author of *The Truly Disadvantaged*, Canada was convinced that the gap was caused by poverty and social inequality. He knew that the kids he worked with were just as smart as any others, but they were held back by the effects of poverty and entrenched racism. In order to really make a difference, as well as prove his case for the capacity of black children to succeed, he decided he would have to start small. He assembled a team and raised funding to create a model demonstration project in a limited geographical area: a children's zone of twenty-four blocks, where Canada and his team would show that children in Harlem, given a fair start, could compete in the race for success.

Canada decided his past interventions had been too diffuse and had come too late. He also had a hunch that there was a tipping point where the problems of a neighborhood became so severe and intense that it was almost impossible for kids to succeed. Instead of trying to help all of the kids in Harlem, he would create a laboratory out of the twenty-four-block section of Harlem. He would create a comprehensive program of support for kids and families living there, and his team would aggressively recruit expectant parents so that they could change children's environment even before birth. A "Baby College," where expectant parents could learn parenting skills, was the first step, to be followed by high quality preschools and primary schools. The objective was to provide a sample of poor inner-city kids who would arrive at first grade ready to learn, instead of lagging years behind their middle-class peers.

The HCZ kids would be supported throughout their school years with access to counselors and after-school programs. In order to persuade the skeptics, the project's success would have to be measured using quantitative methods, but this could be done by comparing objective test scores of the HCZ children and the numbers who were graduating from high school and enrolling in college with data from the control group of kids who were not in the program.

Early on, Canada became frustrated by the red tape and obstructionism of the New York public school system. So instead of just preparing kids for school, he opted to create a new charter school, called "Promise Academy," in order to have greater control over the content and competency of the children's school experience. The closest equivalent to charter schools in Italy are "*scuole paritarie*" (literally "equal schools") like the Asilo Buon Pastore. Under an Italian law enacted in 2000, private schools that provided a public benefit could be recognized as part of the nationally funded system of public education. In Italy, while there is no official religion, the wall between church and state is less formal, so funding can go directly to religious schools performing a public function without infringing on individuals' constitutional rights. However, the charter school movement in the United States was controversial. It reflected a belief, fueled by economists, that competition is the engine of excellence, and its proponents believed that opening up public funding to support establishment of newly chartered, independent schools with their own curricula would force ossified public school systems to compete.

Geoffrey Canada, like many other Americans, shared some of the widespread concerns that charter schools, instead of fostering healthy competition, might siphon talented pupils and funding away from the traditional public school system. The children most at risk, whose families lacked the skills necessary to advocate for them, would be left behind. But flexibility and control were important to Canada's project. In order to construct a study that would stand up to scrutiny, he needed a randomly selected group and a control group. Charter schools in New York had to be open to all, and a lottery was required to determine which students who applied would be admitted. Canada found himself in a local public school filled with hopeful parents, holding a lottery that would bring joy to a few but result in yet another waiting list for children whose names were not drawn. "What I'm going to remember tonight," he said, "is how those mothers looked at me when their kids didn't get in. When I go home tonight to my kid, whose life is pretty much secure, it's not going to make me sleep well knowing there are kids and families out there that *don't* feel secure. They are just terrified that their child is not going to make it, and they think this is another opportunity that slipped by" (Tough 2009, 20).

The lottery captures the cruel dilemma of the American dream. Americans are taught to believe that any kid can rise from poverty to become the president of the United States. The dark side of our "meritocracy" narrative is that it is inherently exclusionary, built around a system of competition, where you are either a winner or left behind. Success is measured by standardized testing that rates children against their peers, and the only way out is to climb up and away from where you began. But it seems there is never enough space on the ladder to the top.

Paul Tough narrates the struggles and growing pains of the Harlem Children's Zone from its initial conception to the graduation of the first middle-school class in 2008. His book tells many individual children's stories while focusing on the broad sweep of the project. There were more hard choices ahead if the project was to achieve its long-term goals. Initially, Promise Academy admitted two classes—an entering primary-school class (first graders/six-year-olds) and an entering middle-school class (sixth graders/ eleven-year-olds). The plan was to continue adding grades as the first class of sixth graders reached high school level until Promise Academy formed a continuum from preschool programs to twelfth grade. At the same time as it was growing Promise Academy, HCZ was expanding from its original twenty-four blocks to ninety-seven blocks in central Harlem. It was also strengthening its early childhood programs and parenting programs, adding "Harlem Gems" for preschoolers and "Three-Year-Old Journey" as a follow-on to Baby College. These early interventions seemed to be paying off for some but not all of the children. After a rocky start, the primary school was exceeding expectations. But the middle-school students were struggling. Many of them seemed held back not by cognitive problems but by emotional problems, stemming from difficult home environments that sapped their motivation and made it difficult for them to trust.

By the winter of 2008, it was time for a reckoning. Two-thirds of the third graders were scoring at or above the third grade level in reading on state mandated tests and an astonishing 95 percent at or above third grade level in math skills. However, the eighth-grade students, who had been slated to continue at Promise Academy as it expanded to grades nine through twelve, were performing below the median even for schools in equally challenged communities. It seemed that the kind of progress seen in the primary-school kids could only be achieved by starting children on "the conveyor belt" to success at the earliest age possible. Perhaps it had been a mistake to hope that a group of sixth graders who had not had the benefit of early interventions would be able to show the sort of progress that HCZ had promised.

In late March 2008, Promise Academy sent letters home informing the parents of the eighth graders that there would be no ninth grade. Instead, they would have to find high school placements in other New York City schools. Parents and students were crushed; they felt abandoned. Canada too was suffering. He explained to them that he had told them from the beginning that Promise Academy would be not just good but excellent. He could not allow them to continue in a failing school. To achieve the goal of excellence, HCZ was going to have to rethink its approach. The primary school would continue to move forward building new entering classes by lottery, but the middle school would not admit any new students. The current eighth graders would graduate to eighth grade and the current sixth graders to seventh grade. What the students did not know was that Promise Academy's board of directors, which consisted of hard-headed businessmen, some of whom had become billionaires on Wall Street, had drawn a line in the sand. They insisted on proof of success: if the remaining two classes of the middle school failed to improve, the middle school would be closed at the end of 2009 and reopen under management of a large educational corporation with a proven track record.

Despite this sad setback, 2008 was also the year when HCZ caught the attention of rising presidential candidate Barack Obama, and its national profile spread rapidly. There were doubts among some researchers that the data could support a claim that the students' school success was related to HCZ's holistic approach of funding neighborhood-based intensive support and enrichment programs. Some argued that HCZ's results were no better than other high-quality charter-school programs that lacked its holistic approach (Whitehurst and Croft 2010; Center for the Study of Social Policy 2016). But support for the HCZ model remained strong and the model spread to other locations. Under President Barack Obama, a federal program of Promise Neighborhoods replicated the model in demonstration projects in cities in California and Florida, with continued emphasis on cradle-to-career supports, evidence-based programming, and measurable standards. By 2015, HCZ was serving thirteen thousand Harlem children and almost as many adults, providing education plus recreation, nutrition, after-school programs, and college preparation and support. The Promise Neighborhood projects in other cities were also thriving (Center for Study of Social Policy 2016). Scholars like Nancy Dowd have been drawing on the lessons of the HCZ to imagine how an environment that responded to the unique developmental needs of black boys could change the face of inequality in America (Dowd 2018).

Comparing La Sanità and the Harlem Children's Zone

How can you compare apples and oranges? These programs grew in different soils and different cultures. And yet comparisons must be made if we are to learn from our own and others' success and mistakes. There are many ways in which the Harlem Children's Zone and La Sanità projects were similar. Both were founded by charismatic leaders who were dedicated to helping children achieve their full potential. Both took on the tough challenge of working with children and youth trapped in marginalized, violence-ridden communities that offered few positive options. Both took a holistic approach, seeing community resources like day nurseries, parent education, after-school programs, and recreation centers as central components for children's healthy development. Both reached out to all who have a stake in children's future, including family members and community leaders. Both created alliances with existing institutions such as churches and schools. Both mobilized private-sector donors as well as public agencies to cobble together enough resources to launch new programs. Both inspired similar projects in other places and served as models attracting praise from policy-makers and politicians.

There are also many striking differences between these projects. Starting with the charismatic leaders, Geoffrey Canada had grown up in an impoverished neighborhood and had fought his way up and out by grasping the ladder of educational opportunity. Don Loffredo had been born to an affluent family and was called by his faith to disappoint his wealthy father by joining the Catholic social justice movement. It is not a stretch of the imagination to say that each was influenced by the path he had taken and by the path he had not taken. Also different were the scope and size of their projects. One unfolded in a small neighborhood where almost everyone was both white and Catholic. The other began by carving out a section of a large, densely populated city neighborhood where almost everyone was black or Hispanic. Don Loffredo and the youth of La Sanità developed relationships with people and agencies in other parts of the city but largely stayed confined to the traditional boundaries of the neighborhood. Harlem Children's Zone expanded rapidly, not only in Harlem but in programs in other parts of North America. From the start, Canada had his eyes on designing a blueprint that could be replicated and taken to scale.

The differences can be traced to the different macrosystems in which these men were operating. Geoffrey Canada, growing up in the United States, believed in the promise of meritocracy and viewed competition as the pathway to achieving the American dream. Although he was attuned to the importance of family and community, his natural unit was the individual and his or her potential, his focus was on equality of opportunity, and his metaphor was the level playing field. Don Loffredo, coming from the Catholic social justice movement, saw all people as children of God and equal in His sight, but as called to contribute in different ways. His natural unit was the cooperative, which maximized the potential of all members. His focus was on comforting the afflicted and opening minds and hearts, and his credo was "love thy neighbor." The programs also differed in another way. HCZ, although rooted in a community, was primarily a top-down project designed and run by professionals; the hardheaded Wall Street donors on the HCZ board insisted on quantitative metrics of success and were quick to embrace privatization as a model for cutting through red tape and achieving efficiency. The leadership opted for private and charter schools despite widespread and valid concerns that these initiatives would erode support for the public schools, concerns that have only been gaining momentum in the intervening years (NAACP 2017; Strauss 2018).

La Sanità, by contrast, was a bottom-up project, designed and run by the youth themselves. It utilized community services such as public health care and social services networks wherever they existed, and, where they did not exist, it tried to bridge the gaps. From the start, the goals of La Sanità were more qualitative than quantitative—more faith-based than mathematical. Although La Sanità also had a governing board and external support from the Vatican, I found no indication of tampering with the basic communitarian model of Catholic outreach. The proof of success is to be measured by each life touched, as I was reminded many times over by the TV campaign of the Italian Catholic church to build support for its community outreach projects. Each film tells the stories of several people from marginalized communities who have been helped by church projects and ends with the refrain, "Is our work worthwhile? Ask *them*." The faces and voices of the people served are proof enough.

With such different goals and structures, it is not surprising that metrics played very different roles in each setting. Although it may seem counterintuitive, in order to prove to policy-makers that individual black children can succeed given a fair chance, Geoffrey Canada had to rely on group metrics. In *Whatever It Takes* we see how metrics were used to measure group achievement through standardized testing. The unit tested was the individual child, but their destiny was sealed by the failure of the group to reach the necessary benchmarks of success. Metrics are the language of profit and loss, and metrics seemed to dominate and sometimes supplant the interests of the individual child in the HCZ program. In Don Loffredo's book *Noi del Rione della Sanità*, I cannot recall a single mention of group metrics as a means of measuring success; instead, the highest value was group solidarity. It would have been inconceivable for Don Loffredo to abandon a group of adolescents who trusted him in order to begin anew with set of children who would be more successful.

These observations are admittedly a gross oversimplification of very complicated projects and very complex individuals. Geoffrey Canada, despite his decision to focus on creating a blueprint for cradle-to-college success that could be replicated at scale, never gave up his commitment to the hardest cases. He and HCZ continued to work with kids who had fallen off the conveyor belt or never gotten onto it. And Don Loffredo, although proud of all of the young people who found their life's mission and their place in society, was not above bragging about the academically talented ones who graduated from university.

One final difference between these initiatives brings us full circle to a primary theme of the "small is beautiful" movement—sustainability and the linear versus the circular economy. The HCZ model is primarily linear while the Sanità model is primarily circular. The HCZ model is about enabling individual children to move up a ladder of success that takes them to a new level and a better place; all children in the community potentially benefit, but the emphasis is on escaping the bonds of the local to succeed on a larger stage. It resembles the notion of limitless movement, voiced by economist Larry Summers in one of the epigraphs of this chapter. Substituting "individual" for "economy" in Summers' statement, the credo would read: "We cannot and will not accept any speed limit on [an individual's] growth. It is the task of [social] policy to grow the [individual] as rapidly, sustainably, and inclusively as possible." But this approach rests on an assumption of unlimited horizons for expansion, where each generation enjoys a better lifestyle and more opportunity than the preceding generation. We are discovering, to our dismay, that this is an illusion that results in the hollowing out of communities, leaving too many people behind who cannot find a foothold on the ladder. These are the "throwaway" people of the "throwaway" culture condemned by Pope Francis.

Turning to the chapter's second epigraph, taken from *Small Is Beautiful*, substituting the word "individual" for "market" reveals the small is beautiful theory as a critique of the culture of individualism: "[Individuals] . . . represent only the surface of society and [their] significance relates only to [the individual's] situation there and then, There is no probing into the depths of things, into the natural or social facts that lie behind them. In a sense, [it] is the institutionalization of individualism and non-responsibility. [No actor] is responsible for anything but himself."

These perspectives shed a harsh light on the idea that individual success, like a rising stock market, is going to be a tide that lifts all boats. How sustainable is a linear society in which every individual's ambition is to move up and out?

13

Charting the Way to a World Fit for Children

Some people look at things in a big way, and some people have gifts for addressing things in a big way. But I'm more drawn to thinking about things on a small level—that's where my gifts lie. The Gospel message "love thy neighbor as thyself" speaks strongly to me. Loving the people that I meet every day, in my household and my community, is where I focus my energy. If we could all do the small things that contribute to loving our neighbor, each and every day, then I think the big things in the world would move much closer to resolution. Take care of all the small, and you necessarily take care of all the big too, for the big is made up of the small.
—Jim Wright, Christ Church, Cedar Key, Florida, September 9, 2018

Jim Wright, vicar of Cedar Key's Christ Episcopal Church, made the remarks quoted above in a sermon to a very small congregation in a very small church in a very small town. As Father Jim reminds us, "The big is made up of the small." In this book I have argued that the most serious threats we face are not from nature but human activity and are global in scope. Admittedly, we have achieved remarkable victories over some of our natural enemies. But our worst wounds are self-inflicted—the result of poverty, inequality, armed conflict, toxic waste, and greed. Although I have examined the ecology of childhood at the intimate level of the village and its microsystems and mesosystems, I have argued that the problems of these small communities are emblematic—they are the world's problems. People everywhere are adjusting to rapid technological change; struggling to generate sufficient work for the able-bodied while caring for the vulnerable; racing to achieve a sustainable relationship with the natural world before it is too late; coping with the pressures of mass migration and dislocation; and striving to achieve justice, dignity, security, peace, and equality without sacrificing individual liberty. I have called for a fundamental reformation of today's dominant macrosystemic values, at both the local and global levels, to reduce the emphasis on individualism and materialism and to foster the values of solidarity, sustainability, and mutual support on which the survival of the human species depends.

The closing chapter of a serious book like this one is usually the chapter in which readers expect the author to propose grand solutions to the global problems she has identified. I have forewarned my readers that they will be disappointed. There are already many voices proposing a variety of answers to these questions. I have alluded to some of these voices already and will touch upon them again in this chapter. What I won't do, in closing, is propose global solutions to all of the ills I have discussed in this book; I leave that project to those scientists and theoreticians, many of whom I have cited in this book, who have been tilling those vast fields and will continue to do so. In this final chapter I will focus instead on the small and local—things that can be done at the microsystemic and exosystemic levels of family, community, municipality, and region. As Father Jim preaches, if we could all do the small things, each and every day, the big things in the world would move much closer to resolution. These small things are within all of our reach, whatever our age or stage of life. They have meaning and impact at every level of the ecology of childhood, including the macrosystemic. Macrosystemic values like solidarity and generativity begin at home.

Big Ideas That Mattered in Shaping a Plan of Action

This is not to say that "big ideas" are not crucial to the goal of defending children's small worlds. "Small is beautiful" is an example of a big idea, encountered during this project, that has shaped its direction. In another example, as I studied globalization, I began to see how the big idea of globalization could serve as a sort of umbrella for examining many current issues with both global and local impact. Unrestrained capitalism, technological revolution, discrimination, inequality, mass migration, and climate change can all be understood as interrelated dimensions of a process of globalization gone wrong. But globalism itself is not inherently evil. Many of the solutions to globalization's ills are also global in scope. Climate change and mass migration, for instance, defy boundaries and can only be addressed through global cooperation. Globalism is an idea to be engaged with, not rejected.

Other big ideas that I brought to the table, learned about through research, or encountered along the way have seemed especially relevant to mapping a path homeward. I came to this project already oriented in certain directions; I was a nursery school teacher and parent before I ever thought of becoming a lawyer. My belief system, instilled in childhood and nurtured in the Episcopal and Catholic faiths, was strongly aligned with social justice and the injunctions to "love thy neighbor" and care for those in need. Later, as a law student, lawyer, and scholar, I began to develop a larger theoretical framework for thinking about child law and policy. "Ecogenerism" was the result. As explained in chapter 2, ecogenerism puts children at the center of concern, uses an ecological model drawn from child development as its framework, and adopts "generativity," the quality of caring for and nurturing future generations, as its central value and driving force. On my way to developing the concept of ecogenerism, I utilized many other theoretical frameworks, including feminism, environmentalism, and the emerging recognition of children's rights as human rights, all of which influenced and shaped its development.

More recently, vulnerability theory, the path-breaking philosophy pioneered by my Emory University colleague Martha Albertson Fineman, has been a major influence on my work. Vulnerability theory rejects the focus on the autonomous liberal subject that has characterized Western liberal thinking. Instead, it holds that the single unifying characteristic of the human condition is not autonomy but vulnerability. Liberal Western democracies, Fineman has argued, mistakenly posited an abstract autonomous legal subject at the core of liberal theory, an approach that fails to reflect the fundamental reality of the human condition. At every stage of life and in every dimension of life, we are all vulnerable. In her 2017 article, "Vulnerability and Inevitable Inequality," Fineman recounts her intellectual journey from feminist legal theory to vulnerability theory and why she and so many others find it so compelling:

> What vulnerability theory offers is a way of thinking about political subjectivity that recognizes and incorporates differences and can attend to situations of inevitable inequality among legal subjects. In this regard, one advantage of vulnerability theory is that it can be applied in situations of inevitable or unresolvable inequality: it does not seek equality, but equity. A vulnerability analysis incorporates a life-course perspective while also reflecting the role of the social institutions and relationships in which our social identities are formed and enforced. It also defines a robust sense of state responsibility for social institutions and relationships. (143)

These benefits are all highly relevant to thinking about childhood, which is an integral part of the human life course. Vulnerability theory also provides a way of framing and justifying a collective responsibility for cross-generational support.

Another key influence on this project has been the work of my University of Florida colleague Nancy E. Dowd. A prolific scholar who has explored many dimensions of family, child, and juvenile law, in her recent work on equality, difference, and child development she has reimagined inequality through a developmental lens. As she notes, one of the key contributions of the social and neurological sciences to modern family law and children's policy has been the adoption of an evidence-based, developmentally informed perspective on what is good for children and how to meet their basic needs. This has been an important step forward. But, as Dowd points out, the image of "the child" at the center of our ecological diagram is based on a fallacy. Dowd's developmental equality theory examines how the ascendant "race-and-gender-neutral" models of child development have ignored and erased the life experiences of children who are different from and marginalized by the dominant group.

Discrimination is a universal phenomenon, but its targets and hierarchies are culturally constructed. Whether we are talking about a Somalian child in Italy, a Uighar child in China, or an African American child in the United States, different groups of children, depending on the context, face very different risks and challenges. They do not all start on an even playing field, and their developmental trajectories and responses cannot be judged in isolation. Dowd uses the example of black boys in the United States who adopt an aura of hypermasculinity as a coping strategy. Is this maladaptive, or is it a rational response to risks and forces in the environment? As Dowd explains, "By using a developmental equality lens, the source of exacerbated risks is exposed: as long as identity alone, or in combination, triggers heightened developmental challenges or differential developmental support, this analysis exposes continuing inequalities for identifiable groups of children" (2018, 78). While Fineman asks us to reject identity politics, Dowd sees recognizing the role played by identity as essential to achieving equality for children from disadvantaged groups. All humans are vulnerable, but each in their own way. Developmental equality aims to address these differential risks and continuing inequalities at the earliest possible moment, and it builds identity into our responses to vulnerability rather than banishing it to the sidelines or treating it as a wedge that divides us. I welcome Dowd's theory because it encourages us to look at children in social context—the key insight of the ecological model.

I encountered one big idea from economics that has shaped my thinking about this project in reading about climate change and sustainability. This concept, which I discussed briefly in chapter 12, is "the circular economy." Walter R. Stahel, an architect and leading expert on the circular economy, tells a revealing story about our macrosystem to introduce the concept. He writes:

> When my battered 1969 Toyota car approached the age of 30, I decided that her body deserved to be remanufactured. After 2 months and 100 hours of work, she returned home in her original beauty. "I am so glad you finally bought a

new car," my neighbour remarked. Quality is still associated with newness, not caring; long-term use as undesirable, not resourceful. . . . Cycles, such as of water and nutrients, abound in nature—discards become resources for others. Yet humans continue to "make, use, dispose." One third of plastic waste globally is not collected or managed. . . . There is an alternative. A "circular economy" would turn goods that are at the end of their service life into resources for others, closing loops in industrial ecosystems and minimizing waste. It would change economic logic because it replaces production with sufficiency: reuse what you can, recycle what cannot be reused, repair what is broken, remanufacture what cannot be repaired. (2016, 435)

Economic theories about the circular economy may seem far removed from the ecology of childhood, but, as Stahel's commentary shows, there is a connection. The concept of the circular economy grew out of Stahel's work in Europe in the early 1970s, a period of rising energy costs and high unemployment during which public intellectuals like Schumacher were mounting a critique of the throwaway culture of the linear economy. Stahel reveals that he was as interested in creating jobs to meet human needs as he was in conserving resources to meet environmental goals: "As an architect, I knew that it took more labour and fewer resources to refurbish buildings than to erect new ones. *The principle is true for any stock or capital, from mobile phones to arable land and cultural heritage*" (2016, 435, emphasis added). The circular economy is also highly relevant to the quality of life in communities. William McDonough, cofounder of the Cradle to Cradle Products Innovation Institute, writing in *Scientific American*, envisions "positive" cities replacing the negative linear model of take, make, and waste. He sees these clean, sustainable cities as enabling people to work and live in the same place. His vision integrates children and elders into the sustainability web: "Kids could use their optical sensors known as eyeballs" to sort and recycle and get paid in toys. He uses the city of Curitiba, Brazil, as an example. Instead of one big central library, its designers created fifty small "lighthouses of knowledge"—equipped with books and internet and open to all people aged three to eighty—so that every child was within walking distance of a library. "What we are after, for all people," McDonough writes, "is something I would call the 'good life'—a life that is safe, dignified and creative. Positive cities are the places where that can happen. If they are designed and run on this principle, everything gets better. We have to insist on the rights of humanity and nature to co-exist, to bring together the city and its surrounding countryside" (2017, 48). Spurred by the climate change crisis, the concept of a circular economy has become more than a utopian dream; it is a leading force in the quest for sustainability. In June 2018, the European Commission adopted a long-term Circular Economy Action Plan aimed at closing the loop of product life cycles as a key step towards sustainability (Cole 2018; European Union Official Journal L150, 2018).

The pragmatic connections between the circular economy and the ecology of childhood are obvious. As we saw in part 3, an exosystem (the economy) that fails to provide people with work is not child- or family-friendly. Young people need jobs in order to start families and parents need jobs in order to support them. The younger generation needs work in order to sustain the older generation and the older generation, as its physical powers ebb, needs the dignity of useful work that connects elders to their culture, communities, and families. Economies that "make, use, and dispose" of people without heeding the costs are not sustainable. The environmental principles of conservation and sustainability should be embedded in any project for healing the ecology of childhood. These are the direct economic connections.

A less direct connection—the philosophical one between the circular economy and the ecology of childhood—began to dawn on me gradually. I thought about it when I saw the grandparents' brigade patrolling the streets of Lecce, armed only with their moral suasion as elders. I thought about it when I saw the kids in the Future Farmers of America in Cedar Key planting their community gardens to reduce malnutrition among the elderly. I began to see the philosophical principle of circularity as essential to a culture of solidarity and inherent in the philosophy of ecogenerism. The critique of the linear economy as leading to wasted lives and throwaway people transcends efficiency. When we treat human beings as just another material resource to be produced, used, and disposed of, we are not only foolishly and inefficiently externalizing the future costs of wasted lives in the pursuit of present profits; we are also committing a moral evil. This is what Pope Francis means when he places the "instrumentalization of the human person" on par with discrimination and intolerance (2017). As both a practical and a moral matter, sustainability and the circular economy are essential tools for thinking about human society as well as about environmental change.

Those are some of the big ideas that have shaped, and continue to shape, my work and my own personal macrosystem. And, as Father Jim recognized, macrosystems run in both directions, from top down and from bottom up. What we *do*—turning belief into action—in our daily lives can slowly but surely shift the dominant macrosystem. In the final pages of this chapter, I will propose a number of ways in which we can effect change in the macrosystem through actions taken at the local level in the small worlds where children live.

Small World Strategies for Building a New Macrosystem

Building Recognition that Children's Rights Are Human Rights

I have proposed human rights, and specifically the CRC, as the value system that can guide us toward achieving a better world for children. Human rights are often seen as abstract and distant, happening at the UN Headquarters in New York or at the International Court of Justice in the Hague. In the United States we may feel especially powerless to effect change. If Presidents Bill Clinton and Barack Obama, both of whom were strong CRC supporters, could not move the CRC forward toward ratification by the US Senate, what can ordinary Americans do to break the stalemate? Actually, quite a lot.

At the microsystemic levels of family, school, and faith community, we can incorporate an appreciation of children's human rights in our interactions with the children and youth we know and love. Read to children: that was the path that Jonathan Todres and Sarah Higinbotham took in researching *Human Rights in Children's Literature*. They went to children's classes and read aloud to the students to find out what children of different ages took away from the stories they hear. The book provides an excellent roadmap for understanding how children develop values and how human rights already figure in American children's literature.

Another resource is UNICEF. It is not just in New York City—it is everywhere we look, with 85 percent of its posts in field offices around the world. It also has a powerful internet presence; resources for promoting an understanding of children's rights as human rights can be found on the UN Headquarters of UNICEF website. Closer to home for Americans is the Unicef USA site, which lists nine regional offices and provides resources for teachers and advocates.

Schools are an obvious place to teach children. We must encourage the study by children of their rights not in a didactic format but using age-appropriate materials and playful learning. Many of the human rights values in the CRC have their counterparts in US constitutional law. These can be explored by children through a program called iCivics, developed by my former boss Justice Sandra Day O'Connor during her retirement years (iCivics n.d.). In her lifetime, O'Connor had seen civics (the study of our system of government) once a staple of education, forced out of the curriculum to make way for high-stakes testing of math and reading skills. Founded in 2009, iCivics is currently used, free of cost, by over two hundred thousand teachers in schools across the nation. When Justice O'Connor became Chair Emeritus, Justice Sonia Sotomayor joined the board. For a taste of iCivics' engaging style and appeal to children, visit one of its newest web-based units, "Immigration Nation." Offered in both English and Spanish this tech-savvy package of course materials, games, and teacher guides engages students in hands on learning about the path to citizenship. Other recent additions to iCivics are "The Fourth Branch—You!" and "Students Engage!" These curricula help children to understand, to role play and to actually engage in government decisionmaking at the local level.

Make no mistake: working at the grassroots level of schools is not for the fainthearted. Access to schools is not always easy, and not just because of politics. The community's passionate sense of ownership of its schools must be respected, and so must the time crunch faced by teachers who are short on supplies and forced to teach to the test. But I have seen my law students in Philadelphia, Florida, and Georgia find ways to overcome these barriers because of the excitement and enrichment they bring to the classroom. They have helped schools qualify for free school meals for all students so they can eat free of stigma and discrimination; they have organized youth summits in local schools so kids' voices could be heard; and they have taught "know your rights" sessions so that children and youth will understand and can exercise their constitutional rights. Advocates for recognition of children's rights as human rights can adopt similar strategies at the grassroots level.

At the municipal and state levels of government, one very accessible form of citizen action has been to propose resolutions adopting the principles of the CRC. In the United States, cities like Chicago and Los Angeles and states like Hawaii have adopted resolutions recognizing children's rights (Columbia Law School 2012). Civic and professional organizations such as the National Council on Juvenile and Family Court Judges have adopted resolutions supporting ratification of the CRC (NCJFCJ 2010). Taking a cue from the climate change movement, advocates for children can continue to play an active role even when national leaders are obstructing international and national initiatives.

Promoting a Culture of Respect for Children's Voices

The best advocates for children are children themselves. They have the capacity to tell us a great deal (Garbarino 1989). Too often adults lack the skills to listen effectively or are afraid to listen for fear of ceding control or hearing something they don't want to hear. Listening to children's voices is a skill we need to practice and one that should become a basic feature of all our systems of governance, from family on up. There are many examples at the local level of children and youth participating in planning and implementing activities that matter to them and to their communities. Kids are serving on their school's student council and taking leadership roles in local Girl Scout troops and chapters of the Future Farmers of America. What is missing in many American contexts is the official commitment of governing bodies to incorporate children's voices in their deliberations. There is no reason why US communities cannot incorporate the voices of children, and this is one place where children may be the most effective tool for teaching adults the value of listening.

An example of grassroots advocacy by youth that caused a change in the macrosystem at the local and regional levels can be found in Funky Dragon. This was the name that the children of Wales gave to a young people's assembly established in that country in 2002; it refers to the brilliant red dragon that appears on the Welsh flag. Wales, as one of the member nations of the United Kingdom (composed of England, Wales, Scotland, and Northern Ireland) has its own government, located in Cardiff and headed by a First Minister nominated by the popularly elected Welsh National Assembly and appointed by HM Queen Elizabeth. The Welsh government (similarly to those of the US states) has primary responsibility for many areas of child and family law and policy. The CRC, ratified by the United Kingdom but regarded with some skepticism in Westminster, has become deeply entrenched in the laws of Wales. In 2011, Wales became the first area of the UK to make the CRC part of its domestic law, obligating its ministers to have due regard to the CRC's provisions. Wales has a Children's Commissioner, a post established in 2001, whose role is to be an independent champion for children and make sure their voices are heard at the local, national, and international levels (Children's Commissioner for Wales n.d). It also has its own Welsh Observatory on Human Rights of Children located at Swansea University in Wales. Jane Williams, professor of law and codirector of the observatory, tells the story of Funky Dragon's role in advancing children's participation rights (2013). Their work contributed to making Wales one of the leaders in implementing the CRC, including their children's participation rights. But Funky Dragon, in its initial design, lacked a key element—it was dependent on the executive branch for its funding. When a new Welsh government was elected, it reduced the funding drastically, called for competitive bidding and a request for proposals, and awarded the funding to a network of adult-run agencies that would "consult" with children and young people, effectively putting an end to the children's parliament.

Because I was a visiting fellow in the fall of 2014 at Swansea University, where the Welsh Observatory on Children's Rights was based, I observed firsthand how the children and young people of Funky Dragon regrouped to become the Campaign for a Children and Young People's Assembly for Wales (Welsh Youth Parliament 2018). They analyzed the flaws in Funky Dragon's design, researched best-practice models, built an impressive record documenting the capabilities and support of their constituency, and put all of their research into a highly polished document. They also took their report to the Committee on the Rights of the Child in Geneva, where it gained important support. By 2016, they had convinced the Welsh National Assembly to endorse a national youth parliament.

In October 2017, I interviewed one of the young founders of the campaign, Matthew Walker, by then a nineteen-year-old student at Swansea University. Matt is a very serious young man who speaks articulately in full sentences and rounded tones. His interest in politics dates back to his elementary school years, when he ran for office in school elections. He had come up through the ranks of Funky Dragon starting around age twelve, and he had been instrumental in organizing the campaign and drafting its reports. I wanted to hear from him how they were able to turn this demoralizing defeat into a victory. He told me about a moment when they almost gave up: having obtained thousands of youths' signatures on a petition to the National Assembly, they were told when they showed up to present their petition that as minors they had no standing to represent themselves and no business being in the building. Matthew vividly recalled responding, "I am sure in my mind that this is an astonishing breach of children's rights under the UNCRC and our campaign will prove you wrong" (Walker 2017). Matt's prediction came true. One of the most hostile and skeptical of the assembly members, a man who had strenuously opposed the idea of a youth parliament, later confessed to Matt that their advocacy had completely changed the way in which he and his colleagues viewed children's participation rights and their potential contribution to Welsh democracy.

Voting for members of the first Welsh Youth Parliament took place in November 2018. All Welsh youth aged eleven to eighteen were eligible to register to vote and more than twenty thousand exercised their voting rights. Of the sixty youth representatives, forty were elected by the young people in the general population and the remaining twenty were elected by young people in partner youth organizations to ensure diversity and breadth of representation. In December 2018, the names of all sixty inaugural members of the Welsh Youth Parliament were announced on its website. Ignoring or undermining children's voices is no longer an option; as Elin Jones, presiding officer of the National Assembly for Wales, stated at the launch of the elections in May 2018,

The young people elected to the first Youth Parliament in Wales must be allowed to take ownership of the issues that are important to them, and to reflect Wales in its entirety in this regard. They must be allowed to challenge us, the other parliament, and to tell us what their priorities are and where they want changes to be made. It is our responsibility to listen to their voices and to discuss their priorities. (Welsh Youth Parliament 2018)

Having met Matthew Walker and the young representatives from Funky Dragon, reviewed their work product, and observed the quality of their advocacy, I am confident the Youth Parliament will make important contributions to Welsh democracy. Funky Dragon's story demonstrates that building recognition of children's participation rights is a task for which children and young people are uniquely qualified.

It is important to understand that the story of Funky Dragon did not begin with the national victory described above. Instead, it began with the young people's engagement in active advocacy at the local level. Working at the grassroots level in their cities, towns, and villages, they learned the ropes of representative democracy and honed their advocacy skills. They passed their skills along to younger advocates, who moved into place as the older cadre transitioned to work and university. The local impact of their advocacy was very real and visible, to them and to others. The young people of the relatively small city of Swansea, for example, were integral to the 2014 adoption by the Swansea City and County Authority of the Children's and Young People's Rights Scheme, a policy that goes far beyond a resolution of support—it officially commits the Swansea Authority to mainstreaming positive approaches to the rights of children and young people in all its functions, including embedding children's-rights "impact assessments" into its assessment process and requiring participation by children and young people at the formative stages of all policy-making activities (Swansea Council 2014).

Building Support for a "Children's Rights Approach" in Private and Non-Governmental Organizations (NGOs)

Private and nongovernmental organizations are ever-present in children's lives. The category covers anything from a children's hospital or youth orchestra to a local sports club or scouting troop. We might ask, What is a "children's rights approach"? It is less formal than enactment of a law or government policy, but it can have an even more immediate impact. An excellent guide to the children's rights approach—one that could serve advocates of any age and in any location—was published by the Children's Commissioner for Wales in 2017 and is available on the commission's website. Titled *The Right Way: A Children's Rights Approach in Wales*, this handbook provides a blueprint for introducing a children's rights approach into any entity or organization. As the authors point out, while it can be used in the public sector, its utility is not limited to governmental bodies: "A range of organizations in the private and non-governmental sectors . . . have a significant part to play in the implementation of children services, and therefore have an obligation to contribute toward better realization of children's rights. . . . A Children's Rights Approach will help organizations in the private and public sectors give effect to children's rights" (Children's Commissioner for Wales 2017, 4).

Here is one case study from *The Right Way* that illustrates how a child-serving entity in the health, child welfare, or social and recreational sectors can become a site for promoting the voices and perspectives of children. A local health care provider created a Children's Rights Unit (CRU) to ensure that children's rights would be respected and protected in all its activities. The CRU was tasked with providing information and training to help young patients become aware of their rights, which enabled them to assert their rights and make a contribution to the organizations that affect children's lives but have traditionally been adult-only domains. The CRU also created a Young Trustee Project that prepares fifteen-to-twenty-five-year-olds to take leadership positions in governance boards of private and NGO institutions. To date, over sixty children and young people have taken the training, and over thirty young people are on institutional boards of youth-oriented organizations. As the Children's Commissioner commented, "By providing children with the skills required to sit on organizational boards the CRU has contributed to their development as individuals, and has enabled them to participate in decision-making at the highest level, taking decisions that affect the lives of children as well as adults" (Children's Commissioner for Wales 2017, 11).

In another example, a local nonprofit organization adopted a Children's Rights Charter, developed in consultation with children and young people. The charter was endorsed by the nonprofit's leadership and is being implemented as a guide for all planning and operational staff to provide a framework for working with children. The board has worked closely with the Observatory on Human Rights of Children on training of staff and clients and has established a Children's Panel to advise it on children's issues (Children's Commissioner for Wales 2017, 8).

Building Child-Friendly Cities, Towns, and Communities

Another promising movement at the local level addresses the needs and rights of children in planning of housing, design and structuring of living spaces, and restoration of communities. Although this movement takes many forms, the biggest impact has come from the Child-Friendly Cities Initiative, which was launched in 1996 by UNICEF as a result of the second UN Conference on Human Settlements (Habitat II). One of the foundational principles of this movement is that "the well-being of children is the ultimate indicator of a healthy habitat, a democratic society and good governance" (UNICEF 2018b, 8).

A CFC is defined as a city, town or community that strives to ensure that children

> are safe and protected from exploitation, violence and abuse;
> Have a good start in life and grow up healthy and cared for;
> Have access to essential services;
> Experience quality, inclusive and participatory education and skills development;
> Express their opinions and influence decisions that affect them;
> Participate in family, cultural, city/community and social life;
> Live in a clean, unpolluted and safe environment with access to green spaces;
> Meet friends and have places to play and enjoy themselves;
> Have a fair chance at life regardless of their ethnic origin, religion, income, gender or ability. (10)

If this list reads like a litany of the rights of the child, it is no accident. However, there is no need to formally adopt or endorse the CRC to create a child-friendly city or town. While the CFC concept was spearheaded by UNICEF and is based on the principles of the CRC, the principles listed above reflect a widely shared, evidence-based understanding of children's needs and capacities. The path may be easier for communities in countries that have ratified the CRC. Italy has had laws implementing these initiatives since 1997. Law 285/97, titled "Provisions to Promote Rights and Opportunities for Children and Adolescents," has supplied the legal framework for implementing the CRC in Italy; Article 7 of Law 295/97 provides financial and legal support to the Sustainable Cities for Girls and Boys Project launched by the Ministry of the Environment following the commitment made at the Istanbul City Summit (1996) to establish a national CFC program. This set the stage for the creation of the Mayors as Defenders of Children Initiative, a network of cities and communities committed to giving space to children "in roads, schools and town-halls" (UNICEF 2006, 5). But there is nothing to stop US advocates for children from following the CFC model. In 2017, over three thousand cities and communities, reaching over thirty million children in thirty-eight countries were putting the concept of child-friendly cities into practice (UNICEF 2018b, 8). As the handbook states, "Cities and communities that work towards realizing the Convention on the Rights of the Child, but do not partner with UNICEF, can also apply the guidance in this Handbook" (9).

One key principle in building a CFC is the importance of mobilizing a wide range of stakeholders, including government, children and youth, civil society, the private sector, media, academia, volunteers, and networks. The category of civil society organizations includes NGOs, membership organizations, religious communities, and community-based organizations, as well as social movements and popular organizations that include volunteers. The CFC process begins with a Child Rights Situation Analysis involving self-assessment tools and focused on the specific community and its context. Next comes an Action Plan, which translates the Situation Analysis into goals, objectives, and actions. An essential step is formulating a Theory of Change, identifying change pathways and conditions that must be in place to make the desired change happen. The handbook also covers best practices in child participation, capacity building, monitoring, and evaluation. One of the key principles of CFC is to foster the development of spaces and places within the urban landscape that welcome children and are designed on a child-friendly scale. This is the sort of holistic approach to defining stakeholders and developing goals that we saw in La Sanità and the Harlem Children's Zone. The CFC model has a lot to teach us about building child-friendly communities, even if we do not adopt the UNICEF name or follow the UNICEF script.

Building Support for Combatting Climate Change

This is perhaps the most global and yet the most local of issues. The first step is education. Once individuals understand the human contribution to climate change they can begin to take steps to reverse it: recycle, buy organic, reduce dependence on fossil fuels. Sustainability has become the watchword for every form of planning, including initiatives focused on the well-being of children. The Child-Friendly Cities Initiative described above is closely connected to the UN Sustainable Development Goals and the 2030 Agenda for Development. It also reflects the New Urban Agenda developed at Habitat III in Quito, Ecuador, in 2016 that produced the Quito Declaration on

Sustainable Cities and Human Settlements for All (UNICEF 2018b, 14; United Nations 2017). The declaration highlights the growing importance of cities to the future of children, with increasing numbers of children growing up in densely populated urban spaces. It also foregrounds the importance of creating manageable child-friendly communities on a human scale. Clearly, climate change and sustainability are key issues for the ecology of childhood. While adults were busy writing about the crisis, a girl named Greta Thunberg galvanized her peers into a global movement. Even at age eight, Greta had understood the threat climate change posed to her future; at age fifteen, frustrated with adults' inaction, she decided to stage a one-girl sit-down strike outside the Swedish Parliament. She inadvertently started a youth movement that inspired children and youth across Europe and at this writing has spread to 110 countries, with more than a million schoolchildren staging walkout strikes (BBC 2019).

But what if a country's young people are in denial about climate change? In the United States, too many youth have been bombarded with messages from adults in authority who are intent on discrediting the science of climate change; the political stranglehold on kids' minds is one of the worst effects of science denialism. Rather than throw numbers and statistics at readers, let me tell you about what I learned from Amber Nave Philogene. After graduating from college, Amber signed on with an NGO in the United States whose mission was to teach young people about climate change. Alliance for Climate Change (ACE), which is just one of dozens of NGOs focusing on climate education, goes to kids where they are, in schools and clubs, through music videos and YouTube spots. Its message is "You Have a Right to Know" about climate change. ACE emphasizes that "starting small, you can make big change" (Alliance for Climate Change 2013).

Amber is a gifted communicator who loves advocating for a just cause and her work with ACE inspired her to apply to Emory Law School. She used her ACE experience as the basis for a seminar paper in my seminar on children's rights, and she began the in-class presentation of it by engaging us in a mock-up of a typical presentation like the ones she had given to middle-schoolers in the very conservative state of Georgia. Amber is a genius at the skills of child-friendly communication, and she projects and reflects the youth and enthusiasm of the kids she has been teaching. She presented the science to us in vivid charts, using cartoons and other audiovisuals and punctuating her presentation with rapid-fire questions. She motivated us to engage by tossing little bags of candy or snack bars to classmates who volunteered, while teasing us and telling jokes. Amber is a force of nature; in one twenty-minute talk, she can do what hours of didactic instruction would have failed to accomplish—

convert a teenage skeptic whose head has been filled with junk science. In 2015, Amber was named a White House Champion for Change by President Obama for having brought climate change alive to over 45,000 Georgia children and training dozens of youth fellows to carry the campaign forward. She was also honored for her outreach and collaboration with stakeholders and organizations of every type. In honoring her work, her colleagues commented, "Amber empowers diverse students across the state of Georgia to fight climate change in innovative ways, leveraging methods like digital media, video, and music. In her climate work, Amber has built strong relationships with partners in Atlanta, including Georgia Interfaith Power and Light, Clean Air Campaign and Citizens Climate Lobby" (Alliance for Climate Change 2015).

Repopulating Villages and Farming Communities One Family at a Time

Depopulation in Italy and the hollowing out of rural communities is harming the children who are left behind, like Davide, whose poem about being "The Last Child in the Village" introduced chapter 5. Depopulation and migration from small towns to big cities also hurts American kids. Too many children in the United States are growing up in deserted towns whose main streets are boarded up and whose farmlands are lying fallow. At the same time, thousands of families are fleeing war and violence, or simply seeking a better life, and they need safe and healthy places to raise their children. When it comes to housing, open spaces, and population, it seems there is a terrible mismatch between supply and demand.

A number of initiatives have sought to reverse depopulation and mitigate falling birth rates by matching those seeking a new life with places where people are the missing piece. Of course, there must be work for these people, but the geography of work is changing. Just as the supposed efficiency of monoculture, huge factory farms, and big-box stores sucked the life out of smaller communities, the move toward a more circular economy and sustainable use of land and resources can revitalize them.

By their very nature, these initiatives are highly individualized and shaped by local geography, history, and culture. They tend to share an environmentalist, back-to-the-land philosophy along with a commitment to social solidarity. They also tend to favor small- over large-scale enterprises. In Italy, one such group is a coalition of local initiatives called the Movimento per la Decrescita' Felice (literally, the movement for happy de-growth). This movement got its start in economics, the same field in which the word "growth" had been "arbitrarily freighted with positive meaning"; as social critic and environmentalist Maurizio Pallante describes in his book *La Decrescita' Felice*, the term has evolved from an academic concept into a philosophical grassroots movement (2011). Founded in 2007 by Pallante, the movement hosts a website of the same name and convenes workshops and events around the country (Decrescitafelice.it n.d.). It is one of many movements, both in the United States and in Europe, that are seeking to translate principles of sustainability into action on the ground. Among the goals shared by such groups are reuse of existing buildings, reclamation of abandoned fields for small-scale agriculture, and the development of technologies that assist rather than displace human labor. Another common thread is the preservation and restoration of sustainable crops that have been displaced or abandoned because of mega-farming practices. In addition to movements mentioned earlier to revitalize farming of sheep for wool and cheese, Scanno is home to a movement to restore ancient grains and legumes such as the *fagiolo bianco di Frattura* (white bean of Frattura) and the ancient grain called *solina* that was almost lost in the 1970s when newly created high-yield grains swept away traditional grains (Polizzi 2018; Slow Food Foundation for Biodiversity n.d.; Pianetta Pane 2018).

Some of these ideas for preservation and restoration have been implemented by regional governments. For example, the Region of Campania in southern Italy has created a Banca della Terra Campana (Campana Land Bank). This part of Italy has seen massive outmigration as small farmers unable to compete with mega farms and foreign imports leave for distant lands or migrate north to work in factories. As more people seek a return to the land, Campania has launched a plan to "bank" unused public lands or farmlands which is deposited by owners into the land bank so it can be can be given to agricultural associations and especially to people under the age of forty who want to start farms (Di Miele 2018). Other initiatives take the form of cooperatives; the members of Terra della Resilienza (Resilient Lands), founded in 2012 in the depopulated rural region south of Salerno, are putting into practice their belief in the resilience of the land and its capacity for endogenous growth. They consider themselves part of a dual cultural and agricultural revolution (Terra di Resilienza 2018). Perhaps the most widely publicized Italian effort at resettling rural towns came from the town of Riace in Reggio Calabria. Riace was dying a slow death from depopulation when its mayor invited refugees from Africa and the Middle East to travel to the town via church-sponsored *corridoi umanitari* (humanitarian corridors of volunteers who assist migrants in gaining legal entry). Over one hundred migrants settled in the town as long-term residents and were employed in sheep herding, street sweeping, agriculture, and in local crafts enterprises. The project earned the town's mayor a spot on the *Forbes* list of the fifty most influential leaders (Sewell 2017). But in October 2018 the mayor, Mimmo Lucano, was placed under arrest and banished from his village under the pretext of misuse of funds. When Italian Interior Minister Matteo Salvini announced his intention to expel all refugees from the town, most refugees fled and Riace's workshops and farming cooperatives were shuttered (Gostoli 2018a and 2018b). While judicial decisions in April and May 2019 by the national Corte of Cassazione and of the regional Administrative Tribunal for Calabria subsequently exonerated the mayor, the damage was done (Cavalli 2019).

In the United States, in a similar backlash against refugee resettlement, the Trump administration has made massive cuts to the US Refugee Resettlement Program, threatening one of the nation's most successful humanitarian efforts. But one bright spot in terms of repopulation of fallow lands comes from New Hampshire, where the Organization for Refugee and Immigrant Success has purchased unused farmland to allow fourteen refugees to get a start in farming. The project dovetails with sustainability and community development initiatives like Community Supported Agriculture (CSA), which promotes distribution of local fresh produce, and SNAP accessible farm stands (Sampadian 2018). These little "points of light," to borrow a phrase coined by the late President George H. W. Bush, are not the global answer to the migration crisis nor to depopulation, low birth rates in rich countries, or high birth rates in poor ones. But they are small steps that have the potential to change some children's worlds for the better.

Is it fair to "discriminate" in favor of left-behind places as opposed to creating equal opportunity for all people and let the market take care of leveling the playing field? A defense of place-based policies has been mounted by the Brookings Institution in a report titled "Countering the Geography of Discontent: Strategies for Left-Behind Places" (Hendrickson 2018). This report rigorously analyzes the history, causes, and effects of a phenomenon that is clearly national in scale. While it advocates reforms at federal and state levels, it issues a call for "place-sensitive" approaches to mitigate "place-based disparities." The authors believe that turning the clock back to a time of traditional mining and manufacturing is no solution, but neither is laissez-faire neglect:

> We have tested the alternative to nostalgia—namely, neglect based on the assumption that the market would suffice to spread opportunity across the country. It has not and cannot do so. While our place-sensitive policies must build on the economy of the present and future, not the past, they must also push against the forces that have produced—and, if left unchecked, will sustain—the Great Divergence that has polarized our politics and constrained life-chances for millions of Americans. (6)

In other words, instead of pretending that these regional and local disparities between booming and left-behind places can be addressed by "people-based but place-neutral" policies, we must accept that "people-based characteristics are often inextricably linked to place" (Hendrickson 2018, 182, citing Garretson 2013).

Mobilizing Our Individual Civil Rights to Change the Macrosystem

This final and most personal call to action and expression can be captured in three words. Vote! March! Litigate! Adults possess these options by right, and children and youth are steadily gaining their own civil rights.

We can support young people with our votes. Almost fifty years ago, youth advocates succeeded in a decades-long campaign to convince existing voters to lower the voting age from twenty-one to eighteen (US Constitution Amendment XXVI, 1971). Today, youth-led civil rights organizations such as the National Youth Rights Association, founded in 1998, have been gaining traction in campaigns at the local, state, and federal levels to extend the franchise to sixteen- and seventeen-year-olds, a right enjoyed by youth in a dozen other countries (AYRA 2019; Astor 2019). On March 5, 2019, Representative Ayanna Pressley (D-MA) introduced an amendment in the US Congress to lower the federal voting age to sixteen; it surprised its sponsors by getting 126 votes (Connor 2019). Opponents argue that today's youth, in comparison to those of the Vietnam Era, have "no skin in the game" because they are not being drafted into the military. But youth advocates point to issues like gun violence, climate change, student debt, and their status as taxpayers. As one Boston high schooler put it, "The sixteen-year-olds right now will be the ones who live with the choices the adults make right now" (Astor 2019, quoting seventeen-year-old Vikiana Petit-Homme).

We can march beside them. American children have been marching since the labor movements of the 1900s and the civil rights movement of the 1960s, often inspiring reluctant elders to leave the sidelines and march beside them (Woodhouse 2008a). The current generation of school-age climate activists has issued an explicit challenge to older generations to join them in their protests (BBC 2019). In a letter published on the eve of the strike of May 24, 2019, they stated, "This is our invitation. On Friday, 20 September, we will start an action week for climate change with a worldwide strike. We ask you to join us.... Join in the day with your neighbors, colleagues, friends and families to hear our voices and make this a turning point in history" (BBC 2019).

We can litigate beside them. As I teach my law students, litigation should not be the first and is never the best option, but it is not a dirty word. Rather, it is a classic strategy in the battle to make rights a reality and an integral part of our constitutional scheme. The young people who filed the ongoing case of *Juliana et al. v. United States et al.* (217 F. Supp. 3d 1224 [D. Or. 2016]) challenging their government's inaction on climate change are not advocating only for their generation; they are acting on the behalf of future generations (Our Children's Trust 2018). These are all ways in which adults can join forces with youth and magnify the power of their voices.

Rather than belabor the point that these freedoms are solemn responsibilities as well as rights, I will refer you to iCivics.org, where you can brush up on the three branches of government and the avenues they provide for citizen engagement. Better still, join your children or grandchildren in an iCivics game. I assign these games to my law students because playful learning works: it is not just for kids.

* * *

In the grand scheme of human history, the actions I propose in this final chapter may be too little and too late. We might be reaching, or already have passed, a tipping point in the ecology of childhood, much as we seem to be regarding climate change. But, as these examples suggest, perhaps we can build, if even on a very small scale, multiple sustainable environments that fully meet the needs of the children born into them. The ecology of childhood is not only about children: "The well-being of children is the ultimate indicator of a healthy habitat, a democratic society and good governance" (UNICEF 2018b, 8). Children may be the canaries in the coal mine, signaling a toxic environment, but they also hold the secret to achieving a healthy planet. To borrow the phrase coined by the youth delegates to the 2002 United Nations Special Session on Children: "A world fit for children is a world fit for everyone" (UNICEF 2003, 3).

ACKNOWLEDGMENTS

I offer my sincerest thanks to Clara Platter, my editor at New York University Press, and to Nancy E. Dowd, editor of the NYU series on "Family, Law, and Society," for believing in this book and shepherding it on its long journey from proposal to publication. Words are inadequate to express my appreciation for their steadfast support and encouragement. Thanks also to Martin Coleman and the copy editors for their excellent work.

This book would not have been possible without funding and support from Emory University's School of Law, the European University Institute, and the Fredrick G. Levin College of Law at the University of Florida. My deepest thanks to these institutions and their leadership for being so generous and for waiting so patiently to see the fruits of their investments.

Also instrumental in supporting my research were the gifted librarians of the Hugh F. Macmillan Law Library at Emory, especially Richelle Reid and Vanessa King. I am grateful as well to the librarians at the UNICEF Innocenti Research Centre and Universita' degli Studi di Firenze, for making their facilities available to me and guiding me in my search for materials and data.

My heartfelt thanks to my student research assistants, now professional colleagues with doctorates, for their invaluable contributions. I am especially grateful to Dr. Sayali Himanshu Bapat (SJD Emory University), whose ideas and passion for excellence have enriched this project over the past five years. Dr. Elisa Cinini (PhD Universita' di Firenze) contributed enormously to my research and appreciation of Italian law. Thanks are also due to Douglas Waters (SJD candidate, Emory University) for his able assistance. Finally, Maura Cosenza, a daughter of Scanno with a degree in translation and interpretation (Universita' di Genova), assisted in designing and administering the Scanno survey and consulted on issues of English/Italian translation and cultural competence. Along the way, these talented young students and scholars have become friends and colleagues.

I am grateful as well to my academic colleagues, both in the United States and abroad, working in the field of children's rights. I would especially like to thank (in alphabetical order by institution) Jane Spinak and Andrew Shepard, my first mentors at Columbia University Law School; Martha Fineman, Randee Waldman, and Kirsten Widner at Emory University; John Witte and my colleagues at the Center for the Study of Law and Religion at Emory; Nancy Dowd, Robert Jerry, Shani King, Ken Nunn, and Laura Rosenbury at the University of Florida; Jonathan Todres at Georgia State Law School; Elena Urso and her colleagues at Universita' degli Studi di Firenze, with whom I have collaborated for over a decade; my International Society of Family Law colleague Maria Donata Panforti of Universita' di Modena e Reggio Emilia; John Eekelaar at the Oxford Centre for Law and Policy, and Sanford Katz, at Boston College, for their wisdom and example over the past thirty years; Laura Lundy at the Centre for Children's Rights, Queens College, Belfast, for spurring my interest in children's participation rights; Mariaclara Rossi and Marina Garbellotti at Universita' degli Studi di Verona for sharing their expertise in Italian child welfare policy with me; Jane Williams and Simon Hoffman and their colleagues at Hillary Rodham Clinton School of Law, University of Swansea, for modeling excellence in children's rights; and, last but not least, Michael Freeman, Professor Emeritus at University College of London, whose pathbreaking work on children's rights has set the standard for us all to follow.

A book like this one depends on insights of ordinary people even more than on the writings of academics. Countless residents of the two "villages" at the heart of this book have generously shared their memories, thoughts and expertise. It would be impossible to give due credit to every one of them, but here is a partial listing in alphabetical order: sincerest thanks to Stefania Baldoni, Vanda Bocchini, Bill Campbell, Pasquale Caranfa, Grazia Carfagnini, Davide Cetrone, Sue Colson, Ricky Cooke, Brenda Coulter, Ilario Cosenza and family, Claudio d'Alessandro and family, Mario De Crescentis, Dr. Angelo Di Gennaro, Marianna Di Marco, Angelo Di Masso, Pino, Luca Stefano and Valentina Di Masso, Armando Di Rienzo and family, Ezio Farina, Sandro Fronterotta and family, Enzo Gentile, Eustachio Gentile, Roberto Grossi, Doris Hellerman, Gay Lynn and John Langley, Candido Nannarone and family, Cyrce Nelson, Giulia Mancini, Giorgio Morelli, Andrea Petrocco and family, Sabrina Pizzacalla and family, Rita Quaranta, Anna Rizzo, George and Carol Sakellarios, Genny Schiappa, Giuseppe Serafini, Paolo Sera and family, Linda Seyfert, Cesidio Silla, Daniele Tarullo, and Ken Young and family. All have contributed to the living color and the mosaic quality of my portraits of Cedar Key and Scanno, although I take full responsibility for any errors or misconceptions.

The vibrant civic and educational institutions of the two villages also deserve special recognition for helping me explore the ecology of childhood in their communities. In Cedar Key, these institutions include the Cedar Key Chamber of Commerce, Cedar Key Center for the Arts, Cedar Key School, Cedar Key Historical Society, *Cedar Key Beacon*, and Cedar Key Public

Library. Many of Cedar Key's civic activities are aimed especially at young people, including the Future Farmers of America and the CKS athletic teams, as well as the educational programs in arts and sciences at the Arts Center and the Nature Coast Biological Station. In Scanno, the key institutions include the Asilo Buon Pastore, the Scuola Mons. Celidonio and Scuola Romualdo Parente, and the journals *La Foce, Il Gazzetino della Valle del Sagittario*, and *La Piazza di Scanno*, and cultural offerings including Museo di Lana, the Sabati Letterari, and Appuntamento con la Tradizione, also deserve thanks, as does the newest civic institution, the Pro Loco of Scanno, founded by a group of energetic, forward-looking young people. The mayors and elected councils of each of these villages deserve high praise for having fostered a climate that encourages civic engagement.

My sincerest gratitude goes as well to the faith communities in both of these villages. Monsignor Carmelo Rotolo, for thirty years Scanno's parish priest, was the first to welcome me to Scanno, and his reputation for selfless devotion to his flock opened many doors. The Sisters of Maria Ausiliatrice welcomed me to the Scanno nursery school classrooms and Sister Ornella welcomed me to the order's school in Rome, serving the city's poor and immigrant children. In Cedar Key, Father Jim Wright, of Christ Episcopal Church, Pastor Susie Horner of the United Methodist Church and the members of both churches' choirs have served as my gateway to Cedar Key's welcoming, ecumenical faith community described in these pages.

I owe a debt of gratitude to various other communities and projects in Italy and Europe that allowed this foreigner to visit and learn from them. Deepest thanks to Don Antonio Loffredo of the Neapolitan neighborhood called La Sanita', and thanks to all the young people who welcomed me, especially Susi. Thanks also to San Patrignano, a community devoted to those recovering from addiction, and especially Monica Barzanti and Rachele, who guided me on my visits. I am grateful to attorney Agnese Caprioli and the members of the Camera Juvenile of Lecce, in Puglia, who welcomed me into that city's juvenile justice and child welfare community. Special thanks to Jane Williams and Simon Hoffman and the young people of Funky Dragon, especially Matthew Walker, who introduced me to the work of the Observatory on Children's Rights at Swansea University. Dr. Elisa Cinini, in addition to providing expert research assistance, arranged visits to schools in her hometown in Toscana. Sergio Capitanucci and his wife Tiziana were my guides to schools and civic institutions in the communities of San Sisto and Lacugnano in the Province of Umbria. At the ARAI in Torino, Anna Maria Colella educated me on Italy's innovative intercountry adoption programs. Attorney Paolo Solimeno and his wife, attorney Maria Chiara Perrone, gave us entrée into the courts of Firenze. Maria Chiara, together with its President Dr. Elena Urso, was a founder of the Italian nonprofit CONTACT (Centro studi e ricerche sull'infanzia e l'adolescenza), which advocates for children's rights in Italy and beyond.

Since so much of this book is about family, I must not forget to thank my own families, in both Italy and the United States, for all they have contributed to my understanding of the meaning of family and of place. In Scanno, Orazio Di Zillo and his family have become our family, especially his cousin Vanda, who at ninety-four years of age is our role model for aging. To quote a recent message from Orazio, "We are bound together by mutual ties of respect and affection as if we had known each other forever." Our other Italian family is the Capitanicci family from Perugia in the province of Umbria, and I really have known them "forever." For more than fifty years and across five generations, they have served as models of the open-hearted, multigenerational, extended Italian family, embracing even total strangers. Back in 1964, Luigi and Peppina welcomed an eighteen-year-old stranger (with a two-year-old's vocabulary) into their home. They taught me how to speak and cook Italian. I stayed with them for almost three years during my studies at the Universita' per Stranieri. In 1980, their son Sergio and his bride Tiziana honeymooned at our home in the United States. In the early 1990s, our daughter spent a year with them. In 2015, my husband and I traveled to Lacugnano for the baptism of Sergio and Tiziana's first grandchild, Aurora. Without doubt, we are family.

It goes without saying that these pages owe a huge debt to my family of origin in the United States and to my lifelong friends who have taught me so much. I am grateful for all I have learned from my children, Ken and Jessie; my grandchildren, Sacha and Zoe; my father-in-law, Henry Chandler (who celebrated his ninety-ninth birthday in 2019) and all the Chandler clan; my brother Charlie and my Bennett-Dyer nephews and nieces; my cousin Brooke; my aunt Else and all the Bennett descendants; my nephews, Matt and Kelly, and their wives, Antje and Jen; my sisters-in-law, Dale, Joanne, and Victorine. I will always be grateful to Sally and David, my dearest childhood friends, as well as my sisters-in-life Michiko, Betty, Molly, Kate, and Susan. Special thanks to Betty's daughter Carol for modeling beauty, strength, and courage in adversity. Although my parents, Anne and Boyd, and my oldest brother, John Tony, are gone, they remain with me in memory and affection. All of the people I have named above have taught me the meaning of "family," "community," and "place": concepts that are central to this study of the ecology of childhood.

Finally, my deepest and most heartfelt thanks go to my spouse of fifty-two years, Charles Woodhouse, and to our pug dog, Jane. They have been my constant traveling companions and cultural ambassadors, sticking with me throughout this decade-long journey. Everywhere we have gone, they have been making friends and spreading a good impression of Americans. My husband, thanks to his cell phone, laptop, excellent management skills, and ability to communicate in multiple languages, has also managed to maintain his busy international food law practice throughout our travels. Jane, who speaks and understands every language, has been my secret weapon in starting conversations with both adults and children. I cannot thank Charley and Jane enough for putting up with stuffy airplane flights, hot train rides, hair-raising drives on winding roads, and other indignities, almost always without complaint.

And a thank you to all of the individuals, young and old, named and unnamed, who shared their thoughts, experiences, and expertise with me during the past ten years. Their insights have enriched these pages. Any responsibility for errors, omissions, or misinformation is entirely my own.

BIBLIOGRAPHY

60 Minutes. 2015. "60 Minutes Report on Rosewood Massacre." YouTube. https://www.youtube.com.
Aaron, Henry J. 2017. "Don't Be Fooled, Trump's Budget Proposal Is Very Much 'Undead.'" Brookings Institution, June 12, 2017. www.brookings.edu.
Acciari, Paolo, Alberto Polo, and Giovanni L. Violante. 2017. "'And Yet, It Moves': Intergenerational Mobility in Italy." Fondazione Rodolfo Debenedetti, May 14, 2017. www.frdb.org.
ADNKronos. 2017. "Pope Francis Calls for an End to Racism." July 18, 2017. https://adnkronos.com.
AEI-Brookings Working Group on Paid Family Leave. 2017. "Paid Family and Medical Leave." AEI Brookings Working Group on Paid Family Leave. www.brookings.edu.
Alexander, Michelle. 2009. *The New Jim Crow: Mass Incarceration in the Era of Colorblindness*. New York: New Press.
Alliance for Climate Change. 2013. "We Have the Right to Know." YouTube, November 13, 2013. www.youtube.com.
Alliance for Climate Change. 2015. "Amber Nave Named Whitehouse Champion for Change." ACE Blog, February 15, 2015. https://acespace.org.
Altintas, Evrim, and Oriel Sullivan. 2016. "Fifty Years of Change Updated: Cross-national Gender Convergence in Housework." *Demographic Research* 35, no. 16: 455–70.
American Academy of Pediatrics. 2009. "Policy Statement—Media Violence." *Pediatrics* 124, no. 5: 1495–503.
American Academy of Pediatrics. 2016a. "AAP Agenda for Children." www.aap.org.
American Academy of Pediatrics. 2016b. "American Academy of Pediatrics Announces New Recommendations for Children's Media Use." News release, October 21, 2016. www.aap.org.
American Academy of Pediatrics. 2018. AAP Council on Community Pediatrics. "Poverty and Child Health in the United States." Pediatrics 137, no. 4: www.aap.org.
American Heritage Dictionary of the English Language. 5th ed. S.v. "method." https://www.thefreedictionary.com.
American Heritage Dictionary of the English Language. 5th ed. S.v. "model." https://www.thefreedictionary.com/model.
American Heritage Dictionary of the English Language. 5th ed. S.v. "neighborhood." https://ahdictionary.com.

American Heritage Dictionary of the English Language. 5th ed. S.v. "value." https://ahdictionary.com.
American Psychological Association. 2015. "Resolution on Violent Video Games." www.apa.org.
Amnesty International. 2016. "Amnesty International Report 2015/16—Italy." www.refworld.org.
Anderson, Craig A., with Douglas A. Gentile and Katherine E. Buckley. 2007. *Violent Video Games' Effects on Children and Adolescents: Theory, Research, and Policy*. New York: Oxford University Press.
Angeli, Francesca. 2015. "Fecondazione assistita, ecco le nuove regole Sì anche all'eterologa." *Il Giornale*, July 2, 2015.
ARAI-Piemonte. 2018. "Agenzia regionale per le adozioni internazionali-Regione Piemonte." www.Arai.piemonte.it.
Ariès, Philippe. 1962. *Centuries of Childhood*. New York: Vintage Books.
Arnold, Sean. 2018a. "Senior Sharks Prepare to Seize the Day." *Cedar Key Beacon*, May 31, 2018.
Arnold, Sean. 2018b. "CKS Hoops Standout Surpasses 1,000 Points." *Cedar Key Beacon*, December 6, 2018.
Asher, Janet, and Beth O. Daponte. 2010. "Human Development Research Paper 2010/40: A Hypothetical Cohort Model of Human Development." United Nations Development Programme. Human Development Research Paper Series 2010/40. https://econpapers.repec.org/paper/hdrpapers/hdrp-2010-40.htm.
Associazione Culturale Il Sentiero della Liberta/Freedom Trail. 2009. *E si divisero il pane che non c'era*. Sulmona: Associazione Culturale Il Sentiero della Liberta/Freedom Trail.
Associazione Difesa Orientamento Consumatori. 2016. "Asili Nido e Mense Scolastiche, in media il costo è di 329 euro/mese." February 19, 2016. www.adocnazionale.it.
Astor, Maggie. 2019. "16-Year-Olds Want a Vote. Fifty Years Ago, So Did 18-Year-Olds." *New York Times*, May 19, 2019. https://www.nytimes.com.
BabyCenter. 2016. "How Much You'll Spend on Childcare." www.babycenter.com.
Bapat, Sayali Himanshu, and Barbara Bennett Woodhouse. 2016. "Is There Justice for Juveniles in the United States, India, and Italy?: Towards a Framework for Transnational Comparisons." In *The Future of Juvenile Justice: Procedure and Practice from a Comparative Perspective*, edited by Tamar R. Birckhead and Solange Mouthaan, 81–110. Durham, NC: Carolina Academic Press.
Baldwin, Eleonora. 2017. "School lunches in Italy: setting a healthy pattern for adult life." Gambero Rosso, August 31, 2017. www.gamberorosso.it.
Baraldi, Claudio. 2005. *Cities with Children: Child-Friendly Cities in Italy*. Florence, Italy: UNICEF Research Centre.
Baraldi, Claudio, and Giuliano Piazzi. 1998. *La comunitá capovolta: Bambini a San Patrignano*. Milano: FrancoAngeli.
Baraldi, Claudio, and Guido Maggioni. 2003. "Introduzione generale: Il significato della promozione della partecipazione sociale di bambini e adolescent." In *I diritti*

di cittadinanza dei minori tra partecipazione e controllo, edited by Claudio Baraldi, Guido Maggioni, and Fabrizio Pappalardo, 3–22. Urbino: Edizione Goliardiche.
Batista-Pinto Wiese, Elizabeth. 2010. "Culture and Migration: Psychological Trauma in Children and Adolescents." *Traumatology* 16, no. 4: 142–52.
BBC News. 2018. "Migrant Crisis: Italy Minister Salvini Closes Ports to NGO Boats." June 30, 2018. www.bbc.com.
BBC News. 2019. "School strike for climate: Protests staged around the world." May 24, 2019. www.bbc.com.
Begley, Sarah. 2015. "Pope Francis to Families: Get Off Your Screens and Actually Talk to Each Other." *Time*, January 23, 2015. http://time.com.
Bellotti, Valerio. 2011. *Costruire senso, negoziare spazio: ragazze e ragazzi nella vita quotidiana: Centro nazionale di documentazione e analisi per l'infanzia e l'adolescenza*. Quaderno 50. Firenze: Istituto degli Innocenti.
Bertolini, Paola, Marco Montanari, Vito Peragine. 2008. "Poverty and Social Exclusion in Rural Areas." European Commission. http://ec.europa.edu.
Bennett, William J., with John Diullio and John Walters. 1996. *Body Count: Moral Poverty—and How to Win America's War against Crime and Drugs*. New York: Simon & Schuster.
Bhagwati, Jagdish. 2007. *In Defense of Globalization*. New York: Oxford University Press.
Blake, William, David V. Erdman, and Harold Bloom. 2008. *The Complete Poetry and Prose of William Blake*. Newly revised edition, with a new foreword and commentary by Harold Bloom. Berkeley: University of California Press.
Blankenhorn, David. 1996. "The State of the Family and the Family Policy Debate." *Santa Clara Law Review* 36, no. 2: 431–38.
Borger, Julian. 2018. "US Quits UN Human Rights Council—'A Cesspool of Political Bias.'" *Guardian*, June 19, 2018. www.theguardian.com.
Brainard, Lael, and Robert E. Litan. 2004. "'Offshoring' Service Jobs: Bane or Boon and What to Do?" Brookings Institution. www.brookings.edu.
Brazelton, T. Berry, and Stanley I. Greenspan. 2000. *The Irreducible Needs of Children: What Every Child Must Have to Grow, Learn, and Flourish*. Cambridge, MA: Perseus.
Breda, Marzio. 2018. "L'Italia non sia un Far West." *Corriere della Sera*, July 27, 2018.
Bronfenbrenner, Urie. 1979. *The Ecology of Human Development: Experiments by Nature and Design*. Cambridge, MA: Harvard University Press.
Brooks, Trica. 2018. "CHIP Funding Has Been Extended, What's Next for Children's Health Coverage?" Health Affairs Blog, January 30, 2018. www.healthaffairs.org.
Brooks-Gunn, Jeanne, William Schneider, and Jane Waldfogel. 2013. "The Great Recession and the Risk for Child Maltreatment." *Child Abuse & Neglect* 37, no.10 (October): 721–29.
Buffet, Jimmy. 2009. "Cheeseburger in Paradise." YouTube. http://youtube.
Bullaro, Grace Russo. 2010. "Introduction: From Terrone to Extracomunitario: A Snapshot of Italian Society in a Globalized World." In *From Terrone to Extracomunitario:*

New Manifestations of Racism in Contemporary Italian Cinema—Shifting Demographics and Changing Images in a Multi-Cultural Globalized Society, edited by Grace Russo Bullaro, xiv–liv. Kibworth, Leicester: Troubador.

Bureau of Labor Statistics. 2016. "Employment Characteristics of Families—2015." News release, April 22, 2016. www.bls.gov.

Bureau of Labor Statistics. 2017a. "Employment Characteristics of Families Summary." News release, April 20, 2017. www.bls.gov.

Bureau of Labor Statistics. 2017b. "Employment Characteristics of Families—2016." News release, April 20, 2017. www.bls.gov.

Cahn, Naomi. 2009. *Test Tube Babies: Why the Fertility Market Needs Legal Regulation.* New York: New York University Press.

Cahn, Naomi, and June Carbone. 2010. *Red Families v. Blue Families: Legal Polarization and the Creation of Culture.* New York: Oxford University Press.

Canada, Geoffrey. 1995. *Fist, Stick, Knife, Gun: A Personal History of Violence in America.* New York: Beacon.

Cantillon, Bea, with Yekaterina Chzhen, Sudhanshu Handa, and Brian Nolan. 2017. *Children of Austerity: Impact of the Great Recession on Child Poverty in Rich Countries.* New York: United Nations Children's Fund/Oxford University Press.

Caranfa, Pasquale. 2010. "From the Middle Ages to Modern Times." In *Scanno: Art and History Guide to the Town and District*, edited by Raffaele Giannantonio, 122–32. Pescara: Carsa Edizioni.

Carbis, Lion. 2018. "Empowering Democracy in Wales by Launching a Youth Parliament." *Welsh Youth Parliament News*, June 19, 2018. www.youthparliament.wales.

Carnovali, Sara. 2017. "The Right to Inclusive Education of Persons with Disabilities in Italy: Reflections and Perspectives." *Athens Journal of Education* 4, no. 4: 315–26.

Casonato, Carlo, and Jens Woelk, eds. 2008. *The Constitution of the Italian Republic*. Trento: Centro Stampa.

Catholic World Report. 2018. "Pope Francis says Trump's 'Zero-Tolerance' Migrant Policy Is 'Immoral.'" June 20, 2018. http://catholicworldreport.com.

Cavalli, Giulio. 2019. "Ora qualcuno chiede scusa a Mimmo Lucano." TPI News, May 22, 2019. www.tpi.it.

Cedar Key Beacon, 2018. "A Good Sport: CKS Claims Sixth Sportsmanship Award." June 21, 2018.

——— "Free Summer Meals at CKS." June 21, 2018.

——— "Eagles Spaghetti Dinner Fundraiser." August 16, 2018.

——— "Pirates to Invade Cedar Key." November 29, 2018.

——— "Lions Club Donates to CKS Students for Seafood Parade Floats." December 6, 2018.

Cedar Key Historical Society. 2018. "Welcome to the Cedar Keys and the Cedar Key Historical Museum." https://cedarkeyhistoricalmuseum.org.

Cedar Key News. 2018. "The Smithsonian Returns." July 18, 2018. www.cedarkeynews.com.

——— "Cedar Key Old Timers' Reunion." March 13, 2018. www.cedarkeynews.com.

Cedar Key Sharks. n.d. Cedar Key School Facebook. https://www.facebook.com.
Cedar Key Homecoming Court. January 15, 2019. Cedar Key School Facebook. www.facebook.com.
Cedar Key Welcome Center. 2018. "Cedar Key: City at the End of the Road." YouTube. https://www.youtube.com.
CENSIS. 2014. *Diventare genitori oggi: Indagine sulla fertilità/infertilità in Italia*. Edited by Concetta Maria Vaccaro. Rome: Carocci Editore.
Census Reporter. n.d. "Cedar Key, Florida." https://censusreporter.org.
Center for the Study of Social Policy. 2016. *Postsecondary Success in Promise Neighborhoods*. Washington, DC: Center for the Study of Social Policy.
Center on Budget and Policy Priorities (CBPP). n.d. "Chart Book: The Legacy of the Great Recession." www.cbpp.org.
Center on Budget and Policy Priorities. 2016. "Policy Basics: Introduction to the Supplemental Nutrition Assistance Program (SNAP)." www.cbpp.org.
Center on the Developing Child. 2007. "A Science-Based Framework for Early Childhood Policy: Using Evidence to Improve Outcomes in Learning, Behavior, and Health for Vulnerable Children." Center on the Developing Child, Harvard University. http://developingchild.harvard.edu.
Centers for Disease Control and Prevention. 2010. "Adverse Childhood Experiences Reported by Adults—Five States, 2009." *Morbidity and Mortality Weekly Report* 59, no. 49; 1609–13. www.cdc.gov.
Centers for Disease Control and Prevention, for National Center for Health Statistics. "FastStats: Unmarried Childbearing." www.cdc.gov.
Central Intelligence Agency, for the World Factbook. "Country Comparisons: Total Fertility Rate." www.cia.gov.
Central Intelligence Agency, for the World Factbook. "Mother's Mean Age at First Birth." www.cia.gov.
Cesari, Claudia. 2007. "The Juvenile Justice System in Italy." In *European Juvenile Justice Systems,* edited by V. Patané, n.p. Milano: Guiffré.
Cha, Ariana Eunjung. 2017. "The US Fertility Rate Just Hit a Historic Low: Why Some Demographers Are Freaking Out." MSN News, June 30, 2017. www.msn.com.
Chemin, Anne. 2015. "France's Baby Boom Secret: Get Women into Work and Ditch Rigid Family Norms." *Guardian*, March 21, 2015. www.theguardian.com.
Chetty, Raj, and Nathaniel Hendren and Lawrence f. Katz. 2015. "The Effcets of Exposure to Better Neighborhoods on Children: New Evidence from the Moving to Opportunity Experiment." NBER Working Paper No. 21156. National Bureau of Economic Research. Issued May 2015, revised September 2015. www.nber.org.
Chetty, Raj, and Nathaniel Hendren. 2018a. "*The Impacts of Neighborhoods on Intergenerational Mobility: Childhood Exposure Effects*." *Quarterly Journal of Economics* 133, no. 3: 1107–62.
Chetty, Raj, and Nathaniel Hendren. 2018b. "The Impacts of Neighborhoods on Intergenerational Mobility II: County-Level Estimates." *Quarterly Journal of Economics* 133, no. 3: 1163–228.

Child Care Aware of America. 2016. "Parents and the High Cost of Child Care." http://usa.childcareaware.org.
Child Care Aware of America. 2017. "2017 State Child Care Facts State of Florida." http://usa.childcareaware.org.
Child Guard. n.d. "Internet Crime and Abuse Statistics." www.guardchild.com.
Child Trends Databank. 2014. "Food Insecurity." http://childtrends.org.
Child Trends Databank. 2015. "Early School Readiness: Indicators of Child and Youth Well-Being." http://childtrends.org.
Child Welfare Information Gateway. 2018. "Child Maltreatment 2016: Summary of Key Findings." www.childwelfare.gov.
Children's Commissioner for Wales. n.d. "About Us: Who is the Children's Commissioner for Wales." www.childcomwales.org.uk.
Children's Commissioner for Wales. 2017. "The Right Way: A Children's Rights Approach in Wales." www.childcomwales.org.uk.
Children's Defense Fund. 2014. "The State of America's Children: 2014." www.childrensdefense.org.
Children's Defense Fund. 2015. "Ending Child Poverty Now." www.childrensdefense.org.
Children's Defense Fund. 2018. "Child Poverty in America 2017: National Analysis." www.childrensdefense.org.
Church of England Education Office. 2017. "Valuing All God's Children: Guidance for Church of England Schools on Challenging Homophobic, Biphobic, and Transphobic Bullying." 2nd ed. www.churchofengland.org.
Ciancio, Antonella. 2015. "Renzi and Obama Agree on Europe's Need to Embrace Expansionary Policies." ItalyEurope24, April 18, 2015. www.italy24.ilsole24ore.com.
City of Chicago. 2009. "City of Chicago Resolution Adopting the UN Convention on the Rights of the Child." http://www.law.northwestern.edu.
Climate Mayors. 2017. "407 US Climate Mayors Commit to Adopt, Honor, and Uphold Paris Climate Agreement Goals." https://medium.com.
Cohen, Nancy L. 2013. "Why America Never Had Universal Child Care." *New Republic*, April 24, 2013. https://newrepublic.com.
Cole, Rob. 2018. "EU Circular Economy Package Becomes Law." *Resource Magazine*, June 20, 2018. https://resource.co.
Coles, Robert. 1986. *The Moral Life of Children*. New York: Atlantic Monthly.
Coletto, Diego. 2010. "Effects of Economic Crisis on Italian Economy." Eurofound, May 31, 2010. https://www.eurofound.europa.eu.
Collins English Dictionary. S.v. "jus sanguinis." www.collinsdictionary.com.
Collins English Dictionary. S.v. "jus soli." www.collinsdictionary.com.
Columbia Law School, Human Rights Institute. 2012. "Bringing Human Rights Home: How State and Local Governments Can Use Human Rights Advocacy to Advance Local Policy." https://web.law.columbia.edu.
Common Sense Media. 2013. "Zero to Eight: Children's Media Use in America 2013." www.commonsensemedia.org.

Common Sense Media. 2017. "The Common Sense Census: Media Use by Kids Age Zero to Eight." www.commonsensemedia.org.

Conca, James. 2018. "Children Change the Climate in the US Supreme Court—1st Climate Lawsuit Goes Forward." *Forbes*, August 3, 2018. www.forbes.com.

Connor, Brian. 2019. "Congress Votes on Lowering Voting Age to 16." National Association for Youth Rights, March 15, 2019. www.youthrights.org.

Cook, John T., Maureen Black, Mariana Chilton, Diana Cutts, Stephanie Ettinger de Cuba, Timothy C. Heeren, Ruth Rose-Jacobs, Megan Sandel, Patrick H. Casey, Sharon Coleman, Ingrid Weiss, and Deborah A. Frank. 2013. "Are Food Insecurity's Health Impacts Underestimated in the U.S. Population? Marginal Food Security Also Predicts Adverse Health Outcomes in Young U.S. Children and Mothers." *Advances in Nutrition* 4: 51–61.

Cooper, Bob. 2018. "Notes on the Song 'Tin Roof Shanties,' Cedar Key's Very Own Ballad," Cedar Key News, August 15, 2018. www.cedarkeynews.com.

Council of Europe. 2010. "Guidelines of the Committee of Ministers of the Council of Europe on Child-Friendly Justice." www.coe.int.

Cunningham, Paige Winfield. 2018. "The Health 202: CHIP Won in the Government Shutdown. But Community Health Centers Did Not." *Washington Post*, January 23, 2018. www.washingtonpost.com.

Cunnyngham, Karen E. 2016. *Reaching Those in Need: Estimates of State Supplemental Nutrition Assistance Program Participation Rates in 2013*. Washington DC: Mathematica Policy Research, USDA Food and Nutrition Service. www.fns.usda.gov.

Curry, David. 2017. "More US Kids in Foster Care: Parental Drug Abuse a Factor." Associated Press, November 30, 2017. www.apanews.com.

Curtin, Sally C., Stephanie J. Ventura, and Gladys M. Martinez. 2014. "Recent Declines in Nonmarital Childbearing in the United States." NCHS Data Brief, no. 162, National Center for Health Statistics. http://cdc.gov.

D'Alessandro, Flavio. 2017. "Voglio un'infanzia spericolata." *La Foce*, April 2017.

Daly, Aoife, Sandy Ruxton, and Mieke Schuurman. 2016. "Challenges to Children's Rights Today: What Do Children Think?" Committee of Experts on the Council of Europe: Strategy for the Rights of the Child. https://edoc.coe.int.

Dasgupta, P. S., V. Ramanathan, and R. Minnerath. 2014. *Sustainable Humanity, Sustainable Nature: Our Responsibility*. Rome: Pontifical Academy of Sciences.

Daugherty, Jill, and Gladys Martinez. 2016. "Birth Expectations of US Women Aged 15–44." NCHS Data Brief, no. 260, October 2016. National Center for Health Statistics. http://cdc.gov.

Davidai, Shai, and Thomas Gilovich. 2015. "Building a More Mobile America—One Income Quintile at a Time." *Perspectives on Psychological Science* 10, no. 1: 60–71.

Davis, Julie Hirschfeld. 2018. "President Wants to Use Executive Order to End Birthright Citizenship." *New York Times*, October 30, 2018. www.nytimes.com.

Dean, Stacy, and Dottie Rosenbaum. 2013. "SNAP Benefits Will Be Cut for Nearly All Participants in November 2013." www.cbpp.org

Decrescitafelice.it. n.d. "Politics." www.decrescitafelice.it.

DeGregory, Lane. 2018. "The Last House in Rosewood: Owner Is Ready to Move but Worried about Drawing Attention." *Tampa Bay Times*, June 6, 2018.

Del Frate, Claudio. 2018. "I bimbi stranieri di Lodi esclusi dalla mensa." *Corriere della Sera*, October 14, 2018. www.corriere.it.

Delude, Cathryn. 2014. "The Epigenetics of Child Abuse." *Yale Medicine* 40, no. 3: 17.

DeNavas-Walt, Carmen, Bernadette D. Proctor, and Jessica C. Smith. 2013. *Income, Poverty, and Health Insurance Coverage in the United States: Current Population Reports*. Washington, DC: United States Census Bureau.

Desilver, Drew. 2014. "American Unions Membership Declines as Public Support Fluctuates." FactTank: News in Numbers, Pew Research Center, February 20, 2014. www.pewresearch.org.

Detrick, Sharon. 1999. *A Commentary on the United Nations Convention on the Rights of the Child*. Leiden: Martinus Nijhoff.

Di Gennaro, Angelo. 1981. *Scannismo overro sul Rapporto tra Personalitá ed Ambiente*. Sulmona, Italy: Stampa Editrice La Cittá.

Di Masso. 2018. "Dolci di Natura." www. dimassoscanno.net.

Dimick, Dennis. 2014. "As World's Population Booms, Will Its Resources Be Enough for Us?" *National Geographic*, September 21, 2014. http://news.nationalgeographic.com.

Di Miele, Chiara. 2018. "Terreni pubblici incolti ai giovani imprenditori. La Regione istituisce la Banca della Terra Campana." *Ondanews*, September 4, 2018. www.ondanews.it.

Di Rienzo, Filippo. 2012. "Amicizie." In *Voci Antiche: Antologia di poesia e prose premiate al concorso regionale di poesia dialettale "Romualdo Parente" Scanno*. Istituto Comprensivo Valle del Sagittario Introddaqua. Torre dei Nolfi (AQ): Edizione QUALEVITA.

Dowd, Nancy. 1997. *In Defense of Single-Parent Families*. New York: New York University Press.

Dowd, Nancy. 2018. *Reimagining Equality: A New Deal for Children of Color*. New York: New York University Press.

Dowd, Nancy, Dorothy Singer, and Robin Fretwell Wilson. 2006. *Handbook of Children, Culture, and Violence*. Thousand Oaks, CA: Sage.

Duffield, Barbara, and Phillip Lovell. 2008. "The Economic Crisis Hits Home: The Unfolding Increase in Child and Youth Homelessness." NAEHCY and First Focus. https://naehcy.org.

Durden, Tyler. 2016. "Baby Bust: US Fertility Rate Unexpectedly Drops to Lowest On Record." ZeroHedge, June 10, 2016. www.zerohedge.com.

Dye, R. Thomas. 1996. "Rosewood, Florida: The Destruction of an African American Community." *Historian* 598, no. 3: 605–22.

Easterbrook, Gregg. 2018. *It's Better Than It Looks: Reasons for Optimism in an Age of Fear*. New York: Public Affairs.

Easton, David. 1953. *The Political System: An Inquiry in the State of Political Science*. New York: Alfred A. Knopf.

Economist. 2012. "Monti's Medicine: Mario Monti Has Restored Italy's Credibility but Much More Must Be Done to Restore Its Fortunes." December 8, 2012. www.economist.com.

Edelman, Marian Wright. 2016. "The Early Childhood Infrastructure Our Children and Nation Urgently Need." Child Watch Column: Children's Defense Fund. www.childrensdefense.org.

El Arbaoui, Yasmin. 2018. "Ius soli, in Italia oltre 8000 mila bambini e ragazzi sono 'italiani senza cittadinanza.'" *Il Sol 24 Ore*, May 15, 2018. https://alleyoop.ilsole24ore.com.

Elder, Glen H., Jr., and Richard C. Rockwell. 1979. "The Life Course in Human Development: An Ecological Perspective." *International Journal of Behavioral Development* 2, no. 1: 1–21.

Ellen MacArthur Foundation. 2018. "The Circular Economy." http://ellenmacarthurfoundation.org.

Emory University. "Vulnerability and the Human Condition Initiative." http://web.gs.emory.edu/vulnerability.

Erikson, Erik H. 1963. *Childhood and Society.* 2nd ed. New York: W. W. Norton.

Erikson, Erik H. 1976. "Reflections on Dr. Borg's Life Cycle." *Daedalus* 105, no. 2: 1–28.

European Commission, for summaries of EU legislation. "The Pecautionary Principle." http://eur-lex.europa.eu.

Eurostat. 2017. "Immigrants, 2016 (per 1,000 Inhabitants)." https://ec.europa.eu.

Evans, Richard I. 1995. *Dialogue with Erik Erikson.* Lanham, MD: Rowman & Littlefield.

Federal Wildlife Service. 2015. "Shell Mound Trail: Before Written History." https://fws.gov.

Feeding America. n.d. "Hunger and Poverty Facts and Statistics." www.feedingamerica.org.

Ferrario, Paolo. 2018. "Scuola e web. Ragazzi sempre piu' connessi. Ma attenzione ai rischi." *Avvenire*, January 29, 2018. www.avvenire.it.

Filastrocche.it. 2002. "I bambini d'Italia." June 19, 2002. http://filastrocche.it.

Filosa, Maria Anna. 2017. "Applicazione della legge sulla procreazione medicalmente assistita (legge 40/2004)." Diritto e Diritti. www.diritto.it.

Fineman, Martha A. 2008. "The Vulnerable Subject: Anchoring Equality in the Human Condition." *Yale Journal of Law and Feminism* 20, no. 1: 1–23.

Fineman, Martha A. 2010. "The Vulnerable Subject and the Responsive State." *Emory Law Journal* 60, no. 1: 251–75.

Fineman, Martha A. 2013. "Equality, Autonomy, and the Vulnerable Subject in Law and Politics." In *Vulnerability: Reflections on a New Ethical Foundation for Law and Politics*, edited by Martha Albertson Fineman and Anna Grear, 13–27. Surrey: Ashgate.

Fineman, Martha A. 2017. "Vulnerability and Inevitable Inequality." *Oslo Law Review* 4, no. 4: 133–49.

Fineman, Martha A., and George B. Shepherd. 2016. "Homeschooling: Choosing Parental Rights Over Children's Interests." *University of Baltimore Law Review* 46, no. 1: 57–106.

Finkelhor, David, Kei Saito, and Lisa Jones. 2016. "Updated Trends in Child Maltreatment, 2014." Crimes Against Children Research Center, University of New Hampshire. www.unh.edu.
Fischer-Baum, Reuben, Darla Cameron, Sahil Chinoy, and Kevin Schaul. 2017. "Which of Your Family Members Could Visit under the Travel Ban." *Washington Post*, July 19, 2017. www.washingtonpost.com.
Florida Channel. n.d. "Florida Portraits: Cedar Key Museum State Park." https://thefloridachannel.org/videos.
Florida Department of Education. n.d. "Levy County Schools: Cedar Key High School." http://doeweb-prd.doe.state.fl.us.
Florida Department of Health. 2018. "Income eligibility guidelines, free meal scale." http://floridahealth.gov.
Forum Nazionale delle Associazioni Studentesche. 2002. "IoStudio, Carta Dello Studente." http://iostudio.pubblicaistruzione.it.
Fowler, Jonathan. 2014. "Pope Francis Has More Clout on Twitter Than Any Other World Leader: Study." *Huffington Post*, June 25, 2014. www.huffpost.com.
Freeman, Michael. 1997. *The Moral Status of Children: Essays on the Rights of the Child.* The Hague: Kluwer Law International.
Freeman, Michael. 2017. *Human Rights.* 3rd ed. Cambridge: Polity.
Fulton, L. 2015. "Worker Representation in Europe." Labour Research Department and ETUI. http://worker-participation.eu.
Galway-Witham, Julia, and Christopher Brian Stringer. 2018. "How Did Homo sapiens Evolve?" *Science*, June 2018, 1296–98.
Garbarino, James. 1985. *Adolescent Development: An Ecological Perspective.* Columbus: Merrill.
Garbarino, James. 1989. *What Children Can Tell Us: Eliciting, Interpreting, and Evaluating Critical Information from Children.* San Francisco: Jossey-Bass.
Garbarino, James. 1995. *Raising Children in a Socially Toxic Environment.* San Francisco: Jossey-Bass.
Garretson, Harry, and Philip McCann, Ron Martin, and Peter Tyler. 2013. "The Future of Regional Policy." In *Cambridge Journal of Regions, Economy, and Society* 6, no. 2: 179–86.
Gatti, Uberto, and Verde, Alfredo. 2002. "Comparative Juvenile Justice: An Overview of Italy." In *Juvenile Justice Systems: International Perspectives*, edited by J. A. Winterdyk, 297–315. Toronto: Canadian Scholars.
Gentile, Douglas A., and Craig A. Anderson. 2006. "Violent Video Games: Effects on Youth and Public Policy Implications." In Dowd et al. 2006, 225–46.
Giannantonio, Raffaele. 2010. *Scanno: Art and History Guide to the Town and District.* Pescara: Carsa Edizioni.
Giannarelli, Linda, Kye Lippold, Sarah Minton, and Laura Wheaton. 2015. "Reducing Child Poverty in the US: Costs and Impacts of Policies Proposed by the Children's Defense Fund." Urban Institute. www.childrensdefense.org.

Giuffrida, Angela. 2018. "Matteo Salvini Orders Removal of Refugees from Riace." *Guardian*, October 14, 2018. www.theguardian.com.

Goldberg, Jonah. 2018. "We Shouldn't Ignore Systemic Discrimination in China." *National Review*, August 22, 2018. www.nationalreview.com.

Goldberg, Michelle. 2018. "Want More Babies? You Need Less Patriarchy." *New York Times*, May 25, 2018. www.nytimes.com.

Goodloe, Trevor. n.d. "Rosewood Massacre (1923)." BlackPast.Org: Remembered and Reclaimed. www.blackpast.org.

Goodstein, Laurie, and Sharon Otterman. 2018. "Catholic Priests Abused 1,000 Children in Pennsylvania, Report Says." *New York Times*, August 14, 2018. www.nytimes.com.

Gostoli, Ylenia. 2018a. "'Riace Was Destroyed': Pro-refugee Village Broken after Mayor Ban." Al Jazeera, November 1, 2018. www.aljazeera.com.

Gostoli, Ylenia. 2018b. "Salvini Law Could Make Thousands of Refugees Homeless." Al Jazeera, December 17, 2018. www.aljazeera.com.

Government of Canada. 2018. "Canadian Citizenship." www.canada.ca.

Grabar, Henry. 2018. "Minneapolis Confronts its History of Housing Segregation." Slate, December 7, 2018. https://slate.com.

Grubb, W. Norton, and Marvin Lazerson. 1988. *Broken Promises: How Americans Fail Their Children*. Chicago: University of Chicago Press.

Guerra, Simona, and Mario Giacomelli. 2016. *Il Bambino di Scanno*. Rome: Postcart.

Guzman, Gloria G. 2017. "Household Income: 2016." www.census.gov.

Hamilton, Brady, Joyce Martin, Michelle Osterman, Anne Driscoll, and Lauren Rossen. 2018. "NVSS Vital Statistics Rapid Release, Report No. 004, May 2018, Births: Provisional Data for 2017." Centers for Disease Control and Prevention. www.cdc.gov.

Hanna, Kirsten, Ian Hassall, and Emma Davies. 2006. "Child Impact Reporting." *Social Policy Journal of New Zealand* 29: 32–42.

Hanson, Claudia, Jonathan Cox, Godfrey Mbaruku, Fatuma Manzi, Sabine Gabrysch, David Schellenberg, Marcel Tanner, Carine Ronsmans, and Joanna Schellenberg. 2015. "Maternal Mortality and Distance to Facilty-Based Obstetric Care in Rural Southern Tanzania: a Secondary Analysis of Cross-Sectional Census Data in 226,000 Households." Open Access. https://researchonline.lshtm.ac.uk.

Hanson, Kenneth, and Victor Oliveira. 2013. *Economic Conditions Affect the Share of Children Receiving Free or Reduced-Price School Lunches*. Washington DC: USDA Economic Research Service.

Hendrickson, Clara, Mark Muro, and William A. Galston. 2018. "Countering the Geography of Discontent: Strategies for Left-Behind Places." Brookings Institution. www.brookings.edu.

Holger, Gorg. 2011. "Globalization, Offshoring, and Jobs." In *Making Globalization Socially Sustainable*, edited by Marc Bacchetta and Marion Jansen, 1–47. Geneva: WTO.

Holland, Sally. 2016. "Welsh Commissioner for Children—Sally's Blog: A Youth Parliament for Wales: A Welcome Addition for Our Democracy." www.childcomwales.org.uk.

Holt, Marilyn Irvin. 1994. *The Orphan Trains: Placing Out in America*. Lincoln: University of Nebraska Press.

Horowitz, Jason. 2017. "Immigration Moves Front and Center in Italy's Local Elections." *New York Times*, June 24, 2017. www.nytimes.com.

Horowitz, Jason. 2018. "Vatican Power Struggle Bursts into Open as Conservatives Pounce." *New York Times*, August 27, 2018. www.nytimes.com.

Huang, Mary I., Mary Ann O'Riordan, Ellen Fitzenrider, Lolita McDavid, Alan R. Cohen, and Shenandoah Robinson. 2011. "Increased Incidence of Nonaccidental Head Trauma in Infants Associated with the Economic Recession: Clinical Article." *Journal of Neurosurgery: Pediatrics* 8, no. 2: 171–76.

HuffPost Business. 2012. "Reagan-Appointed Judge: Deregulation Movement Made a 'Fundamental Mistake.'" Huffington Post, August 24, 2012. www.huffpost.com.

Human Development Index. 2018. "2018 Statistical Update." http://hdr.undp.org. Accessed May 24, 2019.

iCivics. n.d "iCivics Is Reimagining Civil Learning." www.icivics.org.

Il Messagero. 2018. "Nave Diciotti a Trapani, Mattarella chiama Conte, sbloccato lo sbarco dei migranti. "Stupore: al Viminale." July 12, 2018. www.ilmessagero.it.

Indexmundi. For Italy birth rate, crude per 1000 people. www.indexmundi.com.

INPS. 2017a. "Come richiedere il premio alla nascita—800 euro." INPS Comunica: Notizie. www.inps.it.

INPS. 2017b. "Indennità per congedo obbligatorio di maternità/paternità per lavoratrici e lavoratori dipendenti e per iscritti alla Gestione Separata." www.inps.it.

INPS. 2017c. "Relazione Annuale del Presidente INPS." June 4, 2017. www.inps.it.

Invernizzi, Antonella, and Jane Williams, eds. 2011. *The Human Rights of Children: From Visions to Implementation*. New York: Routledge.

Isaacs, Julia B. 2008. "International Comparisons of Economic Mobility." In *Getting Ahead or Losing Ground: Economic Mobility in America*, edited by Julia B. Isaacs, Isabel V. Sawhill, and Ron Haskins, 37–46. Brookings Institution, Economic Mobility Project. www.brookings.edu.

Isaacs, Julia B. 2012. "The Ongoing Impact of Foreclosures on Children." Brookings Social Genome Project Research Series. Washington DC: Brookings Institution and First Focus. brookings.edu.

Isaacs, Julia B., and Olivia Healy. 2012. "The Recession's Ongoing Impact on Children, 2012: Indicators of Children's Economic Well-Being." Urban Institute and First Focus. www.urban.org.

ISTAT. 2011. "Childhood and Daily Life." www.istat.it.

ISTAT. 2014. "Birth and Fertility of the Resident Population." www.istat.it.

ISTAT. 2016. Annuario Statistico Italiano 2016. "Capitolo 10 Cultura e Tempo Libero." wwww.istat.it.

ISTAT. 2017. "Indicatori Demografici: Stime per l'anno 2016." www.istat.it.

ISTAT. 2018a. "La Poverta' in Italia Anno 2017." www.istat.it.
ISTAT. 2018b. "Anno 2017 Report on Natalitá e Feconditá della Popolazione Residente." www.istat.it.
ISTAT-FUB. 2018. "Internet@Italia 2018: Domanda e offerta di servizi online e scenari di digitalizzazione." Fondazione Ugo Bordoni. www.istat.it.
Jacobs, Andrew. 2018. "Opposition to Breast-Feeding Resolution by US Stuns World Health Officials." *New York Times*, July 8, 2018. www.nytimes.com.
Jan, Tracy. 2018. "Redlining Was Banned 50 Years Ago. It's Still Hurting Minorities." *Washington Post*, March 28, 2018. www.washingtonpost.com.
Jordan, Miriam. 2019. "Family Separations May Have Hit Thousands More Migrant Children Than Reported." *New York Times*, January 17, 2019. www.nytimes.com.
Karaca-Mandic, Pinar, Sung J. Choi Yoo, and Benjamin D. Sommers. 2013. "Recession Led to a Decline in Out-of-Pocket Spending for Children with Special Health Care Needs." *Health Affairs* 32: 1054–62.
Kaufmann, Paulus. 2011. "Instrumentalization: What Does it Mean to Use a Person?" In *Humiliation, Degradation, Dehumanization: Human Dignity Violated*, edited by Paulus Kaufmann, Hannes Kuch, H., Christian Neuhaeuser, and Elaine Webster, 57–65. Dordrecht: Springer.
Keith-Jennings, Brynne. 2012. "SNAP Plays a Critical Role in Helping Children." Center on Budget and Policy Priorities. www.cbpp.org.
Kells, Paul. 1997. "A Statistic of One." *Injury Prevention* 3: 305–6.
Kenney, Genevieve M., Joan Alker, Nathaniel Anderson, Stacey McMorrow, Sharon K. Long, Douglas Wissoker, Lisa Clemans-Cope, Lisa Dubay, Michael Karpman, and Tricia Brooks. 2014. "A First Look at Children's Health Insurance Coverage under the ACA in 2014." Urban Institute Health Policy Center. www.urban.org.
Kington, Tom. 2010. "For a Real Italian Getaway, Follow the Herd." *Guardian*, February 6, 2010. theguardian.com.
Kirkpatrick, David D. 2015. "Migrants Face Hellish Limbo in Libya before Journey towards Italy." *Irish Times*, April 29, 2015. www.irishtimes.com.
Knoema. For GDP per Capita by Country: Statistics from IMF, 1980–2002. https://knoema.com.
Kohler, Hans-Peter. 2015. "Six Myths and Truths about Fertility in the West." Institute for Family Studies. https://ifstudies.org.
Kohn, Nina A. 2014. "Vulnerability Theory and the Role of Government." *Yale Journal of Law and Feminism* 26, no. 1: 1–28.
Kornelson, Jude, Shiraz Moola, Stefan Grzybowski. 2009. "Does Distance Matter? Increased Induction Rates for Rural Women Who Have to Travel for Intrapartum Care." *Journal of Obstetrics and Gynecology of Canada* 31, no. 1: 21–27.
Kraus, Michael W., Shai Davidai, and A. David Nussbaum. 2015. "American Dream? Or Mirage?" *New York Times*, May 1, 2015. nytimes.com.
Krugman, Paul. 2012. *End This Depression Now!* New York: W.W. Norton.
Krugman, Paul. 2015. "That Old-Time Economics." *New York Times*, April 17, 2015. www.nytimes.com.

Krugman, Paul. 2017. "Voodoo Too: The GOP Addiction to Deregulation." *New York Times*, November 26, 2017. www.nytimes.com.
Kunkel, Dale, and Larta Zearun. 2006. "How Real Is the Problem of TV Violence." In Dowd et al. 2006, 203–24.
Kuo, Lily, and Xueying Wang. 2019. "Can China Recover from its Disastrous One-Child Policy?" *Guardian*, March 2, 2019. www.theguardian.org.
Kurukulasuriya, Sharmila, and Solrun Engilbertsdottir. 2011. "A Multidimensional Approach to Measuring Child Poverty." UNICEF Division of Policy and Practice: Social and Economic Policy Working Briefs. www.unicef.org.
Associazione Culturale L'Appuntamento con La Tradizione. "Vivi il Costume." www.facebook.com
La Foce. 2018. "A scuola tutti insieme: Gli alunni riuniti finalmente nel plesso di via Napoli." *La Foce*, September 2018.
Lami, Giuseppe. 2017. "Paolo Gentiloni dice che un nuovo voto sullo ius soli avrebbe 'archiviato' il tema per anni." *Il Post*, December 28, 2017. www.ilpost.it.
Landrigan, Philip J. 2016. "Children's Environmental Health: A Brief History." *Academic Pediatrics* 16, no. 1: 1–9.
Lavilloti, Massimiliano. 2018. "Scanno ancora senza scuola." *Il Centro*, September 2, 2018. www.ilcentro.it.
Leonhardt, David, Amanda Cox, and Claire Cain Miller. 2015. "An Atlas of Upward Mobility Shows Paths Out of Poverty." *New York Times*, May 4, 2015. www.nytimes.com.
Leventhal, John M., and Julie R. Gaither. 2012. "Incidence of Serious Injuries Due to Physical Abuse in the United States: 1997 to 2009." *Pediatrics* 130, no. 5: 847–52.
Levi, Carlo. 1983. *Cristo si è fermato ad Eboli*. Torino: Einaudi.
Liptak, Adam. 2012. "Supreme Court Upholds Health Care Law, 5–4, in Victory for Obama." *New York Times*, June 28, 2012. www.nytimes.com.
Lisa, Elena. "Eterologa, cento coppie torinesi sono già in lista di attesta." *La Stampa Torino*, September 9, 2014. www.lastampa.it.
Litvinov, Amanda. 2014. "As Homeless Student Rate Soars, House Republicans Propose Cuts to Life-changing Services." *EducationVotes*, May 16, 2014. http://educationvotes.nea.org.
Livingston, Gretchen. 2016. "Growth in Annual US Births since 1970 Driven Entirely by Immigrant Moms." In *Births Outside of Marriage Decline for Immigrant Women*, 13–15. Pew Research Center. www.pewsocialtrends.org.
Local.it. 2018. "Immigration to Italy: A Look at the Numbers." www. thelocal.it.
Loffredo, Antonio. 2013. *Noi del Rione della Sanità*. Milan: Mondadori.
Longman Dictionary of Contemporary English. 6th ed. S.v. "faith community." www.ldoceonline.com.
Lopez, Linette. 2012. "poll: Warren Buffett Says Kids Born in the US Today Are the Luckiest People in the World—Do You Agree?" *Business Insider*, June 12, 2012. www.businessinsider.com.
Losito, Alessandra. 2016. "Bonus bebè 2016 INPS: modulo domanda requisiti dove come e quando." *Guida Fisco*, June 17, 2016. http://guidafisco.it.

Louv, Richard. 2008. *Last Child in the Woods: Saving Our Children from Nature-Deficit Disorder*. Chapel Hill, NC: Algonquin.

Lucas-Thompson, Rachel G., Wendy A. Goldberg, and JoAnn Prause. 2010. "Maternal Work Early in the Lives of Children and Its Distal Associations with Achievement and Behavior Problems: A Meta-Analysis." *Psychological Bulletin* 136, no. 6: 915–42.

MacKenzie, James. 2015. "Pope Francis Rails Against 'Throwaway Culture' of Globalization." Huffington Post, March 1, 2015. www.huffpost.com.

Magliano, Tony. 2013. "Pope Francis Condemns Profit-centered Economy." *National Catholic Reporter*, December 23, 2013. www.ncronline.org.

Maron, Dina Fine. 2017. "Maternal Health Care is Disappearing in Rural America." *Scientific American*, February 15, 2017. www.scientificamerican.com.

Marro, Enrico. 2017. "Senza immigranti all'Inps mancano 38 miliardi." *Corriere della Serra*, July 3, 2017.

Mascheroni, Giovanna, and Kjartan Ólafsson. 2018. "Accesso, usi, rischi e opportunita' di internet per I ragazzi italiani: I primi resultati di EU Kids Online 2017." Governo Italiano. https://miur.gov.it.

Mastrogiovanni, Alessandra. 2010. "Calendar." In Giannantonio 2010, 86–89.

Mathews, T. J., and Brady E. Hamilton. 2016. "Mean Age of Mothers Is on the Rise: United States, 2000–2014." NCHS Data Brief, no. 232. National Center for Health Statistics. www.cdc.gov.

Matthews, Dylan. 2018. "Paul Ryan Is Lying to You About the Children's Health Insurance." *Vox*, January 19, 2018. vox.com.

Mazzini, Silvia. 2018. "Italy's Election Should Be a Wake-up Call for the EU." Al Jazeera, March 8, 2018. www.aljazeera.com.

McCarthy, Kevin M. 2007. *Cedar Key Florida: A History*. Charleston, SC: History.

McDonough, William. 2017. "How Cities Could Save Us." *Scientific American*, July 2017, 44–48.

McIntyre, Lisa J. 2014. *The Practical Skeptic: Core Concepts in Sociology*. 6th ed. New York: McGraw Hill.

McKibben, Bill. 2018. "Big Oil CEOs Needed a Climate Change Reality Check. The Pope Delivered. At a Gathering of Fossil Fuel Executives at the Vatican, Pope Francis Spoke Much-needed Common Sense about Climate Change." *Guardian*, June 14, 2018. www.theguardian.com.

Meadows, Rachel, Kate Sell, Elias Blinkoff, Narissa Williams, and Laura Repcheck. 2015. "The Effect of the Great Recession on Child Well-Being: A Synthesis of the Evidence by PolicyLab at the Children's Hospital of Philadelphia." Edited by Kathleen Noonan, David Rubin, and Maureen Byrnes. PolicyLab and FirstFocus. https://firstfocus.org.

Mentzelopoulou, Maria Margarita, and Costica Dumbrava. 2018. "Acquisition and Loss of Citizenship in EU Member States: Key Trends and Issues." P.E. 625.116, European Parliamentary Research Service, European Parliament. http://europarl.europa.eu.

Meta, Ermal. 2017. "Amara Terra Mia (Con Testo)." YouTube. https://www.youtube.com.

Mignot, Jean-Francois. 2015. "Why Is Intercountry Adoption Declining Worldwide?" *Regulation & Societies* no. 519: www.ined.fr.
Mikkola, Reetta. 2018. "First European Symposium of Child and Youth Councils Assembles in Spain." https://childfriendlycities.org.
Miller, Claire Cain. 2018. "Americans Are Having Fewer Babies. They Told Us Why." *New York Times*, July 5, 2018. www.nytimes.com.
Miller, Mark D., Melanie A. Marty, and Philip J. Landrigan. 2016. "Children's Environmental Health: Beyond National Boundaries." *Pediatric Clinics of North America* 63, no. 1: 149–65.
Mittica, M. P. 2003a. "Una cornice giuridica per partecipare: La Legge 285/97." In *I diritti di cittadinanza dei minori tra partecipazione e controllo*, edited by C. Baraldo, G. Maggioni, and F. Pappalardo, 29–46. Urbino: Edizione Goliardiche.
Mittica, M. P. 2003b. "La partecipazione e' un diritto dal punto di vista dei bambini?" In *I diritti di cittadinanza dei minori tra partecipazione e controllo*, edited by C. Baraldo, G. Maggioni, and F. Pappalardo, 97–122. Urbino: Edizione Goliardiche.
Moore, Gary. 1982. "Rosewood." *St. Petersburg Times*, July 25, 1982.
Moore, Heidi. 2013. "Pope Francis Understands Economics Better than Most Politicians." *Guardian*, November 27, 2013. www.theguardian.com.
Museum on Main Street. 2018. "Crossroads." https://Museumonmainstreet.org.
NAACP. 2017. *Quality Education for All . . . One School at a Time*. Report of NAACP Task Force on Quality Education. www.naacp.org.
NAEHCY. n.d. "Welcome." http://naehcy.org.
NAEHCY and First Focus. 2010. "A Critical Moment: Child and Youth Homelessness in Our Nation's Schools." http://naehcy.org.
Nanni, Davide. 2012. "Castrovalva." In *Voci Antiche: Antologia di poesia e prose premiate al concorso regionale di poesia dialettale "Romualdo Parente" Scanno*, 16. Torre dei Nolfi, Aquila, IT: Edizione QUALEVITA.
Natali, Luisa, Bruno Martorano, Sudhanshu Handa, Goran Holmqvist, and Yekaterina Chzhen. 2014. "A Cross-country Comparative Perspective: Trends in Child Well-being in European Union Countries during the Great Recession." Innocenti Working Paper 2014-10. UNICEF Office of Research. www.unicef-irc.org.
National Center for Health Statistics. 2017. "Unmarried Childbearing." www.cdc.gov.
National Center for Health Statistics. 2018. "Births: Provisional Data for 2017." Report No. 004. www. cdc.gov.
National Center for Health Statistics. 2019. "Births: Provisional Data for 2018." Report No. 007. www.cdc.gov.
National Center for Homeless Education. 2019. "Federal Data Summary: School Year 2014–15 to 2016–17." University of North Carolina, Greensboro.
National Conference of State Legislatures (NCSL). 2016. "Foster Care Bill of Rights." www.ncsl.org.
National Council of Juvenile and Family Court Judges (NCJFCJ). 2010. "Resolution on the UN Convention on the Rights of the Child." www.ncjfcj.org.
National Geographic Encyclopedia. S.v. "Neighborhood." www.nationalgeographic.org.

National Immigration Law Center. 2018. "Status of Current DACA Litigation." www.nilc.org.

National Park Service. 2017. "Timucuan." www.theclio.com.

National Research Council and Institute of Medicine. 2000. *From Neurons to Neighborhoods: The Science of Early Childhood Development*. Committee on Integrating the Science of Early Childhood Development—Board on Children, Youth and Families: Commission on Behavioral and Social Sciences and Education, edited by Jack P. Shonkoff and Deborah A. Phillips. Washington, DC: National Academy.

National Scientific Council on the Developing Child. 2010. "Early Experiences Can Alter Gene Expression and Affect Long-Term Development." Working Paper No. 10, National Scientific Council on the Developing Child. Center on the Developing Child, Harvard University. http://developingchild.harvard.edu.

National Catholic Reporter. 2014. "Pope's Quotes: Youth Unemployment.", September 1, 2014. https://ncronline.org.

Nelson, Charles A. III, Nathan A. Fox, and Charles H. Zeanah. 2014. *Romania's Abandoned Children: Deprivation, Brain Development, and the Struggle for Recovery*. Cambridge, MA: Harvard University Press.

New Economics Foundation. 2012. "Happy Planet Index: 2012 Report." https://neweconomics.org.

Newcomer, Daniel. 2016. "Cedar Key Historical and Archeological District." www.theclio.com.

Newland, Kathleen, and T. Alexander Aleinikoff. 2017. "Commentary: The US Refugee Resettlement Program Is an Unsuitable Target." Migration Policy Institute. http://migrationpolicy.org.

Nickel, James W. 1993. "The Human Right to a Safe Environment: Philosophical Perspectives on Its Scope and Justification." *Yale Journal of International Law* 18, no 1: 281–95.

Nickel, James W. 2008. "Rethinking Indivisibility: Towards a Theory of Supporting Relations between Human Rights." *Human Rights Quarterly* 30, no. 4: 984–1001.

Niezen, Ronald. 2013. *Truth and Indignation: Canada's Truth and Reconciliation Commission on Indian Residential Schools*. Toronto: University of Toronto Press.

Nixon, Richard. 1971. "Veto of the Economic Opportunity Amendments of 1971." American Presidency Project. www.presidency.ucsb.edu.

Nord, Mark. 2009. "Food Insecurity in Households with Children: Prevalence, Severity, and Household Characteristics." USDA Economic Research Service. www.ers.usda.gov.

Notarmuzi, Marco. 2005. *La Pastorizia a Scanno: Cultura e Terminologia*. Sulmona: La Moderna.

Notarmuzi, Marco. 2010. "Religious Festivals." In Giannantonio 2010, 90–92.

Obama, Barack. 2014. "Pope Francis." *Time*, April 23, 2014. http://time.com.

Odobescu, Vlad. 2015. "Half a Million Kids Survived Romania's 'Slaughterhouses of the Soul.' Now They Want Justice." Public Radio International, December 28 2015. www.pri.org.

OECD. 2007. "OECD Offshoring and Employment: Trends and Impacts." wwwoecd.org.
OECD. 2009. "Doing Better for Children." https://read.oecd-ilibrary.org.
OECD. n.d. For OECD family database indicators: public policies for families and children—enrollment in childcare and preschool. www.oecd.org.
OECD. n.d. For Income Distribution Database (IDD): Gini, poverty, income—methods and concepts. www.oecd.org.
OECD. n.d. For Household Savings indicator: 1996–2015 data for Italy. https://data.oecd.org.
Oishi, Shigehiro, and Ulrich Schimmack. 2010. "Residential Mobility, Well-Being, and Mortality." *Journal of Personality and Social Psychology* 98, no. 6: 980–94.
Oliveira, Victor, Laura Tiehen, and Michele Ver Ploeg. 2014. *USDA's Food Assistance Programs: Legacies of the War on Poverty*. Washington DC: USDA Economic Research Service.
Our Children's Trust. 2018. "Mission Statement." www.ourchildrenstrust.org.
Paletta, Damian, and Erica Warner. 2018. "Trump Calls on Congress to Pull Back $15 Billion in Spending, Including on Children's Health Insurance Program." *Washington Post*, May 7, 2018. www.washingtonpost.com.
Pallante, Maurizio. 2011. *La Decrescita' Felice: La Qualitas' della Vita non Dipende dal PIL*. Rome: Editori Riuniti.
Pazé, Piercarlo. 2011. "Le novita' nell' ascolto del bambino." *Cittadini in Crescita* nos. 2–3: 14–24.
Perry, Bruce D, and Maia Szalavitz. 2006. *The Boy Who Was Raised as a Dog: And Other Stories from a Child Psychiatrist's Notebook: What Traumatized Children Can Teach Us About Loss, Love, and Healing*. New York: Basic Books.
Pfanner, Eric. "Europe's Economic Slump Deeper than Expected." *New York Times*, February 13, 2009. www.nytimes.com.
Piaget, Jean. 1958. *The Growth of Logical Thinking in Children from Childhood to Adolescence*. New York: Basic Books.
Pianetta Pane. 2018. "Pan dell'Orso. A Scanno nasce la prima boulangerie del Parco Nazionale d'Abruzzo." March 13, 2018. www.pianettapane.it.
Piketty, Thomas. 2014. *Capital in the Twenty-First Century*. Translated by Arthur Goldhammer. Cambridge, MA: Harvard University Press.
Pilkington, Ed. 2018. "Nikki Halley Attacks Damning UN Report on US Poverty under Trump." *Guardian*, June 21, 2018. www.theguardian.com.
Pilkington, Hugo, Beatrice Blondel, Nicolas Drewniak, and Jennifer Zeitlin. 2014. "Where Does Distance Matter? Distance to the Closest Maternity Unit and Risk of Fetal and Neonatal Mortality in France." *European Journal of Public Health* 24, no. 5: 905–10.
Pivas, Claudia. 2018. "Decisivo l'aiuto dei miei, Da sola con ce l'avrei fatta." *Corriere della Sera*, July 21, 2018.
Polizzi, Donatella. 2018. "Feeding Italy for Millennia: The History of Ancient Grains." *L'Italo-American*, July 18, 2018. https://italoamericano.org.

Pope Francis. 2013. "Apostolic Exhortation *Evangelii Gaudium* on Some Challenges of Today's World." Vatican. http://w2.vatican.va.

Pope Francis. 2015a. "Francis: To Care for the Poor Is Not Communism, It Is the Gospel." Interview by Andrea Tornielli and Giacomo Galeazzi. *Vatican Insider*, January 11, 2015. www.lastampa.it.

Pope Francis. 2015b. "Message of His Holiness Pope Francis for the 49th World Communications Day: Communicating the Family: A Privileged Place of Encounter with the Gift of Love." Vatican, https://w2.vatican.va.

Pope Francis. 2015c. "Laudato Si': Encyclical Letter on Care for Our Common Home." Vatican, http://w2.vatican.va.

Pope Francis. 2017. "We Must Overcome All Forms of Racism, Intolerance, and Instrumentalization of the Human Person." Twitter *@pontifex*, July 18, 2017. https://twitter.com.

Pope Francis. 2018. "Message of His Holiness Pope Francis for the 104th World Day of Migrants and Refugees 2018." Vatican. http://m.vatican.va.

Pope Pius XI. 1931. "Quadragesimo Anno Encyclical on Reconstruction of the Social Order." Vatican. http://w2.vatican.va.

Porter, Eduardo. 2015. "Income Inequality Is Costing the US on Social Issues." *New York Times*, April 28, 2015. www.nytimes.com.

Poushter, Jacob. 2016. "American Public, Foreign Policy Experts Sharply Disagree over Involvement in Global Economy." FactTank: News in Numbers, Pew Research Center. www.pewresearch.org.

Querzé, Rita. 2017a. "Materne vuote e nidi pieni: ecco gli effetti del calo demografico." *Corriere della Sera*, July 9, 2017. www.corriere.it.

Querzé, Rita. 2017b. "Premio alla nascita: 200 mila domande in due mesi." *Corriere della Sera*, July 6, 2017. www.corriere.it.

Querzé, Rita. 2018. "Non e' un Paese per mamme: Per le donne e' sempre piu' difficile riuscire a conciliare lavoro e maternita' e molte delle misure per aiutare quante riescono a resistere sono in scadenza." *Corriere della Sera*, July 21, 2018. www.corriere.it.

Reeves, Richard R. 2014. *Equality, Opportunity, and the American Dream (The Brookings Essay)*. Washington, DC: Brookings Institution.

Reich, Robert B. 2015. *Saving Capitalism: For the Many, Not the Few*. New York: Alfred A. Knopf.

Reich, Robert B. 2018. *The Common Good*. New York: Random House.

Reitz, John. 1998. "How to Do Comparative Law." *American Journal of Comparative Law* 46, no. 2: 617–36.

Rete degli Studenti. 2010. "Rete degli Studenti." www.retedeglistudenti.it.

Rideout, Victoria J., Elizabeth A. Vandewater, and Ellen A. Wartella. 2003. "Zero to Six: Electronic Media in the Lives of Infants, Toddlers, and Preschoolers." Henry J. Kaiser Family Foundation. https://kaiserfamilyfoundation.com.

Rideout, Victoria, and Elizabeth Hamel. 2006. "The Media Family: Electronic Media in the Lives of Infants, Toddlers, Preschoolers and their Parents." Henry J. Kaiser Family Foundation. https://kaiserfamilyfoundation.com.

Rideout, Victoria J., Ulla G. Foehr, and Donald F. Roberts. 2010. "Generation M^2: Media in the Lives of 8- to 18-Year-Olds." Henry J. Kaiser Family Foundation. https://kaiserfamilyfoundation.com.

Roberts, Dorothy. 2002. *Shattered Bonds: The Color of Child Welfare*. New York: Basic Books.

Robertson, Lori. 2018. "Illegal Immigration Statistics." The Wire: FactCheck.Org, www.factcheck.org.

Rodrik, Dani. 2011. *The Globalization Paradox: Democracy and the Future of the World Economy*. New York: W.W. Norton.

Roosevelt, Eleanor. 1999. "Where Do Human Rights Begin?" In *Courage in a Dangerous World: The Political Writings of Eleanor Roosevelt*, edited by Allida M. Black, 190. New York: Columbia University Press.

Root, Leslie. 2019. "Racist Terrorists are Obsessed with Demographics. Let's not Give Them Talking Points." *Washington Post*, March 18, 2019. www.washingtonpost.com.

Rosenbaum, Dottie. 2014. "SNAP Caseloads Down—as Expected." Center on Budget and Policy Priorities. www.cbpp.org.

Rosenbaum, Dottie, and Brynne Keith-Jennings. 2014. "SNAP Costs Falling, Expected to Fall Further: Trend Reflects Shrinking Caseloads and Recent Benefit Cut." Center on Budget and Policy Priorities. www.cbpp.org.

Ross, Casey. 2017. "A Pain in the Night and a Harrowing Drive: A Crisis in Rural Health Care Puts Mothers-to-Be on a Risky Road." STAT, April 17, 2017. www.statnews.com.

Rossi, Valentina, and Maria Teresa Tagliaventi. 2011. "L'aquila: un esempio di progettazione partecipata in un territorio vittima di un evento sísmico." *Cittadini in Crescita*, nos. 2–3: 65–69.

Rudowitz, Robin, Samantha Artiga, and Rachel Arguello. 2014. "Children's Health Coverage: Medicaid, CHIP and the ACA." Henry J. Kaiser Family Foundation. https://kaiserfamilyfoundation.com.

Sacchetti, Maria. 2018. "Trump Administration Seeks More Time to Reunite Some Migrant Families Split at Border." *Washington Post*, July 6, 2018. www.washingtonpost.com.

Sadeghi, Mohammed Reza. 2012. "Low Success Rate of ART, an Illusion, a Reality, or Simply a Too High Expectation?" *Journal of Reproduction & Infertility* 1, no. 3: 13–123.

Salera, Ludovico. 2017. "Amara Terra Mia' tra cultura populare abruzzese, slava, Albanese e . . . Modugno." *Avezzano Informa*, February 2, 2017. www.avezzanoinforma.it.

Sampadian, Hannah. 2018. "New Roots: Story Hill Farm Offers Refugees Chance to Grow Food, Build Community." *Concord Monitor*, March 4, 2018. www.concordmonitor.com.

Save the Children. 2017a. "End of Childhood Report 2017." Save the Children. www.savethechildren.org.

Save the Children. 2017b. "US Complement to the End of Childhood Report 2017: Stolen Childhoods." Save the Children. www.savethechildren.org.

Save the Children. 2018a. "End of Childhood Report 2018: The Many Faces of Exclusion." Save the Children. www.savethechildren.org.
Save the Children. 2018b. "End of Childhood US Complement to the End of Childhood Report 2018: Growing Up Rural in America." Save the Children. www.savethechildren.org.
Save the Children (Italy). 2017. "Le Equilibriste: La maternità tra ostacoli e visioni di future, Rapporto mamme 2017." Edited by Giovanna Badalassi and Federica Gentile. Save the Children Italy. www.savethechildren.it.
"Scanno, Abruzzo." n.d. In Wikipedia. ttps://en.wikipedia.org.
"Scanno: un borgo nel cuore dell'Abruzzo." https://scanno.webnode.it
Schäuble, Wolfgang. 2015. "Wolfgang Schäuble on German Priorities and Eurozone Myths." *New York Times*, April 15, 2015. www.nytimes.com.
Scherer, Steve. 2018. "In Italian Election Campaign, Facebook, Twitter Replace Posters, Piazzas." Reuters, March 1, 2018. https://uk.reuters.com.
Schneider, Carl E. 1992. "The Channeling Function in Family Law." *Hofstra Law Review* 20, no. 3: 495–532.
Schumacher, E. F. (Ernest Friedrich). 2010. *Small Is Beautiful: Economics as if People Mattered*. With a foreword by Bill McKibben. New York: Harper Collins.
Scott, John. 2014. *A Dictionary of Sociology: Oxford Quick Reference*. 4th ed. Oxford: Oxford University Press.
Searchinger, Tim, Craig Hanson, Richard Waite, Brian Lipinski, George Leeson, and Sarah Harper. 2013. "Achieving Replacement Level Fertility: Creating a Sustainable Food Future, Installment Three." World Resources Institute. www.wri.org.
Sell, Katherine, Sarah Zlotnik, Kathleen Noonan, and David Rubin. 2010. "The Effect of Recession on Child Well-Being: A Synthesis of the Evidence by PolicyLab, The Children's Hospital of Philadephia." PolicyLab, First Focus, and Foundation for Child Development. http://policylab.chop.edu.
Sewell, Abby. 2017. "A Small Town in Italy Was Losing Its Population. Now Syrian Refugees Are Key to Its Survival." *Los Angeles Times*, May 1, 2017. www.latimes.com.
Siegler, Robert, Nancy Eisenberg, Elizabeth Gershoff, Jenny R. Saffran, Judy DeLoache, and Campbell Leaper. 2017. *How Children Develop*. 5th ed. New York: Worth.
Slow Food Foundation for Biodiversity. n.d. "Frattura White Bean." www.fondazioneslowfood.com.
Smerconish, Michael. 2012. "'You didn't build that!' in Context." Huffington Post, July 30, 2012. www.huffpost.com.
Smith, Jessica C., and Carla Medalia. 2013. "Health Insurance Coverage in the United States: 2013." United States Census Bureau. www.census.gov.
Smith-Spark, Laura, and Hada Messia. 2017. "Italy Avalanche: Hotel Search Ends with 29 Dead, 11 Rescued." CNN, January 26, 2017. www.cnn.com.
Smyth, Patrick. 2018. "Migration and 'Dublin Regulation' Concerns Continue to Simmer." *Irish Times*, May 10, 2018. www.irishtimes.com.

Social Trends Institute. 2017. "The Cohabitation-Go-Round: Cohabitation and Family Instability Across the Globe." Social Trends Institute and Institute for Family Studies, World Family Map 2017. http://worldfamilymap.ifstudies.org.

Solomon, Josh. 2016. "Dazed Cedar Key Deals with the Aftermath of Hurricane Hermine." *Tampa Bay Tribune*, September 3, 2016. www.tampabay.com.

Solomon, Susan, and Gian-Kasper Plattner, Reto Knutti, and Pierre Friedlingstein. 2009. "Irreversible Climate Change due to Carbon Dioxide Emissions." *Proceedings of the National Academies of Sciences of the United States* 106, no. 6: 1704–9.

Spazioconsulte. n.d. "Notizie dal Ministero." https://spazioconsulte.it.

Specter, Francesca. 2017. "Hope or Hype?: The Chilling Truth about Freezing Your Eggs." *Guardian*, November 6, 2017. www.theguardian.com.

Sprenger, Anne-Sylvie. 2019. "La Liberte de conscience ne commence pas a 18 ans!" Reformes. www.reformes.ch.

Stack, Carol. 1974. *All Our Kin: Strategies for Survival in a Black Community*. New York: Harper & Row.

Stahel, Walter R. 2016. "Comment: Circular Economy." *Nature*, March 24, 2016, 435–38.

Stalford, Helen, and Eleanor Drywood. 2011. "Using the CRC to Inform EU Law and Policy." In *Human Rights of Children: From Visions to Implementation*, edited by Antonella Invernizzi and Jane Williams, 199–218. Farnham, UK: Ashgate.

Stapinski, Helene. 2017. "When America Barred Italians." *New York Times*, June 2, 2017. www.nytimes.com.

Stark, Barbara. 2018. "Introduction: The Trump Administration and Children's Human Rights." *Family Court Review* 56, no. 2: 283–86.

Steger, Manfred B. 2017. *Globalization: A Very Short Introduction*. 4th ed. Oxford: Oxford University Press.

Steiner-Adair, Catherine, and Teresa H. Barker. 2013. *The Big Disconnect: Protecting Childhood and Family Relationships in the Digital Age*. Kindle edition. New York: Harper Collins.

Stiglitz, Joseph. 2002. *Globalization and Its Discontents*. New York: W. W. Norton.

Stiglitz, Joseph. 2012. *The Price of Inequality: How Today's Divided Society Endangers Our Future*. New York: W. W. Norton.

Stiglitz, Joseph. 2015. *The Great Divide: Unequal Societies and What We Can Do About Them*. New York: W.W. Norton.

Stiglitz, Joseph. 2016. *Rewriting the Rules of the American Economy: An Agenda for Growth and Shared Prosperity*. New York: W. W. Norton.

Stiglitz, Joseph. 2017. *Globalization and Its Discontents Revisited: Anti-Globalization in the Era of Trump*. New York: W. W. Norton.

Stone, Lyman. 2018. "How Many Kids Do Women Want?" Institute for Family Studies, June 1, 2018. https//ifstudies.org.

Strauss, Valerie. 2018. "Why It Matters Who Governs America's Public Schools." *Washington Post*, November 4, 2018. www.washingtonpost.com.

Stuckler, David, and Sanjay Basu. 2013. *The Body Economic: Why Austerity Kills*. New York: Basic Books.

Swansea Council. 2014. "Children and Young People's Rights Scheme." https://swansea.gov.uk.
Swanson, Ana. 2015. "The Incredible Decline of American Unions, in One Animated Map." *Washington Post*, February 24, 2015. www.washingtonpost.com.
Tebano, Elena. 2018. "Feondazione eterologa, alla Corte Costituzionale il recorso che potrebbe aprirla alle coppie lesbiche." *Corriere della Sera*, July 4, 2018. www.corriere.it.
Terra di Resilienza. 2018. "Chi Siamo." www.terradiresilienza.it.
Thakrar, Ashish P., Alexandra D. Forrest, Mitchell G. Maltenfort, and Christopher B. Forrest. 2018. "Child Mortality in the US and 19 OECD Comparator Nations: A 50-Year Time Trend Analysis." *Health Affairs* 37, no. 1: 140–49.
Tocqueville, Alexis de. [1835] 2003. *Democracy in America and Two Essays on America*. London: Penguin Books.
Todres, Jonathan. 2006. "The Importance of Realizing 'Other Rights' to Prevent Sex Trafficking." *Cardozo Journal of Law and Gender* 12, no. 3: 885–907.
Todres, Jonathan, Mark E. Wojcik, and Cris Revaz. 2006. *The United Nations Convention on the Rights of the Child: An Analysis of Treaty Provisions and Implications for US Ratification*. Leiden, Netherlands: Brill/Nijhoff.
Todres, Jonathan, and Sarah Higinbotham. 2015. *Human Rights in Children's Literature: Imagination and the Narrative of Law*. New York: Oxford University Press.
Torbati, Yeganeh and Mica Rosenberg. 2017. "Trump Administration Reverses Policy on Fiancés as Travel Ban Takes Effect." Reuters, June 29, 2017. www.reuters.com.
Tough, Paul. 2009. *Whatever It Takes: Geoffrey Canada's Quest to Change Harlem and America*. New York: First Mariner Books.
TravelFeel. 2015. "Scanno, Aquila." YouTube. https://www.youtube.com.
Trisi, Danilo, and Ladonna Pavetti. 2012. "TANF Weakening as a Safety Net For Poor Families." Center for Budget and Policy Priorities. www.cbpp.org.
Tuttitalia. 2018. "Scanno." www.tuttitalia.it.
UN General Assembly. 2018. "Report of the Special Rapporteur on Extreme Poverty and Human Rights on His Mission to the United States of America." UN document A/HRC/38/33/Add.1, HRC, 38th Session, May 4, 2018. https://documents-dds-ny.un.org.
UNDP. 2011. "Human Development Report 2011–Sustainability and Equity: A Better Future for All." http://hdr.undp.org.
UNDP. n.d. For Human Development Index and its components. http://hdr.undp.org.
UN IGME. 2017. "Levels and Trends in Child Mortality Report 2017, Estimates Developed by the UN Inter-agency Group for Child Mortality Estimation." United Nations Children Fund. https://childmortality.org.
UNESCO. 2018. Glossary: "Globalisation." https://unesco.org.
UNICEF. 2000. "A League Table of Child Poverty in Rich Nations: Innocenti Report Card Issue No. 1." UNICEF Innocenti Research Centre. www.unicef-irc.org.
UNICEF. 2001a. "A League Table of Child Deaths by Injury in Rich Nations: Innocenti Report Card Issue No. 2." UNICEF Innocenti Research Centre. www.unicef-irc.org.

UNICEF. 2001b. "A League Table of Teenage Births in Rich Nations: Innocenti Report Card Issue No. 3." UNICEF Innocenti Research Centre. www.unicef-irc.org.
UNICEF. 2002. "A League Table of Educational Disadvantage in Rich Nations: Innocenti Report Card Issue No. 4." UNICEF Innocenti Research Centre. www.unicef-irc.org.
UNICEF. 2003a. "A League Table of Child Maltreatment Deaths in Rich Nations: Innocenti Report Card Issue No. 5." UNICEF Innocenti Research Centre. www.unicef-irc.org.
UNICEF. 2003b. *Building a World Fit for Children: The United Nations General Assembly Special Session on Children, 8–10 May 2002.* New York: UNICEF.
UNICEF. 2005. "Child Poverty in Rich Countries 2005: Innocenti Report Card 6." UNICEF Innocenti Research Centre. www.unicef-irc.org.
UNICEF. 2006. "Cities with Children: Child-Friendly Cities in Italy." www.unicef-irc.org.
UNICEF. 2007. "Child Poverty in Perspective: An Overview of Child Well-being in Rich Countries: Innocenti Report Card 7." UNICEF Innocenti Research Centre. www.unicef-irc.org.
UNICEF. 2008. "The Child Care Transition—A League Table of Early Childhood Education and Care in Economically Advanced Countries: Report Card 8." UNICEF Innocenti Research Centre. www.unicef-irc.org.
UNICEF. 2010. "The Children Left Behind—A League Table of Inequality in Child Well-Being in the World's Rich Countries: Innocenti Report Card 9." Florence: UNICEF Innocenti Research Centre. www.unicef-irc.org.
UNICEF. 2012. "Measuring Child Poverty—New League Tables of Child Poverty in the World's Rich Countries: Innocenti Report Card 10." UNICEF Innocenti Research Centre. www.unicef-irc.org.
UNICEF. 2013. "Child Well-Being in Rich Countries—A Comparative Overview: Innocenti Report Card 11." UNICEF Innocenti Research Centre. www.unicef-irc.org.
UNICEF. 2014a. "Background on Human Rights." www.unicef.org.
UNICEF. 2014b. "Children of the Recession—The Impact of the Economic Crisis on Child Well-being in Rich Countries: Innocenti Report Card 12." UNICEF Innocenti Research Centre. www.unicef-irc.org.
UNICEF. 2016. "Fairness for Children: A League Table of Inequality in Child Well-being in Rich Countries: Innocenti Report Card 13." UNICEF Innocenti Research Centre. www.unicef-irc.org.
UNICEF. 2017. "Building the Future—Children and the Sustainable Development Goals in Rich Countries: Innocenti Report Card 14." UNICEF Innocenti Research Centre. www.unicef-irc.org.
UNICEF. 2018a. "An Unfair Start—Inequality in Children's Education in Rich Countries: Innocenti Report Card 15." Florence: Innocenti Research Centre. www.unicef-irc.org.
UNICEF. 2018b. Child-Friendly Cities Handbook. https://childfriendlycities.org.
UNICEF Data. n.d. For maternal mortality; statistics by topic and country https://data.unicef.org.

UNICEF Data. n.d. For under-five mortality rates in Italy and the United States; statistics by topic and country. http://data.unicef.org.
UNICEF Office of Research. 2014. *The Challenges of Climate Change: Children on the Front Line*. Florence: Innocenti Insight, UNICEF Office of Research.
Unicef USA. n.d. "Unicef USA." www.unicefusa.org.
United Nations. 2017. *New Urban Agenda*. United Nations Conference on Housing and Sustainable Urban Development. Quito, October 17–20, 2016. A/RES/71/256. http://habitat3.org.
US Census Bureau. For Annual Estimates of the Resident Population: April 1, 2010 to July 1, 2016 Population Estimates. https://factfinder.census.gov.
US Census Bureau. n.d. For Statistical Abstract of the United States: 2012—Section 30 International Statistics: Table 1355–Births to Unmarried Women by Country. www.census.gov.
US Climate Alliance. n.d. "States United for Climate Change." https://www.usclimatealliance.org.
US Zip Codes. n.d. www.unitedstateszipcodes.org.
University of Florida/Institute of Food and Agricultural Sciences. 2018. "Nature Coast Biological Station." https://ncbs.ifas.ufl.edu.
US Citizenship and Immigration Services. 2013. "US Citizenship." www.uscis.gov.
US Department of Education. 2015. *A Matter of Equity: Preschool in America*. Washington DC: US Department of Education. http://www2.ed.gov.
US Department of Health and Human Services. 2000. "Child Welfare Outcomes 1998: Annual Report." Washington DC: US Department of Health and Human Services, Children's Bureau. acf.hhs.gov.
US Department of Health and Human Services. 2013. "AFCARS Report No. 20: Preliminary FY 2012 Estimates as of November 2013." US Department of Health and Human Services, Children's Bureau. www.acf.hhs.gov.
US Department of Health and Human Services. 2015. "The Health and Well-Being of Children in Rural Areas: A Portrait of the Nation, 2011–2012." US Department of Health and Human Services, Health Resources and Services Administration, Maternal and Child Health Bureau. https://mchb.hrsa.gov.
USDA Economic Research Service. n.d. "Definitions of Food Security." www.ers.usda.gov.
USDA Food and Nutrition Service. 2011. "SNAP Participants by Age: Distribution of SNAP/FSP Participants by Age and Year." USDA.www.ers.usda.gov.
USDA Food and Nutrition Service. 2014a. "Supplemental Nutrition Assistance Program." www.fns.usda.gov.
USDA Food and Nutrition Service. 2014b. "Supplemental Nutrition Assistance Program Participation and Costs." www.fns.usda.gov.
Vatican Radio. 2014. "Pope at Audience: If We Destroy Creation, It Will Destroy Us." News release, May 21, 2014. http://en.radiovaticana.va.
Vatican Radio. 2015. "Pope Francis: Economy Must Have Human Person at Its Heart." News release, January 11, 2015. http://en.radiovaticana.va.

Veerman, Philip E. 1992. *The Rights of the Child and the Changing Image of Childhood*. Leiden: Martinus Nijohff.

"The Village of Castrovalva." n.d. http://italia.indettaglio.it.

Voyles, Karen. 2003. "Up from the Ashes." *Gainesville Sun*, October 31, 2003. www.gainesville.com.

Waldfogel, Jane. 2006. *What Children Need*. Cambridge, MA: Harvard University Press.

Walker, Matthew. 2017. Unpublished interview of Matthew Walker of the Campaign for Welsh Youth Parliament by Barbara Bennett Woodhouse, October 16, 2017.

Wall, John. 2010. *Ethics in Light of Childhood*. Washington DC: Georgetown University Press.

Wall, John. 2016. *Children's Rights: Today's Global Challenge*. Lanham, MD: Rowman & Littlefield.

Walt, Stephen M. 2011. "The Myth of American Exceptionalism." *Foreign Policy*, October 11, 2011. http://foreignpolicy.com.

Warren, Elizabeth. 2017. *This Fight Is Our Fight: The Battle to Save America's Middle Class*. New York: Metropolitan Books.

Watts, Jonathan. 2019. "Greta Thunberg: Schoolgirl Climate Change Warrior: 'Some People Can Let Things Go. I Can't.'" *Guardian*, March 11, 2019. www.theguardian.com.

WCJB Television. 2019. "TV 20 Meldon Scholar Athlete Jasmin Jackson (Cedar Key)." January 23, 2019. www.wcjb.com.

Welsh Youth Parliament. 2018. "Hi, We're the National Youth Parliament." http://youthparliament.wales.

Whelan, Daniel J. 2010. *Indivisible Human Rights: A History*. Philadelphia: University of Pennsylvania Press.

Whitehurst, Grover J., and Michelle Croft. 2010. "The Harlem Children's Zone, Promise Neighborhoods, and the Broader, Bolder Approach to Education." Brown Center on Education Policy, Brookings Institution. www.brookings.edu.

Wikipedia. 2016. "August 2016 Central Italy Earthquake." https://en.wikipedia.org.

Wikipedia. 2018a. "Cedar Key, Florida." https://en.wikipedia.org.

Wikipedia. 2018b. "Palio di Siena." https://en.wikipedia.org.

Wikipedia. 2018c. "Scanno, Aquila." at https://en.wikipedia.org.

Wikipedia. 2018d. "Sulmona, Aquila." https://en.wikipedia.org.

Wikipedia. 2018e. "Questo nostro amore." https://it.wikipedia.org.

Wikipedia. 2018f. "One Child Policy." https://en.wikipedia.org.

Wikipedia. 2018g. "Romanian Orphans." www.wikipedia.com.

Wikivoyage. 2016. "Scanno." https://it.wikivoyage.org.

Wilcox, W. Bradford. 2018. "Renewing Family in Working-Class America." Institute for Family Studies, November 29, 2018. https://ifstudies.org.

Wilcox, W. Bradford and Laurie DeRose. 2017. "The Cohabitation Go Round: Cohabitation and Family Instability Across the Globe." World Family Map, Social Trends Institute and Institute for Family Studies. https://worldfamilymap.ifstudies.org.

Williams, Jane. 2013. "Funky Dragon's Children as Researchers Project: A New Way of Enabling Participation." In *The United Nations Convention on the Rights of the Child in Wales*, edited by Jane Williams, 195–206. Cardiff: University of Wales Press.

Wilson, William Julius. 1987. *The Truly Disadvantaged: The Inner City, the Underclass, and Public Policy*. Chicago: University of Chicago Press.

Wilts, Teresa. 2015. "Q and A: How the Great Recession Affected Children." Stateline: An Initiative of the Pew Charitable Trusts. www.pewtrusts.org.

Witt, Terry. 2018. "Board Members, Superintendent, Defend Transfer of Cedar Key Principal to Williston." Spotlight on Levy County Government, June 12, 2018. www.spotlightonlevycountrygovernment.com.

Wood, Joanne N., Sheyla P. Medina, Chris Feudtner, Xianqun Luan, Russell Localio, Evan S. Fieldston, and David M. Rubin. 2012. "Local Macroeconomic Trends and Hospital Admissions for Child Abuse, 2000–2009." *Pediatrics* 130, no. 2: 358–64.

Woodhouse, Barbara Bennett. 1992. "'Who Owns The Child?': *Meyer* and *Pierce* and the Child as Property." *William and Mary Law Review* 33, no. 4: 995–1122.

Woodhouse, Barbara Bennett. 1993. "Hatching the Egg: A Child-Centered Perspective on Parents' Rights." *Cardozo Law Review* 14, no. 6: 1747–865.

Woodhouse, Barbara Bennett. 1999. "The Constitutionalization of Children's Rights: Incorporating Emerging Human Rights into Constitutional Doctrine." *University of Pennsylvania Journal of Constitutional Law* 2, no. 1 (Symposium): 1–52.

Woodhouse, Barbara Bennett. 2001. "Youthful Indiscretions: Culture, Class Status, and the Passage to Adulthood." *DePaul Law Review* 51, no. 3: 743–768.

Woodhouse, Barbara Bennett. 2002. "Making Poor Mothers Fungible: The Privatization of Foster Care." In *Child Care and Inequality: Rethinking Carework for Children and Youth*, edited by Francesca M. Cancian, Demie Kurz, Andrew S. London, Rebecca Reviere and Mary C. Tuominen, 83–98. New York: Routledge.

Woodhouse, Barbara Bennett. 2004. "Reframing the Debate about the Socialization of Children: An Environmentalist Paradigm." *University of Chicago Legal Forum* 2004 (2004): 85–165.

Woodhouse, Barbara Bennett. 2005. "Ecogenerism: An Environmentalist Approach to Protecting Endangered Children." *Virginia Journal of Social Policy and Law* 12, no. 3 (Symposium): 409–47.

Woodhouse, Barbara Bennett. 2006a. "Cleaning Up Toxic Violence: An Ecogenerist Paradigm" in Dowd et al. 2006, 415–36.

Woodhouse, Barbara Bennett. 2006b. "The Family-Supportive Nature of the UN Convention on the Rights of the Child." In Todres et al. 2006, 37–49.

Woodhouse, Barbara Bennett. 2008a. *Hidden in Plain Sight: The Tragedy of Children's Rights From Ben Franklin To Lionel Tate*. Princeton NJ: Princeton University Press.

Woodhouse, Barbara Bennett. 2008b. "Individualism and Early Childhood in the US: How Culture and Tradition Have Impeded Evidence-Based Reform." *Journal of Korean Law* 8, no. 1: 135–60.

Woodhouse, Barbara Bennett. 2009a. "A World Fit for Children Is a World Fit for Everyone: Ecogenerism, Feminism, and Vulnerability." *Houston Law Review* 46, no. 3 (Symposium): 817–65.

Woodhouse, Barbara Bennett. 2009b. "The Courage of Innocence: Children as Heroes in the Struggle for Justice." *University of Illinois Law Review*, 2009, no. 5: 1567–90.

Woodhouse, Barbara Bennett. 2010. "An Ecogenerist Model of Vulnerability, Resilience, and the Responsive State." Paper presented at "Vulnerability, Resilience and the State: A Feminism and Legal Theory Project Workshop," Emory University School of Law, Atlanta, Georgia, March 2010.

Woodhouse, Barbara Bennett. 2014a. "Listening to Children: Participation Rights of Minors in Italy and the United States." *Journal of Social Welfare & Family Law*, 36, no. 4: 358–69.

Woodhouse, Barbara Bennett. 2014b. "Intercountry Adoption in Italy and the United States: Divergent Approaches to Privatization, Discrimination, and Subsidiarity." In *Parents and Children in a Narrowing World: Adoption in Comparative Perspective*, edited by Maria Donata Panforte, 66–86. Modena, IT: Mucchi Editore.

Woodhouse, Barbara Bennett, and Charles F. Woodhouse. 2018. "Children's Rights and the Politics of Food: Big Food Versus Little People." *Family Court Review* 56, no.2: 287–307.

World Bank. For adolescent fertility rate: births per 1,000 women ages 15–19 for the United States and Italy; accessed May 22, 2015. https://data.worldbank.org.

World Bank. For birth rate, crude per 1,000 people; accessed June 18, 2016. https://beta.data.worldbank.org.

World Bank. For birth rate, crude per 1,000 people—1960 to 2016; accessed January 9, 2018 http://data.worldbank.org.

World Bank. For fertility rate, total, births per women 2016; accessed January 19, 2019. https://data.worldbank.org.

World Bank. For GDP per capita (current US$): 2015 World Bank national accounts data, and OECD National Accounts data files; accessed May 20, 2017. https://data.worldbank.org.

World Bank. For Gini index World Bank estimate, accessed July 4, 2018. https://data.worldbank.org.

World Bank. For health expenditure per capita; accessed June 17, 2016. https://data.worldbank.org.

World Bank. For life expectancy at birth, total (years) for United States, high income: OECD, Italy; accessed April 22, 2016. https://beta.data.worldbank.org.

World Bank. For mortality rate, infant, per 1,000 live births; accessed January 7, 2019. https://data.worldbank.org.

World Bank. For population density (people per sq. km. of land area); accessed May 10, 2019. https://data.worldbank.org.

World Bank. For unemployment, youth total 2016; accessed July 22, 2017. http://data.worldbank.org.

World Economic Forum. 2011. "Global Competitiveness Report: 2011–2012." Edited by Klaus Schwab. http://reports.weforum.org.
World Economic Forum. For Global Competitiveness Index; accessed July 4, 2018. http://reports.weforum.org.
World Economic Forum. For Global Competitiveness Index 2017–2018 Edition: Italy; accessed July 4, 2018. http://reports.weforum.org.
World Health Organization. For Global Health Observatory Data: country profiles for Italy and the United States; accessed June 17, 2016. http://apps.who.int.
World Health Organization, UNICEF, UNFPA, World Bank Group, and United Nations Population Division. 2015. "Trends in Maternal Mortality: 1990–2015: Estimates by WHO, UNICEF, UNFPA, World Bank Group, and the United Nations Population Division." WHO Document Production Services. http://apps.who.int.
World Population Review. 2019. "Florida Population." http://worldpopulationreview.com.
"World Population Trends." United Nations Population Fund; accessed July 22, 2017. www.unfpa.org.
Wu, Tim. 2018. "Be Afraid of Bigness; Be Very Afraid." *New York Times*, November 10, 2018. www.nytimes.com.
Yanovich, Liza. 2015. "Children Left Behind: The Impact of Labor Migration in Moldova and Ukraine." Migration Policy Institute. www.migrationpolicy.org.
Yogman, Michael, Andrew Garner, Jeffrey Hutchinson, Kathy Hirsh-Pasek and Roberta M. Golinkoff. 2018. AAP Committee on Psychosocial Aspects of Child and Family Health, AAP Council on Communication and Media, "The Power of Play: A Pediatric Role in Enhancing Development in Young Children." Pediatrics 142, no. 3: https://pediatrics.aapublications.org.
Zagorsky, Jay, Michelle Schlesinger, and Robert Sege. 2010. "What Happens to Child Maltreatment When Unemployment Goes up?" Paper presented at the 2010 National Conference and Exhibition of the American Academy of Pediatrics, San Francisco, California, October 2010. https://aap.confex.com.
Zakaria, Fareed. 2018. "The 'Yellow Vest' Protests Add to a New Dividing Line in Western Politics." *New York Times*, December 13, 2018. www.nytimes.com.
Zero to Three. 2013. "Building a Secure and Healthy Start: Family Leave in the Early Years." March 11, 2013. www.zerotothree.org.
Zero to Three. 2017. "The Child Development Case for a National Paid Family and Medical Leave Program." February 7, 2017. www.zerotothree.org.
Zumbrun, Josh. 2016. "Behind the Ongoing US Baby Bust, in 5 Charts." *Wall Street Journal*, June 7, 2016. https://blogs.wsj.com.

STATUTES

Constitution of the Republic of South Africa, adopted May 8, 1996, amended October 11, 1996. justice.gov.za.
European Union Official Journal, L150, Vol. 61, June 14, 2018. https://eur-lex.europa.eu.
Family and Medical Leave Act, 29 USC §2601(1993).

Legge 19 febbraio 2004, n. 40 (It.).
Legge n. 113/2018. https://temi.camera.it.
National Environmental Policy Act, 42 USC 4321(1970).

BRIEFS

Brief of Child Advocacy Organizations as Amici Curiae in Support of Petitioners on the Minimum Coverage Provision Question, Department of Health and Human Services v. State of Florida, 132 S.Ct. 1133 (2012) (No. 11–398).

GRAND JURY REPORTS

Commonwealth of Pennsylvania Statewide Investigating Grand Jury. August 14, 2018. Fortieth Statewide Investigating Grand Jury, Report 1, Interim—Redacted. http://media-downloads.pacourts.us. Accessed August 29, 2018.

CASES

Brown v. Board of Education of Topeka, 347 US 483 (1954).
Brown v. Entertainment Merchants Association, 564 US 786 (2011).
Corte Cost., 30 gennaio 2002, n.1, 2002a (It.)
Corte Cost., 22 novembre 2002, n. 467, 2002b (It.) (asilo nido and right to education).
Corte Cost., 27 gennaio 2010, n. 4, 2010 (It.) (aides for children with disabilities).
Corte Cost., 9 aprile 2014, n. 162, 2014 (It.) (assisted conception).
Corte Const., 6 aprile 2018, n. 107, 2018 (It.) (asilo nido antidiscrimination and education rights).
DeShaney v. Winnebago County Department of Social Services, 489 US 189 (1989).
Endrew F. v. Douglas County School District, RE-1, 580 US ___ (2017).
In re Gault, 387 US 1 (1967).
Juliana v. US, 217 F. Supp. 3d 1224 (D. Or. 2016).
King v. Burwell, 135 S. Ct. 2480 (2015).
National Federation of Independent Business v. Sebelius, 132 S.Ct. 2566 (2012).
Palmore v. Sidoti, 466 US 429 (1984).
Parents Involved in Community Schools v. Seattle School Dist. No. 1, 551 US 701 (2007).
San Antonio Independent School District v. Rodriguez, 411 US 1 (1973).
SH v. Austria, App. No. 57813/00, Eur. Ct. HR (2010).
Village of Euclid v. Ambler Realty Co., 272 US 365 (1926).

MULTILATERAL TREATIES

Association of South East Asian Nations (ASEAN), ASEAN Human Rights Declaration, adopted November 18, 2012.
Convention on the Rights of the Child, entry into force September 2, 1990, 1577 UNTS 3.
Convention relating to the Status of Refugees, entry into force April 22, 1954, 189 UNTS 137.

Optional Protocol to the Convention on Rights of the Child on a Communications Procedure, entry into force April 14, 2014, A/RES/66/138.

Organization of African Unity (OAU), African Charter on the Rights and Welfare of the Child, July 11, 1990, CAB/LEG/24.9/49 (1990).

Organization of American States (OAS), Additional Protocol to the American Convention on Human Rights in the Area of Economic, Social and Cultural Rights ("Protocol of San Salvador"), A-52 (November 16, 1999).

Protocol relating to the Status of Refugees, entry into force October 4, 1967, 606 UNTS 267.

United Nations Declaration on the Rights of Indigenous Peoples, adopted September 13, 2007, A/RES/61/295.

Universal Declaration on Human Rights, GA Res. 217A, UN Doc. A/810 (1948).

INDEX

AAP. *See* American Academy of Pediatrics
abortions, 110–11
abuse. *See* child abuse
ACA. *See* Affordable Care Act
ACE. *See* Alliance for Climate Change
ACEs. *See* adverse experiences in childhood
addiction treatment, 249–51
adolescent birth rates, 168
adolescent fertility rate, 102
adoption (*kafala*), 22; family reunification or, 250; right to, 253–56. *See also* intercountry adoption
adulthood, 27
adverse experiences in childhood (ACEs), 9
AFDC. *See* Aid to Families with Dependent Children
Affordable Care Act (ACA), 145–46
Africa, 100, 136–37, 209
African Americans, 198–99, 221; communal identity of, 85; Mokgoro, 136–37; Rosewood Massacre of, 68–69. *See also* Harlem Children's Zone
African Union, 209
"after-tax and transfer income" (ATTI), 159
age, 217, 242, 244; childhood development stages related to, 16–17, 18, *18*; laws related to, 16–17; mothers' reproductive, 101–2, 110; sandwich generation and, 106; in school grouping, 79–80
age sets, 80–81
agrarian society, 17

Aid to Families with Dependent Children (AFDC), 149, 159–60
Albertson, Martha, 27–28
Alexander, Michelle, 198
Alliance for Climate Change (ACE), 297
All Our Kin: Strategies for Survival in the Black Community (Stack), 24
Alston, Philip G., 163–66
"Amara Terra Mia," 192
American Academy of Pediatrics (AAP), 182, 227
"American dream," 187
American law, 15
American Recovery Act, 178
American Recovery and Reinvestment Act of 2009 (ARRA), 142, 144, 145
Ancient Voices (*Voci Antiche*), 97, 98
animals, 42–43; rights of children accused of crimes and, 243–44
Anthony (saint), 46, *46*, 47
anti-immigrant populism, 73, 107, 109
anti-Semitism, 69
Anversa degli Abruzzi, Italy, 179–80, 192, 228, *228*
architecture, 287
ARRA. *See* American Recovery and Reinvestment Act of 2009
ART. *See* "assisted reproductive technology"
Article 12, of CRC, 223–24, 236
Asilo Buon Pastore (nursery school), 59, *59*, 88, 229
asilo nido (shelter nest), 125–26; system system, 79
ASL (*azienda sanitaria locale*), 120

341

342 | INDEX

"assisted reproductive technology" (ART), 108
ATTI. *See* "after-tax and transfer income"
authenticity, 41
autism spectrum, 256–57
azienda sanitaria local (ASL), 120

"Baby Bonus," 122–23
"Baby Bust," 106, 161–62
"Baby College," 276
baby-making, 112
Baby Milk Action, 169
Banca della Terra Campana (Campana Land Bank), 299
bancarella, 231, 231–33, 232
Barbarino, James, 18
Barker, Teresa H., 180–81
bartering, 179–80
Barzanti, Monica, 251
Basilica of Santa Maria della Sanità, 269
The Bell Curve (Murray), 276
Benedetto XVI (pope emeritus), 176
Bennett, William, 199
Bergoglio, Jorge. *See* Francis I
Berlusconi, Silvio, 178
"best interest," 217
The Big Disconnect (Steiner-Adair and Barker), 180–81
"bigness," 260–61. *See also* smallness
Bill of Rights, US, 25–26, 210
birthplace, 192; identity related to, 174–75
birth rate decline, 168; ART for, 108; "child free" choice in, 113; choice and, 97; economics and, 97–98, 113–14, 118; Italian public policy in, 117–19; in US, 106–8
birth rate factors: adolescent fertility rate as, 102; crude birth rates, 100; domestic labor gender as, 105–6; mothers' marital status as, 102–3; mothers' reproductive age as, 101–2; workforce women percentage as, 103–4
birthright citizenship (*jus soli*), 108–9

boat migration, 193–94
boats, 65
Body Count: Moral Poverty (Bennett, Diullio, and Walters), 199
Boeri, Tito, 104, 107
bonfires, 89–90
"bonus babysitter," 122–23
The Boy Who Was Raised as a Dog and Other Stories from a Child Psychiatrist's Notebook: What Traumatized Children Can Teach Us About Loss, Love, and Healing (Perry and Szalavitz), 175–76
breast feeding, 168–69
Brexit, 169
Bronfenbrenner, Urie, 3, 18
Brown v. Board of Education (1954), 210, 223, 274
Brown v. Entertainment Merchants Association (2011), 185
Buffett, Jimmy, 57, 58
Buffett, Warren, 131
Bush, George H. W., 300
Bush, Jeb, 69

Campaign for a Children and Young People's Assembly for Wales, 291–92
Campana Land Bank (Banca della Terra Campana), 299
Canada (nation), 99
Canada, Geoffrey, 275–77, 279; Loffredo compared to, 280–82
capitalism: death related to, 176; in economics, 36–37; "finding America" in, 179; in globalization, 176–79; triangulation and, 179–80; "trickle-down theories" in, 176, 177; after World War II, 178, 179–80
caregivers, 116–17. *See also* grandparents
Carter, Jimmy, 263
Casa del Monacone, Naples, Italy, 273
Castrovalva, Italy, 97, 98
Catholic Church, 44, 58–59, 87–88, 266; child abuse within, 37; first commu-

nion in, 32, 44, 47–48, 252; outreach of, 281. *See also* Francis I
Cedar Key, Florida, 12, *52*, *62*; authenticity in, 41; buildings in, 55, 56; culture of, 24, 25; demographics of, 51, 53–54; history of, *49*, 49–51; home in, 35–36; hurricanes in, 51–52; land in, 55–56; location of, 34–35, *35*, 48–49, *49*, 51; Native Americans of, 49–50; pride in, 41; race in, 53, 68–69, 70–72; racism and, 68–69, 70–72; in Reconstruction, 51; religion in, 60, *60*; researcher in, 36; Seminole Wars and, 50; status in, 36; surrogate parents in, 61–62; tourism in, 56, 57, *57*; tradition in, 56; in US Civil War, 51. *See also* comparisons
Cedar Key children, 52; education of, 53, 54–55, *55*, 60; playing by, 54–55, 56
Cedar Key School: church and, 82–83; Homecoming Spirit Week at, 86, *86*; Madrigal Dinner at, *82*, 82–83; Sharks at, 54–55, 71, 81–82, 86, 91–92
CENSIS study, 113–15, 117–19
CFC. *See* child-friendly cities
charisma, 275
charter schools, 276–79
child, definition of, 217
child abuse, 148–50; within Catholic Church, 37
childbirth, 120–21. *See also* birthplace
child development: "educare" and, 124; globalization and, 174–76; mothers' employment and, 104
"child free" choice, 113
child-friendly cities (CFC): Child Rights Situation Analysis in, 296; definition of, 295
child-friendly language, 213–16
childhood, 4; research on, 28–30
childhood development stages: age related to, 16–17, 18, *18*; ecological model and, 17–18; "social construct" of, 18
"Childhood Enders," 166–69
childhood environment, 9–10
child mortality rates, 21
child neglect, 150
child poverty: in Report Card Twelve, 153–54; in United Kingdom, 154
child poverty measurement, 135–39
child protection programs, 148–49
Child Protective Services, 6
Children of the Recession: The Impact of the Economic Crisis on Child Wellbeing in Rich Countries (Innocenti Centre). *See* Report Card Twelve
Children's Health Insurance Program (CHIP), 145, 147, 166
children's literature, 225–26
Children's Rights Charter, 294
Children's Rights Convention (CRC), 12, 190; African Union and, 209; Article 12 of, 223–24, 236; basic principles of, 213; CFC and, 295–96; child development integration in, 222–24; in child-friendly language, 213–16; "ecogenerism" from, 14; implementation of, 218–20; indivisibility of, 220–21; "legal fiction" related to, 222–23; majority age in, 17; overarching principles of, 217–18; parents' rights related to, 223; positive rights in, 222; public-private divide and, 221–22; reports in, 219; resolutions on, 290; "rights" in, 25, 214; smallness related to, 261; States Parties in, 213, 218, 219, 223–24, 234; variations on, 222; in Wales, 291
Children's Rights Unit (CRU), 294
children's voices, 290–91; in CRC affects, 225–26; in playing, 233–34; in right to participation, 240
Child Rights Situation Analysis, 296
child soldiers, 219–20
child well-being self-reports, 155
China's one-child policy, 110–11
CHIP. *See* Children's Health Insurance Program

Christian denominations, 87
church, 82–83. *See also* Catholic Church
Church of England, 212
Ciambella, 227–29, *228*, 233
circular economy, 267–68, 286–88
citizen protests, 121, 188
citizenship: in EU, 109; *jus soli*, 108–9; in US, 108–9
Civil War, US, 51
climate, 261–62
climate activists, 301–2; Philogene as, 297–98; science denialism and, 297
climate change, 235; Francis on, 200–201, 203; globalization and, 200–203, 208; Obama and, 298; smallness, economics and, 267; solidarity and, 200, 203
Clinton, Bill, 123, 149, 260, 289
Clinton, Hillary, 162
Colella, Anna Maria, 255–56
communal identity, 84–85
communication, 243, 245; languages, 66–67, 213–16, 257, 271
communities, 269–70; farming, 298–300; in rights to identity and family, 249–51. *See also* faith community
Community Supported Agriculture (CSA), 300
comparative method, 14, 20; "functional equivalent" in, 22; intergenerational support in, 22–23; "other" in, 22; principles of, 21–22
comparisons, 36; of demographics, 52–53; beyond description, 58; early childhood socialization and education in, 58–60, *59*, *60*; economic trauma and resilience in, 67–68; on "educare," 125; free play space access in, *59*, *60*, 60–62, *61*; Great American Recession related to, 131–32; land in, 55–56; natural disasters in, 63–65; racism in, 68–73; sense of history and place in, 65–67, *66*; from UNICEF, 21; value systems in, 62–63

competing social structure and institutions, 85–87, *86*
competition, 277–78; GCI, 134, 169–70; Global Competiveness Report, 133
conflict avoidance, 24
confraternita' (confraternity), 88
Constitution, of Italy, 118, 178, 188, 210
Constitution, of US, 209–10
constitutional rights, 209–11
contrade. *See* neighborhoods
Convento di San Antonio, *228*, 229
Cooper, Bob, 41
cooperatives, 270
"core household chores," 105
corruption, 178
Cosenza, Maura, 24
costs: of "educare," Italy, 125; of "educare," US, 129–30
Council of Europe, 225, 241
"Countering the Geography of Discontent: Strategies for Left-Behind Places," 300
CRC. *See* Children's Rights Convention
CRC affects: children's literature and, 225–26; children's voice in, 225–26; music related to, 225; right to play as, 226–34, *228*, *231*, *232*
Creation, 37
crimes, 17; gang violence, 275; in La Sanità, 269. *See also* rights of children accused of crimes
"Crossroads: Change in Rural America," 63
CRU. *See* Children's Rights Unit
crude birth rates, 100
CSA. *See* Community Supported Agriculture
culture, 16, 73, 230; "Amara Terra Mia" in, 192; of Cedar Key, 24, 25; globalization and, 171
custody, 221, 241

day care, 110; "bonus babysitter" as, 122–23; in "educare," US, 127–28, 129–30
deaths: abortions, 110–11; adoption and, 250; capitalism related to, 176; child mortality rates, 21; from earthquakes, 64; infant mortality rates, 119, 163–64, 166, 167; maternal mortality rates, 119; suicide, 168, 219
Declaration of Independence, US, 210
Defenders of Children Initiative, 295–96
DeGregory, Lane, 72
demographers, 11
demographics: of Cedar Key, 51, 53–54; comparisons of, 52–53; of Scanno, 42, 52–53. *See also* fertility demographics
depopulation, 299–300
destinies, 202–3
developmental equality theory, 285–86
dialect, 61; poetry in, 66–67, 227, 253, 255, 255
Di Gennaro, Angelo, 230–31
disabilities. *See* right to children with disabilities inclusion
discrimination, 286
Diullio, John, 199
Doek, Jaap, 219
domestic labor gender, 105–6
Donna de Scanno statue, 229, *231*, 232
Dowd, Nancy E., 198, 279, 285–86
Down syndrome, 258
"Dreamers," 109–10
dropouts, 167
drug addiction, 249–51
Duncan, Arne, 126–27
DuPree, Sherry, 72
Durkheim, Emile, 23

Earned Income Tax Credit (EITC), 159–60
earthquakes, 48, 63–64, 236, 238
Easton, David, 135
"ecogenerism," 14, 27, 208, 212–13, 285

ecological model: American law related to, 15; childhood development stages and, 17–18; definition of, 15; development of, 14–15; exosystems in, 19; laws related to, 15, 20; macrosystem in, 19–20; mesosystems in, 18–19; methods and, 20–21; microsystems in, 18; triangle of, 15; values in, 20
ecology, 15, 92
ecology of childhood diagram, 5, *5*
economic crisis, 7–9
economic mobility, 21
economics, 74, 260; "Baby Bonus" in, 122–23; bartering and, 179–80; birth rate decline and, 97–98, 113–14, 118; Brexit, 169; capitalism in, 36–37; Francis on, 174, 176; GCI in, 134, 169–70; Gini coefficient in, 133, 134; globalization and, 171; social welfare programs in, 92–93. *See also* inequality
economic trauma and resilience, 67–68
"educability," 78
"educare," 165–66; benchmarks for, 124–25; comparisons on, 125; as requirement, 124
"educare," Italy: *asilo nido* in, 125–26; children's centers in, 126; cost of, 125; *scuola d'infanzia* in, 125, 126
"educare," US: affluence and, 128; child labor and, 127; costs of, 129–30; day care in, 127–28, 129–30; Head Start in, 127, 128–29; lag of, 126–27; nursery schools in, 128; pre-kindergarten in, 127; race and, 128; risks in, 130
education, 58–59, *59*, *60*, 216; of Cedar Key children, 53, 54–55, *55*, *60*; dropouts in, 167; NEET and, 155, 161, 174; rights to, 246–49; right to participation on, 239; in Scanno, 42, 48, 184, *184*
EITC. *See* Earned Income Tax Credit
Elder, Glen H., Jr., 20
elder-care, 106

346 | INDEX

elderly, 153
employment protection, 178–79. *See also* unemployment
entitlements, 210
Erikson, Erik, 18; "ecogenerism" and, 27, 212
ethnography, 21, 24–25
EU. *See* European Union
Euclid v. Ambler (1926), 189
Europe: Brexit in, 169; family size in, 103. *See also specific countries*
European Court of Human Rights, 241
European Union (EU), 5, 194; citizenship in, 109; crude birth rates in, 100; economic crisis in, 8
evolution, 191
exclusion, 186
exosystems, 4, *4*, 5, *5*, 207; in ecological model, 19
exploitation, 216; from globalization, 173–74
"extra-communitarians," 197
"extreme poverty," 138, 163

fairness, 217
faith community: definitions of, 77; in solidarity, 77, 87–89
family, 75, 218; definitions of, 76; solidarity and, 76–77; stereotypes of, 116–17. *See also* rights to identity and family
Family and Medical Leave Act, 123
family law, 218
family life, isolation of, 32–33
family reunification, 249–50
family size, 103
family-supportive policies, 119–20
farming communities, 298–300; Future Farmers of America and, 288
fertility demographics: future related to, 99; Nanni on, 97, 98; in *National Geographic Atlas*, 98–99; social insurance in, 99–100

fertility measurement: crude birth rates on, 100; replacement rate fertility, 101; total fertility rate, 100–101
fertility rate decline, 97
"finding America," 179
Fineman, Martha Albertson, 28, 285
Finland, 138
first communion, 32, 44, 47–48, 83–84, *84*, 252
fishing, 67–68
Fist, Stick, Knife, Gun (Canada), 275
Five Star Movement (Movimento Cinque Stelle), 8–9
Florida High School Athletic Association, 82
food, 168; preservation of, 299; restoration of, 299; in school, 78–79, 143
"food deserts," 143
food insecurity, 140; malnutrition and, 167; NSLP and, 143; SNAP in, 141–42, 159, 166; stress of, 141, 143–44; WIC and, 142–43
food stamps. *See* SNAP
foreclosure, in housing instability, 144
foster care, 149
Fourth of July parade, 87
France, 170
Francis I (pope), 288; on climate change, 200–201, 203; on economics, 174, 176, 186; on environment, 38; on globalization, 172; on inequality, 186; on mass migration, 190–91, 193; against racial and ethnic discrimination, 196; on science, 37; on solidarity, 37–38; on technology, 180
free play space access, 59, 60, *60–62*, *61*
"Friendships," 226–27
Frozen, 151–52
Funky Dragon, 291–93
Future Farmers of America, 288

Gaddafi, Muammar Al, 193–94
Galbraith, John Kenneth, 266

gang violence, 275
GCI. *See* Global Competitiveness Index
GDP. *See* gross domestic product
gender, 105–6; age sets and, 80; Le Glorie di San Martino and, 90–91; in playing, 230–33, *231, 232*; of Sharks, 91–92
generativity, 27, 285
Genny, 234–37, *235*
Gentile, Enzo, 47–48, 66, 90
geography, 300; inequality related to, 189–90
Gini coefficient, 133, 134
Global Competitiveness Index (GCI), 134, 169–70
Global Competiveness Report, 133
global ecological model, 211–13
globalism, 202, 284
globalization, 10–11, 284; apocalypse of, 172; benefits of, 173; capitalism in, 176–79; child development and, 174–76; climate change and, 200–203, 208; definition of, 171–72; dimensions of, 172–73; employment and, 176; exosystems and, 173; exploitation from, 173–74; Francis on, 172; mass migration in, 190–95; playing and, 233; racial and ethnic discrimination in, 196–200; unemployment and, 173, 174. *See also* technology
Globalization: A Very Short Introduction (Steger), 171, 172–73
Le Glorie di San Martino (bonfire), 89–91, *90*
goals, 208, 224
Good Shepherd Nursery, 33, 58–59, *59*
Google Earth app, 98–99
Gore, Al, 202
grandparents, 22; *Nonni di Strada*, 244; in Scanno, 115–16
Great American Recession, 157, 172; child poverty measurement in, 135–39; comparisons related to, 131–32; dates of, 139; exceptionalism and, 131–32; factors related to, 132; GDP in, 132; well-being measurement in, 133–35
Great American Recession children: food insecurity of, 140–44; housing instability of, 144–45; maltreatment of, 148–50; poverty of, 139–40
Great American Recession children's health: ACA in, 145–47; CHIP in, 145, 147; "churning" for, 147; pregnancy in, 147–48
Great Recession, across Atlantic: ATTI in, 159; dominoes in, 158; EITC in, 159–60; "fiscal adjustments" in, 156; household income in, 157–58; industry in, 151; monetary policies in, 158–59; "one percenters" related to, 156; social exclusion in, 158; social protection systems in, 159; sovereign-debt crisis in, 157; TANF in, 149, 159–60; unemployment in, 151. *See also* Report Card Twelve
Great Recession, aftermath: mitigation in, 162; neurology in, 162; policies in, 162
Greece, 154, 156
Grillo, Beppe, 8–9
gross domestic product (GDP), 132
Growing up Rural in America, 166–69
Grubb, Norton, 75
Grusky, David, 189

Haley, Nikki, 165
Halloween, 89
Happy Planet Index (HPI), 133
Harlem Children's Zone (HCZ), 12, 268; Canada in, 275–77, 279–82; commitment to, 282; lottery in, 277–78; meritocracy in, 275–78, 280–81; metrics in, 281–82; privatization in, 281; replication of, 279, 280; results in, 278–79; La Sanità compared to, 280–82; segregation related to, 274
HCZ. *See* Harlem Children's Zone

HDI. *See* Human Development Index
Head Start, 127, 128–29
health, 119, 121, 166; of Great American Recession children, 145–48
health care, 119–20, 145–46, 166, 215
Higinbotham, Sarah, 225–26, 289
history, 71–72; of Cedar Key, 49, 49–51
history and place, sense of, 65–67, 66
Homecoming Spirit Week, 86, 86
Homeland Security, US, 76
homeless children, 144–45, 166
"home-schooling," 243–44
Hospital of the Innocents (Ospedale degli Innocenti, Innocenti Centre), Florence, Italy, 152
household income, 157
household median income, 153
housework, 105–6
housing instability, 144–45
HPI. *See* Happy Planet Index
Human Development Index (HDI), 110, 133, 134
human rights, 207, 220; constitutional rights compared to, 209–11; as global ecological model, 211–13. *See also* Children's Rights Convention
Human Rights in Children's Literature: Imagination and the Narrative of Law (Todres and Higinbotham), 225–26, 289
human rights law, 209
Hurricane Hermine, 64–65
hurricanes, 51–52, 64–65

Iceland, 153
iCivics, 289–90, 302
identity, 84–85, 92–93, 214, 286; birthplace related to, 174–75; faith communities and, 87–89; names in, 75; parades and, 86–87. *See also* rights to identity and family
immigration, 44, 73, 163, 170, 215; refugee resettlement, 299–300; in US, 76, 107–10

Immigration and Naturalization Act of 1965, 76
inclusion, 186
indigenous children, 209, 216, 221
individualism, 190
industry, 151
inequality: CRC and, 190; exclusion and, 186; Francis on, 186; geography related to, 189–90; individualism and, 190; opportunity related to, 187–88; upward mobility and, 187, 188–89, 199–200
infant mortality rates, 119, 163–64, 166, 167
Innocenti Centre (Hospital of the Innocents, Ospedale degli Innocenti), Florence, Italy, 152
Innocenti Report Card 8, 124–25, 139–40
Innocenti Research Centre, 3, 4
In re Gault (1967), 211
"instrumentalization," 196
intercountry adoption, 255–56; of Nannarone, G., 251–52
intergenerational support, 22–23
interviews, 23–24
iPhone, 184
IQ tests, 276
Island Hotel, Cedar Key, Florida, 57, 57, 58
ISTAT. *See* Italian National Institute of Statistics
Italian Corte Costituzionale (Constitutional Court), 241, 257
Italian National Institute of Statistics (ISTAT), 183
Italian public policy, 117–19
Italy, 100, 235; anti-immigrant populism in, 73, 107, 109; Anversa degli Abruzzi in, 179–80, 192, 228, 228; birth rate in, 32; citizenship in, 109; Constitution of, 118, 178, 188, 210; corruption in, 178; Five Star Movement in, 8–9; mass migration and, 191–94; multiple generations in, 16, 16; Northern League in, 9, 194, 197; PIGS related to, 156–57; in Report Card Twelve, 153–55; as

research subject, 5–6; rights to identity and family in, 249–51; right to participation in, 234–40, 235; social media in, 185–86; social-welfare policies in, 6–7, 8–9, 93; sociocultural diversity in, 73; total fertility rate of, 101; workday in, 105. *See also specific cities*

Jackson, Jasmine, 71
Japan, 219
Jews, 69
Johnson, Lyndon, 146
Jones, Elin, 292–93
Ju' Catenace (traditional marriage procession), 258
Juliana et al. v. United States et al. (2016), 302
jus soli (birthright citizenship), 108–9

kafala. See adoption
Keillor, Garrison, 88
King v. Burwell (2015), 146–47
Kohler, Hans-Peter, 110
Krugman, Paul, 160

languages, 66–67, 213–16, 257, 271. *See also* dialect
La Sanità. *See* La Sanità (under 'S')
Latin America, 195
Lauzi, Bruno, 41
laws, 209, 218; age related to, 16–17; ecological model related to, 15, 20
Lazerson, Marvin, 75
Leaf, Munro, 226
Legal del Nord (Northern League), 9, 194, 197
legal custody, 221
"legal fiction," 222–23
Lello, 272–73
Leonhardt, David, 188
LGBTQ parents, 108
libertarian philosophy, 177
Libya, 193–94

literature, 225–26; on right to participation, 237–38. *See also* poetry
litigation, 301–2
Loffredo, Antonio, 268–72, 274; Canada compared to, 280–82
lottery, 277–78
love, 283

macrosystem, 4, *4*, 5, *5*, 202–3, 207–8; in ecological model, 19–20; in smallness, 280–81, 283–84, 288, 289–302
Madonna delle Grazie, 46, 47, 88
"the Madonna effect," 115
Madrigal Dinner, 82, 82–83
majority age, 17
Malinowski, Bronislaw, 24
malnutrition, 167
maltreatment, 148–50
maritime heritage, 65
"market child-poverty rate," 137
marriage, 66–67, 258
Martin (saint), 47–48
Mary (saint), 47
mass migration: DNA technology and, 191; Francis on, 190–91, 193; in globalization, 190–95; from Libya, 193–94; from Scanno, 192; in smallness, economics, 264; Trump and, 191, 195; "unaccompanied minors" in, 195
maternal mortality rates, 119
Mattarella, President, 73
"A Matter of Equity," 126–27
McDonough, William, 287
McIntyre, Lisa J., 23
McKibben, Bill, 200–201, 263
McKinney Vento Act, 144–45
Mead, Margaret, 24
Medicaid, 146, 166
men: parenthood for, 114–15; in Scanno, 115
meritocracy, 275–78, 280–81
mesosystems, 3–4, *4*; in exosystem, 18–19. *See also* solidarity

messa alla prova (put to the test), 243–44
Meta, Ermal, 192
methods: comparison, 20–21; definition of, 14; ethnography in, 24–25; sociology in, 23–24
microsystems, 3, *4*, *5*, 5, 18
millennials, 113
model, 14
Modugno, Domenico, 192
Mokgoro, Justice Yvonne, 136–37
Montessori schools, 128
Monti, Mario, 161, 178
Moore, Gary, 69, 71
mothers' employment, 104
mothers' marital status, 102–3
mothers' reproductive age, 101–2, 110
movement for happy de-growth (Movimento per la Decrescita' Felice), 298–99
Movimento Cinque Stelle (Five Star Movement), 8–9
Movimento per la Decrescita' Felice (movement for happy de-growth), 298–99
Murray, Charles, 276
music, 192, 225; jazz artists, 274
Muslim Ban, 76
Muslims, 76, 195

names, 75, 175, 214, 251–52
Nannarone, Angela, 83, 84, *84*
Nannarone, Candido, 44, 83, 84, *84*, 252
Nannarone, Gaia, 83, 253, 254; first communion of, 84, *84*, 252; intercountry adoption of, 251–52; in traditional costume, 253, 255, *255*
Nannarone, Massimo, 83, 253–54, *254*; first communion of, 84, *84*, 252; name of, 251–52
Nanni, Davide, 97, 98, 111
Naples (Napoli), 271. *See also* La Sanità
Napoleonic Empire, 268
Natali research paper, 156–57

National Federation of Independent Business v. Sebelius (2012), 146
National Geographic Atlas, 98–99
national health program, 119
nationalism, 193
national paid leave policy, 122–23
National School Lunch Program (NSLP), 143
National Trust for Historic Preservation, 71–72
National Youth Rights Association, 301
Native Americans, 49–50, 65
natural disasters: earthquakes, 48, 63–64, 236, 238; hurricanes, 51–52, 64–65
nature and nurture, 9
Nature Coast Biological Station, 65, 91, *91*
Nazis, 69
NEET. *See* "Not in Education, Employment or Training"
neighborhoods (*contrade*), 199; allegiance to, 89; definitions of, 77; San Martino festival related to, 89–91; in solidarity, 77, 89–92, *90*, *91*, 188
neurology, 162
neuroscience, 124, 140, 223; pre-school and, 126–27; on violent media content, 185
Newfoundland, Canada, 99
New Hampshire, 300
NGOs. *See* nongovernmental organizations
Nixon, Richard, 129
Noi del Rione della Sanita' (We of the Sanita') (Loffredo), 270
nongovernmental organizations (NGOs), 219
Nonni di Strada (street grandparents), 244
Northern League (*Lega del Nord*), 9, 194, 197
"Not in Education, Employment or Training" (NEET), 155, 161, 174
NSLP. *See* National School Lunch Program

nursery schools, 88, 229; in "educare," US, 128; Good Shepherd Nursery, 33, 58–59, *59*

Obama, Barack, 38, 135, 161, 279, 289; climate change and, 298; health care from, 145–46
obstetrical unit (*punto nascita*), 120–21
O'Connor, Sandra Day, 289
OECD. *See* Organization for Economic Cooperation and Development
"one percenters," 156
opportunity, 187–88
Organization for Economic Cooperation and Development (OECD), 5, 125, 163–64
Organization for Refugee and Immigrant Success, 300
Ospedale degli Innocenti (Hospital of the Innocents, Innocenti Centre), Florence, Italy, 152
overall poverty rate, 137

Pallante, Maurizio, 298–99
parades, 86–87
parenthood: incentives for, 117, 122; Italian perspective of, 113–15; for men, 114–15; social construction of, 112–13; technology related to, 180–81; for women, 114–15
parenting social supports, 104
parents' rights, 223
parrocchia (parish), 88
passeggiata (recreational stroll), 116
peer group, 80–81
peer-to-peer teaching, 257
People of the Shell Mounds, 50
Perry, Bruce D., 175–76
Pescatore, Doctor, 69
Philogene, Amber Nave, 297–98
Piaget, Jean, 18
Piazza della Santissima Grazia, Florence, Italy, 151

Piazza Santa Maria della Valle, Scanno, Italy, 112
PIGS (Portugal, Italy, Greece, and Spain), 156–57
Pirate Festival, 65
Pius XI (pope), 266
place-based policies, 300–301
playing: *bancarella*, 231, 231–33, *232*; by Cedar Key children, 54–55, *56*; children's voice in, 233–34; in *Ciambella*, 227–29, *228*, 233; free play space access, *59*, *60*, 60–62, *61*; gender in, 230–33, *231*, *232*; globalization and, 233; learning by, 232–33; "Mother, May I?" as, 231; soccer as, 231; technology related to, 182–85. *See also* right to play
poetry: "Castrovalva," 97, 98, 111; in dialect, 63, 227, 255, *255*
politics, 63, 121, 188; Republican Party, 144; Tea Party movement, 177. *See also* Trump, Donald
Porter, Eduardo, 187–88
Portugal, 156
positive rights, 222
Posner, Richard, 177–78
poverty: child, measurement of, 135–39; child neglect related to, 150; of Great American Recession children, 139–40; race related to, 138–39; in Scanno, 74
"poverty gap," 138
poverty line, 135–36
poverty rates, 119–20, 163–64
power, 176–77
The Practical Skeptic: Core Concepts of Sociology (McIntyre), 23
pregnancy, 147–48
pre-kindergarten, 127
pre-school, 126–27
Pressley, Ayanna, 301
privacy, 212–13
private schools, 276
privatization, 281
Promise Academy, 276–79

Promise Neighborhoods, 279
protests, citizen, 121, 188
public health policy, 121
punto nascita (obstetrical unit), 120–21
put to the test (*messa alla prova*), 243–44

Quito Declaration on Sustainable Cities and Human Settlements for All, 296–97
race: in Cedar Key, 53, 68–69, 70–72; poverty related to, 138–39
racial and ethnic discrimination: against "extra-communitarians," 197; Francis against, 196; "instrumentalization" in, 196; regional bias in, 196; on television, 196–97; in US, 197–200
racism, 50–51, 170, 274; Cedar Key and, 68–69, 70–72; in comparisons, 68–73; Scanno and, 69–70, 73
Reagan, Ronald, 263
Reconstruction, 51
recreational stroll (*passeggiata*), 116
redlining, 274
Reeves, Richard, 187
reformation, 13
refugee resettlement, 299–300
refugees, 215
regionalism, 264
Reitz, John, 21–22
"relative income poverty," 165
relative poverty line, 136, 154
religion: in Cedar Key, 60, *60*; Muslims, 76, 195. *See also* Catholic Church
religious festivals, 45–48, *46*; San Martino festival, 89–91, *90*
Renzi, Matteo, 161
replacement rate fertility, 101
"Report Cards," 3, 4–5
Report Card Twelve, 152; case studies in, 159; child poverty in, 153–54; child well-being self-reports in, 155–56; elderly in, 153; household median income in, 153; Italy in, 153–55; NEET in, 155; US in, 154, 155
"Report of the Special Rapporteur on extreme poverty and human rights on his mission to the United States of America," 163–66
Republican Party, 144
resolutions, 290
Rienzo, Filippo Di, 226–28
"rights," 25, 203, 208, 214. *See also* Children's Rights Convention
rights of children accused of crimes, 241; after-school youth center in, 243–44; age in, 242, 244; animals and, 243–44; communication in, 243, 245; *messa alla prova* in, 243–44; team for, 242–43; in US, 244–45
rights to education, 246–49
rights to identity and family: community in, 249–51; family reunification in, 249–50; foster care and, 251; in Italy, 249–51; in US, 251
rights to support, 217–18
right to adoption, 253–56. *See also* Nannarone, Gaia; Nannarone, Massimo
right to be heard in judicial and administrative proceedings, 240–41
right to children with disabilities inclusion: autism spectrum in, 256–57; Down syndrome and, 258; teacher's assistants in, 256–57
right to participation: children's voice in, 240; economic crisis in, 239; on education, 239; by Genny, 234–37, *235*; legal structures, 239; literature on, 237–38; political participation, 238–39; on projects, 238; retention of, 235; social justice in, 240; social participation in, 237–38; Sport Center in, 234, 236; UN Special Session on Children, 236–37; Young People's Assembly in, 236
right to play: "Friendships" on, 226–27; spaces in, 227–29, *228*, 233

"right to work," 177
The Right Way, 293–94
rituals and relationships, 81–84, *84*
Roberts, Dorothy, 197
Roma, 197
Roosevelt, Eleanor, 207
Root, Leslie, 108
Rosewood Heritage Foundation, 72
Rosewood Massacre (1923), 68–69
Rotolo, Carmelo, 33, 46, 62, 88, 258
rural poverty, 166–67
Ryan, Paul, 144

Salvatore, 271–72
Salvini, Matteo, 194
Sandlin, Virgil, 65
sandwich generation, 106
San Gaudio Catacombs, Naples, Italy, 270–71
La Sanità (Naples): benefit gala in, 273; bridge over, 268–69; commitment in, 273–74; cooperatives in, 270; crime in, 269; curiosity in, 272–73; festival in, 269; Fondazione San Gennaro for, 270; foster home in, 273–74; goals of, 281; HCZ compared to, 280–82; infrastructure of, 269; Loffredo in, 268–72, 274; San Gaudio Catacombs in, 270–71; sustainable community creation in, 269–70; travel related to, 270, 273; visits to, 271–74
Sanitensemble, 273
San Martino festival, 89–91, *90*
San Patrignano, 249–51
Santa Maria della Valle (St. Mary of the Valley), 33
Save the Children study, 105–6; End of Childhood Index in, 166
Scalia, Antonin, 185
Scannismo (Scannism) (Di Gennaro), 230–31
Scanno, Italy: agriculture in, 44–45; children's centrality in, 32, 41, 45, 46, 46–48; demographics of, 42, 52–53; earthquakes in, 48, 63–64; education in, 42, 48, 184, *184*; employment in, 43; first communion in, 32, 44, 47–48, 83–84, *84*; friendly environment of, 32; Good Shepherd Nursery in, 33, 58–59, *59*; grandparents in, 115–16; immigration in, 44; invasions of, 43–44; land in, 55–56; location of, 30–32, *31*, 42; mass migration from, 192; migration from, 43; modernity in, 34; photography in, 45; poverty in, 74; pride in, 41; religious festivals in, 45–48, *46*; research contacts in, 33–34; research on, 30–32, *31*; sheep related to, 42–43; social class in, 230; solidarity of, 230; sports in, 44; tourism in, 44, 45; town center of, 32; tradition in, 34, 45, *46*, 46–48; World War II and, 43–44, 67. *See also* comparisons
Schäuble, Wolfgang, 160
scherzetto o dolcetto (trick or treat)., 89, 90, *90*
Schnieder, Carl, 241
school, 289–90; definitions of, 78; food in, 78–79; in solidarity, 78–80. *See also specific types*
school anxiety, 219
school grouping, 78, 79–80
school of childhood (*scuola d'infanzia*), 125, 126
"the school-to-prison pipeline," 245
Schumacher, E. F., 260, 263–67, 282, 287
science, 37, 264–65. *See also* neuroscience
science denialism, 202, 297
scuola d'infanzia (school of childhood), 125, 126
Seminole Indians, 50
Seminole Wars, 50
sense of history and place, 65–67, *66*
Sessions, Jeff, 195
Seuss, Dr. (fictitious name), 225–26
"severe material deprivation," 153

sexuality, 216; technology related to, 185–86
Sharks, 54–55, 71, 81, 86, 91–92
sheep, 42–43
shelter nest (*asilo nido*), 125–26
Sicily, 196–97
Six Myths and Truths about Fertility in the West (Kohler), 110
Slemp, Joshua, 70, 71
Small Is Beautiful (Schumacher), 260, 263, 282
smallness: climate for, 261–62; CRC related to, 261; integration of, 262; limitations of, 262; love related to, 283; macrosystem in, 280–81, 283–84, 288, 289–302; solidarity and, 262; yearning for, 262
smallness, economics: balance of, 263–64; circular economy in, 267–68, 286–88; climate change and, 267; emotional attachment and, 263; identification in, 265; mass migration in, 264; motivation in, 266; "private" enterprise and, 266–67; regionalism in, 264; solidarity in, 268; structure diversity in, 263–64; subsidiarity in, 265, 266; technology and science in, 264–65; urbanization and, 267–68; vindication in, 265; virtue of, 267
small worlds, 11–12, 203
SNAP (Supplemental Nutrition Assistance Program), 141–42, 159, 166
social class, 118; in Scanno, 230
social exclusion, 158
social institutions, 74–75
social insurance, 99–100
social media, 37; Francis on, 196; in Italy, 185–86
social mobility, 187
social protection systems, 159
social structures, 75, 85–87, 86; globalization and, 171
social-welfare policies, 6–7, 118–19

social welfare programs, 92–93
sociocultural diversity, 73
sociology, 23–24
solidarity, 37–38, 74; climate change and, 200, 203; communal identity in, 84–85; competing social structure and institutions in, 85–87, 86; definition of, 77; faith community in, 77, 87–89; family and, 76–77; neighborhoods in, 77, 89–92, 90, 91, 188; peer group in, 80–81; rituals and relationships in, 81–84, 84; of Scanno, 230; school in, 78–80; smallness and, 262; social institutions in, 74–75; village identity erosion and, 92–93
song, 192
South Africa, 136–37
Spain, 156
Special Supplemental Nutrition Program for Women, Infants, and Children (WIC), 142–43
Sport Center, 234, 236
sports: race and, 71; in Scanno, 44. *See also* Sharks
Stack, Carol B., 24
Stahel, Walter R., 286–87
"state action," 222
States Parties, 213, 218, 219, 223–24, 234
status, 217
Steger, Manfred B., 171, 172–73
Steiner-Adair, Catherine, 180–81
stereotypes, 115; of family, 116–17
"Stolen Childhoods," 166
street grandparents (*Nonni di Strada*), 244
strike, 301
subgroups, 85, 91. *See also* neighborhoods
sub-Saharan Africa, 100
suicide, 168, 219
Sulmona, Italy, 235
Sulmona *punto nascita*, 120–21
Summers, Larry, 160
superheroes, 86, *86*

Supplemental Nutrition Assistance Program. *See* SNAP
Supreme Court, US, 15, 76, 185, 189, 198, 222
surrogate parents, *61*, 61–62
surveys, 23–24
survival, 11
Susi, 271–73
sustainability, 13
sustainable community creation, 269–70
sustainable crops, 299
Swanson, Ana, 177
Szalavitz, Maia, 175–76

TANF. *See* Temporary Assistance to Needy Families
teacher's assistants, 256–57
Tea Party movement, 177
technology, 191; AAP on, 182; digital divide of, 182; hurricanes and, 65; ISTAT on, 183; mixed blessing of, 180; ownership of, 181–82; parenthood related to, 180–81; playing related to, 182–85; screen time with, 181–82; sexuality related to, 185–86
television, 196–97
Temporary Assistance to Needy Families (TANF), 149, 159–60, 166
Tenth Annual Conference on the Rights of the Child, 73
Thunberg, Greta, 297
Timucua Indians, 50
Tocqueville, Alexis de, 174
Todres, Jonathan, 225–26, 289
total fertility rate, 100–101; in US, 106–7
Tough, Paul, 276, 278, 281
tourism: in Cedar Key, 56, 57, *57*; in Scanno, 44, 45
tradition: in Cedar Key, 56; of "core household chores," 105; Halloween, 89; Pirate Festival, 65; in Scanno, 34, 45, 46, *46–48*;

traditional costumes, *66*, 66–67; Nannarone, G., in, 253, 255, *255*
traditional cultures, 16
traditional marriage procession (*Ju' Catenace*), 258
trauma, 9
treaties, 212
triangulation, 23–24, 70–73; capitalism and, 179–80; of Sulmona *punto nascita*, 120–21
"trickle-down theories," 176, 177
trick or treat (*scherzetto o dolcetto*), 89, 90, *90*
The Truly Disadvantaged (Wilson), 276
Trump, Donald, 8, 10, 72, 107, 109–10, 135; hostility toward children by, 162–63, 168–69; mass migration and, 191, 195; wealth inequality from, 164–65
trustees, 294

UN. *See* United Nations
UNDRIP. *See* United Nations Declaration on the Rights of Indigenous Peoples
unemployment, 151; child maltreatment related to, 149–50; globalization and, 173, 174
UNESCO, 171
UNICEF, 3, 152, 213–14, 220, 289; comparisons from, 21
union membership, 177
United Kingdom, 154; Wales, 291–94
United Nations (UN), 13, 211; Human Rights Council, 163, 165; Special Session on Children, 236–37, 302
United Nations Convention on the Rights of the Child. *See* Children's Rights Convention
United Nations Declaration on the Rights of Indigenous Peoples (UNDRIP), 109

United States (US), 51; Bill of Rights of, 25–26, 210; birth rate decline in, 106–8; citizenship in, 108–10; Declaration of Independence, 210; Homeland Security, 76; immigration in, 76, 107–10; mass migration and, 191, 195; oil consumption of, 201; racial and ethnic discrimination in, 197–200; in Report Card Twelve, 154, 155; rights of children accused of crimes in, 244–45; rights to identity and family in, 251; right to participation in, 237; Supreme Court of, 15, 76, 185, 189, 198, 222

Universal Declaration on Human Rights, 207

upward mobility, 187, 188–89, 199–200

urbanization, 267–68. *See also* La Sanità

Urso, Elena, 69, 85

values: definition of, 14; environmentalist on, 26–27; for parenthood, 114

value systems, 62–63; development of, 25–26

village identity erosion, 92–93

violence, 168, 185

Voci Antiche (*Ancient Voices*), 97, 98

voting, 301

vulnerability theory, 27–28, 285

Waldman, Randee, 245

Wales, 291–94

Walker, Matthew, 292–93

Wall Street crash, 7

Walters, John, 199

Warren, Elizabeth, 267

welfare programs, 92–93

well-being measurement, 135; GCI in, 134; HDI in, 133, 134

Welsh Observatory on Children's Rights, 291–92

Welsh Youth Parliament, 292–93

Whatever It Takes (Tough), 276, 278, 281

white supremacy, 108

WIC. *See* Special Supplemental Nutrition Program for Women, Infants, and Children

Wilson, William Julius, 276

women: parenthood for, 114–15. *See also specific topics*

workday, 105

workforce women percentage, 103–4

working poor, 153

workplace, 19

world problems, 92

World War II, 67; capitalism after, 178, 179–80; in Scanno, 43–44, 69

worldwide strike, 301

Wright, Jim, 283–84

Wu, Tim, 260

ABOUT THE AUTHOR

Barbara Bennett Woodhouse is LQC Lamar Professor of Law at Emory University Law School and author of *Hidden in Plain Sight: The Tragedy of Children's Rights from Ben Franklin to Lionel Tate*. She is also David H. Levin Chair in Family Law (emeritus) at the University of Florida, where she founded the Center on Children and Families. Educated in Italy and fluent in Italian, she obtained her law degree from Columbia University. She clerked for Associate Justice Sandra Day O'Connor at the US Supreme Court before joining the faculty of University of Pennsylvania, where she cofounded the multidisciplinary Center for Children's Policy Practice and Research. Author of over seventy-five articles and book chapters in several languages, plus numerous legal briefs, she utilizes methods from a range of disciplines, including comparative legal and cultural studies, child development, sociology, ethnography, and history to explore the legal and social ecology of childhood. She was recognized in 2005 as a "human rights hero" by the *ABA Journal on Human Rights*. In 2013, she founded the Emory Child Rights Project and she has authored or coauthored numerous briefs in cases involving the rights and needs of children.